Masters *of* Violence

The Carolina Lowcountry and the Atlantic World
Sponsored by the Program in the Carolina Lowcountry and the Atlantic World of the College of Charleston

Masters *of* Violence

The Plantation Overseers of Eighteenth-Century Virginia, South Carolina, and Georgia

Tristan Stubbs

The University of South Carolina Press

Published by the University of South Carolina Press
Columbia, South Carolina 29208

www.sc.edu/uscpress

Manufactured in the United States of America

27 26 25 24 23 22 21 20 19 18
10 9 8 7 6 5 4 3 2 1

ISBN: 978-1-61117-884-5 (hardcover)
ISBN: 978-1-61117-885-2 (ebook)

This book was printed on recycled paper
with 30 percent postconsumer waste content.

For Gertrud, Hanna, and Elias

Contents

Acknowledgments

By far my greatest debt of acknowledgement is to Betty Wood, who offered sage advice, friendship, and professionalism. My work owes an incalculable debt to her inspiration. Professor Tim Lockley, Dr. Ben Marsh, and Professor Michael O'Brien provided valuable comments on my early writing on plantation overseers and helped me identify certain weaknesses and potential new avenues of research. Looking further back Clive Trebilcock and Mark Kaplanoff introduced me to ideas that have shaped my understanding of social history, agricultural history, and American colonial history; it is a matter of regret that they and Professor O'Brien will not see the finished product. Neil Whiskerd was the reason that I ever decided to study history. Though his modesty would prevent him from acknowledging the impact that his teaching continues to have, he can be sure that his influence runs through this work.

During the last few years, Toyin Falola, Amanda Warnock, Edward E. Baptist, and Alan Johnson have published small sections of my research. For the invitation to present papers and the opportunity to have my ideas challenged and tested, I am grateful to the organizers of the "Atlantic Slavery in the Age of Revolution" conference at the University of Leeds; the "Slavery: Unfinished Business" conference at the University of Hull; the Scottish Association for the Study of the Americas conference at the University of Edinburgh; the British Society for Eighteenth-Century Studies conference at the University of Oxford; and the "Consent in Early America" conference at the Rothermere American Institute. I am indebted also to the conveners and members of research seminars at the following institutions for their helpful and constructive responses to my work: the University of Sussex, the Colonial Williamsburg Foundation, the University of Cambridge, and the Virginia Historical Society. The College of Charleston's Program in the Carolina Lowcountry and the Atlantic World was kind enough to award this work the Hines Prize for the best first manuscript on lowcountry or Atlantic history, to invite me to the college's beautiful campus to give a Wells Fargo lecture, and to name me an affiliate faculty member. The feedback that I received at that lecture and at subsequent meetings in Charleston—and the comments and support of Alex Moore, Linda Fogle, and the anonymous reviewers of the University of South Carolina Press—have shaped the final manuscript for the better. Olivia Durand of the University of Oxford was an exemplary indexer, and I look forward to reading her future work.

Staff at archives in two countries were exceptionally helpful, and this book would never have appeared without their conscientiousness and enthusiasm. I am indebted to librarians and archivists at the South Caroliniana Library at the

University of South Carolina; the Virginia Historical Society; the South Carolina Historical Society; the Georgia Department of Archives and History; the Georgia Historical Society; the University of Georgia; the Library of Virginia; the Earl Greg Swem Library at the College of William and Mary; the University of Virginia; the Southern Historical Collection at the University of North Carolina; the Warwickshire County Record Office; Birmingham Central Library; the Vere Harmsworth Library at the University of Oxford's Rothermere American Institute; and, of course, Cambridge University Library.

For their invaluable contributions to the funding needed to complete my research, I am sincerely grateful to Pembroke College, and especially to Michael Kuczynski and Jon Parry, who encouraged me to apply for a variety of crucial bursaries and travel grants. My gratitude extends to the University of Cambridge, who awarded an Allen Meak and Read studentship and a Worts traveling scholarship; to Cambridge history faculty, who awarded a Prince Consort and Thirlwall Fund studentship and a Sarah Norton Fund travel grant; to the Sir John Plumb Charitable Fund, who provided a young historian's grant; and to the Arts and Humanities Research Council. The Rothermere American Institute at the University of Oxford awarded me a Visiting Research Fellowship that gave me access to the institute's wonderful library and the resources that I needed to finish the manuscript.

At vital stages in my research, a host of institutions in the United States appointed me to research fellowships. These included a Gilder Lehrman Fellowship at the Colonial Williamsburg Foundation; an Andrew W. Mellon Fellowship at the Virginia Historical Society; a Lewis P. Jones Visiting Research Fellowship at the South Caroliniana Library; and a fellowship at the University of South Carolina Institute for Southern Studies. The staff who offered guidance on everything from archival research to the location of supermarkets are too numerous to mention. I hope that by giving the following individuals the special credit that they deserve they will be encouraged to pass on my thanks: Jim Horn in Williamsburg; E. Lee Shepard in Richmond; and Herb Hartsook and Thomas Brown in Columbia. Taking over Trevor Burnard's lecture program at the University of Sussex taught me a very great deal, and I thank him, Clive Webb, and my former students for that invaluable experience.

Barb and John Orsolits were the consummate hosts in Atlanta—welcoming, generous, and forgiving of a callow visitor's ignorance of his surroundings. Barb also shared the plat that is reproduced below, as well as countless fascinating observations on southern landscape and agriculture. My sincerest thanks go to the Orsolitses, as they do to John Houghton, who was kind enough to lend me his house during my stay in Athens. Also in Athens Professor Allan Kulikoff provided me with lunch and invaluable comments, and Professor John Inscoe gave me a warm welcome, counsel, and dinner. For taking the time to discuss my work, I am grateful to David Barry Gaspar, Fredrika Teute, Michael Trinkley, and Chuck Lesser.

I owe a significant debt to friends who gave me something else to talk about during the course of the research. This applies in particular to John Bew, who put me up in Cambridge and supplied advice whenever I needed it, as well as to Sean McGovern, Stuart Snelus, Ben Rabb, Mathieu Apotheker, Martin Brown, Mike Franklin, Pete Hall, Richard Plumb, John Cummings, Jeff Knezovich, Liam Thompson, John Clarke and Chaminda Seneviratne. It applies, too, to the many other friends that I have made through my work at four think tanks and two parliaments in London and Brussels and to Anthony Seldon and Guy Lodge, who trusted me to manage the research team for their book on Gordon Brown. I hope that my understanding of slavery has improved since I began working in politics; my conviction that enslaved resistance is fundamentally a political act has certainly been fortified by the epistemic linkages that I have drawn between the two halves of my career.

My family's support has been remarkable Though my maternal grandparents died before the project was complete, they and my paternal grandparents would have been delighted to read the finished project. My sister, Tara, not only typed up research notes but offered sound guidance on American literature. Her intelligence and diligence make her an inspiration for her twin. Without the incredibly generous spiritual, material, and financial support provided by my parents, this book would never have seen the light of day. I hope that they are as happy with the final outcome as I am. My father and sister were brave enough to proof the final draft—any remaining mistakes are mine alone. Last, for her unwavering encouragement and unstinting belief in me and this project, I owe my wife, Gertrud Malmersjö, much more than she could know.

A Note on Terminology

The proliferation of contemporary terms that describe overseeing and its practitioners often cause difficulties for the researcher. Overseers are variously referred to as "overlookers" or "bailiffs"; at other times they are called "managers," a term that this book employs as an alternative to "overseer."[1] Sometimes the same employer would even use the names interchangeably. Yet they often overlapped with terms for various other supervisory positions on southern plantations, such as stewards or agents. The sources also record an assortment of professions that either were related to overseeing, or might be confused with it: in particular, when enslaved overseers worked on plantations, the distinction between "driver," "overseer," and "foreman" was nebulous, and the application of terminology imprecise.

The term "overseer" frequently referred to occupations involving the direction of small groups of enslaved people involved in nonagricultural labor. In 1764 an advert appeared in the *Georgia Gazette,* stating: "AN OVERSEER is wanted by the subscriber. Any person properly qualified for taking charge of a few pair of sawyers, and [who] can be well recommended for his diligence, sobriety, and honesty, may meet with good encouragement."[2] Conversely, when subscribers advertised explicitly agricultural management positions, sometimes the term "overseer" did not appear. In 1767 a "man, that understands planting and mowing [was] wanted, on a plantation near Charles Town [Charleston], where there are but few negroes employ'd."[3] Another advertiser similarly "WANTED ON HIRE, A MAN, capable of tending the MARKET, and managing a small FARM about a mile from Charles Town, with a dozen of hands thereon."[4] This was likely a result of scale: superintendents were often known by terms other than "overseer" on smaller quarters. Scale also affected the terminology used to describe superintendents on the biggest plantations. In a 1767 issue of the *Virginia Gazette,* an advert appeared for "a farmer who will undertake the management of about 80 slaves."[5] The term "farmer" was also common on large or small quarters that raised grain as opposed to tobacco.[6]

Planters such as the Virginians George Washington, Landon Carter, and Thomas Jefferson, as well as the South Carolinian Henry Laurens, each employed stewards.[7] Absentee landlords in particular instituted a hierarchical structure with stewards at the peak, especially if they owned a number of plantations or large tracts of land. The Earl of Dunmore employed at least three overseers under his steward, Edward Snickers, on his Virginia plantations in 1774.[8] Robert Carter III of Nomini Hall, Virginia, summed up the steward's working relationship with overseers. John Ridout was to "engage the overseer to live their ye suceding year; tell him to cloth the Negroes, to reserve corn [etc.] f[o]r [the]m & ye stocks; [and] to sell [tha]t part of ye Crop [tha]t be superfluous."[9] An indication of the greater level of responsibility that devolved to stewards was offered by Richard Henry Lee, in a *Virginia Gazette* advert from 1776: "as the business is considerable, and the trust great, any person willing to undertake the same will meet with the most generous and satisfactory encouragement."[10] The term "steward" appears infrequently in the records, however: more common were "overlooker," "manager," and "agent."[11] Although, with the exception of the last, these terms also referred to overseers, more commonly they denoted employees with a broader managerial role. A steward working on a plantation in Hanover County, Virginia, where a slave uprising took place in 1769, was described in the *Virginia Gazette*'s report as "overlook[ing]" the quarter.[12] When George Washington and Robert Carter III wrote of their "managers," they generally referred to their stewards.[13] Similarly Henry Laurens advised Richard Oswald that he should "provide a proper manager & an inferior Overseer" to supervise fifty men and women.[14] The presence of stewards increased the distance between slave owners and overseers, and therefore stewards played a key role in the development of anti-overseer prejudices. William Cash, steward to sometime Georgia governor Edward Telfair, wrote that he had been unable "to leave home . . . owing to the . . . bad beheaviour of my overseer, which required my Constant Attention."[15]

As slavery became more securely established, the records describe stewards and agents less frequently as overseers.[16] By late century Bataille Muse worked as an agent in upcountry Virginia on behalf of Robert Carter III, supervising the work of overseers and stewards on numerous plantations and collecting rent from Carter's tenants. George Newman, employed to superintend overseers on a couple of Virginian plantations, was also described as an agent.[17] The scope of stewards' and agents' responsibilities varied within colonies. Virginian stewards were charged with facilitating relations between overseer and slaveholder and across plantations; with ensuring that all quarters under their control were well provisioned; and with collecting and marketing the crops grown.[18] Agents in Virginia had a wider role, involving the protection and management of all their employers' interests, agricultural or otherwise, within the scope of their remit. They also deputized for their employers when they went abroad.[19] Given the smaller number of bondpeople working under each overseer in Virginia, stewards there were more involved in everyday plantation management than their more southerly counterparts. George Washington's favored term "manager" summed up the Virginian steward's role well. His responsibility, similar to that of a company manager, was to ensure the smooth running of a number of plantation units in line with his employer's interests.[20] Washington also assumed that his stewards would be wealthier than general overseers. The president thought, pessimistically, that stewards would not "labor in [the] manner [that] one would do whose living depended upon it."[21]

In South Carolina Henry Laurens advised Richard Oswald to employ a "proper manager" to purchase a "small stock of cattle, Hogs, Horses, Waggons, &ca., &ca."[22] Eliza Lucas Pinckney, on discovering that her "plantations wanted but every thing and [were] every way in bad order," employed a "good man . . . to undertake the direction and inspection of the overseers."[23] Stewards in the lowcountry undertook similar tasks to their counterparts in Virginia. But the greater size of plantation units and prevalence of absenteeism in the more southerly colonies sometimes blurred the distinction between steward and agent. The volume of rice produced by landholdings with very large economies of scale meant that some stewards liaised directly with the commissary factors on the Charleston and Savannah waterfronts, while the isolation of lowcountry slave quarters led many more tasks surrounding the marketing of the end crop to devolve to the steward. Josiah Smith's correspondence with George Austin in Shropshire, England, demonstrates this difference.[24]

At the other end of the spectrum, some overseers found themselves in charge of subordinate overseers, referred to variously as "under-overseer"s or "suboverseers."[25] Such men worked on plantations that were large enough to require an extra layer of management and would have had more contact with enslaved people than the overseers above them in the hierarchy. These lowlier superintendents, sometimes illiterate and often having little contact with their employers, usually appear in the primary sources only as passing references.[26] Yet it was to these men that elite commentators would also refer when they came by late century to discuss overseers' general incompetence, their penchant for cruelty, and their shaming dependence. Superior overseers attempted to avoid association with the stereotype by placing themselves in a more exalted position in the eyes of their employers: for example James Kerr, an overseer for Francis Jerdone, stressed that he had "Overseers under him."[27]

They did this by underlining the importance of their own contribution—suboverseers in both regions were less likely to be tasked with the vital daily allocation of work to enslaved people, and with ensuring that the distribution of provisions, tools, and other resources was founded on the most equitable balance between necessity and profit. Whatever their level of responsibility, for overseers, stewards, and suboverseers alike it was the role that they played in striking this balance that determined how successful they would be in performing their everyday duties.

Introduction

To "treat them . . . inhumanly"— Overseeing in the Eighteenth Century

The overseer performed a role of singular importance to the plantation economies of the eighteenth-century South. Ultimately the responsibility for a profitable return on his employer's investment in land and human property fell to him, ahead of the estate steward or planter's agent, both of whom were superior in the management hierarchy. In the course of a single day, the overseer undertook a large number of duties germane to this responsibility and vital to the requisites of the plantation. He would rise early, earlier even than the enslaved people, whom he would awaken with the ring of a bell or a blow from his horn.[1] After they had gathered he would dispense tools, and send the people into the fields to begin their daily toil. There he would allocate tasks, following the instructions or interpreting the wishes of the plantation owner, which were described to him in written missives that were often sent from many miles distant.

Different crops were cultivated in different regions, and plantation management differed accordingly. In Virginia, depending on the season, the overseer would put gangs of enslaved people to work clearing new ground, building soil hills to receive the tobacco plants, or stripping and stemming the freshly grown crop.[2] In lowcountry South Carolina and Georgia, where rice culture was dominant, the overseer would give men and boys the tasks of digging, draining, or clearing the "flushes," the irrigation channels stemming from the great rivers that dissected the lowcountry.[3] To women and children he assigned the less arduous (but no less tedious) jobs associated with the planting and harvesting of rice.[4]

The overseer's role was broader still. The eighteenth century saw South Carolina develop a majority black population, and Virginia claim the largest number of enslaved people of any of the thirteen mainland colonies.[5] Whites everywhere were continually uneasy at the prospect of rebellion, and the numerous, if ultimately unsuccessful, uprisings of the eighteenth century made fears that they were living on top of a volcano all the more concrete. In the view of the colonial jurists who responded to these anxieties, the tactics that the overseer employed in keeping enslaved people to the hoe, shovel, and axe should be adapted to the defense of white society itself. Yet paranoid white southerners felt that some overseers tipped the balance too far. They expressed few greater concerns than that enslaved people might become accustomed to "lenity and indulgence[s]," such as the right to time off work or to cultivate their own meager plots. They argued that after the enslaved had developed a taste for such "liberties," however small, their appetites never would be sated.[6]

Faced with twin responsibilities for economic success and societal order, the overseer contrived to circumscribe every part of the lives of the enslaved, thereby delineating the spatial and temporal boundaries designed to keep black people in bondage.[7] With his employer often far away, theoretically it was the overseer who claimed the last word on when the bondpeople got up, when they went to bed, when they worked, when they could rest, whether or not they could amuse themselves at parties or through other forms of entertainment, and whether or not they could talk the languages and practice the religions that they had brought from Africa.[8] It was the overseer who could disrupt relations between members of enslaved families, by reporting to the planter conjugal visits to neighboring plantations or by suggesting family members for sale. Women lived in fear of rape by overseers flaunting all the venal authority that accrued to them. Their husbands had little redress or outlet for their anger since laws ensured that attacks on overseers could be punishable by death, while flight left their wives and daughters to confront alone an even greater threat.

The overseer purchased food for these people and distributed clothing and shoes when their owner saw fit to send them. But although these measures went some way to keeping the men and women healthy, they represented little more than another means used by the overseer in his quest for control over the bondpeople. Many overseers and planters convinced themselves that a good profit followed a straightforward equation. If enslaved people received sufficient provisions and were kept warm and well, a tractable work force might result. Yet the prescriptions and proscriptions of plantation life were sustainable only with so-called moderate correction from time to time.[9] Especially on absentee quarters, where they had much more autonomy of action, overseers became the primary arbiters of this delicate trade-off between provision and punishment.

Lurking behind the promise of profit was, then, the threat of violence—sometimes unspoken, but nonetheless constant.[10] And so all the while the bondpeople labored on the plantation, the overseer stood above them, whip in hand, his dark presence intended euphemistically to "keep them at their work."[11] Enough people had experience of the overseer's lash to understand the real meaning of this term: the tattered backs of men, women, and children underlined it. When whippings came they were often prolonged, sometimes fatal, and always brutal. Floggings of fifty or one hundred strokes were not unusual; if the person survived, the overseer might then rub salt into their lacerations and pour tar onto the wounds.[12] Chastised, the alleged troublemaker was returned to work, despite the unbearable agony of his or her burning, flailed skin.

Some slaveholders attempted to draw a line between violence that they believed was acceptable and that they believed represented excessive punishment of enslaved people. When Newyear Branson, overseer of one of his Virginian plantations, beat two young enslaved boys in 1790, Robert Carter of Nomini Hall counseled against savage punishment: "I recommend moderate correction in every case and . . . make proper allowance for the feelings of the mother."[13] Planters also highlighted overseer violence against women: another Virginian described in a runaway advert how a "Negro Woman named BETTY . . . ha[d] a Scar on a Breast occasioned by a Stroke from her Overseer."[14] Frederick Wiggins, overseer to the South Carolinian slave trader turned planter and future president of Congress Henry Laurens, was reported to "whip Wenches till they misscarry."[15] Violence was not a trait that was believed simply to infect individual overseers. Alexander Hewatt, the first historian of South Carolina and Georgia, who held lands in the latter colony, averred that overseers in general were "ignorant and cruel."[16] Looking back in 1815 to his plantation experiences, Thomas Jefferson claimed that overseers were an "unprincipled race," while George Washington noted how most overseers seemed to "consider a Negro much in the same light as they do the brute beasts, on the farms, and oftentimes treat them as inhumanly."[17]

As vivid as these characterizations were, and despite the brutality of physical chastisement, real or threatened, the implacably violent, sadistically capricious overseer was largely atypical. Relations between overseers and bondpeople were more nuanced: while the menace of violence was always maintained, supervisors knew that the most effective way to guard against the truculence of the enslaved was not rigidly to enforce plantation discipline but to award "petty privileges" to those who followed the rules.[18] Unhappy, abused, and injured bondpeople labored with less alacrity than those who had a material incentive, however small, while the rebukes of their employers were usually enough to discourage overseers from the most barbarous actions. And there was no reason why overseers should have been any more or less violent than planters who directly supervised their own enslaved people.[19]

For the most part this was a stereotype, a "preconceived and oversimplified idea of . . . [typical] characteristics" that developed in the later decades of the 1700s.[20] Like many stereotypes, however, it was founded on and strengthened by eyewitness accounts. Slaveholders in Virginia, South Carolina, and Georgia patented (meaning that they received ownership of land in return for developing it) an increasing acreage of absentee property throughout the century, and this trend reached its peak at century's end. Absenteeism devolved to the overseer much more autonomy of judgment in the punishment of enslaved people; some overseers responded to this development not by granting privileges, but by using more and crueler violence. Enslaved people bore tales of cruelty to the more solicitous planters in an attempt to undermine their supervisors.

Whether exaggerated or not, such reports reinforced slaveholders' preconceived ideas, which had themselves resulted from a change in the ideological and intellectual architecture of slavery. Late eighteenth-century Virginia, South Carolina, and Georgia witnessed a significant conceptual shift regarding the use of violence against enslaved people. In the first few decades of the 1700s, patriarchal masters and mistresses saw violence as an acceptable means of disciplining bondpeople and white indentured servants. For a number of ideological reasons (the most influential of which was enlightened patriarchal sentiment), toward the end of the century, and particularly in the years following the Revolutionary War, some began to raise their voices against violent punishment. In a departure from the belief that profit arose from a compromise between provision and punishment, enlightened patriarchism now viewed reciprocated affection for bondpeople as the reward of the slaveholder, substituted emotional for material provision, and claimed to regard violence as inhumane.

But these planters recognized at the same time that in a system of forced labor, violent punishment remained necessary; and their need to profit from the plantation business only grew stronger. The use of force that inhered in patriarchism survived long after the eighteenth century: it was merely subsumed into gentler rhetoric.[21] So as they began to turn away from the more brutal side of slavery, enlightened patriarchs salved their collective guilt over the continued use of violence by performing an effective diversionary trick. In practical terms increasing managerial devolution over the course of the 1700s allowed enlightened patriarchs to avoid administering violence. Those men—namely plantation overseers—who continued to practice violence against enslaved people they now despised as being inherently, implacably brutish and sadistic. This was, these planters told themselves, the rational explanation for those who would savagely whip other human creatures. And in claiming concern for their bondpeople, slaveholders implicitly cursed their lack of control over distant employees, declaring overseers incapable of directing the loving, if firm, regimes that they themselves advocated.

Southerners leveled three further denunciations at overseers: first, that they were incompetent agriculturists; second, that they had little prospect of ever attaining the propertied independence enjoyed by others in the South; and third, that they were untrustworthy, dissolute, thieving scoundrels. In a letter of 1782, George Washington related how he wished to employ a "good steward"—a farm manager who supervised overseers—"the advantage of which, every person who has had any thing to do with Overseers, and Plantations at a distance, must be amply convinced of."[22] In the short period between his tenures as governor of Virginia, secretary of state, and vice president, Thomas Jefferson grumbled in a letter to Washington that the abandonment of his lands for the previous ten years had given "the unprincipled ravages of overseers" free rein.[23] Other planters, only slightly more kindly, favored a distinction between the few competent and the larger number of "common overseers."[24] On their dependent status, Jefferson claimed that overseers were "the most abject, degraded . . . race."[25] And patriarchal rhetoric insisted that because they were dependents, overseers were not to be trusted. Washington discussed with James Mercer in a letter of 1774 what should be done with a surplus of corn. He concluded that it should be sold, "but who is to be entrusted with this, unless you can confide in your New Overseer, I know not."[26] Likewise Eliza Lucas Pinckney, the widowed South Carolinian slave mistress, blamed "ignorant or dishonest Over Seers" for the mismanagement of her late husband's affairs.[27]

Planters made their indictments all the more humiliating by combining accusations of overseer incompetence and untrustworthiness. In 1776 one Matthew Marable was moved to report in the *Virginia Gazette* that he had determined no longer to trust a "set of people calling themselves *overseers*" with the management of his "plantations and slaves," a course of action that never produced "anything but ruin and destruction," and so had resolved to split up his land into tenements.[28] Correspondingly George Washington advised that the overseers be moved off the plantation of his niece, Frances B. Washington, and replaced by a farmer and two ploughboys.[29] These prejudices appear to have held such widespread credibility that Marable felt no need to cite the source of his grievances, prompting a correspondent—calling himself "Overseer"—to ask a month later, "why did not mr. Marable inform that *wealthy fraternity* [of overseers] of the grievous complaints he had to lay against them at the bar of the publick?"[30]

Similar to the violent overseer stereotype, these characterizations developed only in the later decades of the eighteenth century.[31] There is little evidence of comparable general prejudices existing early on in the 1700s. In fact the opposite was sometimes the case: overseers were ascribed positive normative characteristics. Robert Beverley, a historian of colonial Virginia in a tract designed partly to encourage new immigrants to the colony, remarked in 1705 that "an Overseer is a[n] [indentured servant], that having served his time, has acquired the Skill and Character of an experienced Planter."[32] In Beverley's estimation an overseer's lowly status did not preclude him from carrying out his duties successfully. A slightly later commentator presented overseeing as a reward for agricultural aptitude and, tellingly, compared it to other options available to the ambitious, who could "rent a small Plantation . . . or else turn Overseers, if they are expert, industrious, and careful."[33]

Again structural changes to the plantation system fuelled and supported this transformation in opinions. Increasing absenteeism disbarred planters from extending the patriarchal control over their plantations that their forebears had enjoyed, but their addiction to land in the Virginian piedmont and Georgian and South Carolinian backcountry meant that they continued to invest ever greater sums of capital further and further away. The latter half of the century also saw some plantation owners experiment with the productive, but expensive, innovations of the English agricultural revolution, which developed in a different climatic and topographical context. Consequently, while managerial responsibilities grew, many overseers struggled to cope. As a reward for their increased workload overseers received only poor pay; a number of the more competent sought other employment. Weakened and more infrequent proprietorial intervention also meant more opportunities for overseers to steal from and defraud their employers. Though Matthew Marable was not inclined to reveal the motivation behind his complaints, that his correspondent demanded he do so shows how the relationship between individual errors and a reputation for ineptitude, between sporadic deceit and general distrust was dialogic: representation could never entirely be divorced from reality.[34]

A final consequence of the rampant patenting of land was that lowlier Virginians, South Carolinians, and Georgians were increasingly unable to purchase real estate. At the start of the eighteenth century, men who entered the overseeing profession could still reasonably expect to become independent heads of household on leaving. Yet opportunities for economic and social advancement soon reduced.[35] Dependents had been stigmatized in the Anglo-Saxon mindset long before the eighteenth century. Women, children, the poor, the young, and men without independent means were all believed to be incapable of rational thought and action. Without the constraint of reason, these individuals were thought to be governed by their passions; without the guidance of a more reasoned individual, they were considered prone to desultory behavior. Planter distrust of overseers' capacity to manage plantations, and their assumption of overseer dishonesty, should be judged against this background.[36]

But why, by the late eighteenth century, were overseers stigmatized by figures such as Jefferson as much for their membership in a dependent "class," or "race" of overseers as for belonging to a broader class of dependents?[37] Overseers were acutely aware of this trend: Matthew Marable's adversary mocked how the planter had vented "his scribbling itch on the pestilent *Race of Overseers*"; claimed that Marable's fulmination was indicative of a "new mode of libelling a whole society of men"; and enquired as to why such libel was not "severely punishable by the laws."[38] The explanations for this new prejudice were threefold and, with the ideological rejection of violence, form part of another conceptual shift with ramifications for southern opinions of overseeing. First, as long as their social mobility remained relatively attainable, overseeing was not associated irredeemably with dependence, as Beverley's quotation intimates. Since early modern and Enlightenment conceptions of dependence recognized its transitory nature, prejudices regarding their behavior and reason dissolved when overseers' prospects changed.[39] The unfortunate counterpoint to this belief in the mutability of status was that when overseers' chances of social betterment became generally and irreversibly calcified, their reputation was doomed. Hence Jefferson viewed all overseers as naturally indigent and subservient, with no possibility of a change in their characters. Second, prejudices regarding dependence sharpened at a time when vociferous demands for independence from Great Britain precipitated the Revolutionary War. And third, as the new nation arose from the ashes of conflict, overseeing appeared to betray America's nascent republican values. Working for another, with little hope of heading a household, the overseer represented the antithesis of the yeoman farmer, vaunted by Thomas Jefferson and contemporaries as the type of landed, independent citizen whom all virtuous male citizens should try to emulate.

Historians have long recognized the significant role that oversight played in the plantation economies of the South: Kenneth Stampp opined that the overseer was "an indispensable cog in the plantation machinery."[40] Yet few have studied the daily lives and work of overseers.[41] An exception is the preeminent work on antebellum overseeing, William K. Scarborough's *The Overseer: Plantation Management in the Old South.* Scarborough attempted a complete survey of nineteenth-century oversight, utilizing plantation records from across the South.[42] William E. Wiethoff's *Crafting the Overseer's Image* seeks, like the present study, to enrich comprehension of "the rhetoric of [the overseer's] reputation and the actuality of the historical overseer" yet limits its discussion to antebellum managers and does not research the centrality of negative overseer stereotypes to the construction of antebellum paternalism.[43] A large number of secondary works on slavery in the 1700s make mention of oversight.[44] Here overseers often take on the role of amanuenses, assigning tasks, providing food, and whipping bondpeople at the behest of the slave master or mistress. The poor literacy of many eighteenth-century overseers has rendered them almost silent in the historical record: their employers' voices frequently drown them out.[45] There are very few broader descriptions of overseers in the 1700s.[46] A portrayal of eighteenth- and early nineteenth-century overseers appears in a dissertation written at Johns Hopkins University by James Baird.[47] The concern of Laura Sandy's doctoral thesis on eighteenth-century overseers in Virginia and South Carolina is with the social and economic function of overseers on southern plantations.[48]

In light of the paucity of secondary literature on overseeing, and in recognition of the importance of oversight to plantation agriculture, the first significant contribution of this book is its attempt to reconstruct as full a picture as possible of the eighteenth-century overseer. It seeks to record every aspect of overseers' lives and work, from their recruitment, to their dismissal and future careers. It differs from previous approaches in aiming to map the changes that the overseer system underwent in the eighteenth century.[49] At a time when historians of slavery have called for more and broader comparative studies, and despite the importance of the overseer in delineating the contours of eighteenth-century slavery in all its cruel pettiness to hundreds of thousands of the institution's victims, labor relations during the first expansion of the slave system are often neglected.[50] American slavery was founded long before the antebellum period, and overseers and bondpeople were negotiating their relative positions on the plantation almost from its inception.[51] The second major contribution of what follows is to describe and analyze relations between these two parties.[52]

This study also engages with a number of broader debates. By placing overseers at the center of eighteenth-century intellectual currents, it highlights how these men were unique in that they acted as receptacles for planters' fears and frustrations. It considers literature on dependence and deference in the colonial South and elsewhere and suggests that studying overseers more closely can enliven the debate about the pervasiveness of these ideas. Set against this background, the growing development of the idea of an overseer "profession" is viewed as a rejection of attempts to group overseers with other dependents.

What is most important, the book contends that eighteenth-century overseeing is integral to understanding the development of slaveholder paternalism in the nineteenth century. The forerunners to the paternalists—the enlightened patriarchs—made claims to emotional relationships with bondpeople on outlying quarters just as they did for those with whom they had a face-to-face relationship. Traditionally home plantations have been seen as the locus of the development of an emotionalist language to describe southern power relations.[53] Through focusing on the centrality of overseer stereotypes in providing the rhetorical space for the development of such language, this study reasserts the importance of the periphery in the growth of these influential ideas. And by emphasizing the importance of overseeing to planter self-fashioning, it argues for prejudices toward overseers to be assessed as central to the development of republican manhood in the South.[54]

— *Chapter One* —

A "continual exercise of our Patience and Economy"

The Structure of Oversight, Patriarchism, and Dependence in Pre-Revolutionary Virginia, South Carolina, and Georgia

> Besides the advantage of a pure Air, we abound in all kinds of Provisions without expence (I mean we who have Plantations). I have a large Family of my own, and my Doors are open to Every Body, yet I have no Bills to pay, and a half-a-crown will rest undisturbed in my Pocket for many Moons together. Like one of the Patriarchs, I have my Flocks and my Herds, my Bond-men and Bond-women, and every Soart of Trade amongst my own Servants, so that I live in a kind of Independence on everyone but Providence. However this Soart of Life is without expence, yet it is attended with a great deal of trouble. I must take care to keep all my people to their Duty, to set all the Springs in motion and make every one draw his equal Share to carry the Machine forward. But then "tis an amusement in this silent Country and a continual exercise of our Patience and Economy."[1]

William Byrd II's panegyric to the glory of patriarchism likened the plantation hierarchy to a well-constituted machine.[2] At its head, naturally, sat Byrd, who took "care to keep all [his] people to their Duty, to set all the Springs in motion and make every one draw his equal Share to carry the Machine forward." Two hundred and thirty years later, Kenneth Stampp's description of the overseer as "an indispensable cog in the plantation machinery" drew an equivalent comparison.[3] Yet there is little evidence that Byrd would have agreed with this analysis. As a "Patriarch," he viewed himself customarily as the only valid source of plantation authority; he had, moreover, little faith in the abilities of overseers. Nor would he have admitted a second observation. Dreamily depicting himself at the center of a pastoral idyll, a watchful master of his "Flocks" and "Herds," Byrd imagined plantation agriculture to be an exercise in disinterested benevolence. His explicit calling was to rule dependents, not manage assets.[4]

But like all machines, eighteenth-century Chesapeake and lowcountry plantations were designed for a specific task—in this case to turn a healthy profit from capital investment. The thin fabric of Byrd's bucolic sketch now and again reveals this problematic truth. He had "Bond-men and Bond-women, and every Soart of Trade amongst [his] own Servants," so that he could "live in a kind of Independence on everyone but Providence"; indeed, although he had "a large Family of [his] own, and [his] Doors [were] open to Every Body, yet [he had] no Bills to pay, and a half-a-crown [would] rest undisturbed in [his] Pocket for many Moons together." For all his ostentatious exasperation at the "great deal of trouble" inherent in patriarchal "Duty," and for all his claims that plantation management represented an "amusement," Byrd's freedom from economic worries derived ultimately from his exploitation of dependent and enslaved labor.

The eighteenth-century South was a "remarkably underinstitutionalized world."[5] Long before diffuse political power was subsumed into the modern centralized state, throughout the Anglophone world much political authority and legitimacy derived from the idealized figure of the household patriarch.[6] Societal maturation led to the domination by elite whites of the primary means of production in plantation society—the enslaved workforce.[7] William Byrd II had spent much of his early life studying and working in London, but in his ambition to define himself as a patriarch he was typical of the rich colonists of his age.[8] His fellow elites developed patriarchal control over their households (which included white employees as well as black people) and kinship circles and were able to maintain oligarchic rule of the government of North American colonies.[9] Putting to work ever-greater numbers of enslaved and indentured dependents over the course of the century further aggrandized plantation owners' conception of the power and extent of their dominions.

Reflecting the importance of such ideas for the growth of prejudices against overseers, the first five chapters of this book look at overseeing in the patriarchal era (defined here in broad terms as the seven decades before the Revolution—though a few examples appear from beyond 1775). The views of planters were so central to the popular understanding of oversight that negative opinions of the profession are impossible to understand without reference to this discourse, while patriarchism represented the dominant model of political economy, at the center of which overseers found themselves. So although it is often extraordinarily difficult to discern overseers' voices above the noise of planter prejudice, understanding exactly why slave owners cleaved so tightly to the stereotype reveals much about the society that overseers helped to create. Linking these chapters is a more prosaic theme. For all the late-century rhetoric that suggested otherwise, the impetus to turn a good yield from their plantations remained paramount in slaveholders' minds. Throughout the pages below, overseers' involvement in realizing a profit is discussed concurrently with slaveholder ideology; it was the dichotomy between the two that informed much anti-overseer sentiment.

As a means of rationalizing planter rule, patriarchism first developed in the earliest slave colony, Virginia. Owing to the relatively small size of the Chesapeake plantation, in the early years of the colony's history there was regular contact between patriarchs and subordinates.[10] The nature of tobacco production, which involved small groups of laborers working under supervisors, meant that there was a "patriarchal, intimate quality about its work."[11] From its beginnings the ideology was defined by a Lockean code of material reciprocity. As sovereign of his household, the patriarch provided for its members.[12] In return he expected loyalty and their dedicated labor.

Elite men invoked the language of the biblical ancients and their Roman successors when describing their unique positions. They put themselves at the head of a tribe, like "the Patriarchs of old," or gave themselves the Latin title paterfamilias.[13] In so doing they aped a tendency that was current among other Anglophone men of high status. Just as household relationships within Britain's empire were conceptualized in familial terms, so the head of the empire, the king, named himself paterfamilias of all subject territories and peoples. Because the personal was so political, other political relationships were also described in the same terms as household relationships. To the metropolis, and in the regretful eyes of many of the colonists, Virginia, South Carolina, and Georgia were as much dependents as the indentured servants who first peopled them.[14]

Elite whites in North America constructed a formulation that rationalized the unbreakable linkages between varying strata in the social and political hierarchy, a formulation that bound the lowliest enslaved person to God Himself.[15] The "Chain of Being," while describing a simple hierarchical ordering of power from top to bottom, also contained within it diverse definitions: there were as many different types of patriarchy and dependence as there were of patriarchs and dependents. And since everyone (with the exception of the divine) was dependent on someone else, southerners developed an acute sense of the expected rights and privileges, and duties and responsibilities, associated with their specific social positions. The patriarchal cultural ethos positioned enslaved people at the bottom of this network of relationships.

Long before southerners saw a need to justify slavery, they explained social distinctions with reference to a seemingly natural ordering that ranked people according to intelligence.[16] Patresfamilias not only adopted the titles of the ancients; they claimed to have the wisdom of the ancients, too. As in Greece and Rome, mature, elite white men alone possessed sufficient mental faculties to contend with the burden of responsibility that the management of dependents placed on them, because mature, elite white men alone possessed sufficient reason for the task. Patriarchal southern societies contained hierarchies of rational capacity to match their hierarchies of power. Reason itself provided the rationale for the societal and economic inequalities that pervaded Virginia, South Carolina, and Georgia during the first seventy years of the eighteenth century.

In essence a rationalization of unequal labor relations, patriarchism rationalized additional inequalities of wealth and status by calling on unsympathetic character assumptions. Elites believed dependents to be dissolute and untrustworthy, led more by their passions than by reason. The Virginian Huguenot minister

Peter Fontaine explained how, unless "ye Impetuosity of ye Passions" was quelled, "they should run Into Riot, if Left unsubdued, and unemploy'd."[17] Such prejudices claimed a long heritage in the Anglophone Atlantic world. They traced their earliest roots to seventeenth-century civic humanism and the liberalism of John Locke (who had penned the 1669 *Fundamental Constitutions of Carolina*) and were fortified by a contemporary discourse on personal morality known in North America through the writings of David Hume and Adam Smith.[18] Both William Cabell and his fellow Virginian planter George Washington read Francis Hutcheson, Smith's onetime tutor and a contemporary progenitor of the revived language of passions.[19]

If mastery and dependence were deemed integral facets of the natural order of things, confirmation was provided by America's idiosyncratic labor practices. The sparsely populated seaboard colonies contained a higher proportion of legal dependents than early modern Britain and western Europe. Enslaved people were seen to possess the lowest level of reason of any eighteenth-century southerners. But along with bondpeople, indentured servants and women and children generally were supposed to be irrevocably incapable of their own self-rule; they therefore "deserved to be subjected to power."[20] Because women were widely believed to be in hock to their passions, they were not permitted the responsibility of exercising political rights. More than this, dependence among males was itself feminized, while independence was bound up with ideals of masculine self-worth.[21] A Virginian book of aphorisms from the 1760s counseled that "if thou goest about any Thing in a Passion, thou takest on thee to do a *manly Act,* when thou art not a Man."[22]

Dependency also encompassed other sizeable groups of southerners—the poor, those who were not heads of households, and, by extension, those who worked for others. Their lack of material wealth meant that such people were motivated by baser instincts than disinterested patriarchs, and likely to be dominated by more powerful individuals. A sympathetic commentator described just before the Revolution the bind that this network of prejudices created: "an humble man is generally accounted *base,* if otherwise, he is esteemed *proud;* a bold look is looked upon as *impudence;* if modest, then . . . he must be *hypocritical.*"[23]

The English understanding of liberty, from medieval jurist Henry de Bracton's *De legibus angliae* onward, sprang from the idea that subjects were free as far as they yielded to no power other than the law.[24] For John Locke liberty meant personal autonomy: freedom from another man's command.[25] Depending on anyone else's will, as overseers depended on the will of their employers, meant "forfeit[ing] [their] liberty."[26] The first edition of the *Encyclopaedia Britannica,* printed in 1771, defined "LIBERTY" as "a state of freedom, in contradistinction to slavery. According to Cicero, liberty is the power of living as a man please, or without being controlled by another," while "FREE . . . is used in opposition to whatever is constrained or necessitated. When applied to things endowed with understanding, it more peculiarly related to the liberty of the will."[27] "SLAVE," on the other hand, was "a person in the absolute power of a master."[28] The Virginian planter Joseph Ball, who evinced a strong patriarchal attitude in all areas of plantation management, read Cicero as well as the influential English theorists of dependence and patriarchy Hobbes and Coke.[29]

Such strength of feeling arose because as slavery became more widespread, and "servile work and dependence" came to be identified with slaves, all men ideally should have owned land, the "hallmark of independence."[30] The relative abundance of land in the eighteenth century cemented the importance of property ownership in defining membership of the elite. Property not only brought civic freedoms such as the ability to vote; it reduced men's reliance on other people and guarded against arbitrary passions and the vagaries of fate. In 1722 lieutenant governor of Virginia John Spotswood linked prosperity with this understanding of freedom when he planned to "make Such Settlement of a part of my Estate which may be for ever a Supply to our posterity, and thereby be not onely Screened from the fear of wanting means of Living but also freed from the chances of fortune & Dependence on others."[31] The Virginian Peter Fontaine believed that "a Small Estate" through "a mans Industry" would "maintain himself and family and Set him above ye necessity of Submitting to ye humours & Vices of others."[32] Landon Carter bragged in 1759 that he was virtually invulnerable in his "excellent little fortress . . . built on a Rock . . . of *Independency.*"[33] The John Page's "Virginia Almanack" for the year that the Revolution began described "the blessings" that the author "desired in life": "a moderate, but independent fortune, business enough to secure [him] from indolence, and leizure enough to have always an hour to spare. [He] would have no master. . . . [He] would not be led away by ambition."[34]

Although the exigencies of absentee management devolved to many overseers a great deal more freedom of action than most dependent employees could expect, underpinning the overseer-slaveholder relationship were familiar negative cultural assumptions. These men still counted among dependents, and their hierarchical duty was to execute planter demands. Every such assumption would have significant consequences for overseers, meaning that the patriarchal cultural metaphor determined the tenor of interactions between overseers, their subordinates, and their superiors. Many slaveholders found difficulty in striking a balance between noninterference and control. Unwilling to jettison patriarchal values, planters clashed with overseers who took an autonomous approach to oversight; when plantation affairs went awry, they betrayed familiar prejudices against dependents. Without the brake of reason, overseers were deemed mistrustful and avaricious, and likely to defraud their employers if given the opportunity. Much prewar anti-overseer criticism evolved from discrepancies between patriarchal ideals and plantation returns.

Patriarchism developed against a specific agricultural and topographical background in Virginia; in South Carolina, and later Georgia, it had distinguishing features that also derived from local structural idiosyncrasies. The ideology exhibited a protean ability to explain African slavery on the vast rice plantations of the Southeast, account for white dependence on tobacco farms to the north, and answer the desires of planters everywhere in America to exercise monocratic authority over their lands and servants. Indeed the social, economic, and political conditions under which overseers worked varied not simply from colony to colony but between regions within those colonies.[35] Variations were already evident by 1700 and grew increasingly marked as the century wore on. The plantation experience of overseers and enslaved people who worked in Tidewater and lowcountry regions differed from that of people who cultivated the higher elevations of the Virginian piedmont and South Carolinian backcountry. And two broader regions—Virginia, and South Carolina and Georgia—were sufficiently far removed to have had distinct crop mixes, which played a significant role in creating variations between slave societies. The cultivation of different plants (rice and indigo in South Carolina and Georgia, tobacco and wheat in Virginia) "powerfully shaped [bondpeople's] lives, influencing everything from daily and seasonal rhythms to basic working conditions, from the variety and nature of work to labor organization."[36] By comparing these two societies, it is possible more effectively "to identify the independent forces" that shaped them.[37] Different settlement patterns, differing demographics, and regional disparities in the degree to which absenteeism was practiced all had a bearing both on the work of overseers and bondpeople and on how southerners regarded overseers.

Yet there were similarities as well as differences between the two regions. As much as the crops that an overseer planted determined the annual rhythm of his life, a South Carolinian overseer could expect to be idle in winter, when cold weather also stalled his Virginian counterparts. The agricultural cycle decreed that work in both regions begin again in spring, and that overseers secure a yearlong position before then. Though regional variations in the structure of plantation slavery had a bearing on forms of enslaved resistance, the aims and motivations of bondpeople's oppositional activity were comparable in all three colonies.[38] Prejudices against overseers seem to have converged across both regions toward the end of century, as new Americans sought to construct for themselves new understandings of the ideal republican citizen. The "othering" of plantation managers also formed one of the key buttresses to antebellum paternalism, an ideology that, like patriarchism, paid little heed to regional distinctions and extended across the South from the Eastern Seaboard to Texas. Unsurprisingly the earliest stirrings of such sentiment led slaveholders from Virginia, South Carolina, and Georgia to voice common rhetorical ideas.[39]

Most important were the similarities between each colony's founding and later development. With the exception of Puritan New England, every Anglo-American colony in the West Indies and on the mainland was established "for the central purpose of enriching the individuals who sponsored and settled them."[40] In Virginia the first successful English North American possession, and in South Carolina, set up by wealthy Barbadian émigrés, the quest for personal enrichment precipitated the introduction of African slavery. For a while Georgia held out against the temptation to enslave, but in 1750 it submitted to petitioning by its citizens, envious of their slaveholding neighbors' extraordinary riches. The first mainland colony established in the 1700s thereby became the last to permit the ownership of slaves.

Virginia was the original plantation economy of mainland North America. By 1700 the colony was thriving. A number of factors had proved integral to Virginia's success. The introduction of tobacco as Virginia's staple (and trade in the commodity with the metropolis) had largely provided subsistence, while the headright system of landholding, introduced in 1618 and extant for almost a century, encouraged settlement by granting fifty acres to anyone owning servants.[41] The former encouraged the growth of larger plantations, run entrepreneurially, while the latter supported westward expansion and the patenting of land in the piedmont. In motivating the colony's founding—and providing for its continued existence—profit, landholding, and dependent labor had joined in important ways before the 1700s. That century saw tobacco planters' fortunes vary. Though prices increased moderately between 1700 and 1800, there was significant secular fluctuation about this trend, with slumps occurring with "appalling regularity" between 1680 and 1750; in the years preceding the Revolution, similar price depressions were frequent.[42] In spite of this cycle, the cultivation of tobacco remained broadly profitable, and investment in land and enslaved people economically viable. The Virginian planter Joseph Ball could report in 1755 from England that tobacco "is the Greatest Drug in the world here now."[43] Yet the tendency for tobacco cultivation to exhaust soils developed in Virginians a strong desire to diversify their agricultural mix. Of the crops mentioned in Virginian overseer recruitment adverts, none was predominant; the notices most frequently required of overseers an aptitude for raising wheat and corn, closely followed by barley, tobacco, and flax.

The first area of Virginia to be planted (and the most mature example of a slave society in the three colonies) was the Tidewater region. Tidewater Virginia encompassed those counties aligned along the low-lying plain of the Chesapeake Bay's western shore, between the Atlantic Ocean and the fall line.[44] It was the location of the greatest plantations and grandest domiciles in the colony, seats of quasi-aristocratic families like the Byrds, Lees, Carters, and Balls. This region experienced earlier than its neighbors the alterations in societal characteristics that accompanied the stabilization of slave societies.[45] Changes including a higher life expectancy and a lower age at first marriage aided the creation of a patriarchal family system; society became more stratified as classes developed, and the Virginian planter gentry came to dominate government.[46] Further inland lay the piedmont, an area of more undulating topography and less fertile soil, beginning at the fall line and rising gradually to meet the Blue Ridge section of the Appalachians.[47] Here marginal agricultural conditions traditionally had entailed smaller plantations, or farms where no bondpeople were worked. Like George Washington and Thomas Jefferson, the largest planters of this region tended to see themselves more as agriculturists than aristocrats.

Whether they called the Tidewater or piedmont home, slaveholders from both regions shared a fixation with purchasing and developing new acreage on the colony's frontier. Although tobacco surpluses magnified the impact of price depressions, planters tended to respond to downturns by overproducing.[48] Set in train by men such as Robert "King" Carter of Lancaster County, who early in the century already owned vast tracts of land, and following both an enlarged influx of African bondpeople and a rapid natural increase of the native enslaved population in the first half of the eighteenth century, planters believed that superior production was best achieved through a greater investment in land and labor.[49] The frontier continually shifted as Virginia removed Indians or purchased their land, surveyed its gains, and offered tempting incentives to prospective cultivators. During the early 1700s, most westward expansion went as far as the piedmont; at midcentury, the frontier extended to Lunenburg County and the "southside" on Virginia's borders with Carolina, then north along the Appalachians into the region that would become West Virginia.[50] Meanwhile large planters consolidated their slaveholdings. Thomas Jefferson owned forty-one bondpeople by the early 1770s; in 1774 he inherited eleven more people from his mother and gained control of 135 who had passed down to his wife from her father.[51] George Washington's acquisitions followed a similar course. Through his marriage to Martha Custis, a significant number of "dower" slaves came into his possession.

Nonlandholders suffered both from the development of frontier areas and from the maturation of older regions to the east. Encouraged by affordable prices and the availability of land, numerous Virginians migrated westward in the hope of establishing farms or plantations of their own.[52] Yet during the seven decades before the Revolutionary War, Virginia offered lowlier inhabitants ever-decreasing opportunities to achieve this ambition.[53] Large landowners had already cleared or already owned most eastern land; and tobacco culture exhausted fecund Tidewater soils after only seven years' cultivation.[54] Even at the beginning of the century, declining fertility led slave owners to criticize the way plantations were run. Robert Bristow complained in 1714 that "in my Grandfa[the]rs time [his lands] hath clear[e]d 2 or 300 [hogsheads of tobacco] a year & can there be such a different without bad management[?]."[55] But the abundance of unpatented land in frontier regions offered little inducement to slaveholders to improve what acreage they already possessed. Blessed with the capital profitably to enhance undeveloped plots, they gradually usurped poorer planters there.

Like slavery itself North American overseeing began in Virginia. After 1619 the Virginia Company employed men to oversee white indentured servants and

African bondpeople in Jamestown.[56] Prefacing later juridical pronouncements on the overseer's role, a very early statute established that his hierarchical position sat squarely between planter and laborers: "all overseers of workmen, shall be careful in seeing that performed, which is given them in charge, upon paine of such punishment as shall be inflicted upon him by a martiall Court."[57] The demands of forging a society in a new land required seventeenth-century overseers to possess as varied a set of abilities as their counterparts in the 1700s. Within a few years of the development of the profession, the overseer had become both agriculturist and craftsmen, akin to the bailiffs who worked on landed estates in the mother country.[58]

At the outset of the eighteenth century, slaveholders such as Robert "King" Carter employed overseers to supervise bondpeople and indentured servants, and to run the plantations that lay scattered around their principal lands.[59] Later the establishment of slaveholdings in the piedmont and on the frontier saw distances between home plantations and outlying quarters stretch further than before, and greater levels of responsibility devolve to overseers. Seventeenth-century Virginia established a convention for "eight or ten" indentured servants to be placed under the supervision of an overseer.[60] Ratios had not altered much by the 1700s. John Spencer oversaw eleven enslaved men (including his own bondman, Jack) and eight women for Francis Jerdone in 1757, while William Berry supervised eight bondmen and his own bondwoman, Doll, the same year.[61] In 1760 Colonel Dudley Digge put David Chisholm in charge of six men and five women on his plantations in Louisa County.[62] Between 1762 and 1766, Jerdone's managers were charged with an average of ten people each, and each supervised an average of just under fourteen hundred acres of land.[63] The overseer under steward Charles Dabney was in charge of eight people in 1773, and John Page's overseers supervised between five and twelve bondpeople three years later.[64]

Late eighteenth-century ratios between overseers and the enslaved in Virginia seem not to have changed much from the late seventeenth century. John Gollehorn managed eleven adults (plus fifteen children, thirty-three cows, and four horses) in 1782; Thomas Appling "overlooked" six hands for William Cabell in 1792; and Ralph Smith in 1798 was contracted to supervise "Seven Hands and four Work Horses" for one Hugh George.[65] Sometimes overseers were employed to manage bondpeople spread across more than one plantation—Cabell hired Theodorick Scruggs "to be an Overseer at my two upper plantations over 18 or 20 hands."[66] There is some suggestion that the ratio of enslaved people to overseers had intraregional variations, owing to differences in crop mix.[67]

And yet the presence of larger numbers of bondpeople presents a more complex picture. In 1732 John Hurst supervised sixteen enslaved people for Robert "King" Carter at his Hamstead Quarter in Stafford County, while John Leathead was in charge of twenty-six at Carter's Indian Town plantation in Lancaster County.[68] Like Carter other planters worked different numbers of people on different quarters, their decisions reflecting the individual circumstances of each. Francis Jerdone employed one overseer for eleven of his hands at his plantations in Albemarle County in 1762, although by the following year he had hired four supervisors for the same number of bondpeople.[69] At his home plantation, however, Jerdone was prepared to allow his overseer to manage nineteen enslaved, presumably since the shorter distance between owner and overseer meant that Jerdone would have taken on at least some managerial responsibilities himself, and because he could directly control this superintendent.[70]

Characteristic of eighteenth-century Virginian agriculture were smallholdings that sat alongside large plantations. On the majority of these, the owner employed no overseer and worked in close proximity with his bondpeople. This situation pertained throughout the century in the piedmont, where in 1775 a few counties had half the enslaved population of some Tidewater equivalents.[71] Yet plain data can misrepresent oversight's institutional importance. In Lancaster County overseeing became the preeminent occupation for dependent white males during the third quarter of the eighteenth century.[72] By the later decades of the century the overseer was a highly visible figure for Tidewater bondpeople. As many as one half of them lived on units headed by these men.[73]

In some cases even small plantations hired overseers. This was especially true in the piedmont, where absenteeism was more prevalent. Planters in Tide water Virginia were as likely as not to employ a free dependent—most probably an overseer—when they owned seven enslaved men and women. Resident planters in the piedmont tended to deploy a free dependent, again in all likelihood an overseer, when they had just four to six taxable bondpeople.[74] Absenteeism was also more significant that traditionally thought. By 1739 thirty-seven slave quarters in Orange County were run by overseers for nonresidents, chiefly members of prominent Tidewater families.[75] Some absentee slaveholders even directed their plantations from Great Britain.[76] While absentee plantations were in no Virginian county more prevalent than resident quarters, they contained a very sizeable proportion of the enslaved population, and particularly in newly settled areas. Thirteen percent of tithable slaves were owned by absentee land owners in Tidewater Lancaster County in the middle of the eighteenth century; well over twice that proportion of bondpeople were claimed by nonresident taxpayers in Goochland, a piedmont county, just a few years later.[77] Absentee plantations came to rely more on overseers and stewards the longer they were established. Overseers ensured the quarter's self-sufficiency by facilitating a trade in crops and provisions with those living nearby.

As in Virginia South Carolina's earliest developers envisaged lucrative returns from their colonial investments. The crown issued grants to the Carolina territory (which included North Carolina) as early as 1629, but it was not until 1663 that a group of eight proprietors—most of them men of great wealth and power—began to colonize the area. The proprietors hoped to grow silk in the warm climate of the

Carolinas, but all efforts to produce that valuable commodity failed.[78] It proved difficult to attract settlers; it was not until 1718, after a series of violent Indian wars had subsided, that the population began to increase substantially. Once begun the pattern of settlement diverged. North Carolina, largely cut off from the Atlantic trade by its unpromising coastline, developed into a colony of small to medium farms. The Atlantic littoral would also prove formative to South Carolina. Merchants, and the owners of plantations on its long coast, enjoyed cultural and familial ties to Barbados and Europe, and the colony possessed deep-water ports such as Charleston (through which would eventually pass 40 percent of all North American enslaved people).[79]

The rice trade formed one of two main buttresses to South Carolina's success, bringing its richest inhabitants greater wealth than any of Britain's other American subjects.[80] In the eighteenth-century Americas, only in South Carolina and Georgia was rice ever the principal cash crop.[81] Carolina's earliest white inhabitants had learned to trade in sugar in Barbados and transplanted their mercantile expertise to the mainland.[82] Rice was a natural option for them, its production requiring similar cultivation methods to sugar. Even in the beginning it was a profitable option too. From the seventeenth century rice enjoyed British imperial preference under the Navigation Acts; and ready markets existed in the Mediterranean and the Caribbean (where the plant was used as a food for enslaved people).[83] Prices received by rice planters nearly doubled between 1720 and 1738, and by a factor of more than 6.5 by 1740.[84] Total Carolina exports increased by 50 percent from around 1760 to around 1775, suggesting productivity gains from greater investments in land and labor; an increase in the skills of the enslaved force; technical improvements in cultivation and processing; and the growth of average plantation sizes with related returns to scale.[85] Rice revenues and the rewards of other commercial activities brought certain Carolinian families a privileged status in the cities and plantations along the coast. The Pinckney, Rutledge, and Lowndes families controlled much of the trade passing through Charleston. Later many of their number would be involved in the debates leading to the Declaration of Independence, and in the legislature of the new nation. One of the suggestions that the Continental Congress made before the American Revolution was a program of economic pressure culminating in a policy of nonexportation; tellingly this tactic was to be employed only after the rice harvest had been exported.[86]

The second buttress to South Carolina's wealth was indigo. Mainland North American planters came relatively late to this valuable dye and may never have attempted its cultivation without the efforts of a pioneering British American plantation mistress, Eliza Pinckney (née Lucas).[87] The "new Staple" was "of very great Advantage" to planters; "a Valuable Commodity," "it will always bear the high Charges of Freight & Insurance," wrote one slaveholder, while Josiah Smith in 1772 expected to make a return of "Fifteen pr Cent" on a purchase of the dye.[88]

Britain's rapidly growing textile industry and inadequate imperial supplies explain why, despite a shaky start, the crop became so valuable during the 1740s.[89] By 1754, following a parliamentary decision to subsidize indigo, the colony was exporting more than one million pounds (454,000 kilograms) annually.[90] Planters like William Ancrum soon turned to producing indigo as their main crop.[91] Illustrative of the growing importance of indigo and rice, between 1750 and 1775 16 percent of lowcountry recruitment adverts requested overseers with the ability to cultivate the former crop, while 20 percent of the advertisements required men with knowledge of the latter. Eight percent of advertisers grew both plants (though "hybrid" rice and indigo plantations were "very rare," largely because of the costs associated with developing successful indigo production).[92] By 1770 indigo accounted for about one-quarter of South Carolina's exports; the colony eventually grew 25 percent of the exports of indigo from the New World to Europe.[93]

In 1732 King George II granted proprietorship of the eponymous Georgia to General James Oglethorpe, a member of Parliament, and twenty trustees. The grant covered the land in South Carolina between the Savannah and Altamaha Rivers. Their charter directed that the proprietors would make no profits, and that the colony would come under crown rule after twenty-one years. Most significantly the territory initially forbade slavery. In 1733 the first 114 settlers disembarked at the mouth of the Savannah River; Parliament and the trustees subsidized the migration of around twenty-five hundred people over the following decade, while self-financed settlers also immigrated. The trustees experimented with silk at first, but, as in South Carolina, rice and indigo soon thrived. However, without an enslaved workforce, output remained low, and the settlers began to balk at the prohibition of slavery. Bondpeople started to be imported illegally, especially by migrating South Carolinians. In 1747 the antislavery laws were tacitly relaxed; in 1750 the trustees finally revoked the ban, before surrendering to crown rule the following year, a year early. The numbers of the enslaved in Georgia rose from five hundred in 1751 to fifteen thousand, nearly half the colony's population, by 1775. In the same period, rice production increased tenfold.[94]

These two colonies had many features in common.[95] They share a border, they have a similar climate, and Georgia, like South Carolina, relied heavily on the Atlantic and Caribbean trade. Much work on eighteenth-century slavery focuses on the lowcountry, a 250-mile strip of coastline running from Georgetown in South Carolina in the North, through Georgia to St. Marys on the Florida border in the South.[96] Because rice and indigo formed a staple in both colonies, considering them jointly provides more evidence on—for instance—overseers' agricultural competence. But there were also discrepancies between areas within South Carolina and Georgia, meaning contrasts can be drawn as well. Life on the South Carolinian and Georgian frontiers differed as much from the genteel, established, and quasi-aristocratic lowcountry as did Virginia's Tidewater from its backcountry areas.

South Carolina imported to the lowcountry a facsimile of the hierarchical Barbadian society that many of its earliest settlers had left. And although Savannah shared numerous cultural similarities with Charleston (indeed many South Carolinian planters' business activities crossed colonial borders), especially at midcentury the city held little in common with the more egalitarian, less slave-based economies toward the interior of Georgia. This was because Georgia's slave society was still in the early stages of development compared with its northern neighbor.[97]

During the 1700s the Southeast, like the Chesapeake, underwent social and economic transformations resulting in large part from extensive agricultural developments. Before the first half of the eighteenth century, planters grew rice in inland swamps. Afterward they became aware of the potential of the tidal flow of rivers to irrigate their plantations and moved cultivation in the direction of the coast. Advances in flooding and draining permitted a return to swampier lands toward the west and further down the shoreline, making swampy land the most valuable.[98] Fields could be flooded regularly to prevent the growth of weeds, and draining meant that bondpeople ideally were no longer forced to hoe while standing in water. From the 1750s onward, further innovations lessened the amount of manual labor required. Pounding machines and water mills driven by wind fans and livestock began to appear on some plantations.[99] Backcountry areas of South Carolina offered lowlier inhabitants novel opportunities for patenting lands, and South Carolinians moved to new acreage in Georgia. Yet, as in Virginia, large planters also improved the frontier, their capital resources squeezing out those without the same capacity to purchase. Only forty years after the introduction of slavery to Georgia, by 1790 over half of that state's enslaved lived on absentee plantations in the backcountry.[100]

The Caribbean experience of the many planters who bought land in South Carolina taught them that larger groups of enslaved people (and, early on, indentured servants) worked most effectively under the supervision of overseers. In the early 1700s some bondpeople were imported from the Caribbean with their indentured supervisors, a practice that recognized the often highly personalized relationships between individual overseers and enslaved people, and which would be echoed in later contractual arrangements requiring overseers to accompany hired groups of enslaved people to new plantations.[101] There was a further reason for lowcountry planters to employ overseers. The hierarchical arrangements to which large Carolinian slaveholders had grown accustomed on their island plantations assumed an intermediary between themselves and the workforce. Growing rice involved large economies of scale that called for resident supervision of the enslaved, both to encourage efficient cultivation and to guard against potentially catastrophic slave revolt in a colony that—through the sustained importation of African labor—had a black majority population. Rice cultivation and the introduction of indigo demanded new skills of Lower South supervisors, some of whom came from older colonies to the north, and all of whom had scant experience of managing these exotic floras.[102]

A zeal for absenteeism was more widespread among southeastern planters than those who owned lands in the Chesapeake region. South Carolina and Georgia struggled to produce a coherent societal grouping equivalent to the piedmont slaveholders of Virginia: gentleman aristocrats preferred the urbane delights of Savannah and Charleston to isolation in remote inland counties or a life of disease on the Sea Islands of the Atlantic coast. The wealthy Charleston resident William Ancrum was typical of his class in owning at least two plantations in the South Carolina backcountry.

Fig. 1. "An Overseer Doing His Duty, Sketched from Life near Fredericksburg [Virginia]," 13 March 1792, Benjamin Henry Latrobe, sketchbook, 3:33. Courtesy of the Maryland Historical Society, 1960-108-13-21.

Small to medium-sized quarters, which were in the majority in the colonial lowcountry, were often too small to employ overseers.[103] The incompleteness of extant South Carolinian and Georgian tax documents and plantation records makes a definitive analysis of the ratio of overseers to slaves difficult. Many burned in the War of 1812; Virginian planters took more detailed accounts of the number of enslaved people subordinated to overseers because they tended to pay managers using the share system, which linked remuneration to the number of bondpeople supervised. But it seems clear that more bondpeople were subordinated to each overseer in South Carolina and Georgia than in Virginia. By 1720 perhaps more than half the plantation overseers in South Carolina had twenty or more laborers working for them.[104]

Three factors explain this difference. First, the task system that produced rice and indigo (where bondpeople did specific jobs, either individually or in small groups) required less supervision than Virginia's gang system (where groups of people carried out the same work at the same time—see fig. 1). Second, plantation units were larger since rice cultivation was less labor intensive than that of tobacco. Third, the costly draining and ditching required before rice planting could begin disadvantaged smaller landholders in the tidal areas and particularly in Georgia, where after 1750 established South Carolinian slaveholders and Savannah merchants rushed to patent the land.[105] The traditional picture of the overseer as "the only White Face" on the plantation, surrounded by tens or even hundreds of bondpeople, was therefore most true of overseers in lowcountry South Carolina and Georgia.[106]

Absenteeism would represent oversight's salvation and its condemnation. The elites' lust for landholdings and slaveholdings meant that there was abundant work. But such was the demand for overseers that the incompetence of many individuals who managed to find employ did a lot to fuel prejudices against their capabilities; such was the level of authority devolved that only the most competent were able to cope. Another component of the anti-overseer stereotype was how fellow southerners perceived overseers' backgrounds. Ethnicity, country of origin, and social status each contributed to normative ideas about managers. Eighteenth-century Virginian overseers had names that originated in England, Germany, Italy (Lombardy), Wales, Scotland, Sweden, the Baltic countries, and Ireland.[107] As a ledger kept by the South Carolinian Isaac Hayne attests, many overseers were born in Europe. Out of sixteen that he recorded, fewer than half his overseers were "Carolinian"—indicating that they were born in the colony. Four were "German"; two were Dutch (one "Hollander" and one "Dutchman"); and there was one "Scotchman," one "Englishman," and one "Pennsylvanian."[108] Other lowcountry overseers' names came from Wales, Ireland, Scotland, England, Germany, and Switzerland.[109] Henry Laurens employed two Huguenot protégés, James Theodore Rossel and John Lewis Gervais, as managers on his South Carolinian plantations. These men were from the Palatine, the same part of Germany to which Laurens traced his roots. Some overseers hailed from the peripheries of Great Britain. John Harrower, author of a noted diary and for a while overseer to Colonel Dangerfield, came to Virginia from Lerwick in Shetland.[110] John Pressley, who oversaw for Margaret Colleton, arrived from Scotland in 1772 before patenting three hundred acres in Granville County, South Carolina.[111] In 1754 Virginia, John Barton hired William Griffin as an overseer; Griffin was "thought to be an Irish lad."[112] Although Griffin was born in the colony, his Irish ancestry was deemed paramount when describing his origins. English settlers, like their metropolitan brothers, loathed

Irish Catholics.[113] Griffin's ethnicity was used to cement others' perception of him as a dependent "lad," and to set non-Irish elites apart from the lower classes.

The motivation for Europeans who entered overseeing was primarily a desire to make money. James Barclay, who took employment on a South Carolina plantation at the culmination of a voyage from England, had lofty ambitions: he hoped that his adventure would "bring him a fortune in a short time," allowing him "to return to my native country, there to spend the remainder of my days in ease and affluence."[114] Others had more prosaic wishes. A "Young Man," who had "just arrived from England," advertised his services in the *South Carolina Gazette* in 1754. He claimed that he was used "to Farming" and had served in a "Compting House," declaring simply that he "want[ed] employment; and would be glad to serve any gentleman, merchant, store keeper, or planter, in quality of clerk, book-keeper, or overseer, &c."[115]

Some candidates traveled between colonies to find employment as overseers. Burgess Mitchell came from Maryland to work for George Washington in 1762; in 1749 he had served as a private in the Prince George's County militia.[116] The "Man and his Wife" who in 1754 were "desirous of being employed on some good gentleman's plantation, in the capacity of overseers or otherwise" described themselves in the *South Carolina Gazette* as being "well recommended from the Northward."[117] Interregional migration occurred in the opposite direction—Henry Laurens bemoaned the loss of "Several of our best Overseers" to "the Virginians"; they had been "tempted by their high wages . . . to go and instruct them in [the] manufacture" of indigo.[118] The technical skills possessed by some overseers were evidently transferable. Generous remuneration made the long journey worthwhile and serves as an indication of the value and desirability of this new staple.

However, given the difficulties and expense of covering even short distances in eighteenth-century Virginia, South Carolina, and Georgia, overseers in most areas were likely to have derived from the local population.[119] In general managers came from the lowest reaches of white society. Social status gained in importance in determining how overseers were perceived by southerners, and how they perceived themselves. Especially in the seventeenth and early eighteenth centuries, indentured overseers were made responsible for black enslaved as well as white servants.[120] The suggestion made by Robert Beverley at the beginning of the 1700s—that an overseer was a servant who, having served his time, had acquired the "Skill and Character of an experienced Planter"—seems to indicate that indentured servitude was widespread among Virginian overseers.[121] William Griffin, the "Irish lad" who worked for John Barton, was one such servant.[122] Although immigrants paid for their Atlantic passage through indentured servitude less and less frequently as the century wore on (making foreign-born overseers less common), John Harrower was an example of an indentured overseer from the late eighteenth century, who, "'[r]educed to the last shilling' . . . felt 'obliged to engage to go to Virginia for four years.'" Harrower later worked as an indentured tutor and teacher but died before his indenture was up.[123]

Following the introduction of indentured overseers with groups of African bondpeople to South Carolina in the early 1700s, unfree overseers continued to work across the lowcountry. After dismissing Mark Noble for a number of misdemeanors, Henry Laurens left the day-to-day running of his Broughton Island estate to the indentured servant Conrad Fabre.[124] In Georgia John Gibbons employed an indentured servant "as an Overseer on the plantation of the Estate," thereby giving "him up his Indentures by which he had been bound for four years."[125] The year 1774 saw a prospective overseer advertise the services of himself and his wife, stating (with some temerity) that "there will be a Necessity of their Employers advancing a Trifle of Cash, to defray the Expenses of their passage from England, as they have each of them 4 Years to serve, in recompence for their Passages."[126] Despite the late-century calumny that the overseeing profession received, clearly employers deemed some overseers sufficiently competent that they paid off their employees' indentures. Slaveholders' recompense derived from the overseer's service: he was obliged to work for the planter in return. For the price of freedom, these managers subjected themselves to another form of dependency. And because they had been indentured, they brought oversight and servility further together in the public mind.

Others transferred to overseeing from different occupations, with carpenters, coopers, and blacksmiths the most numerous in this group.[127] Such men developed experience of plantations from working on them in these other capacities. After he had dismissed the overseer Mark Noble, Henry Laurens chose Matthias Zophi, a "carpenter who seems to be a careful Fellow."[128] South Carolinian "Mr. Brown," contracted by Josiah Smith in 1770, was from a rope-making family but was "perswaded" by a fellow overseer "to attempt the planting Business."[129] Some Georgian overseers were former plantation workers displaced after 1750 by the widespread introduction of slave labor.[130] Other overseers previously had been farmers and sought employment only for a short time. Although the wish—if not necessarily the practice—of many managers was to abandon oversight and invest in land when they had accrued enough savings, some small farmers temporarily moved away from agricultural pursuits and became overseers in an attempt to earn more capital and expand their holdings. Similarly former overseers who had left the profession to establish a farmstead sometimes decided to return in order to augment failing incomes. Few intended to become overseers for good, particularly once the profession began to attract social disesteem, though a plurality of both Henry Laurens's and George Washington's overseers had an agricultural background.[131]

Examples of men of high status who worked in managerial roles offer an indication of the importance of social status in determining how contemporaries perceived overseers. The planters who employed them addressed these men, the sons of large planters and other members of the gentry, in honorific terms. When George Washington was looking for an overseer, the "young gentleman" John Pendleton was recommended to him, his title indicating the status of the Pendleton family.[132] Robert Hamilton worked as an overseer for Landon Carter of Sabine Hall, Virginia. Hamilton was left land and bondpeople in Carter's will, after Carter had taken a duty of care over Hamilton following the death of Hamilton's father, Gilbert, who had once been a county sheriff. After Carter's own death, Hamilton became overseer for Carter's son, Robert Wormeley Carter.[133] For such men overseeing meant a preparation for later independent careers in planting; their respectable background gave them a better reputation than other managers.[134]

This practice was current in the Lower South as well. In South Carolina John Couturier, who oversaw for John Ewing Colhoun, was a member of a Huguenot family with sizeable landholdings and slaveholdings; John Grinninger, a cousin, also worked for Colhoun.[135] Joseph Fogartie was in 1758 an overseer in St. James Santee, South Carolina; his father was Stephen Fogartie, a large planter in St. Thomas Parish.[136] Henry Laurens intended the employment that he gave to James Theodore Rossel and John Lewis Gervais to be edifying, as Rossel and Gervais both had designs on owning their own plantations. Laurens admitted of Rossel and Gervais that "they are no Planters I can easily perceive" but still encouraged their ambitions, Rossel eventually managing Laurens's Broughton Island plantation.[137] Also arrived in the colony from Germany was Peter Horlbeck, a master mason who would eventually build the Exchange, the customs house in Charleston, with his brother John Adam Horlbeck. Laurens took Peter under his wing and made him overseer at Mepkin plantation, giving him advice and encouragement in his desire to advance, economically and socially, in South Carolina.[138] Managers like these were far removed from the "common mercenary overseers" that planters such as Henry Laurens and George Washington deplored.[139] Compare how slaveholders sometimes voiced strong reluctance to deal with lowlier overseers, requiring instead direct interaction with elite counterparts. A neighbor of the Georgian James Habersham objected to the planter sending his overseer to issue a message rather than Habersham delivering it himself: "I am not to be threatened by Overseers of any person else . . . I was the proper person to have been applid to."[140]

Large numbers of locally born white managers in both regions were the sons of small farmers.[141] Thomas Lawson, overseer to Landon Carter, was the son of Daniel Lawson, a farmer in Richmond County.[142] Sons of overseers also became overseers themselves, as in the case of James King the younger, who served as a manager to Landon Carter.[143] The Virginian William Cabell employed Thomas Appling and his son together.[144] John Fox sent a recommendation to Francis Jerdone on behalf of his eldest son, James, who had been working for John as his assistant in Virginia and now sought to strike out on his own.[145] In Georgia Matthias Binder was employed with his son for one year to oversee a plantation belonging to William Gibbons; perhaps the son was intended to receive an apprenticeship in overseeing.[146] Also in Georgia the sons of Bennet Wheeler's overseer were charged with collecting and delivering crops.[147]

Overseers from different social groupings held one thing in common. Whether they were indentured servants, or sons of planters or small farmers, most overseers seem to have been young men. Few planters referred specifically to their managers' ages, though Thomas Jefferson described a prospective employee as being "about 30. years of age."[148] Nearly three quarters of a group described as "sons of householders or overseers" in the 1776 census of Maryland, the neighboring colony to Virginia, were between twenty and twenty-eight years old.[149] In the lowcountry John Couturier was in his early thirties when he oversaw for John Ewing Colhoun.[150] Josiah Smith described an overseer as "a very Sober, honest & Industrious man," though he "want[ed] a few years more Experience to make an able Planter."[151] Young men also reached greater heights in the plantation structure—for example Billy Beale was just eighteen when he became a steward for Landon Carter.[152]

Yet some overseers were much older. While many planters held to the practice of annually dismissing overseers, others employed proficient managers for long periods. Joseph Valentine, hired by Daniel Parke Custis in 1755, was overseer of the Custis estates when George Washington married Martha Custis in 1759; in 1771, while still an overseer, he advertised a runaway slave in the *Virginia Gazette*.[153] Planters appreciated the reliability implied by old age. One old man who handled the "house people" and ditchers for George Washington was "honest, sober, well-meaning and 'something knowing,'" though Washington admitted that this overseer was "not accustomed to Negroes, who[,] since they were in no sort of awe of him[,] of course do as they please."[154]

The presence of enslaved people in the overseer role also contributed to prejudices against superintendents. Not only did white overseers spend the majority of their time in the company of enslaved people; bondpeople could also perform the managerial role capably and effectively. One of the key components in the strengthening of eighteenth-century prejudices against overseers was the association of overseeing and servility. The terminology that described enslaved overseers, foremen, and slave drivers was often just as imprecise as that used to denote white superintendents. In 1769 Henry Lee advertised an enslaved foreman, Tom Salter, who had "managed several years as an overseer . . . under Capt. Robert Downman."[155] Yet the range of tasks carried out by enslaved overseers differed from foremen's typical duties. These overseers, like their white counterparts, were "more akin to managers than mere gang leaders," whereas the main task for foremen was to set the pace for a group of laborers.[156] One of George Washington's foremen, also named Tom, gained his role because he was "exceeding healthy, strong and good at the hoe": his attributes were similar to those of the average bondman, an indication of the nature of the work that he was required to do. Enslaved overseers usually did not undertake physical labor. Edmund Bagge, of Essex County, Virginia, allowed "Negro Cromwell overseer" to take charge of all aspects of his tobacco production in 1730; he produced more pounds of tobacco per hand than a white overseer managed two years later.[157]

Virginia differed from South Carolina and Georgia in not legally proscribing the employment of enslaved overseers.[158] In 1704 the Virginian Henry Thacker recommended in his will that one of his bondmen work as an overseer, while Ralph Wormeley used his bondman, "Captain," in a similar role on his Rosegill estate in Middlesex County.[159] There is evidence that planters such as George Washington hired bondmen specifically for their expertise in oversight, though he and Landon Carter at one time or another expressed doubts about the wisdom of such decisions.[160] When these slaveholders perceived that newly promoted men were taking liberties such as working too slowly, both men came to feel that "they had made a mistake in their judgment." Carter expressed a sense of betrayal as he began to view the very men that he had chosen as "cursed villains."[161] The enslaved overseer won opportunities to influence other bondpeople that were unavailable to those outside the managerial cadre. Carter complained that Jack Lubber, a bondman whom he had made overseer, not only had lied and stolen but had allowed other enslaved people to evade their "responsibilities."[162]

Owing to the relatively large and growing size of plantations; the widespread absenteeism of masters and mistresses, particularly during summer; and the small and declining pool of available white overseers, many lowcountry planters opted to have slave drivers (the equivalent of Virginian "foremen") perform some managerial tasks in defiance of legal censure.[163] Bondpeople with prior managerial experience also gained full promotions to overseer level. In Georgia John-Martin Bolzius recorded the presence of "Negroe Overseer[s]," while in South Carolina, Ralph Izard was advised to transfer more authority to enslaved managers on discovering pleasing productivity results from this course of action.[164] South Carolina immigrant James Barclay recounted that under him "there was a black overseer, whose business it was to measure off the work to the rest, and see it performed during the day."[165] When Henry Laurens fired the white overseer Mark Noble, he left his South Carolinian New Hope plantation under the care of Old Cuff, a trusted bondman who had probably been a driver.[166] Thomas Owen, establishing a new plantation in the same colony, had similar intentions for "2 Sawyers who are . . . old slaves accustomed to planting and all business of a country life."[167]

The advantage of this approach was that an enslaved person would know the needs of the plantation better than a neophyte free overseer.[168] At the end of the century, one South Carolinian advertiser even assured applicants for a managerial position that they would have time to carry on another trade if they had one, as the actual "business of the plantation is conducted by a black man," while other planters opted to do away with overseers altogether, relying solely on drivers.[169]

Experienced enslaved people could fill short-term managerial gaps. The overseer John Couturier wrote to his employer, South Carolinian planter John Ewing Colhoun, also at the end of the century, "I dont expect to move away & If I did, it will be at least a Month afore I do in which time you may depend I will take as much Care of the Plantation as if I meant to Stay. There is no reason to fear Of getting a good hand to manage for you If I Should Quit as Mr Cahusac will be Glad to Undertake it."[170]

Bondpeople in the South Carolina and Georgia lowcountry were twice as likely to work under enslaved drivers as their Chesapeake counterparts.[171] Around midcentury in a typical lowcountry parish at least two-thirds of the adult enslaved worked under drivers.[172] The result of these local circumstances was that the terms "driver" and "overseer" were often confused.[173] Adding to this complexity, Henry Laurens employed free black overseers but confessed that an overseer's race made his position all the more dangerous. He advised one such overseer to "carry a steady command . . . for of all Overseers they [the enslaved people] love those of their own colour least."[174] Bondpeople must have viewed as treacherous the assumption by nonwhites of the overseer's symbolic role for the defense of white racial hierarchy.

The presence of bondmen in a range of supervisory roles can lead historians to overestimate the number of enslaved managers at work on plantations across the South.[175] Enslaved overseers were in fact generally few in number: the majority of supervisors were white, which southern plantation societies regarded as socially and legally necessary.[176] As members of a subordinated racial caste, enslaved overseers were stigmatized in different ways to their white counterparts, and for different reasons. Those bondmen who found themselves in a position of authority over other enslaved people might have escaped the day-to-day drudgery of fieldwork but not the racial debasement to which the white South subjected them.

One intriguing case yields a glimpse of possible female involvement in plantation management. Economic forces made societal constraints on women of lower status more malleable than is often assumed: the demands of an expanding market economy brought with them a popular image of lower-class women that did not preclude hard labor.[177] Against this background there were opportunities for such women to pursue more unusual careers. In 1778 a Georgia plantation owner stated a preference for a single male overseer but conceded that "if a prudent woman cou'd be got I shou'd have no Objections as she might be usefull on the Plantation."[178] A considerable level of stigmatization would have attached to any woman engaged in work so deeply associated with men. This example is, however, the only mention of women involved in overseeing to appear in the sources consulted here.

Robert Beverley's suggestion that overseers could gain the "Skill and Character of an experienced planter" seems to indicate a more fluid social position for managers at the start of the eighteenth century and hints at more benign attitudes toward the profession then. Beverley's work was partly promotional: in attempting to portray the advantages of Virginia to prospective settlers, he likely would have downplayed the hardships experienced by white people. There are indeed examples of successful early managers, such as one of Robert "King" Carter's overseers, John Buckles, who owned 135 acres by 1721.[179] For many overseers, although such rhetoric might have been kinder at the beginning of the 1700s, the reality was different. The most valuable possessions owned by Timothy Stamps, who died in 1731—also after overseeing for Robert "King" Carter—were seven horses and a sheep.[180] Those who passed away with relatively sizeable estates owned little in the way of land or human property. The possessions of Charles Stagg, a long-standing overseer for Carter, were valued in 1736 at just over £211, but he owned only one "Negro-woman," an "old blind Negro Man," and two indentured servants.[181]

Young, lower-class, or indentured, sometimes foreign, and occasionally Catholic overseers possessed traits that were deemed undesirable in the patriarchal mind. These traits restricted the enfranchisement of overseers across the South—the colonies studied here banned from voting men who were under age twenty-one, those who owned fewer than fifty acres unimproved or twenty-five acres improved land, Catholics, and newcomers to the colonies.[182] The growth of absenteeism and the diminishing availability of land brought with them not only an increase in the physical distance between overseers and elites, but also a widening of social status. Five years after Timothy Stamps's death, the voting qualification for white men in Virginia was the possession of a freehold of one hundred acres of unsettled land.[183]

Overseers also rejected the undesirable connotations of their position. Individuals resisted attempts to group them with other dependents as well as together with other overseers. They viewed independence and dependence not as discrete, self-exclusive categories, but rather as poles on a continuum of relative degrees.[184] Managers' responses to accusations of dependence often included attempts to ameliorate their status. The short length of overseer contracts enabled members of the profession to move away from communities where they might otherwise experience "shaming dependence." This type of movement might be described as honor-led migration. Moving permitted overseers to establish some degree of the personal credit that southerners considered vital for interpersonal relationships.[185] Two-thirds of householders in Goochland County, Virginia, from 1752 were recorded in tax records two years later, though only one-third of those who identified as overseers remained.[186] Some overseers associated migration with the life stages that they linked to the eventual gaining of independence. One of George Washington's managers outlined in 1765 his intention to move to York County, Virginia, "because I of Late Seem determed to marry and there I imagine I may probably meet with Some Girl that may make an agreeable wife."[187] It is true that many white migrants who appear in colonial Virginian tax records under their own name—meaning that they were heads of household—had traveled to other, often outlying counties, in order to establish themselves. Unfortunately the data from colonial tax lists for South Carolina and Georgia is too incomplete to draw similar conclusions. Only a few lists survive for South Carolina before 1808, while the federal census of 1790 lists heads of households and numbers of enslaved people but does not include the names of all property owners or describe all property owned.

It seems likely, however, that many overseers stayed in the profession until they had put aside enough capital to purchase a smallholding or become a tenant. Those who rented plantations attempted to make money on their own account while working for someone else.[188] Indeed overseeing was viewed in certain quarters as a route to advancement. Lewis Gray, the early historian of American agriculture, argued that poor whites, if they desired to "escape" their situation, thanks to competition with enslaved labor could aspire only to be overseers or small commercial farmers.[189] In 1770 South Carolinian merchant Josiah Smith wrote that one overseer, Wadingham, had decided to "quit the management of [George Austen's] plantation as he found it rather too fatiguing to attend the Business of that and his own new Settlement."[190] A few years later, Robert Carter of Nomini Hall in Virginia recorded that "John Crabb . . . is going to his own Plantation and does not intend to serve me longer than the present year," while another overseer left Carter's service after his father died and bequeathed him fifty acres.[191] Some overseers enjoyed rights that were denied to other dependents. Although only a small proportion voted, they made up a higher share of the Virginian electorate than, for instance, tenant farmers. A few overseers were jury members, others became magistrates and burgesses, and there is evidence that some managers fraternized with members of the gentry.[192]

The ownership of slaves was another sign of social advancement. Buying humans and putting them to work held a particular cachet—it meant that a man became a "master and, in a slave society . . . a member of the ruling class."[193] While many white men had dependents—wives, children, indentured servants, and free employees—not everyone could afford to buy bondpeople. Owning black people enabled overseers to demonstrate that they were further removed from the enslaved underclass than patriarchal rhetoric tried to suggest. Slaveholding overseers could advertise their own independence in opposition to the racially and legally subjugated group of people that they placed beneath them. James Harrison, who oversaw for the Virginian Robert Carter just after the Revolutionary War, owned an enslaved woman.[194] Henry Laurens's overseer at Mepkin, John Smith, owned two enslaved men; in total Laurens employed at least eleven slaveholding overseers.[195] James Barclay recounted how an acquaintance was offered bondpeople for sale: "the overseer of Mr. Verin's plantation . . . agreed to take two of them."[196] By the time of his death in 1771, Joseph Valentine, who had been overseer to Daniel Parkes Custis in York County, Virginia, since 1755, owned twelve enslaved men, women, and children who made up £400 of the £600 value of his estate, an indication of the importance of slave ownership to capital accumulation.[197] When overseers worked on shares, owning their own bondpeople gave them an extra share of the crop per man, or half a share if the enslaved person was a female, though managers usually had to provide subsistence for their own people.[198] Some overseers bought enslaved people on credit and paid off their debts by working the bondpeople on shares.[199] Slaveholding overseers could also rent their bondpeople's labor to their employers. Michael Boinneau supplemented his year's salary of £50 with £16 hire for each of his four enslaved men.[200]

Yet even if some overseers were able to win material advancement, the restricted social opportunities for the majority of their counterparts and their need to work for other men underpinned negative opinions of overseers. Even in the early stages of the 1700s, despite Beverley's platitudes, managers were starting to receive vitriol. William Byrd I vociferously denounced the marriage of his neighbor's daughter to an overseer: "to stoop to a dirty Plebian, without any kind of merit, is the lowest Prostitution. I found the Family justly enraged at it."[201] More dramatically, in Middlesex County, Virginia, a militia colonel suggested that one of his men, Davis, work for him as an overseer. This provoked Davis; the men dueled, and Davis was killed.[202]

Virginians in particular began to set overseeing in explicit contrast to independence. George Tucker reflected that in the colonial Tidewater, "there was no such thing as *Dependence,* in the lower counties, except in the case of overseers."[203] When as governor in 1786 Thomas Jefferson eliminated primogeniture in Virginia, breaking up established estates, John Randolph of Roanoke complained: "the old families of Virginia will form connections with the low people, and sink into the mass of overseers' sons and daughters."[204] In like manner the debate over the introduction of slavery to Georgia in 1750 referred to the consequent introduction of overseeing as a profession. Opponents claimed that "a low Set of Men" whom, they believed, had "been promised to be made Overseers" of any bondpeople brought to Georgia had organized one proslavery petition. The petitioners must have come to the conclusion that "the less well-off settlers would be deprived of their economic independence and left with little choice but to work as hired hands or overseers" following observations of the slave system in other colonies.[205]

The very fact that overseers managed agricultural work also damned them in the eyes of their upper-class employers. Again taking a cue from their classical forebears, southern elites told themselves that slavery allowed them a life devoted to cerebral pursuits such as art and philosophy, rather than the mundanities of plantation business—though this was more a planter ideal than plantation reality. Furthermore their moral aversion to physical labor meant that both male and female slaveholders were not supposed to handle the planting, tending, or harvesting of the crop, tasks that could instead be delegated to an overseer.[206]

Though it was in the post–Revolutionary War decades that southerners made permanent the comprehensive negative image of the overseer, the late-century "new mode of libelling a whole society of men" built on a raft of prejudices against dependents that had a long pedigree in the colonial South. Despite Robert Beverley's self-serving description of overseer advancement, the indications are that there were managers who were able to escape their situation. Precisely because overseers faced stigmatization as a result of their dependent status, the few who were lucky enough to progress might have won the respect of colonial society eventually. Yet these successes had little effect either on halting the development of the anti-overseer stereotype, or on contemporary opinions about the less fortunate, dependent majority of superintendents. The tension between patriarchism and profit weighed heavily on the overseer and the way that he was perceived, heaping onto dependence myriad further reasons for stigmatism.

— *Chapter Two* —

"Douptfull of my Diligence"

Overseer Recruitment and Character Requirements

Jarring with his wistful desire to live like "one of the Patriarchs," the prosaic economic foundation to William Byrd's existence is clear even within his sketch of bucolic rapture. Byrd, it has been pointed out, explicitly opposed "money" to "patriarchy" in his idyll. Nearly all the trappings that he enjoyed as a patriarch—refined dress, furnishings, diet, and his grand plantation house at Westover—"owed their existence to a form of money, namely credit." Byrd viewed matters of money and markets only as means to his patriarchal ends.[1] In the European political tradition, for centuries elites had attempted to separate the domestic from the public sphere. Greeks talked of the competing claims of the *oikia* and *polis,* Romans of drawing a distinction between *otium et negotium.* In eighteenth-century plantation America, the principal unit of economic production was the household, but it was also the principal unit of political control: *oikia* had merged with *polis.* Moreover a continued commitment to *negotium*—commerce or business—was vital both for plantation success and for slaveholders like Byrd to imagine that they lived a life of *otium,* or disinterested pleasure.[2]

Byrd's obfuscation of his true economic imperatives is representative of slaveholders' public reactions following the expansion of the North American market economy. In one of the founding texts of political philosophy, Aristotle had drawn an explicit contrast between the ignoble subsistence activities for which the household was designed, and virtuous political engagement in the public sphere. For the sake of a truly free politics, the polis strictly excluded all questions of personal welfare or private concern. This arrangement provided male heads of household with a position of freedom from need, allowing an engagement in politics based on purely ethical or philosophical concerns.[3] But, as Hannah Arendt suggested, whereas for the ancients the notion of political economy would therefore have been "a contradiction in terms," the consumer revolution of the eighteenth century caused the economy to break loose of the shackles that had tied it to an ancillary role within feudal society and transform the public realm into a "sphere for the satisfaction of . . . material needs" through commercial exchange.[4] In the economic context of eighteenth-century Virginia, South Carolina, and Georgia, private interests invaded the public sphere, just as political relationships were subsumed into, played out in, and tested in slaveholders' private households.

One source of managerial stigmatization was that to slaveholders, overseers represented a daily reminder of their commercial imperatives. In their dealings with managers planters were forced to acknowledge the limitations of their idyll. Unlike their ancient forebears, the demands of the market economy prevented eighteenth-century planters from taking advantage of the slave (and hence the overseer) system to devote themselves entirely to leisure pursuits and the cultivation of the arts: *negotium* had an unfortunate tendency to scupper plans for *otium*. Since responsibility for plantation returns often devolved to the overseer, he was able to amend the fundamental tension between slaveholders' ideological preoccupations and their need to realize a sustained profit from capital investments. In return he might be given wages, food, and lodging, but with them he received prejudice, mistrust, and dishonor.

Another source of stigmatization was the fact that overseers represented an intrusion into plantation life from the commercial world outside the patriarch's household. Many overseers were recruited through advertisements in eighteenth-century gazettes and often were hired on very short contracts. They thus did not fit completely into the patriarchal body politic. Although a manager might draw "an equal Share to carry the Machine forward," his position, as a white, often non-indentured male—though one who was nonetheless seen as dependent owing to his failure to establish his own household—sat uneasily within this political model. The overseer usually was not owned by, or related to, his employer. According to patriarchal reasoning, the likelihood that the overseer would fulfill his obligations was therefore less assured. Slaveholders found their managers either by advertising in newspapers or through recourse to "word of mouth" systems—personal recommendations, information-sharing between planters, and consultation with trusted employees. Employers demonstrated an obsessive wish to make sure that they were hiring the right man. Partly their attention to detail arose from commonly held prejudices against dependents; partly it derived from slaveholders' recognition of the importance of the managerial position to their profit margins. Increasingly it also derived from planters' growing antipathy toward the overseer class.

Why did slaveholders invest so much time and effort in what their prejudices were starting to suggest was a futile exercise? The answer lies in their continuing desire for other members of the elite to regard them as having full control of their dependents and plantations. Faced with the intellectual and philosophical barrage that the market economy had released on their patriarchal bubbles, overseer recruitment became another effective way for slave owners to demonstrate their mastery. They strove to redesign patriarchal rhetoric for these new conditions and to reposition themselves at the head of organizations that, especially in the lowcountry, came in this period to resemble "factories in the field" more than they did traditional patriarchal households.

Slaveholders' profit margins nevertheless were of greater concern than their more ephemeral pretensions to the moral order of the plantation. In the end it was of more importance that overseers be efficient workers than morally upright. The same was not necessarily true of those men who oversaw for plantation mistresses. As southerners grew wealthier over the course of the century, and as they employed enslaved people to carry out the tasks associated with agriculture, most white women, like most white men, were able to avoid shaming physical labor. Elite women in particular devoted themselves to the pursuit of domesticity: in line with the stipulations of the eighteenth-century division of labor, commerce and industry were a male preserve.[5] But those women who found themselves in charge of large plantations—widows, for example—perceived a tension between this ideal and a need successfully to manage their plantations. For these women an overseer could represent a means to avoid the stigmatization of involvement with the commercial male world.

Some planters of both sexes explicitly sought married overseers, while other slaveholders desired single men. Wives fulfilled a valuable economic role, since they were able to manage dairies, perform domestic chores, or care for sick enslaved children. On the other hand, single men were cheaper. For women planters overseers' wives were of significant practical use in providing mediation between the fields and the Big House. Since the overseer was a male representative of the brutal side of plantation life, to spend too much time in his company was unthinkable for many elite women. Taking a spouse had natural advantages for managers too: it was essential in constructing overseers' identities as free white men.

Planters recruited overseers at certain times throughout the year, depending on the tasks that they expected them to perform. Changes in land and cash crop prices also affected the employment of overseers, especially the significant fluctuations in the value of tobacco over the course of the eighteenth century. But in Virginia, South Carolina, and Georgia, the peak recruitment time fell in the autumn and winter.[6] George Washington aimed to hire in the autumn, "the season at which our Overseers are engaged, and the plans for the ensuing Crop must be formed."[7] Washington recruited overseers in the natural break in the agricultural year: the tobacco harvest and the cutting of wheat were finished by September.[8] The planting of both crops would then begin anew in January, the month in which plantation accounts were settled, and when, having found suitable candidates, George Washington would offer his overseers a contract.[9] An analysis of Chesapeake and lowcountry newspapers (the *Virginia Gazette,* the *South Carolina Gazette,* the *Georgia Gazette,* and a number of minor publications) confirms that the period when most overseeing positions were advertised centered on January.[10] In the southern colonies, as in Virginia, planters began the recruitment process in early autumn, advertising for overseers "in time to prepare land for the next crop," and after the rice harvest was finished.[11] A number of other subscribers, with their minds set on specific tasks, advertised for managerial recruits before particular dates in the planting calendar, “by the first of March” for instance, or “in August next.”[12]

In all three colonies, overseer recruitment notices were placed in newspapers either by planters or their agents, or by overseers requiring employment. The format of one such advertisement from the *Virginia Gazette* is comparable to those published in South Carolina and Georgia. Placed by Lemuel Riddick, it outlines the number of bondpeople under supervision, the plantation, and the crop (grain) grown on it (see fig. 2).[13] Because planters believed that only the most experienced overseers were equal to such challenges, they tried to make recruitment adverts sound appealing in a competitive market. This tactic increased the pool of candidates and thereby maximized slave owners’ chances of finding a good overseer. Thirteen out of 140 lowcountry notices described plantations as situated near large towns such as Charleston.[14] Just as slaveholders did, overseers preferred the relative comfort, the sociability, and the career opportunities provided by an urban environment to a lonely and sickly life in the malarial swamps, a life defined by shaming contact with enslaved people.[15] One plantation was located in a “pleasant, healthful situation”; another had “but few negroes employ’d.”[16] According to a contemporary, Charleston itself was “filled with the richest planters of the province, who resort hither in quest of health and pleasure.”[17] Adverts placed by overseers reinforce the impression that a position away from the coastal swamps was preferable—a Georgian overseer desired a “plantation up the country, on the salts, or in Carolina.”[18] But one “PERSON . . . [who] understands the Management of Negroes,” perhaps cognizant of the improved opportunities for land ownership on the frontier, averred that he “would rather be placed in the Country than Town.”[19]

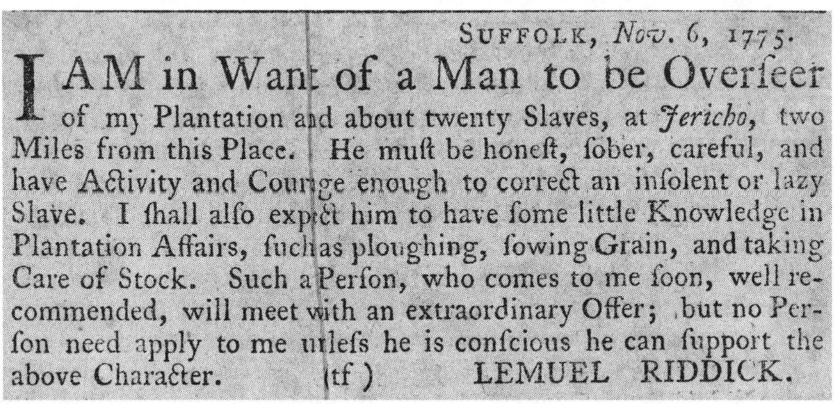

SUFFOLK, *Nov.* 6, 1775.

I AM in Want of a Man to be Overſeer of my Plantation and about twenty Slaves, at *Jericho*, two Miles from this Place. He muſt be honeſt, ſober, careful, and have Activity and Courage enough to correct an inſolent or lazy Slave. I ſhall alſo expect him to have ſome little Knowledge in Plantation Affairs, ſuch as ploughing, ſowing Grain, and taking Care of Stock. Such a Perſon, who comes to me ſoon, well recommended, will meet with an extraordinary Offer; but no Perſon need apply to me unleſs he is conſcious he can ſupport the above Character. (tf) LEMUEL RIDDICK.

Fig. 2. Advert for overseer, *Virginia Gazette* (Dixon and Hunter), 18 November 1775, p. 3. Courtesy of Virginia Historical Society.

Would adverts have attracted managers who were more literate (and perhaps better educated) than those recruited by word of mouth? Conversely could written notices disadvantage employers by excluding potential, but illiterate, candidates? Some of the features of the gazettes suggest that their readership was at least erudite. As part of the pre-Revolutionary debates held on their front pages, Latin, French, and Greek are often used.[20] In one issue of the *South Carolina Gazette,* an advertisement appears entirely in Latin.[21] In all likelihood the majority of overseers would not have appreciated the ornate literary allusions peppering the gazettes. Most lacked the classical education that members of the gentry and elites enjoyed. Although republican discourse played out on the pages of the modern newspaper media, it reinforced for patriarchs the ideal of an intellectual lineage dating back to Greece and Rome. Its intended audience did not include overseers. Yet although only two out of every five poor farm tenants in eighteenth-century Virginia were able to read and write (and even those who learned to do so "gained only minimal literacy"), and some managers do appear to have been illiterate, most overseers were expected to have at least elementary literacy skills.[22] One South Carolinian notice advertised its author as a manager who "writes a good legible Hand," and planters frequently corresponded with their overseers.[23] Basic numeracy was also essential for the job (and might have been required for enslaved managers as well): an advert in South Carolina demanded "an overseer, who . . . can write and cypher sufficient to measure boards and timber."[24] For tax purposes overseers were required to make a list of the tithables on each quarter—the owner was responsible if the overseer failed to turn in the list on time—while managers generally compiled the plantation accounts contained in the papers of men like Landon Carter.[25]

For a slaveholder to rely solely on newspaper advertising was not perforce to set him or her at a disadvantage. Advertisements did not have to be seen by all who were part of their "target audience." Readers might inform colleagues who had not read the gazettes of vacancies listed therein.[26] Eighteenth-century Americans' low level of access to newspapers meant that such networks were essential if recruitment notices were to be effective.[27] A Virginian subscriber deemed an advert to be the "method of address . . . more immediate than any other I could take" to reach a "Mr *Whiting* who has the direction of part of Mr. *Fitzhugh's* business in the *Northern Neck,*" whose assistance he hoped to solicit in finding a suitable overseer.[28] Further "the contents of the fine print" could reach overseers "through reading aloud and through conversations at courthouses, ordinaries (pubs), and other places of assembly."[29] Most gazette advertisements (but particularly those for overseeing positions) were laid out simply and lent themselves to being read out to a listening, interested audience. This was especially relevant because the difficulties associated with transporting newspapers meant that they did not always reach those who had paid a subscription. One Virginian complained that "subscribers to said Papers began to murmur, saying that a News Paper was a very uncommon thing among them, and threatened to have their names erased out of the [newspaper's] Books."[30]

Notices often combined an advertisement for saleable goods with an appeal for overseers. By broadcasting to the planting community as a whole, even across colonial borders (the *Georgia Gazette* and *South Carolina Gazette* were circulated widely and subscribed to in neighboring colonies), advertisers could use written and word-of-mouth methods to maximize their chances of finding a good candidate. Those who saw George Smith's 1766 notice for rum, sugar, and mahogany were informed that he also wanted "an OVERSEER, with a Wife, to take charge of his plantation on Cooper-River."[31] John Parker and William Logan made a similar remark at the end of an advertisement for cattle, corn, and potato seed.[32] Other overseer notices mentioned the sale of land and runaway horses.[33] This last was significant because a principal managerial duty was the retrieval of stray animals.[34] The South Carolinian John Waring's dual need to advertise a lost steed and employ an overseer therefore offered him an opportunity to "highjack" word-of-mouth information-sharing networks.[35] When overseers advertised themselves, they used similar networks. On at least one occasion, George Washington recommended a manager on the basis of an advertisement that he had read.[36]

Despite the links between adverts and word-of-mouth networks, the relative scarcity of recruitment notices in the gazettes suggests that the more informal mechanisms were cheaper, more effective, and more trustworthy. In the peak winter recruitment period, the number of advertisements per issue rarely rose above two, whereas those for runaway bondpeople were far more numerous (bondpeople, of course, were believed to be more crucial to plantation yields than overseers). The examples of adverts that supported a word-of-mouth course of action intimate that planters resorted to advertising only after other options were exhausted.[37] Similarly planters might have used advertising at "crisis" times—when they had fired an overseer for some indiscretion, or when they had acquired a plantation and needed a supervisor.[38] The several advertisements that begin with "*WANTED IMMEDIATELY*, an overseer" are indicative of such pressures.[39]

Subscribers who placed adverts often repeated them two or three times, although a number reappeared with greater frequency. South Carolina planter Rawlins Lowndes advertised his vacancies for two overseers on twenty occasions between October 1764 and May 1765.[40] On the one hand, this could imply that subscribers found adverts ineffectual in securing capable overseers, if, indeed, they found decent candidates at all. On the other hand, that Lowndes was willing to pay to advertise so often might suggest that he was confident that his advertisements would receive an answer. William Gibbons paid three shillings in 1769, and the same amount the following year, to advertise for overseers.[41] And since the majority of notices were repeated only a small number of times, the conclusion must be that a good number of adverts were successful. The amount of subscribers who used the gazettes frequently, but for advertising different available positions, far exceeds the number who repeated their adverts. Planters like Henry Smith, who advertised two different jobs in the *South Carolina Gazette* in 1764 and 1765, are typical.[42] Absentee plantation owners certainly perceived an advantage in advertising, since newspapers publicized their notices across large distances.

Whether or not the notices were effective, slaveholders' lack of faith in the unverifiable qualities of previously unknown overseers led most to favor informal recruitment. Since slaveholders required agricultural skills and strong experience, overseers who placed notices described themselves in flattering terms. One claimed that "whoever wants an overseer . . . [who] can be well recommended for making Indico and Rice, may hear of a person so qualified, on application to Mr. *Thomas Sikes,* Butcher, just without Charles-Town gates."[43] Unlike word-of-mouth networks, adverts could deliver a large group of unreliable hopefuls. And they were expensive. Henry Laurens complained in 1766 that he had: "been abundantly plagued & put at some expence to get an Overseer for Mr. Oswald. Several clever fellows, & a vast number of worthless ones, applied in consequence of my advertisements & with some of the former class I had at different times actually agreed, but all shewed great reluctance to the undertaking when they found that the Plantation to be settled was not on my own account, & by some shabby means or other all gave me the slip."[44]

Advertisers tried to counter these problems. A typical demand that they made of candidates was that "none need apply, except known or brings a proper recommendation."[45] The recommendation was supposed to be a promise of the overseer's integrity penned by a former employer. Advertisers correlated their own (presumably impeccable) ability to judge an applicant's skill with the ability of their fellow slave owners to do the same. The Virginian Robert Brooke demanded that applicants bring with them "the recommendations of any Gentleman of distinguished judgment and candour."[46] One of his counterparts asked for "certificates from gentlemen of character, of [the prospective overseer's] abilities, integrity, and sobriety, without which he need not give himself the trouble of an application."[47] In South Carolina another planter "WANTED, an OVERSEER, for a plantation on Savannah-River," promising that "good encouragement will be given to any who has a good recommendation."[48]

Recommendations attested to an overseer's length of experience, his aptitude, and his style of slave management and sometimes came from fellow managers. A recommendation written toward the end of the century, vouching for the Virginian William Powell, was one such testament. "This is to certify that we have been acquanted with Mr William Powell for several years past Two years of which Time he has livd under are Imidate Notis in the Estate of RobtCarter Esqr & from our knowledge of s[ai]d Powell we beleave him to be an onest industrious Compasinate good Natred man & highly approvd of by the people under his care & Charge."[49]

Demands for recommendations increased over the course of the mid-eighteenth century in South Carolina, an indication of planters' growing dissatisfaction with the quality of available overseers. Mentions of recommendations in adverts went up from 39 percent between 1734 and 1746, to 84 percent between 1746 and 1752 and 72 percent between 1757 and 1768.[50]

In like manner to adverts that used information-sharing networks established by overseers, some masters and mistresses posted adverts only after recourse to their own networks. "*Richard Harris,* formerly an Overseer to *John Drayton,* Esq. [a South Carolinian plantation owner]," was advised that if he should "apply to the Printer, he may hear something to his Advantage."[51] Similarly in 1750 a lowcountry advertiser suggested that "if one *James Lubbuck* (who writes he was overseer for Col. *Bull* in the year 1743) be living, and will apply to Mr. *Thomas Bolton,* he may hear something that may prove to his advantage."[52] Such notices were indicative of a growing skepticism toward not only the utility of recruitment adverts, but also the reliability of written recommendations. Those who brought references with them could not always be trusted to do well on a new plantation. Planter dissatisfaction with the recruitment process increased in tandem with antipathies toward overseers. Henry Laurens had found an overseer for Governor James Grant of the new colony of East Florida but was "sorry to see that Harvie does not behave well. He produced Certificates of his former conduct that were very satisfactory but every Planter experiences such disappointment in that class of people."[53] Employers' cynicism came to affect even the recruitment of men with an exalted position in the management hierarchy. When, just after the Revolutionary War, George Washington discussed the possible employment of a steward, the retired general touched on past difficulties. He affirmed to his correspondent: "I had rather he or they should be personally known to you; or their characters ascertained by a friend in whom you can confide . . . because . . . how often do we find recommendations given without merit to deserve them?"[54]

Why then, in spite of the frequent criticisms that they made both of recruitment adverts and of written recommendations from unknown planters, did some planters continue to rely on the former, and most insist on the latter? The first answer is that both forms of communication represented a pragmatic response to the gradual erosion of face-to-face contact with other planters and their overseers because of the expansion of the plantation economy. A recommendation had to suffice since a personal evaluation of another planter's judgment, or of a manager's aptitude, was often difficult. Furthermore those slaveholders who sought to profit from the skills of overseers from much further afield than before had little choice other than to advertise. The need to place gazette notices became more urgent in the late colonial period as plantations continued to grow and absenteeism increased, resulting in a small and declining pool of available white overseers. In 1768 James Grant's agent reported that he had "sent all over Carolina almost, for Overseers," but had found none.[55]

The second answer is that the continuation of these systems represented another response by patriarchs to absentee plantation ownership. Newspapers, though a modern medium, offered an attractively public means by which patriarchs could demonstrate traditional anxieties for the successful management of their land. In addition slaveholders' insistence on written recommendations points to the survival of long-standing ideological concerns surrounding the probity of dependent overseers. But it seems clear from the testimony of slaveholders like Henry Laurens who attempted to hire managers on behalf of absent counterparts that absenteeism, and its attenuation of former recruitment methods, also played a significant role in turning planters against adverts and written recommendations.

Laurens's problems in securing an overseer for Oswald demonstrate how overseers themselves used the changing nature of recruitment systems in order to assert their authority and bargain for improved conditions. Witness how the "several clever fellows" with whom Laurens "had at different times actually agreed" each "shewed great reluctance to the undertaking when they found that the Plantation to be settled was not on [Laurens's] own account." It is significant that this response came from the better-qualified candidates. Laurens was spectator to a new assertiveness among overseers based on a growing perception of their own professional capabilities, which would become most evident in the years following the Revolutionary War. Yet slaveholder opinions never caught up with overseers' opinions of themselves. While the advertisement that he placed on behalf of Oswald eventually delivered a possible candidate, Laurens could only hope that this man would "not deceive me."[56] Laurens's disappointments with "that class of people" underscore how the middle of the eighteenth century saw southern overseers emerge from the ranks of dependents and take on stigmas of their own. They performed a particular role in a plantation economy that, in its rapid expansion, was changing in a particular way.

To a significant degree, the negative appraisal of overseers was self-perpetuating. Ambitious young men found the prospect of a life following a maligned occupation unenticing, however professional some of its practitioners would eventually become. Some recruiters answered the perceived slippage in the standard of potential candidates by abandoning nonpersonal recruitment methods altogether, depending instead on their own judgment when making a decision. Many planters looked first to their friends and acquaintances. This strategy delivered the advantages that a larger selection of overseers could bring, while at the same time yielding reliable recommendations. James Barclay, a traveler from England who wrote a diary of his time in South Carolina, found employment "with one Mr. Benjamin Verin, to whom after recovery I was sent": the doctor who had treated him during a fever contracted immediately after his arrival in Charleston sent Barclay to Verin's plantation to oversee the bondpeople there.[57] Henry Laurens in 1765 wrote to an acquaintance, Joseph Brown, that he would "be much obliged to you to improve the hint that you were so kind to give me about an Overseer. A capable, discreet Man . . . one that would abide diligently & soberly at his work shall have great encouragement from me."[58] Joseph Ball's intention was presumably to check up on his managers' experience when he said to Joseph Chinn, "I desire to know my overseers names, and whence you had them."[59]

Henry Laurens asked the South Carolinian planter James Marion to "talk a little" to John Smith before Laurens hired him, "& if you have opportunity enquire into his Character."[60] The previous February, on deciding that he required an overseer to replace James Brenard on his Wambaw plantation, Laurens had asked whether Brown knew "of one Myer who served Colonel Horry some Years & lately Mr. Benjamin Smith in your parts. He offers his service but as I am willing to pay well I will have none but such as are at least well recommended."[61] In October of the same year Laurens again advised Joseph Brown that "as to the [overseer]'s behaviour you will . . . have further opportunity of inquiring & seeing into that as well of knowing other peoples opinion of his abilities as a planter. The trust that I shall repose in him if we agree will be very great."[62] Networks of friends and acquaintances with reliable judgment helped to guard against unprofitable managerial incompetence. Plantation mistresses found employees in a similar way. The steward recruited by Eliza Lucas Pinckney to supervise her overseers was "an excellent planter, a Dutchman, originally Servant and Overseer to Mr. Golightly, who has been much solicited to undertake for many Gentlemen," all of whom presumably had given glowing recommendations.[63] Gendered preferences in the recruitment of overseers had a bearing on how slave mistresses scrutinized the character and behavior of applicants. But the requirements of running a plantation efficiently meant that for female, as for male planters, "excellent planter[s]" were always the most sought after.

Once they had proved that they were reliable, some overseers were also trusted to provide recommendations. In 1765, when James Brenard informed Henry Laurens of his intention to leave Wambaw plantation, his employer requested that he "look about & request a person in [his] stead."[64] Laurens would later put faith in another overseer, Frederick Wiggins, manager of the Broughton Island plantation on South Carolina's Ashepoo River, to "recommend to me so good an Overseer as you talk of."[65] Because Wiggins had contact with other overseers, Laurens could also advise one Edward Graham to "enquire . . . of [Wiggins] . . . in a prudent manner if any Overseers . . . are in want of business."[66]

Laurens's caveat to Wiggins on soliciting his recommendation, that the overseer should "send none but honest Men, good planters & such as love work, for I can pick up enough of a different stamp every day," is notable for two reasons.[67] First, Laurens did not have total faith in Wiggins's judgment. And second, the South Carolinian demonstrated a lack of hope that he would find suitable overseers. Both of Laurens's assumptions again hint at his growing antipathy toward overseers as a group and his belief that there were fewer competent overseers available. He and other planters chose to solicit the recommendation of fellow slaveholders because overseers, as dependents, were deemed untrustworthy. Anxious southern patriarchs worried about the ability of dependent overseers to recruit other dependents. Would they mistake an applicant's self-serving flattery for loyalty? Or would they put their own interests ahead of those of the planter and the plantation?

Overseers, unique among dependents, reflected slaveholders' responses to the new moral economy and the changing political economy of the eighteenth-century South. Even as planters attempted rhetorically to defy the blurring of *oikia* and *polis,* their anxieties and preoccupations revealed an understanding that this resistance was futile: that henceforth morality, polity, and economy would be impossible to untangle. But though planters were inspired by this new raft of assumptions, they used overseers in much the same way as they had always used dependents. Slaveholders imposed their deeply held personal fears on managers. Paranoia forced on patriarchs a duty to "be constantly at their guard" to be prepared for the inevitable disobedience offered by preternaturally unruly dependents.[68] A planter's ability to control absolutely everything undergirded political authority in the fragmented institutions of the eighteenth century. It derived not simply from a man's power over wife, children, slaves, and lesser men, but also from his ability to subdue within himself those qualities he attributed to subordinates: "passion, weakness and dependence."[69] Moral, political, and economic worries overlapped with, sustained, and confirmed each other.

Thomas Jefferson's description of overseers as "the most abject, degraded, and unprincipled race" was a clear invocation of the traditional link between dependence and behavior. As an indication of their perceived importance, equivalent concerns often appeared in overseer advertisements before an elaboration of the technical capabilities required by the subscriber. One advert demanded no skills of the overseer, only mentioning the characteristics sought. While a successful applicant should have "Capacity, Sobriety, and Honesty," it was his wife who needed specific technical knowledge—if she "[were] used to manage a Dairy, and raising of Poultry, it will be no Objection."[70] Another went even further, requiring "an honest, sober . . . Man, As an Overseer:—Such, whether he understands the planting business or not, will meet with good Encouragement."[71] Those overseers who advertised that they were seeking work were keen to stress the integrity of their character as well as their many skills: not only did the overseer who placed a notice in the *South Carolina Gazette* "understand . . . Accompts, and the Management of Negroes"; he was also "of unexceptionable Character"; thus "he flatter[ed] himself, he could give satisfaction to his Employers."[72] Another added the following promise to an earlier advert that had not mentioned references: "an unexceptionable Character from the Gentleman in whose Employ [he and his wife] lived last, will be given."[73]

Character guarantees were useful because although a lack of proficiency in farming and slave management was relatively easy to pick out once the overseer had started work, behavioral infractions might take longer to appear. Applicants were warned in the sternest tones that "none need apply, whose character will not bear the strictest scrutiny for soberness and honesty," but it was very difficult to judge whether a prospective manager was in possession of such traits.[74] Written recommendations therefore worked only to the extent that it was possible to describe accurately the characteristics of an overseer, and to predict his future behavior. Because traits such as sobriety and honesty could be denied only if something went wrong, behavioral testimony would never be as verifiable as, for example, an overseer's skill in raising cash crops.

Despite their emphasis on overseers' character, in some cases planters tolerated managerial infractions. Henry Laurens berated Abraham Schad for his impropriety on a number of occasions, but he was the overseer who remained longest in Laurens's service. In like manner Laurens criticized similar behavior in Mark Noble but was happy to reemploy him some years later.[75] Prospective employers made demands on employees' character in advertisements for positions right across the employment spectrum, possibly suggesting that hiring planters followed an insubstantive recruitment code or formula. The South Carolinian William Parker averred that a "person of good character, qualified for keeping a store, and inclinable to live in the country" would "meet with good encouragement."[76] Occupations that necessitated a high degree of practical specialist education were treated similarly—a notice in a 1757 edition of the *South Carolina Gazette* advertised a physician's job with a vague appeal to young men "of good character."[77] This trend for stressing the ephemeral exasperated some planters. In 1775 Robert Carter of Nomini Hall criticized an overseer who vaunted his character above aptitude: "Christopher Bailes, overseer . . . offers to serve me at Coles point plantation, he produced testimonials f[ro]m three persons, whom he had [served], w[hi]ch testimonials speak of Bailes sobriety and honesty, but do not say that he understands either cropping or farming."[78]

How meaningful, then, were the character demands that patriarchs made of overseers? How committed were patriarchs to the values that they expressed when recruiting? To what extent did social convention require that employers demand men of good character? And how far did the hiring process center on the representation of an ideal ahead of the economic realities of southern plantation life? Like the highly visible newspaper adverts, a studied insistence on character traits allowed slaveholders to demonstrate the fretful attention to detail that mastery over dependents obliged, and to convince themselves that it was they who were in charge of plantation affairs, not the market. It was against this background that ephemeral moral concerns such as "Integrity" and "Probity" became intertwined with more pragmatic characteristics such as "Industry" and "Diligence." Henry

Laurens was a planter who valued managerial characteristics with an immediate economic and practical advantage. He reprimanded overseer Mark Noble for his inefficiency and, which was effectively a corollary of this, because he "want[ed] diligence" and was idle; and a concern for utility and efficiency convinced the planter to permit Abraham Schad his foibles.[79] But less prosaic concerns also drove Laurens: he feared that Noble "want[ed] sincerity," and was vain and obstinate. Likewise the Virginian Landon Carter, nephew of his namesake at Sabine Hall, insisted that the overseer John Deatly be a man of "Integrity, Honor & Probity."[80] This language reflected the degree of confidence that absentee owners placed in their managers. Yet it also reflected traditional patriarchal assumptions about dependents' untrustworthiness and laziness.

Lying behind the apparent doublethink were the strong links that bound slaveholders to the Atlantic trade, links that led colonial planters—often the fount of moral and political opinion in the southern colonies—to develop a morbid fear of falling into economic dependence on others, and British merchants in particular.[81] Their trepidation was cut from the same cloth as patriarchal anxieties about dependence and dependents. Embryonic Patriots worried that indebtedness to the British would have a deleterious effect on their personal autonomy by restricting their sphere of economic action.[82] Settlers had been attracted to North America through the promise of personal gain; now they realized that if they were to win economic independence and protect their estates from British creditors, they needed to adopt a simpler mode of living and a more disciplined management of their estates.[83] Virginian planters therefore "counselled each other to practice frugality and simplicity."[84] One of their number, the Chesapeake grandee Richard Corbin, considered personal indebtedness to be one of the principal "Errors of his countrymen" and warned that only "the strongest Efforts of Industry and its attendant Virtue Frugality" could restore the economy to good credit.[85] Fears about debt converged with frustrations over the taxes imposed by the metropolis before the Revolution. Colonials believed that any attempt by an unrepresentative parliament to impose taxes represented a despotic infringement of liberties.[86] Even after the leaders of the Regulators, a group of South Carolinians who protested the "enormous sum for building [a] house for the Governor" had been arrested, "the people in general complain[ed] loudly of the . . . act as a great grievance, as well as that laying a duty on paper, glass &c."[87]

Their parsimony was more than rhetoric—the language was born in often harsh reality. Especially in Virginia the material benefits of frugal attributes were clear: George Washington was one of many planters almost bankrupted by debt during the 1760s.[88] Planters made frequent appeals in adverts and contracts for employees to be "industrious," and to practice "Oeconomy" and "Frugality."[89] In the colonial mind, economics, freedom, morality, and behavior lay on a single spectrum. Indeed they often discussed them in a single breath: when the Virginian planters counseled each other "to practice frugality and simplicity," they also "suggested schemes for general moral reform."[90] A new set of market-oriented moral imperatives had come strongly to influence Virginian, South Carolinian, and Georgian planters. British Enlightenment philosophers, whose work found a wide readership among protorevolutionaries such as George Washington and Henry Laurens, influenced this lexicon. In the mindset of the writers, external economic imperatives joined with internal vice and virtue. The shift from "an abstraction that refer[red] to the external necessity to one that conjure[d] internal experience informed the general project the British moral philosophers undertook: to explain why individuals could be counted on to produce a mutually beneficial society in the process of gratifying themselves."[91] While the demands that planters made regarding overseers' behavior might at first blush appear extraneous—and maybe even pompous—southern elites believed that there were serious reasons for their concern.

The market economy increasingly substituted traditional personal virtues (honor, for instance) with terms that were beginning to have a specifically economic meaning (such as credit).[92] Of growing importance to the patriarchal plantation owner in the mid-eighteenth century was the credit that others were able to place in his capacity to pay off debts. And because the acquisition and protection of property and capital had transformed the moral order, to a large extent the passions that slaveholders believed affected dependents also followed suit. Slaveholders worried that overseers would tarry at their work, would steal from them, and would labor "on their own interest."

For now, however, the old and new terms of vice and virtue sat together in the patriarchal mind, at times overlapping, at others drawing apart. The mid-eighteenth century was a period of rhetorical flux in which patriarchs convinced themselves that the moral and practical demands that they made were equally crucial. Because slave owners were often absent from their plantations, in the recruitment process they attempted to counterbalance potential vice with managerial moral virtue. Yet, as Laurens's lenity with Abraham Schad suggests, planters also reasoned that whatever was best for the plantation as a whole was best for those who worked on it. Recognizing the avowed link between character and successful employment, and understanding traditional patriarchal assumptions about dependents' morals, managers took up their employers' refrain: Humphrey Knight in 1758 was concerned that Washington would be "Douptfull of [his] Diligence."[93] Overseers knew that a good reputation for financial probity was of as much practical benefit to them as it was to their employers. Henry Laurens described in 1766 how John McCullough, whom he had recently employed, was unable to leave George Town province without having first remunerated his creditors. But, "if he is an honest Man his Creditors need not distrust him. He will thrive if they will permit him to go."[94]

The overlap between practical and moral vice and virtue may be glimpsed in slaveholders' insistence on overseer sobriety. Indebtedness and dependence itself were believed to arise from luxurious exuberance.[95] Patriarchs held those that they employed to the same standards as they claimed to hold themselves, especially if overseers' tasks included the frugal allocation of plantation resources. Many planters were anxious that their managers should not demonstrate extravagance. Washington advised one of his overseers against indulging himself at the local still, where "many Idle, drunken and dissolute people . . . continually prid[ed] themselves in debauching sober and welinclined Persons"; another was urged to show himself at all times to be capable of acting "Soberly . . . in all respects."[96] Washington's first reference to sobriety is close to its most common modern definition as the opposite of drunkenness, but his second points up the deeper meaning of the term in the eighteenth century. The sober man contained himself—he did not drink to excess, but he also attempted to control his passions and wastefulness. So whereas one gazette notice declared that a "SOBER, careful MAN" was "wanted immediately," "chiefly to attend a BILLIARD TABLE" (an occupation where the temptation of drink would no doubt have arisen), good recommendations for "sobriety" were also demanded in newspaper adverts for jobs as diverse as wet-nurse and "compting-house" clerk.[97]

The fear when employing superintendents of any type was that unrestrained vices would metastasize among the superintended. A 1750 Virginian advert sought a "sober person, of good morals," who could "depend on meeting with good encouragement, as a school-master."[98] In the underinstitutionalized plantation world, relationships between members of private, patriarchal households were especially prone to corruption by unrestrained vice. Managerial intemperance revealed itself in a number of ways—as a penchant for violence for instance, or as an intemperate sexual appetite. Planters were obliged to call for restraint in their overseers for the sake of their other dependents' moral health. And they were concerned that an untrammeled, passionate demeanor might cause disquiet among the workforce should overseers' advances to enslaved women go unchecked.

Sobriety was also a useful foil to the passions of dissolute bondpeople. In the advert mentioned elsewhere (see fig. 2), the Virginian Lemuel Riddick announced that he was "in Want of a Man to be Overseer," who "must be honest, sober, careful, and have Activity and Courage enough to correct an insolent or lazy Slave." This was clearly of more import than agricultural expertise—Riddick expected his overseer to have only "some little Knowledge in Plantation Affairs, such as plowing, sowing Grain, and taking care of Stock," in order to "meet with an extraordinary Offer."[99] Thus was the necessity of good morals among those who were in political control of others enunciated; along with "Sobriety" advertisers demanded "discretion in the government of slaves."[100] One South Carolina planter's highest praise was to describe a manager as "Sober, Discreet & Industrious."[101] Henry Laurens made an unambiguous link between managerial restraint and supervision of the enslaved when he sought an overseer "of a good moral character and discreet in his Management of Negroes."[102] Discretion required impartiality when dealing with bondpeople, and—what was most important—a dispassionate management style.

An overseer must therefore be sober for two principal reasons—to avoid wasting plantation resources, and to govern enslaved people rationally. Linking practical work with an industrious character, Henry Laurens petitioned Joseph Brown for "an excellent hand at damming & ditching, one that would abide diligently & soberly at his work."[103] Another advertiser echoed Laurens when he requested a "certificate from [the applicant's] last employer, of sobriety," correlating this trait with "ability and industry."[104] But since the practical and moral meanings of sobriety were so strongly related, patriarchs not only underlined the moral definition of the word, but also linked it to aptitude. One advertiser in 1766 requested ability and reason when he called in 1766 for "two Overseers," who "must be both recommended for being capable, sober and not passionate."[105] George Washington summed up how sobriety, management, rationality, and balance sat together in the patriarchal mindset. Describing how individual overseers' regimes often differed, he stated, "let both these managers rise equally early—go equally late to rest—be equally active, sober & industrious—and yet in the course of the year one of them, without pushing the hands which are under him more than the other, shall have performed infinitely more work.—To what is this owing?—Why, simply to contrivance resulting from that forethought and arrangement which will guard against the mis-application of labour and doing it unreasonably."[106] Demands for sobriety gained in importance as planters began to question the character and capability of their overseers. Indeed sobriety does not feature in any South Carolinian overseer advert before 1757; between that date and 1768 it appears in ten.[107]

Along with sobriety marital status was a key factor in determining the suitability of prospective overseers. Forty-seven of the lowcountry recruitment adverts studied, or 34 percent, referred specifically to the marital status of ideal candidates. Twenty-seven of these, or 57 percent, requested single overseers, including two notices by unmarried overseers. Seventeen, or 36 percent, indicated a preference for married overseers or, as in the case of five of them, came from married overseers themselves. Of the remaining three, two suggested that both single and married applicants would be welcome, while one requested an unmarried overseer for one plantation and a married overseer for another. One hundred and twenty-three Virginian recruitment adverts were studied; of these 16 percent requested single overseers, the same proportion requested married men, and one advert stated that marital status did not matter.[108]

The aim of most overseers, like that of most of their countrymen, was to work until they raised sufficient capital to be able to marry and buy land of their own.[109] John McCullough, one of Henry Laurens's overseers, was married in 1764, as were the South Carolinian overseers Andreas Cuhseling, in 1769, and James Jordon, in

1770.[110] A married overseer was part of a more elevated link in the Great Chain of Being than his single counterparts: having dependents himself (a wife and children) made him a little less dependent than other managers. But the cost of married overseers made them less desirable in the eyes of some planters. Potential managers of "a small plantation on Ashley river," South Carolina, were informed that a "middle-aged man without a family will be preferable to one that has a wife."[111] Joseph Ball vowed not to maintain his overseers' "wives and Children . . . for they, I think, do more hurt than Good, taking the hands to wait upon them."[112] George Washington reckoned that "a married man . . . (by keeping a separate house) would add considerably to my expenses. Whereas a single man . . . would with respect to his board, be not more than a drop in the bucket."[113] Similarly Thomas Jefferson wanted to find a "person . . . with a smaller family" than that of the overseer who had recently applied to him for work.[114] Although most lowcountry masters and mistresses did not pay overseers' wives directly, John-Martin Bolzius recorded that their help still came at a price. A typical wife in Georgia was allowed "her food, half the foul [fowl], and half of the third part of the butter [produced on the plantation]."[115] Perhaps it was a sudden realization of the cost of employing a couple that led one South Carolinian advertiser to change his notice from stating that "GEORGE SMITH . . . will want an OVERSEER, with a wife," to read instead, "WANTED . . . a single Man."[116] It is likely that this was also the rationale behind the many adverts specifically requesting single men.

The proportion of notices requesting married overseers is sizeable nevertheless. Because all colonial planters were anxious about frugality, for certain slaveholders there must have been a discernible advantage to hiring such men. In Virginia Landon Carter decided to take on a married man, although he had to "allow him Corn for bread for himself, his wife & Children."[117] Henry Laurens's recruitment history underlined the saliency of marital status. In 1763 he dismissed James Lawrence, his overseer at Mepkin, for his "familiarity with Hagar," a bondwoman. The letter of dismissal explained that Laurens intended, possibly in order to protect his sacked employee's reputation (and his own reputation for control over his plantation), to "assign another reason to anybody that enquires about the matter, that is that I chose to have a Man of more experience & one that has a Wife."[118] As it turned out, Laurens employed someone fitting that description exactly—Abraham Schad.[119]

The episode is revealing for a number of reasons. First, since Schad was married, Laurens perhaps wished to guard against further moral infractions: at the most elementary level, an overseer would have been less likely to stray if his wife was with him to fulfill his more corporal wants. And a wife provided a veil of respectability for the potentially indecorous situation in which a young man found himself when surrounded by perhaps dozens of bondwomen. It is significant that after this event, Laurens insisted on employing married overseers only.[120] Second, Laurens presented the desire for a married overseer as a valid reason for releasing his former employee—acceptable to anyone questioning his decision—indicating that it was common to view married men as making better overseers. Third, Laurens conflates marriage and experience. His marriage meant that Schad was more likely to regard overseeing as a career, as he had a household to provide for.[121] Schad's recruitment possibly represented an attempt to confront a growing patriarchal worry that overseers were incorrigibly flighty. As the Virginian slave owner John Mercer put it, "never . . . trust . . . a Bachelor Overseer."[122]

But there was a more everyday justification for Henry Laurens's employment of the married Schad. Two years later he suggested that Abraham Schad's spouse replace Laurens's own wife in undertaking certain chores: "Mrs. Laurens is not very well & therefore cant make up . . . Cloaths [for bondpeople] but hopes your wife will do that part."[123] Overseers' wives were also vital during crises. Schad was informed in August 1765 that "your own, Mrs. Schads, Mr. Myers, & his Wifes care & constancy at home will be all necessary now at this time of great sickness."[124] In similar fashion Laurens asked his manager at Mepkin, Timothy Creamer, whether "Mrs. Creamer can undertake to make the Negro Cloths this fall."[125] The year 1759 saw the Georgian Clement Martin advertise an overseer's position, suggesting that a "married man will be most agreeable, on account of raising poultry, &c."[126] A 1770 advertisement suggested that if an applicant "has a Wife that understands the management of a Dairy, it will be no objection."[127] And in Virginia in 1777, a subscriber explained that he "could wish the person applying to have a wife who would undertake the charge of a dairy, raise poultry (of which last she may have a share) and also take under her care three or four spinners"—of particular use given wartime embargos on spun textiles.[128] Such aptitude helped to make overseers' households self-sufficient; if a wife produced extra, she might even receive wages or a share of any profits.[129]

Even where planters' recruitment demands had an explicit moral bent, as in Laurens's employment of Schad, the putative sobriety of married overseers would have had some utilitarian effect in averting tensions between slaveholder, overseer, and enslaved workforce. When employing overseers, female planters arguably were more constrained by moral imperatives than their male counterparts. The opportunities for accusations of impropriety were many, since women slaveholders necessarily had close, everyday contact with their managers at a time when frequent dealings with a man of lower status would have raised eyebrows. Did these women employ married overseers to counteract possible opprobrium? The history of female slaveholders in the eighteenth-century South has received less attention from historians than that of their male counterparts. But such women were relatively common in the colonial period. The same expansion of the slave economy that strengthened the ideal of female detachedness from labor, and idealized feminine domesticity, paradoxically required mistresses whose husbands were away to involve themselves more in plantation management. Demographic change had a similar effect, with short male life expectancies atrophying "the normative patriarchy" that had existed in the seventeenth century, meaning that a widow often received a greater share of and a greater control over her husband's estate, and greater responsibility for the welfare of her children and his heirs.[130] This was especially true of those widows left without sons (who could take over some management duties), or with sons still in their minority.[131]

An elite woman's daily routine was supposed to involve staying at home or making visits to neighboring plantations. When Edward Kimber visited the tobacco coast in the 1740s, he noted that the local women's "amusements are quite innocent . . . and within the Circle of a Plantation or two, they exercise all the Virtues that can raise one's opinions of the too light Sex."[132] For some, women planters' "male" obligations therefore became "a burden rather than an opportunity to exercise independent judgment or enrich their lives."[133] Before Eliza Lucas Pinckney's husband, Charles, died in July 1758, though she had been heavily involved in plantation management in advance of her marriage, and was well-known for having introduced indigo production to South Carolina, her correspondence keenly stressed her interests in other topics that were more appropriate for a wife, such as literature and philosophy.[134] According to her own schedule, even after Pinckney had inherited her father's lands in 1747, managing her father's plantations was something that could be fitted in between French lessons, reading, and music.[135] In like manner the Virginian planter Maryann Maury was anxious to portray herself as possessing femininity rather than a head for commerce. She thanked her brother for the agricultural advice that he had given her "for I am but a helpless creature about these Country affairs, never being able to manage planting."[136]

An alternative explanation for women's employment of married overseers is that they were motivated more by the same economic and practical considerations that influenced male planters' recruitment practices. Perhaps their requests simply indicated a desire for extra help. Unused to the burden of plantation work, suddenly widowed women could find solace in the more domestically oriented aid provided by a manager's spouse. Overseers were eager to stress to plantation mistresses their wives' suitability: one man claimed that his spouse was "well acquainted in the Management of a Dairy, and raising of Poultry, &c."[137] Another suggested that his wife could "teach young Ladies to Sew and Mark."[138] It is possible that this overseer was attempting to benefit from the vulnerability of lone women planters,[139] for not only was he "capable of managing a Farm"; like his wife he was also "capable of instructing Children in Reading, Writing, Arithmetic and several Branches of the Mathematics."[140] To a recently widowed planter, this subscriber might have represented an answer to her problems regarding farm management and the education of her children; as a potential instructor of dependents, his "unexceptionable Character" would have been of significant value.[141]

After the death of her husband, Eliza Lucas Pinckney employed an overseer with similarly appealing characteristics. He had "no family but a wife" and was "comfortable enough in his circumstances"; thus he refused "to [oversee] for any but women and children that are not able to do it for themselves." His independence of means and generosity gave him a moral pedigree that Pinckney keenly underlined. He was "a conscientious good man (who by his industry and honesty has raised a fine fortune for 2 orphan children my dear Mr. Pinckney was guardian [to])."[142] Yet although the qualities that Pinckney highlights, especially her overseer's patriarchal disposition to women in need, played on masculine stereotypes regarding women, they clearly worked to her advantage.[143] For the same practical reasons that influenced slave masters when employing overseers, Pinckney found a professed concern for morality to be as useful in the search for good managers as it was for her male counterparts.

The available evidence precludes a complete statistical picture of the influence of overseers' marital status on the choices that women planters made. One difficulty is that because it formed part of plantation management, southerners viewed the task of advertising for and recruiting overseers as unwomanly. Though certain plantation mistresses did advertise oversight positions themselves, there were a number of instances where men found managers on behalf of women planters. In one notable example from just after the Revolutionary War, George Washington recruited an overseer for his mother. Although Washington "ha[d] no earthly inducement to meddle" with the management of his mother's plantation, influenced by patriarchal values he agreed to assist in order "to comply with her wish, and to free her from care." It is difficult to glean much more from this than Washington's own beliefs in the type of overseer who would be suitable for his mother. But Washington used the same mechanisms here that he used when recruiting overseers for himself—he asked someone whom he could trust, his brother, to find a suitable candidate.[144]

A survey of recruitment adverts bears little more fruit. The twenty-five low-country notices seeking single overseers comprise seventeen from male subscribers, and eight from advertisers whose gender is unclear, since they entreated applicants to apply to the printer of the gazettes rather than the planters themselves.[145] One advertiser in a 1774 edition of the *South Carolina Gazette* stated that "great Encouragement will be given to a married Man . . . and none other will be treated with."[146] Ten years earlier another wanted an "Overseer . . . A Single man . . . (none other need apply)."[147] But the gender of neither prospective employer is mentioned. Similar problems beset those adverts requesting married applicants: one was placed by a woman, five were placed by men, and six were from subscribers whose gender is unclear. Because of the stigma surrounding female involvement in plantation affairs, some adverts placed by male advertisers could well have been hiding male agents, relatives, or acquaintances working on behalf of plantation mistresses. Witness the advert that requested potential overseers to apply to "Mrs.

Beresford in *St. Thomas's* parish," but which also mentioned the names of two men as possible contacts.[148]

In the end, of the 140 South Carolinian and Georgian recruitment advertisements analyzed, female names appear on only three, with a similarly small proportion for *Virginia Gazette* adverts.[149] The one notice that definitely was placed by a female subscriber was by Sarah Bullard, who announced in 1769 that a "married man would be most agreeable."[150] However, to confound the issue further the Virginian Mary Jones wanted the opposite: an "OVERSEER (a single Man) . . . that can be properly recommended, for Industry, Diligence, and Sobriety (as he will live in the Family)."[151] Even though convention constricted them more than their male counterparts, women slaveholders still made personal choices when recruiting overseers. Depending on the requirements of their plantations, the resources that they had at their disposal, and the existing social dynamics between the black and white people under their control, plantation masters and mistresses both chose single or married overseers according to their own individual perceptions of what would be the most profitable course of action.

In their recruitment system, planters had created a mechanism with which they hoped to guard against the unprofitable disappointments that so many claimed to have experienced in their managers. But overseers were also one of the most immediate reminders of the blurring of the poetic and prosaic in the slave economy, and in their requirements regarding managers' characters, planters responded to the moral atmosphere of the time. Employers made a further attempt to control managerial profitability and behavior through the contracts that they drew up with their overseers. So much in planter assessments of overseers' characteristics appears contradictory, as do so many planter assessments of the value and role of overseeing itself. The final irony in overseer recruitment is that while slaveholder rhetoric was designed to support and strengthen patriarchal suppositions, it also allowed for the redemption of overseers' characters. In order for planter criticism to work, for every lazy and wasteful manager, the possibility had to remain that overseers could also be diligent and sober. As long as this ambiguity remained in place, it presented employees with the opportunity to demonstrate to their employers that they could rise above the massed ranks of incompetent, dependent overseers. Even as prejudices against overseers calcified toward the end of the century, managers found that through their own aptitude they could make a case to be considered as individuals, to be seen less as dependent employees and more as independent professionals who were worthy of their employers' respect.

— *Chapter Three* —

"Nothing pleases me better than to see them in good order"

Contractual Relationships between Overseers and Planters

Like the overseer system itself, the written agreement underpinning the formal relationship between overseers and their employers had its origins in early modern English employment practices. Generally, when appointed, an overseer received instructions about the care and punishment of enslaved people, cultivation methods, the raising of livestock and other animals, and rules outlining his expected conduct.[1] Also covered were the remuneration that the overseer could expect and the length of time for which he would be employed.[2]

In most colonial plantation relationships, these sorts of obligations formed a central part of the connection between the planter and his workforce. Patriarchism conceptualized relationships in reciprocal terms; in return for doing their "Duty . . . to carry the Machine forward," the "people" (enslaved men and women, but also other dependents) received food and lodging. The ideology also spoke to traditional notions of mutuality and patriarchal care. When plaintively recounting how his "Soart of Life is without expence, yet . . . is attended with a great deal of trouble," William Byrd conceived of himself as being party to a Lockean code that, because of the constant supervision that it required, demanded as much of slaveholders as it did of slaves.[3] Landon Carter heavily annotated his copies of John Locke's works, and few eighteenth-century patriarchs were more anxious about the fragility of his plantation rule than he.[4]

Through these mechanisms planters sought to present themselves as rational, disinterested patriarchal rulers. Yet the relationship between planter and overseer was different. While other dependents were also bound to the planter by contract (indentured servants, for instance), a widely followed practice was for overseer contracts to last for only a short period, after which time they might be renewed, but often were not. In this sense formal written contracts mirrored the types of social contract that patriarchal rulers imagined that they had established with different groups of dependents. Enslaved people did not require a contract since they were unfree, and therefore the slaveholder could punish, attack, and cajole them largely with impunity. Indentured white men and women were subject to the master or mistress's will only while under contract, but that will was often applied forcefully, and violently. The overseer's position was more problematic. Legally he could not suffer physical punishment, but he could face economic chastisement—fines, docking of wages, and so on—and his employer might terminate his contract. Short contracts therefore allowed slaveholders to maintain control over employees whose position did not fit squarely into traditional patriarchal power structures. They gave plantation owners a means to discipline men whom they often regarded as lacking in sobriety, but who had to have more freedom of action, especially in the crucial area of managing other dependents, if absentee land ownership was to work efficiently.

Significantly many overseers took offence at short contracts, thinking that efficient service deserved ample reward. Here again a disconnect was reflected, between eighteenth-century overseers' conception of themselves as proficient agriculturists, and planters' conception of these men as irrevocable dependents. Naturally for planters the most important overseer duties were crop cultivation and the profitable management of enslaved people. Changing agricultural conditions, technological innovations, and the varying makeup of the enslaved workforce made new demands on the overseer's time and activities.

In return for completing these tasks, overseers received compensation from their employer either as wages, a share of the crop, or both.[5] Wages could reflect the employer's opinion of his manager: good service received good compensation. But wages also came to reflect negative planter opinions; as such they mirrored and exacerbated the stereotype of the unprofessional overseer that became more widespread toward the end of the century. Employers offered crop sharing in place of wages to tie in their own success with tangible economic benefits for overseers. When the practice fell into disuse, blamed for exhausting southern soils and falling yields, slaveholders found yet another reason to criticize the managerial profession. Overseers might also receive provisions from the plantation, and many slaveholders provided them with a house. This made overseeing an attractive profession for poor whites, although being dependent on another man for one's very subsistence carried with it other shaming connotations.

Unlike the many planters who contracted overseers for only short periods, some slaveholders kept managers employed for a number of years. Abraham Schad, Henry Laurens's longest server, remained six years in the South Carolinian's employ.[6] John Alton served George Washington at his Northern Neck plantation for more than thirty years.[7] One advertiser in 1771 appealed for a "sedate Person, that does not like changing Places," and this desire also held true for some slaveholders in the immediate post-Revolutionary period: George Hooper oversaw for South Carolinian soldier, planter, and statesman Pierce Butler from 1786 to 1803.[8] There was a discernible advantage to maintaining overseers who knew the peculiarities of a plantation and its bondpeople. Laurens continued to employ Frederick Wiggins, Elias Ball's manager at Ashepoo, after Laurens took over the plantation following Ball's death.[9] This advantage would become clearer as overseeing grew more professionalized in the antebellum period, when terms of fifteen or even twenty years were not uncommon in Virginia and the Carolinas among superior overseers, and when one well-known maxim stated that one should "never change an overseer if you can help it."[10]

In spite of these benefits, the majority of eighteenth-century overseers received short contracts. Henry Laurens employed twenty-five overseers on five plantations between 1763 and 1774, each serving an average of twenty months. In Virginia later in the century, Thomas Jefferson hired ten overseers for only one or two years.[11] Francis Jerdone hired twenty-one overseers between 1762 and 1773, and most stayed fewer than two years.[12] Just before the war, the South Carolinian Isaac Hayne employed fifteen overseers, for an average of twelve months each.[13] Jonathan Godwin took on Richard Smiddall to oversee his plantation at Chuckatuck, Nansemond County, Virginia, in 1776; by 1777, Smiddall was seeking employment again.[14] Some planters employed overseers only at "crisis" times, for example when they needed to leave the plantation for extended periods. And smaller plantations often could afford to hire only when they were prosperous, forced to release their managers during economic depressions.[15] Equivalent motivation perhaps lay behind Isaac Mims's short tenure: he earned "Two Pounds Nine Shillings & six pence Sterling . . . for overseeing for Two Months the Negroes on the Estate of John Gibbons" in Georgia.[16] Recruitment adverts stated specifically that managers would be employed for a short term, such as the 1765 notice that advertised, "I shall want for this ensuing year, TWO or THREE . . . OVERSEERS."[17] Planters' attempts to discover whether applicants were reliable led to the imposition of compulsory short trial periods for a number of candidates; for instance the Georgian William Gibbons had a "months Tryall of the said [Thomas] Moore" inserted into the contract he made with the overseer.[18] Unluckily for Moore in Gibbons's estimation he was of "dubious suitability," and three months later James Guinn was employed to oversee the same plantation.[19]

Overseer contracts could be terminated by either party at any time, although some employers required that managers stay in their service a while after handing in their notice.[20] Henry Laurens intended to employ an overseer in October 1765 yet wrote that "he cannot leave his present place until January."[21] Once a request for severance was accepted, managers usually received a proportion of their annual salary equivalent to time already served; this was also true in cases of overseer dismissal. On sacking James Lawrence for his moral infractions, Henry Laurens made him a "reasonable allowance until you get into some other employment" so that Lawrence did not think his employer "harsh or unkind."[22] The Virginian steward Charles Dabney agreed in 1772 to pay overseers between twenty-five and thirty pounds if they were dismissed.[23]

The threat of dismissal was a viable spur to production used by most slave owners. In a 1765 letter to Joseph Brown, Henry Laurens mentioned that if an overseer whom Brown had recommended were to leave the slaveholder's service, it would "be either [the overseer's] own fault or because of promotion." If he intended, however, to "abide diligently & soberly at his work he shall have great encouragement."[24] The South Carolinian put his words into action; unsurprisingly of all his overseers James Lawrence's tenure was the shortest, lasting only six months.[25] But while on other occasions men like Laurens pragmatically overlooked their overseers' smaller foibles, they also responded to and exacerbated the developing attitude among southern planters that managers should not remain in one place for too long. Even trusted, long-serving overseers would have lived under the shadow of dismissal; the law as yet offered no protection from arbitrary sackings.[26] The basic need to maximize output was a constant; if an overseer failed to achieve this, "he must be dismissed immediately."[27] Similarly, although planters were often obliged to pay severance to an overseer whom they had dismissed early, it was a false economy to avoid payment by keeping him on, thereby risking mismanagement and an attendant drop in profits.[28]

Gibbons's trial periods; Jefferson's record of one or two years' service per overseer; Laurens's promise to sack precipitously any underperforming manager: all assumed managerial incompetence. This assumption was to form the basis of nineteenth-century overseer recruitment practices, where a two-tier system developed between the long-serving professional overseers and the suboverseers who were the main source of antebellum prejudice against the managerial class. By that juncture brevity of tenure among suboverseers had become anything but indicative of ineptitude: "it was the general practice on some plantations in the lower South to change overseers every year no matter how satisfactorily they performed."[29] In the colonial period, a vicious cycle that quickened during the following century was already growing more perceptible, in which "insecurity of [managerial] tenure," leading to "an incapable group of overseers" who were unable to gain requisite planting experience, frequently created "undesirable relations between planter and overseer."[30] George Washington noted at late century this growing division in the managerial ranks. He advised the wife of his nephew that a plantation of the size that she owned was "too small to induce a man of character to engage . . . too small to expect a *good* Overseer."[31] Not only did short contracts ensure that the managerial reputation for incompetence became a self-fulfilling prophecy, but eighteenth-century planters also consistently bemoaned overseers' reputation for constancy. They complained that managers were flighty and unreliable—that they offered no loyalty to their employers, moving on to the next opportunity as quickly as they had arrived.

Why, then, did southern slaveholders institute employment practices that, by exacerbating the incompetence and unreliability of overseers, served largely to confirm their own fears? The answer goes to the heart of the often contradictory intersection of ideology and pragmatism that was shaping overseers' reputations in so many areas. Patriarchs in the Chesapeake and lowcountry believed overseers, as dependents, to be morally incapable of efficiently managing as important an economic resource as a slave plantation. Such men had limited mental capacity for the difficult and sustained political rule that the task required, and for the successful application of complicated agricultural techniques. Short contracts therefore worked to temper the deleterious effects of the necessary yet undesirable decision to put overseers in charge of slave quarters. They also allowed the patriarch to convince his slaveholding counterparts that he was maintaining a grip on his plantation. Short contracts prevented any suggestion that the dependent overseer (unlike the steward, who occupied a different place in the eighteenth-century mindset) was attempting to usurp the planter's strictly defined hierarchical position, through claiming too great a level of ownership of the management of the plantation, or providing an alternative source of authority for the plantation's bondpeople. They prevented overseers from becoming too socialized toward enslaved people, treating them with excessive "lenity," and allowing them too much "indulgence."[32] What is perhaps most significant, short contracts also prevented enslaved people from learning the manager's idiosyncrasies and weaknesses, an education that they needed if they were find an effective way to undermine his regime.

When planters underlined the perceived inconstancy of overseers by offering them short contracts, they likewise attempted to put the manager in his correct place in slave society. Though they wished to place him outside the patriarchal plantation unit in order to reduce any pretence to his dominion over bondpeople, at the same time they branded the overseer a dependent in contrast to his independent, slave-owning employer. Planters made another comparison explicit: by stressing managerial inconstancy, slaveholders portrayed enslaved people as more loyal—more trusted, even—than the white men who supervised them. Patriarchs convinced themselves of the validity of this rhetoric, because if managers were placed outside the household, their contemporaries could not blame planters for overseers' moral turpitude or resistance to patriarchal rule. If planters bemoaned managerial inconstancy as often as possible, their patriarchal credentials were assured. By giving the planter the ability to threaten the overseer with unemployment, short contracts thus aimed to ensure that the slave hierarchy remained rigid.

Set against the complex mindset of American elites at midcentury, a high turnover of overseers appears rational. The short contract was a key element of the patriarchal contribution to normative criticisms of overseers and overseeing yet was never completely successful. The opportunity for managers to "up and leave" enabled them to seek out new opportunities on the frontiers, where they might escape a life of dependence and so challenge hierarchical assumptions.[33] Supervisors viewed in the moment of dismissal an opportunity to underline their reputations as honorable white men, against the prejudices of stewards as well as owners. The Virginian steward Peyton Skipwith claimed that one Neal had falsely accused him of cheating their planter, William Harwood, out of a tract of land. Skipwith believed this "most groundless calumny" to be premeditated: reputedly it was propagated by the "incensed overseer [Neal], who . . . [had] declared, on my threatening to turn him off a plantation of the said *Harwood's* . . . for his insolence and neglect of duty, that he would endeavour by some means or other to avoid being under my direction, for that he was well assured no overseer could please me." In response Skipwith had determined to direct "a suit in the General Court against *Neal*."[34] Canny overseers learned to turn the loose employment law of the time on its head and derived benefits from threatening to withdraw their labor. Even as short contracts provoked southerners into deepening their prejudices against overseers, they performed just as important a role in midwifing the perception among some overseers that, as professional agriculturalists, they deserved better treatment; and they helped to create strong expectations among the broader managerial ranks for basic employment rights.

Employment contracts outlined the structure and nature of oversight on southern plantations. Sometimes they described where the contracted overseer would fit into the management hierarchy. Multiple overseers often superintended large enslaved workforces: in 1762 Francis Jerdone put three overseers in charge of thirty-three bondpeople at his quarter in Albemarle County, Virginia, and by the following year he was employing four managers for the same number of people.[35] Four years later Charles Slathern and James Kerr were overseeing twenty-six enslaved people for Jerdone in the same county.[36] Such practices were also relatively common in the lowcountry, where slave units were bigger. Nine advertisements from South Carolina between 1750 and 1775 requested two overseers for each plantation advertised.

Especially where there was a limited supply of overseers—in frontier districts, for instance—a manager now and again had responsibility for more than one plantation.[37] Thomas Bond oversaw eight enslaved people for Francis Jerdone across two parishes in Albemarle County in 1763.[38] On occasion an overseer might manage two or three plantations that were in the same neighborhood but owned by different planters.[39] Rice districts always suffered from a shortage of qualified overseers, and it was even more common for overseers there to run more than one quarter at once. One South Carolinian advertiser in 1773 "wanted Immediately, *To manage several Plantations,* a . . . MAN, Who is well acquainted with the Management of a Rice Plantation."[40] This course of action was frequently undertaken at "crisis" moments—Henry Laurens placed Broughton Island and New Hope plantations under the overall management of John McCullough after dismissing Mark Noble.[41] Reasons of economy also motivated employers: two gazette notices advertise a position overseeing "two adjoining . . . PLANTATIONS."[42] Such planters risked putting excessive responsibility on untried overseers, who might be in charge of "45 to 50 workers."[43]

Plantation management involved many tasks that varied across space as well as time, but a large number were common to Virginia, South Carolina, and Georgia throughout the eighteenth century. These split into jobs that the overseer forced the bondpeople to carry out, and those that he performed himself. Under the first heading might be put turpentine production, "sawing and squaring" wood, care of livestock, brick making, making pitch, and repairing canoes.[44] Robert Gutritch oversaw enslaved people who looked after forty-seven cows, sixty-four sheep, and one hundred pigs in 1776.[45] Though performed by bondpeople, each of these tasks relied on both the skill of the workforce and the knowledge of the overseer. Planters sought to address the individual needs of their plantation through the employment of experienced managers: hence Peter Papot's agreement to "oversee and do all the Carpenters Business."[46] Other overseers supervised ambitious building projects. William Gibbons settled with James Guinn in 1770 "that the said Guinn doth agree to oversee Doctor Channing's Pleasant Point Plantation, and also manage & carry on the Buildings that are intended to be Built there, and lay out and assist in the Work."[47] Similarly an applicant who answered an advert in a 1766 issue of the *Georgia Gazette* needed to be "capable of erecting rough buildings for his own convenience, and also for negroes."[48]

In both regions men were in high demand who could both oversee enslaved people and adapt plantations to their local topography. Henry Laurens made a plea for "an excellent hand at damming and ditching," and a 1760 gazette notice requested "a good overseer that is acquainted with ditching."[49] In Virginia overseers were involved in reshaping the surrounding environment to harness natural power. Robert Carter of Nomini Hall in 1777 hired John McKenney to overlook his "jobbers." Their agreement required McKenney to produce "a Crop of Corn Pumpkins, Irish Potatoes"; the "s[ai]d Jobbers" were also "to raise Stone to build a tumbling Dam at Dickerson's mill."[50] And superintendents for enslaved sawyers were especially popular: six lowcountry advertisements requested "AN OVERSEER ... who understands Sawing" or one who was "capable of" or "properly qualified for taking charge of a few pair of sawyers."[51] Two further adverts mentioned "planting, [*and*] sawing," another sought "Two Overseers, to manage seven pair of sawyers, and a little planting," and a further notice required "AN OVERSEER, to manage ... 50 working Hands employ'd in Rice and Lumber."[52]

Hiring overseers who owned enslaved people enabled planters to benefit from an established working relationship, together with the manager's knowledge of his bondpeople's aptitude for specific roles. In Virginia William Cabell hired Thomas Appling with "his Negro Boy Lewis" for "nine pounds"; Lewis was "to be considered as a full share in the Crop."[53] In 1770 a gazette subscriber advertised for "A MAN ... [who] has a few Negroes, willing to employ them ... in raising Rice, sawing Lumber, and making Pitch."[54] The gamut of jobs to which the enslaved workforce could be put demonstrates the desirability of such an overseer. Female planters in particular sought managers of this ilk, because they stood to benefit in much the same way as the hiring of a married couple provided an extra pair of hands on the plantation. In 1762 Martha Woodcraft "WANTED, in time to prepare land for the next crop, an overseer who is capable of managing a small plantation. If he has four or five slaves of his own . . . it will be the more agreeable."[55]

Under the heading of tasks that the overseer performed himself were the vital management roles of keeping accounts and selling produce at market, purchasing provisions, making lists of enslaved infants, and advertising the sale of lands. In addition some overseers carried out much less typical tasks such as teaching their employers' children.[56] But a more important responsibility was the welfare and disciplining of bondpeople. On a day-to-day basis overseers apportioned work to slave gangs and supervised their labor; on occasion, when illness broke out, managers needed a good enough knowledge of contemporary medicine to know if ailing enslaved men and women required professional attention, or to be able to treat minor complaints without outside help. Plantation managers conducted periodic inspections of the slave quarters and distributed clothes.[57] The overseer also controlled the bondpeople's workday. He woke them in the morning by blowing a horn, so that they would be ready to labor by the time that daylight arrived.[58] And he directed and devised punishments for those whom he deemed rebellious.

But the manager's own conduct was also strictly delineated, a factor that contributed to the sense that overseers were dependent men. Overseers were expected to follow to the letter the written instructions that they received; the planter was the only arbiter of how well they adhered to his demands. More shamefully for overseers, many were subject to strict codes of discipline: they were not permitted to leave the plantation except when carrying out business for their employer and were not, moreover, allowed to keep private company.[59] These stipulations aimed to discourage overseers from succumbing to insobriety through the temptations of the outside world.

The second principal responsibility for managers was the production of cash crops. Here, overseers' supervisory tasks depended on the region that they lived in and the time of year in which they were employed. In Virginia tobacco beds were seeded in January; the crop would require transplanting in March, cutting in August, and casking in October. If any of the stages were unsuccessful, it could mean "the whole loss of the . . . Cropp."[60] Barley was ready for cutting by the end of June.[61] Other crops were not for sale; instead they fed the animals that worked on the plantation. Planters held fast to this distinction, recognizing the importance of plantation self-sufficiency: one of Francis Jerdone's overseers was informed in 1768 that as part of his contractual provisions he was not to receive any "part of any Oats, which he is every year to Sow from 4 to 6000 Corn hills for the use of my Plantation."[62]

The nature of its cultivation cycle meant that corn and livestock viably could be raised at the same time as tobacco. Many Virginian overseers needed to understand the proper management of all three: one post-Revolution contract allowed the overseer an eighth of the tobacco and a tenth of the corn that he made.[63] Indeed a good number of planters took the decision to grow corn in favor of tobacco, based largely on their experiences of the changeable market in Virginia's traditional cash crop. In 1680 nearly every family in the Chesapeake grew tobacco; but many had abandoned it by 1740, especially in the Tidewater, where the lowest-quality plants grew. In 1750, after two severe depressions, only three-quarters of Chesapeake householders grew tobacco.[64] The cultivation of corn had long been encouraged in Virginian law to provide subsistence for the colony's population, and harvest failures in Europe during the 1760s and 1770s created an increased demand for the foodstuff.[65] Owing to soil exhaustion and market disruptions during the Revolutionary War, between the 1780s and 1790s a significant majority of Tidewater planters came to realize that tobacco was no longer profitable. Planters had to shift to grain farming and herding in order to survive; many did not return their lands to tobacco even after markets had improved.[66] The vagaries of the tobacco trade also encouraged the Virginian assembly to introduce statutes that required the planting of hemp and flax as a further alternative to tobacco.[67]

The changing face of Virginian agriculture represented a challenge for the overseer—the onus was on him to adapt to new crops as quickly as plantation owners responded to the market. Robert Carter of Nomini Hall gave very specific directions about the dimensions, contents, and appearance of a granary he wished to have built. Significantly for his manager, "the Granary should not be very detached from [the overseer's] House."[68] In 1755 Joseph Valentine was already tasked with managing Daniel Parke Custis's grain mill—he was to "have her kept in the best order he can, and to take an exact Account every Week of what Grain the said Mill gets."[69] As planters diversified so did the overseer's work: in March 1776 Robert Gutritch was ordered to "now sow all kinds of pease and seeds, plant broad French beans, set out cabbages and colewarts, the slips of raspberries, and gooseberries, thyme, sage," and fourteen other herbs and vegetables.[70] Diversification was particularly common in this Enlightenment age, as educated planters began to introduce scientific innovation and experimentation to their farming. Thomas Jefferson and George Washington were both interested in the increased yields that agricultural innovations could provide; both recorded in their correspondence experiments with crops such as grain and buckwheat, and the raising of high-yield breeds of sheep and cattle.[71] The damage to his plantations' soils engendered by a tobacco monoculture would induce Washington to remark just after the Revolutionary War that he never rode his plantations "without seeing something which makes me regret having [continued] so long in the ruinous mode of farming which we are in."[72] Washington was prescient—as cotton grew in importance toward the end of the century and at the start of the 1800s, and as newly incorporated western lands adapted to the new crop, Virginia's loss of status as a producer of a valuable cash crop diminished terminally. This decline may well have put a strain on established relations between bondpeople, planters, and overseers.

The "New Agriculture" of the English agricultural revolution strongly influenced the agricultural experiments of noteworthy Virginians. This transformation moved agriculture away from a traditional three-year crop rotation and, in a system pioneered by English agriculturist Jethro Tull, introduced to the rotation forage crops, roots, and "artificial" or nonnative grasses. In 1760 Washington was already a practitioner of Tull's horse-hoeing husbandry; by the time of his death he was devoted to the more sophisticated work of Arthur Young, the famed English agriculturist, and practiced his own seven-year rotation.[73] Other planters found these innovations inspiring. The nitrogen-fixing properties of the plants in John Page's list no doubt benefited cultivation; Washington corresponded frequently with Jefferson about their agricultural experiments and wrote regularly to other slaveholders such as the younger Landon Carter. Jefferson was himself a correspondent of the English agriculturist William Pearce, as Washington was of Young.[74] The number of field crops raised by Washington in his determination to move away from tobacco numbered well above sixty, including barley, carrots, millet, pumpkins, and wheat; he also researched manures for fertilizer, including animal dung and marl.[75]

In South Carolina and Georgia, the most significant agricultural development at midcentury was the introduction of indigo. Production of this crop spread widely and quickly, with many individuals apparently learning how to grow it by word of mouth and often from enslaved people. Because indigo was so profitable when it was first introduced, and because many planters had little personal understanding of its manufacture, the production of this crop became one of the most important aspects of plantation work for many lowcountry overseers. The commodity was so highly prized by customers in the New World and metropolitan Britain that, although it was never more than a marginal crop in the middle colonies, overseers who were skilled in indigo manufacture were much in demand.[76]

Rice was even more important than indigo. Its long growth period meant that overseers in the lowcountry had a different variety of tasks to carry out from those of their counterparts in Virginia. Again unlike in Virginia, the labor- and capital-intensive nature of rice cultivation on the whole discouraged rice planters from devoting valuable resources to experimenting with unproved innovations, especially since they were obliged by the second half of the century to invest in large-scale irrigation schemes if they were to compete with other growers. But novel agricultural technologies were introduced here as well. Overseer John Pressley was recompensed "for making a New Rice Machine" in 1777; Laurens imitated "painstaking" Chinese methods of rice hand transplanting and cultivation; and other planters experimented with automatic rice milling.[77] Investments in experimentation for the world staple market marked out those men who did innovate as nascent capitalists. As sites of production bound to transatlantic markets, plantations were "specialized capital investments in a vanguard form of international commerce." The wealthiest among the planter elite made them into "laboratories for sophisticated agricultural methods" that could "shore up their credentials as participants in a modernizing world."[78]

Indigo's profitability was short-lived. Overseas competition, unsuitable weather, and attacks by pests meant that by the closing decades of the eighteenth century, planters in the United States—who had lost easy access to British markets and the subsidies offered by the crown—had largely abandoned the plant for Sea Island cotton and other crops.[79] Rice, too, began to lose favor once Eli Whitney's cotton gin made that crop more viable, enabling smaller planters and those with marginal soils to invest in a profitable commodity. But this shift began to occur only at the end of the eighteenth century. For most of the 1700s, lowcountry overseers' primary responsibilities therefore centered on the production of rice, or indigo, or both.

Aside from agriculture and the supervision of the enslaved, oversight involved a variety of tasks. Overseers often delivered stray animals to those in authority, a duty required by Virginian law to prevent their theft or misuse.[80] Likewise, in South Carolina, "WILLIAM BROWN, Overseer to Mr. Henry Smith" tolled "a bay GELDING" before "WILLIAM MASON, J.P." in 1770.[81] Other managers placed advertisements in gazettes for runaway bondpeople and servants; many adverts required that the runaway be brought not to the planter, but to the overseer, an indication that these supervisors worked on absentee plantations situated far from the slave owner's residence.[82] In 1773 James Fraser, overseer in South Carolina to Pierce Butler, reported the flight of Johnny, a bondman, and promised that "any Person that will deliver him . . . to the . . . Overseer on said Plantation, shall receive TWO DOLLARS reward."[83]

As free white citizens, overseers were required to assist with slave patrols.[84] Although they and other poor whites bemoaned the sporadic and class-biased nature of the patrols—planters often refused to participate—the authorities levied fines on shirkers.[85] Road maintenance duty was a further obligation. Theoretically this required the regular participation of all males, black and white, slave and free, between the ages of sixteen and sixty, but in actuality the poorest members of society were more likely to be summoned to manual road labor than a supervisory role. Yet overseers, because of their experience as superintendents, tended to fall into the latter category despite having humble origins themselves.[86] Slaveholding managers were also obliged to make their bondpeople available. Timothy Creamer, overseer for Henry Laurens at his Mepkin plantation, received orders in 1764 to bring two enslaved men to work on the parish roads.[87] John Smith was required to do likewise on the road from Watboo to Strawberry in South Carolina.[88] Henry Laurens found mandatory road duty trying, since, by keeping his overseers away from their plantations, it affected production. He assured John Smith that "unless it is your own desire & free will to go, I really cannot consent to it. I am willing to take my full share of every parochial duty . . . but too great a load cannot be borne. I shall therefore Indempnify you."[89] Exactly a year earlier he had beseeched James Cordes Jr. "to postpone the execution of [his road duty] until I have got thro my first cutting of Indigo."[90] Other planters were more anxious to avoid performing their own duty than they were about the effect of their manager's absence. They used a legal loophole that allowed them to nominate someone else—often their overseer—to carry out their civic obligations in their stead.[91]

Overseers came to understand the value of their abilities, but many felt that their employers undervalued them. Far from the respect offered to agriculturists like Arthur Young and William Pearce, managers instead received calumny and the shame of dependency from slaveholders. The managerial contract served largely to exacerbate these tensions by formalizing them. On the one hand, the contract made assumptions about an overseer's lack of reliability and competence; on the other hand, it put the overseer in the most important position on the southern plantation. A particular focus of this uneasy relationship was the payment that overseers received. The amount of remuneration provided in a contract became a tool that overseers could use to dispute their employers' estimation of their worth, and that planters could use to reward good work or punish bad service.

One method of remuneration—payment in wages—was relatively widespread in the eighteenth century. Usually managers received wages at the end of the calendar year (at the same time as overseers completed annual contracts and when the recruitment process was at its zenith). Most managers, however, were given cash advances, sometimes for essential items, which were removed from the balance at the end of their term.[92] Compensation paid to Virginian overseers differed across the century. It ranged from "40 shillings pay[able] to Jeptha Edmunds being part of his wages as an overseer" in 1706; thirty-five pounds for "Randolphs Overseer" in 1763; between twenty pounds and thirty pounds for the Earl of Dunmore's three overseers in 1774; fifty pounds each for two overseers who did a year's work for Benjamin Harrison in 1778; forty pounds per annum paid to John Fairfax, overseer to George Washington in 1784; "seventy pounds current money of Virginia" in 1796 to Landon Carter's overseer, John Deatly; and fifty pounds paid to Archer Christian by Mary Douglass of Louisa County, Virginia, in 1797.[93] The price that William Digges planned to pay to hire from their owner "three pair of good honest SAWYERS" in 1777 offers some comparison—he suggested "ninety pounds a year, or thirty pounds *per* pair."[94] Lord Dunmore's salary payments to overseers accounted for one-sixth of the annual costs of running his plantations.[95]

Although fluctuating currency values and differing exchange rates between colonies mean that a deeper comparison of contemporary prices is problematic, several general factors determined the rate of pay. These included the number of bondpeople maintained, the type of plantation (absentee or resident), the economic condition of the planter, the length of tenure, the overseer's experience, and the geographic location of the plantation.[96] Thus John McKenney, the overseer employed by Robert Carter to take charge of his "jobbers," was "not well paid": he was "to receive for his services . . . 25s/6 per month."[97] Overseers and stewards shouldered greater responsibilities when in charge of a large labor force or an absentee plantation; these responsibilities entailed higher financial rewards and a significant difference in their wage levels in comparison to those of other overseers.[98] In a letter written just after the Revolution, George Washington recognized this fact—he wished to employ a skilled steward but acknowledged that "one who is completely fit for my purposes, wou'd be above my price."[99] Late in the century, Tobias Lear, personal secretary to George Washington as president, explained how wages were determined: "the wages given to those whom [Washington] employs, as well as by other gentlemen in his vicinity who give annual wages instead of a share to the Overseer, vary from 80 to 130 Dollars pr. Year, according to the extent of the farm to be superintended, and the skill of the person in managing the business of it."[100]

In 1771 the Berkeley County, South Carolina, planter John Harleston paid John Bishop "at the rate of Eight pounds p[er] Month."[101] An analysis of overseers' wages in South Carolina has found that they were very poorly paid for the level of responsibility that devolved to them: compared with wages in the metropolis, managers received a salary "only slightly better than an English laborer, far less than a shopkeeper and only a little better than a housekeeper."[102] Managerial salaries in colonial Georgia tended to fall between £25 and £40 per annum.[103] William Gibbons agreed that William May would be paid £25 a year, and Thomas Moore and James Guinn "Forty Pounds Sterling." But he also offered to pay the more experienced Peter Papot "Sixty Pounds money of the State of Georgia a year," apparently in recognition of his skills in carpentry.[104] Each of these overseers received roughly the same amount of provisions and other nonmonetary stipends.

However, other planters in the lowcountry promised "very good," even "extraordinary" wages to successful applicants in an attempt to encourage competent applicants.[105] Charles Cotesworth Pinckney, Eliza Lucas's son, maintained in 1772 that "Good Wages will be given to any person well recommended."[106] Henry Laurens explained to Paul Trapier in 1766 that "whenever a good [overseer] offers I shall be ready to give him good encouragement & something the more."[107] In 1766 truly "extraordinary" wages were offered by Henry Laurens on behalf of James Grant, governor of the temporary British possession of East Florida. Laurens informed his correspondent Edward Graham that Grant had "employment for two" overseers, one of whom was to "go to East Florida to take care of about 40 Negroes to plant Rice, Indigo, &c. . . . his Wages about £180 to £240 per Annum together with maintenance," and proposed that John McCullough be given one of the positions.[108] This significant compensation was due to the great degree of responsibility placed on the manager: McCullough was to be in charge of establishing a new plantation for his employer, which would require command of a large number of bondpeople in a frontier area where the established authority of slave society did not yet reach.

Though Laurens's offer to McCullough was exceptional, his experience underlines how overseeing in rare cases could offer real possibilities for capital accumulation. Yet even where remuneration was less impressive, planters desired to set up a wage scale for their managers—a clear means by which to distinguish competence from incompetence, and to encourage individual overseers to give better service.[109] If a superintendent proved especially industrious, usually he could expect a pay increase. John Beale, who worked on Landon Carter's Virginian plantations, had asked originally for £20 a year but performed so well that he received £50.[110] Returned to his plantations after the Revolution, George Washington explained to the agriculturist William Pearce that this sort of investment was beneficial: Washington intended to "begrudge no reasonable expense that will contribute to the improvement of my Farms . . . for nothing pleases me better than to see them in good order . . . nor nothing hurts me more to find them otherwise."[111] In Georgia Charles Watson was so satisfied with the manner in which John Tebeau had "Discharged the Duty of an Overseer" that in 1769 he gave him an enslaved boy called Griffith.[112]

Along the same lines was the practice of offering bonuses for the successful completion of specific tasks. Henry Laurens told John Smith in 1766 that "as you are so industrious in making Canoes I shall be glad if you could make three more besides that one for your own use & I shall make you a reasonable allowance for your trouble."[113] In addition to his crop share, Francis Jerdone offered James Kerr £15 "for his extraordinary trouble in looking after & managing all my other affairs at the Mountain."[114] Owning one's own capital in humans could also be lucrative. The overseer Michael Boinneau leased seven working bondmen to Charleston lawyer and slaveholder John E. Colhoun for a year. Colhoun agreed to pay £16 for each bondperson and, in addition, contracted to furnish each with clothing and provisions.[115] Here slave ownership had put a manager on a more equal footing in discussions over remuneration.

Later agricultural reformers opposed bonus provisions, arguing with justification that the practice led managers to overwork the bondpeople under their command.[116] The overseer system posed a dilemma that arose from the nature of plantation slavery itself—how to incentivize profitable management in a regime that at its base depended entirely on the forced labor of others. A slaveholder could invest larger sums in the skills of an experienced overseer but had little guarantee that the drive for higher profits would not injure the enslaved men and women to the point where they were no longer valuable as plantation workers. Alternatively a planter might cut corners when recruiting overseers and pay out as little money as possible, especially during the cyclical economic depressions that beset eighteenth-century North American economies. Whatever course they took, planters' actions exacerbated negative overseer stereotypes.[117] By rewarding managers who had had a positive effect on profit margins, planters once more held up some individuals as ideal while condemning the ineptitude of others. If they selected cheaper overseers, planters risked employing men who had little capacity for managing bondpeople without recourse to frequent brutality, or who had little knowledge of cultivation.

Crop sharing, the second main method of overseer compensation, prevailed widely along the Atlantic seaboard during the colonial period.[118] Under this system the overseer earned one share of the crop calculated relative to the time that he had expended on it and the number of enslaved people whom he worked, which he could then market as he saw fit. An early Virginian observer noted that managers received "a Dividend . . . in Proportion to the Number of Hands including himself."[119] In the last decade of the century, George Washington, now president, passed on a description of the Chesapeake crop-share system to an English farmer who wished to manage one of Washington's plantations: "the usual mode of engaging overseers of farms and plantations in Virginia . . . is to give them a share of the Crop as a compensation for their services, for instance, if there should be on a plantation *ten* working hands, the crop is divided into eleven shares, one of which belongs to the Overseer: if a greater or less number of hands is employed, the Overseer's share is in proportion thereto."[120]

Landon Carter of Sabine Hall offered one-twelfth to a prospective overseer in 1771, while his nephew generally paid between one-eighth and one-twelfth of the harvest.[121] John Page engaged Robert Gutrich to be an overseer at Rosewell for one-tenth of the tobacco and corn and one-twelfth of the wheat that he produced.[122] Some planters also included beasts of burden when calculating shares. The crop of tobacco grown by Henry Read, employed on William Cabell's home plantation, was divided into seven shares (five adult bondpeople, two children on half shares, plus Read himself). But this grew to nine shares each for corn and wheat, because Read used two work horses to cultivate these other crops.[123]

A similar calculation determined shares in the lowcountry. As part of "the agreement made Between William Gibbons Planter near Savannah in Georgia, and Matthias Binder labourer of the said place," Binder was allowed "the Use of One Negro Man named Andrew . . . and the Moiety [i.e. the half] of all that [he] and his Son together with the said Negro shall plant & keep on an Island of the said Gibbons."[124] Henry Laurens gave an indication of the volumes of cash crops that shares yielded in a letter to James Brenard, his overseer at Wambaw: "the Wambaw Boat brought down 96 Barrels of Rice & 12 half Barrels. Abram [Schad] wrote that 10 of them were yours but there appear'd to be 13 Mark'd JB so I have thrown them all into one & when the whole is brought down you shall have an equal proportion as to the weight and price."[125]

A further form of crop sharing was unique to the colonial period. Overseers rented developed plantations along with bondpeople and some stock. In return for maintaining the plantation and its enslaved labor force, overseers received one-third of net proceeds from crop sales. Leases were generally long term, sometimes lasting seven to twenty-one years or even longer.[126]

Slaveholding overseers could derive more benefit from crop sharing than those who owned no enslaved people, since they often employed their own bondpeople on shares. Virginian Henry Fitzhugh paid his overseer, William Payne, an extra share for his bondman, Sam, in 1766.[127] Henry Laurens outlined the practice to John Coming Ball: "the Overseer if he employs any Negroes of his own to draw a share of the Crop of Rice in proportion to the number of such his Negroes & no more."[128] Of the ten lowcountry gazette adverts surveyed that requested overseers who owned enslaved people, six suggested that the manager "may join them in shares."[129] While this arrangement could be beneficial to overseers, it meant that they were obliged either to pay their employers for clothing and food for their own bondpeople, or else find such provisions themselves. It also meant that overseers' profits took a hit when enslaved people fell ill or were disabled.[130] Hiring on shares was not the only method of compensation for overseers who employed their own bondpeople. Job-seeking managers were told that their "Negroes . . . will be taken on hire"; another advert promised the applicant that "if he has two or three Negroes, good wages will be allowed for them."[131] Planters needed to weigh up the advantages of employing an overseer with an established relationship with his bondpeople against the cost of paying out more in shares and costs. Pecuniary concerns were undoubtedly the motivation for the more cautionary pleas made by some gazette subscribers. One stated that a "man without negroes will be most agreeable"; another that "no objection will be had to a man who has a few negroes of his own, provided his number does not exceed eight."[132]

As with payment in wages, the crop-share system rewarded managers who shouldered larger responsibilities. Because of the greater numbers of bondpeople that they supervised, overseers in the lowcountry received more sizeable quantities of crop when working on shares than their Chesapeake counterparts. Landowners in England by this point had developed a form of crop-sharing land tenancy that was broadly comparable to the American system in its intention to link the financial success of tenants to the agricultural successes of the lands that they worked. This arrangement had encouraged small farmers to seek out new ways to improve their yield and eventually played a part in inspiring the inventive technologies of the agricultural revolution.[133] Yet in North America, where land was relatively plentiful—if intensive cultivation exhausted their soil, many planters could move elsewhere—and where the most immediate way in which to increase yield was not to innovate, but simply to work enslaved people harder, the system largely failed.[134] A French traveler recorded at the end of the century that "the white overseers overwork [the slaves] detestably, because they get a percentage of the produce."[135]

George Washington was among many who decried "our course of Husbandry in this Country . . . [which] . . . is not only exceedingly unprofitable . . . but destructive to our Lands." Other planters believed that crop sharing, far from tying overseers' interests to that of the plantation, in fact encouraged managers to neglect their day-to-day nonagricultural tasks in favor of their crop-raising duties.[136] Overseers were themselves becoming aware that poor yields meant that crop sharing might not be as profitable as payment in wages, and the more assertive among their number rejected it as a means of payment. Robert Carter of Nomini Hall noted that "Allen and Hickson say tha[t] ye lands there are not proper f[o]r Indian Corn, oats, Rye, Peas & Roots[;] they rejected my Proposal, but offer to serve for standing Wages."[137] By the nineteenth century, crop sharing had fallen largely into disuse.[138]

Because the crop-share system tied salaries so closely to yields, it still represented for many colonial slave owners a better means than cash payments to ensure managerial fidelity to profit margins. But crop sharing should not be viewed as part of an explicit "divide and rule" strategy that separated overseers from their "natural" class allies: other members of the overseeing profession. The strategy might well have limited overseer rebellion against the class structure to small and sporadic acts of disobedience.[139] Yet to ascribe this level of meaning to what was essentially a business decision would require not only the assumption of an unprovable level of false consciousness among those overseers who "collaborated" with planters, but also—by diluting the explanatory worth of resistance—remove political significance from the real and consistent opposition to the slave system that bondpeople effected.[140] Planters and overseers were committed to the preservation of a system that (in theory at least) provided the latter group with the opportunity someday to own land and, crucially, property in humans. Most overseers calculated that the easiest way to achieve this was not through resistance to social superordinates, but through a studied attempt to improve their everyday conditions.

Crop sharing gave some managers greater autonomy than those who were paid wages—the better overseers were rewarded by being able to set a rate at which slaveholders were obliged to buy their crop, which might differ from "market price."[141] It remains true that even when overseers were paid well, only the most diligent savers among the managerial profession would have been able to afford a plantation of their own. A medium-sized tract of land sold in Albemarle County, Virginia, in 1756 cost £200, many times more than overseers' salaries, in wages or shares.[142] The same year one of the overseers from the area earned just under thirty pounds for the tobacco that he had produced over the course of twelve months.[143] Four years later another overseer's reward in the same region was just over nine pounds.[144] Very few, if any, managers would have been able to meet the £750 and £1,000 asking prices for large tracts of land that one Virginian planter advertised in 1773, nor the £455 that Georgian William Gibbons paid for a plantation in 1783.[145]

Remuneration also acted as a constant reminder that managers did not earn their livelihood by working their own lands. Many planters gave material provisions to their overseers: being dependent on an employer for one's very subsistence—sometimes even for one's clothing, shoes, and medicine—deepened managerial shame among the wider plantation community.[146] The accusation of dependence cut especially deep when slaveholders sought to delineate precisely the goods that an overseer was allowed to receive. Close attention to plantation resources motivated the Virginian Francis Jerdone to insist that if one of his overseers were to "make any wheat or oats he is to have no part thereof."[147] Joseph Ball gave precise details from as far afield as London about the number of cows and sheep that were to remain on his plantations.[148] Controlling the allocation of provisions was another means by which patriarchs could guard against the presumed dishonesty of dependent overseers, and claim dominance over their employees.[149]

Many of the drawbacks of receiving provisions were offset by the significant benefits and to some extent must have made up for the relatively meager wages and crop shares that managers earned.[150] Virginian overseers received items including bread corn, cows to provide milk, beef, and pasturage for their horses.[151] Joseph Ball wrote to Joseph Chinn that he was "wellcome to kill Two or Three of the best Lambs every year for [his] own use."[152] In Georgia Matthias Binder was promised by William Gibbons "one half of the Increase of the Hoggs & Poultry, and the Use of [Gibbons's] Beack Cattle, [Gibbons] also allows him the half of all the Garden Stuff that he may make and carry to markett."[153] Gibbons agreed that William May receive "a third part of the Hoggs he raises on the Plantation and also one half of the Poultry"; that Thomas Moore be allowed "the Milk of what cows are on the plantation"; and that he "find the said [James] Guinn such Bread . . . as the Plantation affords."[154] Further north Henry Laurens provided John Smith with rum and offered John McCullough "a reasonable Quantity" of the same libation, as well as pledging to supply him with sugar.[155]

An alternative system of remittance was proposed by the Georgian Charles Wright, who gave John Oakes "an Allowance of Twenty Shillings Sterling per Month in Lieu of Provisions for himself and family."[156] The account book of South Carolinian planter and politician Isaac Hayne reveals frequent transfers of cash and provisions between him and his overseer, James Lewis Culliatte.[157] Cognizant of the effect on productivity that managerial ill health might entrain, some planters paid for their overseers' medical treatment. George Washington recorded just after the Revolutionary War that "Doctr. Craik arrived, on a Visit to John Alton (my Overseer in the Neck [plantation]) who has been ill, & has been confined to his bed for near 3 weeks."[158] And in recognition of the distances that he was required to cover when overseeing two plantations, 1755 saw Joseph Valentine given the use of a horse.[159]

Although John McKenney, the superintendent of Robert Carter's "jobbers," was obliged "to find himself, Board, lodging, Washing &c.," most overseers enjoyed the major advantage of "lodging" provided by employers for managers, and for their families if they were married.[160] Bachelors were often lodged in the same building as the proprietor, but if an overseer was given his own abode, usually it was situated near to the slave quarters, the better to supervise every aspect of bondpeople's lives (see fig. 3).[161] Especially early in the century, overseer housing often did not amount to a lot. Robert "King" Carter did not provide his overseers with much more in the way of provisions than he did his bondpeople and extended his parsimony to managerial dwellings. A 1733 inventory showed that only 33 percent of his overseers had a bed, only 28 percent blankets, and only 5 percent a table, chest or chamber pot.[162] On outlying quarters managers and their families lived in crude houses of similar construction to the enslaved people's homes: the only noticeable difference was that overseers had more space, typically a two-room house measuring sixteen by twenty-four feet.[163]

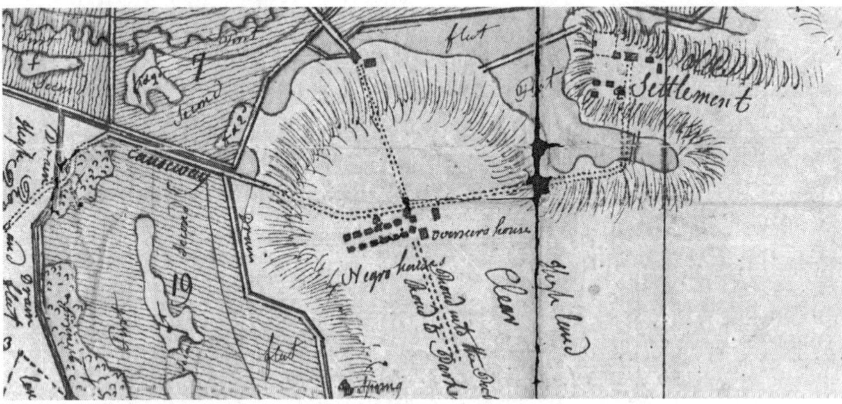

Fig. 3. Plantation belonging to the estate of John Singleton, St. Bartholomew's Parish, South Carolina, May 1795, Theodore Gourdin collection. Courtesy of South Carolina Historical Society.

Later, in 1765, a subscriber to the *Virginia Gazette* who was selling a tract of land described a typical overseer's dwelling. The house had "three rooms below and one large one above."[164] Tobias Lear saw the inclusion of a house in an overseer's contract as another form of remuneration—and claimed that the lodgings that he reserved for managers were far from meager. "To . . . wages [are] added, a comfortable dwelling House on the farm, and a stipulated quantity of provisions, adequate to the support of the Overseer," he wrote at the end of the century.[165] One of George Washington's overseers would have been lucky enough to have lodged near to Washington's own house at Mount Vernon (see fig. 4).

Extra provision increased the cost of employing an overseer and turned planters further against the managerial profession. Henry Laurens commented to Richard Oswald in 1766 how "twenty or thirty industrious families with frugal living at one quarter the expence of your Overseer, & an hundred times the labour that any mere Overseer will be at, might get Bread & even in a course of Years earn some Negroes."[166] Other planters resented paying more than necessary for dependent labor. Joseph Ball complained at midcentury that "I see no reason, why I should keep a Fine House . . . for an overseer."[167] The Georgian senator Josiah Tatnall deducted rent from his overseer's wages (though renting land at least meant that a manager could earn money from growing and marketing his own crops).[168] A list of wages paid in 1780 to Peter Papot by William Gibbons's estate, following this Georgian slaveholder's death, demonstrates well the extra money that a planter might pay an overseer. As well as "one Years wages as overseer" at "£60," also included was a reimbursement of "£35" for "repairing the House & barn & machine house" and compensation of "5/-" and "1/6" for respectively "mending 2 Tables" and "mending the Barn Lock."[169] But, despite Henry Laurens's misgivings about the costs of hiring overseers, even before he employed John McCullough Laurens "paid him £5 expenses & think he ought to be allowed more if he does not accept my present offer." Laurens was prepared to pay over the odds because he was eager to secure McCullough's services—in addition to these expenses and the "extraordinary wages" that he offered, Laurens promised to pay for McCullough's passage to St. Augustine "for him & his family there & back again at the end of the Year if he shall not chuse to continue longer."[170]

Fig. 4. Reconstructed interior of overseer's house, George Washington's Mount Vernon plantation, Virginia (author's own photograph).

Slave owners strove to encourage better management by holding out to overseers the potential for material reward. Yet, in so doing, they also created rods for their backs. The possibility that wages, shares, or provisions might be increased gave overseers a bargaining chip that became more valuable over the course of the century as managerial responsibilities grew larger through the expansion of absenteeism and the introduction of new cultivation techniques. Henry Laurens observed ten years before the Revolution that "every Man thinks himself intituled to the best Wages."[171] This assessment derived from experience: three years earlier Abraham Schad had demanded "as good wages as he can get in the Neighbourhood if he continues another year."[172] By the end of the century, George Washington determined not to take on a manager "at the advanced wages [he] asks, viz £50." He complained, "why *any of them* should think of an *increase* of wages when the produce by which they are to be paid is reduced to half price, and taxes to their Employer (w[hi]ch. they will not feel) are becoming very high, is to me inconceivable, for these causes I am *lower*ing the wages of my Farms."[173] Rejecting Robert Carter III's suggestion of employing a suboverseer, another Virginian overseer also asked for fifty pounds because he felt that he had the requisite "Knowledge . . . of the present arrangement of your Business."[174] Chesapeake planter Joseph Ball grumbled that "the overseers at Morattico and the Forrest are gone off," because their steward "would not allow them more Provisions, than I allow'd them." He concluded, "Let em go."[175] Other overseers spied a gap in the market and advertised themselves as ideal employees for the thrifty planter. One posted in the *South Carolina Gazette* that "as a Salary is but a second Consideration, [he] would give his Service for a small Consideration."[176]

A vignette from the Georgian planter, lawyer, and sometime governor John Houstoun's plantations encapsulates the tension between traditional patriarchal forms of rule and the new influences of a market economy on overseers' choices. Playing the exasperated ruler of dependents, Houstoun declared himself "much surprized . . . at being informed that Mr Gerry had left my Employ—but I did not credit it 'till Yesterday I saw a Letter from Mr Spalding w[hi]ch Speaks of him as the Overseer on Mr Bissits Estate—I am at a Loss to understand this, having heard not a syllable . . . about it." Houstoun had assumed Gerry's constancy: "that he was absolutely fixt in the current Year." Because Gerry's decision conflicted with his employer's plans, Houstoun imagined that the overseer was dissimulating. "I am told his plea is the Mark of Health," he wrote, "but I know there is a better Reason for it, and if there was not, such pretences will not authorize him to trifle with my Interest." Yet he admitted: "some Months Ago I was very indifferent whether he Staid or went, but after . . . his positive Engagement I cannot think myself well used by him or those who tempted him out of my Service by the offer [of] a larger Salary." Wounded, Houstoun now understood the sting in the tail of the annually renewed managerial contract. He blamed Gerry for leaving him adrift "at this critical time just when Negroes are beginning to plant." Such was the lot of the eighteenth-century slaveholder, beset on all sides by subordinates who would disappoint him, to the detriment of his own interest. "It seems to be my fate to meet with something every year to derange my Prospect," Houstoun concluded.[177] Although slaveholders faced novel commercial pressures, they used familiar antidependent rhetoric when criticizing overseers.

Incentivizing profitable management would eventually lead many planters into a race to the bottom, where they sought out the cheapest overseers no matter how incompetent these men eventually might turn out to be. The seeds of the nineteenth-century division between professional and unskilled managers were sown in the eighteenth century and given succor by the overseer contract in which planters recorded their expectations for the plantation and for the manager's activities on it. Clashes between these expectations and managerial performance created frequent disagreements between overseer and slaveholder, hardened attitudes against the managerial profession, and led superintendents by way of a response to underline their agricultural successes.

— Chapter Four —

"Under the shadow of my own Vine & my own Fig-tree"

Relations between Overseers and Slave Owners

As planters in Virginia, South Carolina, and Georgia invested increasingly large sums in their human property and real estate, a particular trope began to gain more prominence in correspondence between employers and their overseers. Slaveholders were continually anxious that managers respect and uphold their "interest." By the eighteenth century, the term "interest" had come to mean anything that was "to or for the advantage of any one"; one's "interest" also referred to one's "good, benefit, [or] profit." When planters spoke of their "interest," it was with prosperity in mind.[1]

A midcentury account from Henry Laurens's South Carolinian plantations demonstrates the vitality of this rhetoric among slaveholders. Because bondpeople tilled the ground and harvested its crops, a break in production due to their ill health could prove costly—and devastating if the sickness was fatal. Laurens insisted to the overseer Peter Horlbeck that "there is nothing of more importance than the care of Sick Negroes."[2] He spoke from experience: in 1763 he had been "indispensably oblig'd to hurry away to [his] Plantation" because "one of my Negroes had . . . broke out with . . . Small Pox to the great danger of my own Interest and the terrour of all the neighbourhood & as I could not trust so important a point wholly to the discretion of an Overseer I was oblig'd to remain there ten days in which time I . . . extinguished the Flame."[3] Five years later the Virginian Robert Carter III, on hearing that "the horned Cattle continue to die," sent "Salt petre[,] [a] Table spoonfu[ll] to be put into a decoction of dogwood bark which I recommend as a proper drink in this case."[4] Few planters had sufficient confidence in their overseers to entrust them with the resolution of potential catastrophes. If a slaveholder's interest was threatened, the overseer could well expect a visit from his employer. Intervention safeguarded the owner's most important resources: the plantation, its stock, and the enslaved people who worked on it.[5]

The first step in assessing the relationship between the two parties is to uncover the motivations of southern planters. In much of the historiography on the political mind of the British colonies before the Revolution, the so-called country ideology (the radical ideas of the Whig country house parliamentary opposition of early eighteenth-century England) is held to have exerted considerable influence. Colonial intellectuals consumed voraciously the works of anti-Court independents within the British Parliament of the 1720s, principally John Trenchard and Thomas Gordon. These Whigs formulated much of their thinking in a volume entitled *Cato's Letters,* which, because it espoused a profound fear of governmental power, would direct fundamentally the nature of American thought and shape the history of the Revolutionary era. In the pages of *Cato's Letters* lay the principles of republicanism as translated by eighteenth-century Englishmen, a republicanism that became one of the most dominant political ideologies in colonial British America.[6] In particular country ideologists adapted the venerable republican notion of virtue to their own ends.[7] According to the Aristotelian moral system, in order to be virtuous a man left his self-interest outside the political sphere—he could be trusted to preserve the traditional distinction between *oikia* and *polis* and thereby enable the growth of virtue in the latter realm. But fuelled by resentment of British government corruption, and adapting the civic republican, Tacitean notion that power and luxury would corrupt existing virtues and destroy established liberty instead (as Aristotle believed) of retarding the original birth and development of these virtues, anti-Court Whigs campaigned for the active removal of enduring special interests from the public political realm.[8] They argued with vigor that the "private spirit," or one's own interest, must yield to the public good.[9]

Yet too deep a focus on the country ideology can obscure the changes that conceptions of political morality underwent in eighteenth-century America and the wider Anglophone world.[10] "Interest" constituted a further entry in an eighteenth-century elite lexicon that was fixated on passions, virtue, and debt. The deep economic fears that underlay this vocabulary demonstrate the shallowness of patriarchal pretensions to the maintenance of social harmony and a disinterested politics; the Lockean reciprocity that planters held in such esteem was, after all, at its base a philosophy designed to protect the sanctity of property. Virginia and South Carolina had become by midcentury two of the three wealthiest colonies in mainland British North America. Turning the logic of the country ideology on its head, promotional literature attracting European emigrants to the new economies began to argue that the private interests of individual adventurers—essentially their dreams of making a fortune—would combine to benefit the entire colony.[11]

This sentiment was characteristic of a shift evident in contemporary political discourse toward the notion that private interest, far from exerting a pernicious influence, could in fact add to the public good. For economist Albert O. Hirschman, during the middle decades of the eighteenth century the new "moral sciences" (the moral and ethical enquiry of Scottish Enlightenment figures such as Adam Smith and David Hume) argued that commercial interests could be counted on to nullify some of the more reckless human passions and ensure moderation and stability. The individual pursuit of self-interest would guard against chaos (which would be in no one's interest) and have the "unintended consequence" of maintaining an autonomous and abstract order in the form of a society.[12] Drawing on

Bernard Mandeville, who believed, controversially, that "private vices" were linked to "public benefits," Adam Smith wrote that it was "not from the benevolence of the butcher, the brewer, or the baker, that we expect our dinner, but from their regard to their own interest. We address ourselves, not to their humanity but to their self-love, and never talk to them of our own necessities but of their advantage."[13]

Such thinking found a ready audience in British America. Many of the great slaveholding families had earned their considerable wealth within only a few generations of their arrival in the New World. Supporting their ties to other regional scions was not heritage, but frequent commercial exchanges. In a social environment where white men were more independent than their cousins in Europe, a civic virtue that derived from one's position in the government of the colony was less important than a moral virtue based on the way that one conducted oneself in relationships with counterparts.[14] A gentleman's virtue was measured in this atmosphere by the value that others put on his commercial attributes. Similarly a patriarchal planter's conception of his self-interest need not make a strict distinction between "good, benefit, [or] profit." He told himself that if his interest was upheld it was not only "to [his] advantage," but to the advantage of his dependents, and of the public good itself.

With public vices exposed and suppressed, the real cause for concern for slaveholders was the intrusion of unfettered competing interests in the person of the overseer into the body politic of the private, patriarchal slave plantation. Their accommodation to the market economy meant that planters had accepted the role that shared private interest played in advancing the public good, but as the country ideologists had tried to do with government, slaveholders still attempted to minimize the corrupting nature of self-interest on the political relationships that they had established on their lands. Seeking thereby to maintain the distinction between *oikia* and *polis,* planters worried that the overseer's desire to shape his working environment to his own ends—cutting corners, taking too much ownership of crop cultivation, tarrying at work, or stealing from the plantation—would gain dominance. As they did when recruiting, in their relations with overseers planters therefore made every effort to prevent managerial influence. They attempted to achieve this by intervening directly when they were able, and through criticism of their overseers if necessary. Planters wished to keep quarters "orderly and regular" and to maintain the stability of the slave system as a whole.[15] Given the amount of responsibility that devolved to overseers on absentee plantations, slaveholders deemed these tactics even more vital there.

In addition to the various mechanisms that slave owners used to intervene in the management of their plantations, planters sought to control their managers through criticism in two broad areas—overseers' agricultural capabilities, and managerial behavior. Criticism reinforced existing, and established new, prejudices against overseers. Censure of managerial agricultural competence derived from planters' anxieties that their interests be upheld, and from their concerns for the value of their investments. Behavioral criticism resulted from traditional fears for the conduct and passions of dependents, and for the fragility of plantation and societal hierarchies. Good relations could, and did, exist between slaveholder and overseer: unsurprisingly, harmonious relations were the most fruitful. With the introduction of agricultural innovations in the late eighteenth century however, planters were more likely to expect better yields from their overseers. Every such development meant one more responsibility for the overseer, one more reason for criticism, and one more addition to the litany of abuses supposedly committed by all overseers.

There was a further crucial dynamic at play. Southern patriarchs voiced pretensions to aristocratic rule. But true aristocracy required not only the attachment of putative aristocrats to this ideal—it needed the fealty of subordinates to the notion that large slaveholders were natural rulers. Throughout the century elites believed that deference to superiors was vital to the maintenance of racial, class, and gender hierarchies. And since white society believed that good management led to good produce, owners were obliged to portray themselves as having control over overseers or else face criticism from their peers for the quality and management of their crop. The reputation of colonial American planters came to be linked to the superiority of the staples that they produced because of the social value of these men's virtue in commercial relations, and because a successful harvest—and a professed love of land and agriculture—indicated a natural mastery both of subordinates and of one's own passions.[16] The author of the Virginia Almanack of 1762 summarized the deep-seated links between reputation, appearance, and virtue. "Virtue," he wrote, "is the highest Proof of a superior Understanding, and the only solid Basis of Greatness: Vice is the natural Consequence of narrow Thoughts; it begins in Mistake, and ends in Infamy."[17] As in overseer recruitment, for planters a reputation for good "character" was all—"Idle Storys whisperd" could amount to "indecent attempts to blast [one's] Charector."[18]

The transition from Old World to New World social and economic relationships already had engendered a reevaluation of the nature of society, of which planter attempts to establish themselves as quasi-aristocrats represented only one manifestation. Overseers, too, perceived these relationships in new ways, leading them to contest their place within social hierarchies. In this context the libertarian impulses that later would be released and sanctioned by the Revolution would play a key role in shaping managerial responses to planter control in the last decades of the eighteenth century. Yet just as overseers were beginning to feel the influence of such impulses, their opportunities for social advancement were decreasing. Because of their lack of alternatives, managerial resistance to slaveholder criticism necessarily was framed by the day-to-day priorities of plantation slavery. Overseers aimed to demonstrate that, far from being bungling and ineffectual, debased and untrustworthy, they were skilled agriculturists and slave superintendents who were due the respect of white society. Managers also bought into the same conception of virtue that their social superiors did. Their relatively independent position made them attuned to the personalized notion of virtue—based especially on one's commercial reputation—that their employers admired. As a key part of white society, overseers were acutely aware of those above and below them. They paid homage to the same mores of deference as their counterparts and respected a hierarchy of symbols and honorific titles designed to tie every member of colonial society in obeisance to the monarch.[19]

Many overseers followed these strictures only on the understanding that their own position was potentially mutable and transitory, and they strove to demonstrate just that. The second step in assessing the relationship between slaveholders and overseers is to outline how managers' reasons for asserting professional control over cultivation, for working on their own interest, for "misbehaving," or for leaving a planter's employ were each linked. This was not only because such actions contributed to the growth of slaveholder prejudices, and hence influenced proprietorial intervention in plantation affairs, but because, what is more important, each course of action represented a strategy of opposition. Depending on a host of individual circumstances, ranging from the employer's lightness of touch to the personal wealth of the overseer, the need for such a reaction varied considerably from one plantation to the next. The widespread vilification of managerial competence is reason enough to view early attempts to professionalize overseeing—far from a betrayal of managers' class counterparts—in fact as a form of defiance to overseer stigmatization as valid as any other attempted by eighteenth-century managers.

Some overseers had dealings not with male heads of the plantation, but with their wives. For a number of reasons, such as urgent political or business obligations, a plantation master might leave his spouse in charge. Many women also became slave owners in their own right following the death of their husbands. Managers represented a means by which mistresses could distance themselves from shaming physical labor, involvement in commerce, and excessive contact with bondmen. Since they usually dealt directly with plantation masters, many overseers regarded women left to run plantations for short periods as an unwelcome interference. The resulting tensions between the two parties, as well as those that developed between overseers and more permanent female employers, were often predicated on traditional notions of female subservience to men.

The economic output of the American colonies increased fourfold in the decades before the American Revolution. Between 1700 and 1710, the colonies exported approximately £265,000 sterling to Great Britain each year. By the 1760s that figure had risen to more than £1,000,000 worth of goods exported annually. As America evolved from subsistence to commercial agriculture, the influential commercial class increased its power in nearly every colony. Though there was no class in Virginia of comparative strength to the merchant families of the lowcountry, those people with the most economic and political power in that colony were commercial farmers who best combined the occupations of trader and agriculturist.

A new mentality formed among Chesapeake tobacco planters in the years prior to the Revolution: they were almost pathologically concerned that their fellow planters would judge their crop negatively. These men and women seemed to have cultivated tobacco as much to gain the respect of merchants and neighbors "as to please the anonymous chewers, smokers and snuffers who ultimately purchased the staple in Europe."[20] Early in the century, following a number of consignments of poor-quality tobacco, Robert Bristow wondered "how it can be clear'd from being a wilfull injuring of me. . . . The Injury . . . extends itself further, it gives a lasting disreputation to [Bristow's tobacco] mark."[21] Crop quality was a particular concern for absentee planters: Joseph Ball wrote from England how criticism of his tobacco "very much Chagrins me . . . for when I lived in Virginia, my Tobacco was so far from being accounted the worst, that it was always very well liked, and sought after."[22] The sentiment was reflected in the relationship between planters and their overseers: Landon Carter criticized a manager for causing his neighbor to scorn Carter's crop.[23] Reputational damage could also lead to a loss of earnings. Edward Ambler complained of "the great Faults the Merchants find with my Tobacco, they say it is not only smoaked to a great degree, but [that] the Overseers Prize [press the tobacco ready for shipment] . . . in a slovenly & unsightly manner."[24]

The link between reputation and crop quality extended south, too. Pierce Butler apologized to London merchant Thomas Fraser, explaining that he could not express "how much I feel hurt that . . . the little rice that was made on my Estate fell short of my managers expectations . . . this disappointment . . . subjects me to a temporary embarrassment . . . I feel doubly hurt that at the Commencement of Our Correspondence there should be an appearance of defficiency on my part." Later that year Butler promised other correspondents that "I think my Rice this season, tho' very small in quantity, as equal in quality to any made in Carolina."[25] Slaveholders also felt competition from producers outside North America. South Carolinian planter and politician John Lloyd thanked Bristol merchant John Champion "for the samples of East India rice" and added smugly, "it afforded me a satisfaction to see that the quality is very inferior to that which is produced in this country."[26]

In both regions the onus was on overseers to deliver the level of excellence that their employers stridently demanded, particularly in the face of British merchants' critiques of South Carolinian indigo.[27] This mentality formed part of a growing tendency across British America to make reputation a central tenet of self-fashioning for elites. The way plantation owners appeared to others was integral to their reputation as free, honorable white men. Partly this obsession with the fragility of reputation derived from an uneasiness among colonial elites that, lacking the bloodlines of European aristocracy, their claims to superiority were built on sand.[28] Partly it was a vestigial remnant of the ancient republican notion that men's fate was inherently unstable—that the course of a life could slip in a heartbeat toward virtual slavery and social death. On hearing that his sister's son was considering a life at sea, Virginian planter Joseph Ball warned: "I think he had better be put aprentice to a Tinker; for a common sailor . . . has by no means the common Liberty of the subject; for they will press him from a ship . . . and cut him & slash him and use him like a Negro, or rather, like a Dog." Ball advised instead that his nephew should become a planter, though he should avoid getting "in the Merchant's Debt," from which he would "never get out again."[29]

Because a slaveholder's reputation was linked directly to the quality and commercial value of the crop, reputation and credit intertwined. Robert Carter III warned his son, "your conduct relative to your creditors is very blameable, and if you continue to neglect their legal claims any longer . . . you will be classed among the careless debtors."[30] (Carter's son died in 1793, a few days after he had got into a fight over gambling debts.)[31] Though the restricting force of debt was felt more keenly in Virginia, where poorer yields and smaller economies of scale meant that planters were hit harder by the vacillations of cash crop prices than in the lowcountry, both regions shared the fear that employers' interests could be undermined fatally. This reflected the unadorned seventeenth-century notion—so formative in the Revolutionary years—that the triumph of competing interests, by restricting the accretion of wealth and the promotion of liberty, was akin to the triumph of despotism.[32] The New World had promised great returns for modest investment, and new freedoms for humble men. Yet the reality for many planters, and for Virginians in particular, was a cycle of low profit margins and shortages. Owners intervened to ensure the frugality and industry of their overseers because bankruptcy and loss of their own status were a real and persistent threat.[33]

Added to these imperatives was a current of thought that hearkened back to traditional European and biblical pastoral ideals. Land represented for southern planters much more than a simple means from which to make money. Many developed a real, visceral love for their holdings, investing in them emotional as well as economic capital. A significant number of George Washington's letters contain an Old Testament passage, chosen to express this attachment. Returned home from his Revolutionary travails, in 1784 Washington wrote to the Marquis de Lafayette that "at length my Dear Marquis I am become a private citizen on the banks of the Potomac, & under the shadow of my own Vine & my own Fig-tree."[34] For Washington the return to his beloved lands, like Roman generals before him, indicated that he was beginning a new peacetime life as an independent republican citizen, and turning away from his former martial career. Further south Continental Army major general William Moultrie confessed once the Revolutionary War was over that he "chearfully [laid] down his sword & uniform . . . and with heartfelt joy retire to the callings of a country life, free from the tumultuous busy times of war: Cincinatus himself never returned to his plow better pleased."[35] Cincinnatus was the early Roman farmer who was called to lead Rome when the city was under threat of invasion, to retire to his lands once he had fulfilled his duty. Later in the century, and echoing William Byrd's description of his bucolic paradise, the South Carolinian John Lloyd reported that his time in retirement on his plantation was "beguiled by rural concerns and the improvement of [his] farm."[36]

There was a further cultural influence encouraging slaveholders to intervene in plantation affairs wherever they could. Management itself was a key indicator of a patriarch's worth, because a well-regulated plantation was as important as a well-regulated household.[37] Leading planters in the Revolutionary period spoke of themselves as managers and crop masters, and many slaveholders viewed their involvement in the allocation of plantation tasks as essential to the construction of patriarchism.[38] One promised a merchant in London that his tobacco was "exceeding good" because "it was made on the plantation w[here] I live & therefore as I saw to the whole mana[age]ment of it my self can with authority recomend it."[39] An ideal overseer for these planters was the one whom Jefferson would describe later on in the century to a correspondent: he "seems as if he would be docile, so that I hope to get my own outlines followed by him."[40] The type of plantation life that William Byrd depicted, "attended with a great deal of trouble," required involvement in plantation affairs at the overseer's expense. Intervention was part of patriarchal self-fashioning because it combined a visible exhibition of the importance of successful cultivation with a demonstrable act of concern for the behavior and putative rebelliousness of dependents.

By the nineteenth century, the distinction between the lowlier overseers on home plantations and those on absentee plantations had grown stark—for William Scarborough, the former group were "little more than . . . glorified driver[s], charged with routine duties under the watchful eye of employer[s]."[41] The first stirrings of this distinction were felt during the 1700s, as planters tested and developed systems to replicate personal control over absentee quarters. In 1729 Robert "King" Carter complained that it was "very difficult for me at this distance to get my plantations tolerably managed."[42] Despite the presence of very large quarters, numerous eighteenth-century landholdings in both regions were relatively small, meaning that heavy proprietorial intervention was common for many overseers: William Byrd was representative of his contemporaries in extolling personal supervision over his estates.[43] A typical entry ran, "I went to the Falls where I did not find things in so good order as I expected . . . I gave the necessary orders, and . . . went in the rain to Appomattox, where I found all things well."[44] The Virginian Landon Carter, born around the time that Byrd wrote his first *Secret Diary,* wrote frequent entries along the lines of: "made a Visit to my Plantations this day . . . that is, looked into every hole and corner of them."[45] Other slave owners made daily inspections. One Huguenot minister and planter liked to "walk much about the family business . . . and ride constantly all over my plantation, giving my servants their several employments."[46]

Some anxious planters determined to make visits in person to their outlying quarters as well. George Washington complained after the Revolutionary War that the time that he had spent away was the cause of the great neglect that he perceived when he came back.[47] The long absences that Thomas Jefferson would spend in Philadelphia (then the federal capital) and France made him more determined to return. He told an overseer of an absentee plantation, "as . . . for arranging the crops of the ensuing year . . . you should make as much as possible of the three weeks stay I make at home"—and of the benefit of Jefferson's advice.[48] Other slaveholders insisted that their manager visit them frequently. Joseph Valentine was "obliged to go as often as his Business will permit him, to . . . [Daniel Parke] Custis's House in Williamsburg."[49]

Washington claimed that if overseers were not supervised, their quarters, "unless it is a very rare instance to the contrary, rather loose annually than gain."[50] But distance usually meant that when George Washington, like Carter, "rid to [his] plantations," he traveled only to those situated close to his home plantation, Mount Vernon. Although, in the words of a contemporary, "his exegecies employ him five days in the week" (and, in fact, Washington died after making such "exegecies," on his return from a visit to his plantations), Washington could not ride to far-flung quarters like Bullskin on the Shenandoah River in the space of a morning.[51] Absenteeism posed challenges to the traditional management model. A routine became more common across the two regions during the eighteenth century, where visits to home plantations supplemented correspondence with stewards and overseers at more distant quarters, often delivered by go-betweens such as agents, or by mail in the areas where a postal service had been established.[52]

Absentee planters were as anxious about their outlying quarters as William Byrd was about his home plantations, and their correspondence networks attempted to reconstruct personal contact with managers. Even in the early 1700s, large landholders had used intermediaries to relay messages to the fields. In charge of a huge Virginian estate—295,000 acres by the time of his death in 1732—Robert "King" Carter kept control of his overseers by having bondpeople carry messages. In July 1724 Carter "sent Billy to the home Quartrs with Order to the Overseers to Trench their Tob[acc]o Ground & Draw of[f] all the Water they possibly Could."[53] Robert Carter's son, Landon Carter, kept a home plantation in Richmond County but owned land as far away as York County; this Carter also sent frequent instructions to his overseers, while George Washington corresponded with supervisors once a week.[54] Their fellow Virginian William Lee acknowledged the hurdles that absenteeism presented: he prefaced a letter to an overseer with "it is not in my power at this distance to be very particular." But he proceeded with very particular instructions regarding foodstuffs for livestock, mulberry trees, fencing, ironworkers and bricklayers, and the care of enslaved people.[55]

James Habersham, a large slaveholder in Georgia, visited his rice fields only once a season. Although he delegated to overseers the responsibility for the daily management of bondpeople, Habersham nevertheless took a keen interest "in every facet of his agricultural operations."[56] The South Carolinian agent Josiah Smith corresponded frequently with his employer, George Austin, in Shropshire, England. Smith kept Austin informed because he suspected the planter to be "anxious respecting the fate of [his] planting Interest."[57] There was a belief that absentee plantations were less profitable than those with a resident owner. Smith wrote to Austin that it could not be "expected that Plantations own'd by Persons who are non residents, should produce so much profit as those constantly under the Inspection of Proprietors who reside on the Spot, & at the same time are able Planters, who are ever employ'd in contriving every thing that can make for their Advantage."[58]

The demands of war did not prevent George Washington from indulging his own interest in agriculture. Throughout the Revolution, Lund Washington, the general's steward-cum-agent, wrote to him every month, "detailing minutely all the events that occurred on the plantations."[59] Even after the war, as president Washington was never disconnected from his plantation operations. In 1789 he sent a lengthy and detailed letter to his overseers, entitled "A View of the Work at the Several Plantations . . . and General Directions for the Execution of It," designed to provide "a full and comprehensive view of my designs, after the [agricultural] rotation is once perfectly established."[60] The year 1793 would bring diplomatic relations with the French almost to breaking point, yet Washington still found time to pore over his steward's weekly reports from Mount Vernon and send off directives.[61]

In similar fashion Robert Carter of Nomini Hall left specific "observations on ye Quality & management of part of my crop of Tobacco, to ye end [tha]t my overseers may follow [the]m for ye future."[62] Because letters were a vital conduit of plantation intelligence, planters depended on responses. Based in London Joseph Ball was especially fearful of the informational deficiencies of his position. He urged Joseph Chinn, "I beg of you . . . to read over all . . . of my Letters of Instructions from the beginning Ever since I left Virginia and see whether you have comply'd with them all."[63] Robert Carter implored his overseer in 1767 to "execute [my] instructions, & to write to me a state of my affairs frequently for an inattention to either will certainly distress me."[64] The year before, Henry Laurens had berated Abraham Schad for failing to correspond: "last Night came down Seven Negroes from Wambaw but no Letter from you. Therefore I am at a loss to know why the eight [bondpeople] that were intended did not come."[65] South Carolina planter William Ancrum complained to one of his overseers that he had failed "to let me hear frequently from You during the whole Season . . . such Indolence & Neglect in You are inexcusable."[66]

Underpinning plantation relationships in both regions was a division of labor in which many planters undertook the commercial side of management, ensuring productivity through the supervision of their managers and the marketing of the end product, while overseers led the "extractive" side of the plantation industry.[67] Because of this approach, as well as the importance of a productive overseer-employer relationship to the civic construction of the patriarchal image, owners were more likely to note when something was going wrong than commend their overseers.[68] Praise could come, however, from the most unlikely sources. Though his denunciations of overseers were legion, George Washington held some individuals in esteem. Just after the Revolution, he would describe one of his managers as "very trusty," and he raised the wages of another, John Fairfax, from £30 to £40 on account of his good service.[69]

Slaveholders also divined an advantage in publicizing successful overseers when selling their crops. In such instances overseers became further exemplars of their employers' good choices in plantation management: praise for managers burnished patriarchs' own credentials. Virginian Henry Fitzhugh wrote that he had been "informed by the Inspectors that [the tobacco] was very good . . . on very good fresh land by an overseer who has the Character of being a neat planter."[70] Later he explained that his tobacco was "made in fresh rich Land by Overseers that I get from the frontiers of James River, where the best tob[acc]o is made."[71] A South Carolinian planter, John Palmer, used positive language when he recommended to Fitzhugh an overseer who was "a Pritty nice Planter of Indigo as I have seen some of his Management in that Line."[72]

Henry Laurens, who had "experienced too many disappointments by Overseers," also acknowledged the competence of some.[73] In 1766 he suggested that his protégés, James Theodore Rossel and John Lewis Gervais, might be transformed into able planters "under the tuition & assistance of a capable overseer for one or two years."[74] Laurens could also be solicitous: when John Smith fell ill, Laurens suggested that he "would gladly pay the expence of an assistant for you . . . until you were quite recover'd."[75] Though worries about a drop in production might have motivated him, Laurens's support indicated his desire to keep hold of a competent overseer. In a similar vein, when James Brenard signaled his wish to leave Wambaw, Laurens told him, "if you stay you shall not want proper encouragement. If you go, you shall not want my good wishes that your change may be for the better."[76] Laurens claimed that he was able to discern "tolerable good rice planters" from "common mercenary overseers," and his contract negotiations saw him grant a significant degree of choice to capable managers who were aware of their own value.[77] He noted in 1768 that William Cantey had "promis'd to become . . . Overseer," but only "if he likes the Land" at Laurens's Georgian plantation.[78] Evidently he did, since Cantey brought "25 or 30 Negroes to begin a . . . Plantation" at Wrights Savannah.[79]

Laurens was especially keen to praise managers with a similar background or status to his own. Peter Horlbeck was "a . . . sensible Man, [with] a general knowledge of farming . . . quick of apprehension."[80] To John Theodore Rossel and John Lewis Gervais, Laurens intended to give "handsome encouragement," to act "without profit . . . to do a service to Men of merit."[81] Even before Rossel became overseer on Broughton Island, and despite his managerial inexperience, Laurens had given him the important task of taking "a very careful & exact Account of every Negro . . . upon Mepkin," stressing that "I cannot make a just payment of my Tax without it."[82] At the other end of the societal scale, it is possible that the greater equality of status found on the small plantations dotting the Chesapeake and lowcountry would have provided more frequent opportunities for close social interaction between planter and overseer. Some employers took meals with their workers, for example.[83]

Yet even for the trusted few, the planter's word was law. The obligation for all managers was to give opinions on planting matters but, if not accepted by the proprietor, to do as they were told.[84] As a result a dynamic underpinned by criticism and conflict was more typical than a harmonious relationship between overseer and planter. To criticism slaveholders added written missives and, on occasion, personal visits, in order to impose their authority from afar. Criticism might be appraised from two perspectives—first, as a response to individual managerial shortcomings; and second, as a contribution to expanding normative critiques of overseers. The most common managerial criticisms centered on the harvest and preparation of tobacco, rice, indigo, or other staples. In 1726 Robert "King" Carter, on finding his overseer's tobacco "basely handled . . . corrected him for it."[85] Joseph Ball, hearing of his managers' failures in providing adequate fencing for his plantations and their tendency to leave the plantation, described them as "slubbering sons of bitches."[86] Thirty years later John Harrower related how his employer had lambasted an overseer for wastefulness: "this day the Col[onel] finding more wheat left among the straw then should be[,] blamed Mr. Lewis the overseer for his carelessness."[87] Henry Laurens, too, was quick to rebuke those overseers who jeopardized plantation efficiency: Mark Noble's failings caused him "the loss of my Canoe, Horses, cattle, tools, etc. etc."[88] A steward on the plantation of his South Carolinian counterpart John Ewing Colhoun berated an overseer: "I doubt you are not frugal in the distribution of Provisions, if you are, you certainly made a Very trifling Crop."[89]

If stewards on absentee estates sometimes delivered criticism, these men were not entirely safe from reproach. George Washington reprimanded Howell Lewis late in the century for having "neglected in the general Report, as the Overseers had before done in their individual ones, to give an account of the stock." The steward's failings required his employer to spell out the tasks for Howell to supervise. Washington "desire[d] all the Overseers to be very regular in penning their stock and not to keep their Pens long in a place. The doing of the latter destroy the use of manure."[90] Joseph Ball similarly accused his nephew, Joseph Chinn, of "one very great omission in not giving me an account every year of what is in your hands . . . you must send me an account of all for the time past, and afterwards a yearly one." On another occasion Ball accused Chinn of being "too Slack in Writing . . . I love to hear how my affairs Stand."[91] With Chinn's employer far removed in London, crucial information must not go missing. Similar anxieties led Robert Bristow to write to overseer Thomas Booth at the beginning of the century, also from the metropolis, that he "desired [Booth] to send [him] a distinct & particular acco[un] t in my last to you of every thing for my Plantation's use which you have not entirely complied w[i]th."[92]

At the base of managerial criticism lay the sentiment that planters were more knowledgeable about the needs of their lands and bondpeople than their overseers. Just after the Revolutionary War, Virginian planter William Lee wrote that he could not "conceive there is any land in Virg[ini]a so bad," that "with tolerable managem[en]t" would fail to make a profit; therefore the blame for any agricultural disappointments must lie with "the Overseers."[93] Though Henry Laurens had only recently become a planter, in 1763 he saw himself as better informed than his overseer when it came to the weighty question of allocating large quantities of foodstuffs. He warned James Lawrence at Mepkin that the enslaved people "will soon consume your little Stock of Corn & pease[,] therefore enquire immediately where I may be supplyed with a sufficient quantity to carry them thro the Year"—Laurens's knowledge clearly did not yet include local intelligence.[94] His South Carolinian counterpart William Ancrum directed Marlow Pryor to "prepare for next Years planting in the Manner you think best until I see you."[95] Sensitive issues such as the treatment of enslaved men and women, where subtle management was often required, called for this putatively greater wisdom. Laurens gave very specific directions for the care of bondpeople when ill and sent medicines. Timothy Creamer, another overseer at Mepkin, received "1 Bottle infused Rhubarb to give in Case of Looseness or Cholics . . . , 2 bottles of . . . Rum, to rub in cases of pains & bruses & sometimes for the Cholic and belly ach."[96] Even minor ailments could incite protests by bondpeople or, at the very least, cause the plantation to lose money if the enslaved people needed to take time off to recuperate.

Though it is uncertain how far broader prejudices against overseers influenced planters' admonishments of individuals, it is possible to understand why these prejudices developed. While advances in agricultural technologies such as new crop rotations, or the introduction of nonnative crops like indigo, transformed the range of tasks that southern overseers were obliged to perform, planters imagined themselves as "men of improvement." They aimed to match the Enlightenment effort to improve manners and morals with a studied program to tame, regulate—and perfect—the American landscape.[97] White plantation culture accordingly "celebrated agricultural expertise." Mastering the techniques that adapted the land for agriculture "stood at the core of planters' self-conceptions as colonists."[98]

Robert Carter III summed up the linkages between improvement and independence when he stressed to the tutor of his sons that "men ought to be practical, for unless we become acquainted with some particular branch of Science[,] husbandry or Mechanics, we are nothing more than dependent men." This course would ensure "the Morals and advancem[en]t of youth."[99] Henry Laurens urged his son, John, to "improve every moment of your time."[100] In Georgia George Walton linked improvement, reason, and landholding when he reported to Seaborn Jones Jr. that he was "glad that you have recovered from the mad contagion caught in Virginia, about that accursed delusion Kentucky. Had you have gone there, I should have concluded, that you had lost your reason . . . to give up such well-grounded [rep]utations in Georgia . . . would have been folly in the extreme." Now that Jones had abandoned plans for land speculation in Kentucky, Walton recommended that he "continue to improve [his] mind by reading, or rather studying some modern author."[101]

Following the cultural metaphor that linked plantations with personality, a slaveholder who exerted sufficient control over dependents and resources to be able continually to make progress had mastered his own internal passions through the continued application of reason. Yet countervailing eighteenth-century ideological currents also flowed across the southern plantation. Even as they took inspiration from a "rationalist spirit of improvement to reshape their region," slaveholders revived bucolic ideals, feeling "early pangs of romantic melancholy over the loss of an untouched, natural order."[102] When planters feared the "ravages of overseers" on their lands, their rhetorical attacks expressed a degree of sadness for this lost pastoral idyll: managers were charged with executing improvements that planters both welcomed and feared.

Not every eighteenth-century planter tried to innovate: Landon Carter, for instance, believed that his managers would become "lazy" through the use of ploughs.[103] Yet those who wrote with disdain about overseers and their incompetence in managing agricultural innovations carried influence as pioneers. Overseers found themselves between two stools, as practitioners of "husbandry" whose contracts required them to implement the findings of "Science." Aside from creating more work, the new technologies increased managerial responsibilities in a number of ways. First, innovation created the expectation among planters that higher yields would result from a smaller relative expenditure of capital and labor, even though agricultural innovation did little to increase yields—and especially in the Chesapeake.[104] Second, since many planters were drivers of agricultural improvement, they considered themselves more proficient in the application of the new methods than their managers.

Overseers were in an unenviable position for another reason. Because many were employed for just a year, they were given insufficient time to perfect even the most basic agricultural innovations, let alone a seven-year crop rotation. The

stud his own livestock—though Thomas West, overseer for Henry Fitzhugh in 1769, made extra money by having his horse cover Fitzhugh's mare.[125]

The primary influence on the development of normative critiques of managerial behavior was again the growth of absenteeism. Now that certain overseers had more latitude to take advantage of their employers, the fear was that the entire managerial cohort was dishonest. Playing the caring patriarchal guardian of women, George Washington suggested to Betty Lewis that an account of all the goods on her plantation be made immediately, "because the Overseer (if he is not a very honest Man), may take advantage of circumstances."[126] On another occasion he accused his mother's overseer of "Knavery."[127] Washington also discussed with James Mercer what he should do with a surplus of corn. Washington concluded that it should be sold, "but who is to be entrusted with this, unless you can confide in your New Overseer, I know not."[128] Landon Carter connoted managerial dishonesty with payment in wages—presumably because he felt that salaried overseers had less personal interest in the success of the plantation than crop sharers: "overseers, especially those on wages, will lie with expectations of great things. Lawson . . . was certain of a better crop of corn than last year, when I am afraid he will not make one half of it."[129] Planters openly voiced their prejudices against overseers—it was up to overseers to prove them wrong. Writing about a manager, one argued that a "man in his situation can never expect either credit, or confidence unless his conduct be such as to deserve it."[130] Distance contributed to the notion that overseers were unreliable, and that they used the planter's time for their own devices.

Landon Carter's fulmination against the managerial class highlights the importance that slaveholders placed in a proprietorial attachment to land and bondpeople: "I cannot but remark the difference between, the Owner and the Overseer of the Crop. Upon Saturday's rain I sent to W. Lawson my Overseer, to be ready before day this morning that we might make a finish; his answer was he would be at it long before day as it was moonshine. I got up before two o'clock, had all the people sent for, but no overseer at home."[131] His fellow Virginian the steward Charles Dabney sought in the contracting process to ensure against overseer unreliability. Dabney insisted that Charles Nicholls and Ancel Clarkson "be Strictly Obedient to the said Dabney's Orders or Directions in every Respect Regarding the management of the Business without either grumbling or feigning Excuses and in all things shall endeavour to promote the Interest of [their] employer in all Respects as is the Duty of an Overseer."[132]

Lowcountry plantation owners expressed comparable sentiments. Henry Laurens leveled the charge of "knavery" against Abraham Schad in 1765 because he "made out only 22 Chords of Wood which he [sold] without any orders."[133] Describing overseers as knaves, rogues, or devils at once associated them with bondpeople (whom patriarchs addressed using the same language); revealed slaveholders' expectations of the inevitability of managerial bad behavior; and provided further justification for patriarchal intervention in plantation matters.[134] Eliza Lucas Pinckney's criticism of "ignorant or dishonest Over Seers," whom she blamed for mismanaging her late husband's affairs, came despite the fact that she understood the difficulties of running a plantation: Pinckney reported that her own "nephew had no management of the planting interest."[135] The negative managerial image had a practical use for some planters, however. Writing to the surveyor William Mayne, Henry Laurens revealed how one Mr. Wright had accounted for discrepancies in an advertisement that he had placed in order to sell land by claiming that "the quantity of . . . Land specified was a mistake owing to a deception of his Overseer." Laurens's dry rebuttal, that he was "not answerable for [Mayne's] Overseer's errors," might imply that he had heard such excuses before.[136]

Yet planter fears were not groundless. Managers carved out a degree of individual autonomy by electing to ignore, adapt, or follow their employer's instructions, their tactics exacerbating the salience of negative stereotypes.[137] And there is little doubt that many overseers engaged in theft. Philip Ludwell put a notice in the *Virginia Gazette* in 1755 announcing, "THERE has been concealed by the Overseer at one of my Plantations, for some Time . . . a Steer which the Owner on ascertaining his property may have of me."[138] Reality sustained rhetoric because stealing represented an immediate means for overseers to improve their income. The opportunities for bending the truth that correspondence networks brought enabled shrewd overseers to disguise their infractions. Even before Timothy Creamer had left Henry Laurens's employ, Laurens accused him of sending false information about the number of hogs that were fit for market, and for making "use of some without asking"; when confronted Creamer "made no better excuse than . . . that you had miscounted, an answer only fit to give to a Child." Since children were dependents, capable only of desultory thought and action, Laurens clearly was affronted by the overseer's defiance and made a veiled threat: "these things ought not to be so, they are very . . . ungenerous & will never be attended with any good consequences to you."[139] For patriarchs like Laurens, "Lying, Servility and Treachery" were among "the most sordid hateful Qualities incident to Mankind."[140] After inefficiency, then, planters most often complained about dishonesty, particularly when, as in Creamer's case, dishonesty threatened profits.[141] William Byrd discounted in 1740 an overseer's protestations of illness, a further area that offered scope for dishonesty. "Most hypercondraick Sir," Byrd wrote, with no little sarcasm, "I had your complaints last night which you drew up into the Form of a letter to save your Blushes."[142]

Dissimulation and theft might be understood to represent forms of small-scale resistance against planter hegemony performed by overseers in lieu of overt rebellion in concert with other members of their class.[143] Planters certainly encouraged divisions between managers: when Laurens began to suspect Abraham Schad of pilfering, he told manager John Smith that "you will be very watchful over all his steps."[144] The above examples demonstrate that overseers had the capacity to do significant damage both to their employers' profits, and to the efficient running of correspondence networks. And as far as the accounts of men like Henry Laurens can be trusted, overseers also attempted to cover up destructive activities. But to what extent should drunkenness, theft, or dissimulation be viewed as political acts? The covert nature of these challenges points to a "hidden transcript" of symbolic and material actions that, in resetting the hierarchical balance in however small a manner, developed greater cultural meaning when directed against planter rule. Slaveholders' anxiety for the security of their property underlines how they bought into the same code. Yet these acts did not presage, in political theorist James Scott's words, a "political breakthrough"—they would make no attempt during the Revolutionary War to transform small-scale deeds into something larger, as enslaved people did.[145]

On the whole the drunken overseer, or indeed the overseer who petitioned for more tools, did not set out deliberately to undermine his employer's position. He wished simply to make his own position more comfortable. To enslaved people and indentured servants, managers were as much a part of the ruling hierarchy as were slaveholders. In developing their own measures to rule over enslaved men and women, overseers themselves sustained the social structures that were created to support and perpetuate the economic relations of patriarchism.[146] Payment in wages or with a share of the crop were both designed to tie managers' aims to those of their masters and mistresses, and the latter especially so. Overseers came from many national, religious, and ethnic backgrounds, as well as from different levels of society. Plus overseers on home plantations would have felt dependence differently to those on absentee quarters.[147] This level of diversity militated against class-consciousness in itself, but what finally put paid to managerial solidarity was that, however damaging the stigmatization of overseers, no white person in Virginia or the lowcountry was held in as much contempt as enslaved people. Though the distinction with blacks did provide some cohesion to white society, the reminder of the arbitrary and hard-won nature of liberty supplied by the presence of the enslaved meant that even slaveholders competed with and were suspicious of one other.[148]

Overseers, then, were restricted by a lack of opportunity first, and by cloying ideology second. The elite's arguments justified social hierarchies: they did not create them.[149] Critical slaveholder rhetoric was not borne lightly by overseers. The invective had the capacity to wound managers' pride in their status as free white males. But dependence was a relative, contested term for early Americans. The uneasiness of the planter class for the permanence of their status and reputation should be a reminder that deference was also a fluid concept. More often than not, it was a conceit that slaveholders enacted for their counterparts as much as for their subordinates.[150] When planters began to talk about an overseer "class," they were not describing a definitive socioeconomic grouping, or a corporate identity created by managers themselves, but an idealized, stigmatized set of dependents on whom they could pin the anxieties and cultural preconceptions of their age.[151] This "othering" of overseers represented one of many attempts to stabilize plantation societies by focusing tensions onto "internal outsiders"—be they dependents, Indians, or bondpeople.[152] One result of this process was that the southern colonies were notably stable.[153] Southerners' treatment of overseers therefore qualifies the conclusion reached by Edmund S. Morgan in his groundbreaking *American Slavery, American Freedom* that elites (in Morgan's study, Virginian elites) structured their society along racial lines.[154] With overseeing so closely associated with slavery—and with managers excluded from some of the most important cultural constructions of white society such as militia service—it would appear that there were some exceptions to racial solidarity.[155]

To focus too narrowly on covert acts of everyday resistance is to miss a more complex range of social dynamics at work on eighteenth-century slaveholdings, and to dilute the role of individual judgment among social actors in eighteenth-century Virginia—bondpeople, overseers, and owners alike. Managers continually disputed their dependent reputations, stressing their rights and cultural inheritance. Necessarily this involved as much of an overt enactment of their freedom as did their employers' symbolic assertions of superiority. Also necessarily it required overseers to enact their freedoms in ways that would be familiar to their bosses and to southern society. One way was to enter into vocal disputes with their employers over the criticism that they leveled at them; another was for overseers to break their contracts and leave the plantation, thereby taking advantage of rights denied other dependents. In 1771 manager Owen Griffith left the employ of Landon Carter, calling him a "boisterous tyrant" and insisting that he would now "lead the life of a gentleman."[156] The most significant reason that overseers gave when asserting their rights was to insist on their abilities as competent agriculturists and managers of the enslaved. This enabled overseers to defy the emergent cultural prescriptions that went beyond stigmatizing these men for their dependent status and instead condemned them because of their membership of the managerial profession.

With the degree of interference and criticism to which overseers' regimes were subjected, tensions often developed with their employers. The two parties argued about a host of issues, ranging from disagreements over payment to unsatisfactory upkeep of plantations. Since few letters survive from overseers themselves, and there is virtually no personal reminiscence, it is difficult to ascertain managerial opinions about their employers. Yet it seems clear that tensions were higher on resident plantations because of greater planter involvement, and because managers resented the dilution of their authority that this entailed.[157] Though the actions of overseers on absentee plantations were more likely to be misunderstood by planters because they had fewer chances to explain their motives, the closeness between the two parties on home quarters would have made disagreements more frequent, and more trying.[158] Overseers' tenures were certainly often much longer on absentee estates.[159]

Whether they were on home or absentee plantations, overseers rarely accepted criticism of their agricultural competence. The earliest years of Virginia's plantation economy saw the first stirrings of their defiance. At the end of the seventeenth century, John Clayton, a parson from Middlesex County, argued with his overseer, Lewis, in favor of a new agricultural technique. Affronted, the overseer replied that Clayton "understood better how to make a Sermon than managing Tobacco," and walked away.[160] Much later a similar reaction greeted the Virginian colonel Dangerfield when he rebuked his overseer for leaving "more wheat . . . among the straw." This reproof made "Mr. Lewis verry much enraged for being spoke to and [he] verry sawcily threw up all the keys he had in charge and went off."[161] The records disclose a sense that managers were both more aware of their centrality to plantation functions following the extension of absenteeism, and more confident in using oppositional strategies. In 1766 Henry Laurens explained how "overseers will not be directed by any body but good planters & . . . bad ones will make a handle of directions from ignorant Masters in order to impose on them."[162]

Slaveholder acceptance of the worth of some overseers implied further stigmatization of the unloved majority. In response overseers stressed a professional bond—recall how Matthew Marable's correspondent in the *Virginia Gazette* resented the "new mode of libelling a whole society of men," and deplored Marable's calumny of the "wealthy fraternity" of managers. Such evidence suggests that, rather than causing fissures between them, planter tactics in fact cemented the growing notion among overseers that they were proud members of a worthy profession, providing a foundation for the full-on professionalization of the upper tiers of management during the following century.[163] In Georgia overseer Jacob Fendin claimed that the merchant and future governor Edward Telfair should be "sensible of [Fendin's] Capacity In the Planting Business."[164] Thomas Mitchell, manager to the Virginian Francis Jerdone in 1789, invoked language familiar from overseer recruitment adverts when he worried that the effects of adverse weather on his crops would cause him to "loose [his] character as an overseer."[165] In the lowcountry William Ancrum urged overseer Marlow Pryor to tell him whether Pryor's "Indico making answers your Reputation."[166] Because of the link between reputed agricultural ability and an independent social status, the focus of such overseers was on distinguishing themselves from other dependents: on gaining the respect of, rather than undermining, the plantocracy.[167] In the new territory of Kentucky, overseer John Lee wrote to George Lewis that "nearly the whole [crop of wheat] has been . . . injured . . . , this I could not prevent as I live a considerable distance of[f] and obliged to trust others to manage it."[168] Simon Sallard looked to distinguish himself from the suboverseers under his control: "I have found Such Loses in our Crops of Corn That I Shall never Truss an Overseer more."[169] The combined managerial rejection of normative critiques (of which the *Virginia Gazette* letter by the "Overseer" formed part) should be taken primarily as a desire to champion an alternative cultural understanding of the overseer profession that stressed the identities and capacities of individuals and resisted planter attempts to homogenize them. It is possible, however, that slaveholder prejudices in fact strengthened against this new and vocal level of confidence among managers.

Whether tensions were rooted in general prejudices or specific misdemeanors, for many overseers their outcome was the same. Sacking represented a decisive solution to the problems that planters encountered in imposing authority. Steward Charles Dabney warned his overseers that should they "fail to comply" with the articles of their contracts, "it shall and may be Lawfull for . . . Dabney to Turn [them] off the plantation at any Time of the Year."[170] Landon Carter fired his overseer, Davis, because the manager's behavior had led directly to a reduction in that important commodity, the quality of Carter's output. He decided "that the bad Crops I have made lately seem . . . to be . . . owing . . . to his idleness occasioned by night drinking."[171] When Mark Noble used another vital commodity, the labor of his employer's enslaved people, to tend his own lands, Henry Laurens "had no hesitation in dismissing him."[172] Converging strands of thought meant that during the second half of the eighteenth century tensions came to hang on those issues that also defined the overseer-employer relationship in the early national and antebellum periods: a volatile combination of class tension, the honor ethic, and racial ideology that made overseers unwilling to be treated like servants.[173] It is apparent that firings in the 1700s saw slaveholders' assessments of their profit margins combine with worries for their own reputation, prejudices against overseers and dependents in general, and dissatisfaction with the performance of individuals.

Even so the ability for overseers to resign at any point led employers to treat overseers with a degree of subtlety. An instance from Henry Laurens's plantations encapsulates the reaction of some managers to perceived slights regarding interference in their management of dependents. John McCullough took exception to Laurens's "friendly Admonition" about his "keeping a Wench in open Adultery" and decided "to Withdraw as soon as [Laurens could] supply his place with another Overseer," though he later rescinded his resignation.[174] This dramatic act of pride sheds light on the perceived realms where overseers might have deemed planter critiques to be acceptable, and where managers rejected them. Although Laurens had gone as far as to sack James Lawrence for a similar infraction, McCullough took issue. Perhaps McCullough's chutzpah at this morally righteous intrusion into his personal life (and indeed his right as a white male to take enslaved females as his own) resulted from his more exalted position in the plantation hierarchy. Laurens had hired him originally to oversee two plantations and attempted to entice him to manage James Grant's East Florida lands through "extraordinary wages" and generous expenses. Or perhaps he had formed a genuine emotional attachment to this woman (though McCullough was already married).[175] Overseers might also leave their employment in response to poor working conditions and in reaction to the level of responsibility that they were expected to shoulder—Landon Carter noted that managers, especially those bedeviled by uncooperative bondpeople, "tire as cornfields do."[176]

Loyalty to an employer could bring rewards. Henry Laurens suggested that because Abraham Schad was "the oldest stander . . . therefore it is but common justice to give him his choice" of dwelling after James Brenard had left the Wambaw plantation.[177] Yet the tradition of short, flexible contracts was a blessing for certain competent overseers since they allowed managers the freedom to play the market and find the best wages available. Even though John Beale had had his salary increased by Landon Carter, he had delusions of independence; according to the slave owner, he was "too great to submit" to Carter's terms.[178] Despite their protestations to the contrary, slaveholders perceived clearly that managers were confident enough in their own agricultural abilities to bargain with their employers. Returning to familiar rhetoric, for Henry Laurens even an overseer who was "a good Planter may have no attachment to me beyond his own Interest."[179] A paradox here was that, while overseers were growing more aware of their new value, slaveholders returned to the traditional notion that managers were disloyal and inconstant.

The eighteenth-century growth in elite landholding and slaveholding led to higher incomes; the implementation of new technologies brought increased productivity; and the expansion of absenteeism and the overseer system meant that involvement in physical labor became anathema for plantation owners. Ideas, it soon proved, disseminated more easily than wealth. In Virginia and the lowcountry these prejudices percolated through societal rankings, as even the lower orders exhibited an aversion to labor.[180] The lengthening distance between the fields and the Big House played no small part in creating the idealized division between female domesticity and male commerce.[181] Philip Vickers Fithian, sometime overseer and tutor to the children of Robert Carter of Nomini Hall, commented that women's value derived from the extent to which they were "ornaments in their family."[182] In implying that the South Carolinian Alexander Gray's wife was involved in plantation work, Florida governor Patrick Tonyn gave great offence: Gray was moved in 1778 to reply that "I never suffered her, nor did she ever shew an inclination to have the least . . . concern relating to . . . the plantations."[183] Whether they were in permanent or temporary control of their quarters, social norms obliged plantation mistresses to demonstrate a wish to continue the domestic life to which they were accustomed.[184]

But the necessities of plantation management often took precedence.[185] On at least one occasion, Eliza Lucas Pinckney had too "many affairs to inspect" to accompany a friend into town.[186] For mistresses trying to shield themselves from dishonorable labor and commerce, overseers were vital conduits of their demands.

In the neighboring state of North Carolina, statesman and planter John Steele summed up to his wife the perceived requirement to delineate clear gender lines in commercial activities: "whilst I am doing my best to make a fortune . . . it is only reasonable . . . that you should . . . preserve . . . *a spotless and unblemished reputation.* You are surrounded by men, and women too, who are enemies to us both . . . you shall not be long among them, not an hour longer than my business and interest render indispensable; but while you do remain I beseech you to maintain that dignity of character which . . . I and all men adore in the female sex."[187]

Cultural imperatives that restricted women perhaps gave managers greater autonomy of action, and more respect, on plantations governed by plantation mistresses—Eliza Lucas Pinckney employed a married overseer because "it requires great care, attention and activity to attend . . . to a Carolina Estate."[188] Autonomy could not extend too far, however. As heads of plantations, mistresses had to undertake decisions concerning the sale of the end product and the hiring and firing of overseers, whether or not they risked the disapproval of their peers.[189] Such capacities gave women their own "version of mastery," which had real "teeth."[190] Overseers played a further role. As interlocutors between the fields and the plantation house, they enabled female employers to avoid contact with enslaved men. Because elite women never wrote about such matters, this function of the overseer-mistress relationship remains cloudy. Yet in the context of widespread worries about intercourse between black men and white women, and the eventual formulation of a myth regarding black men's putative predilection for the rape of white women, the overseer's presence would have afforded the plantation mistress further vital distance from her plantations.[191]

Since the departure of a male employer usually entrained the disruption of established practices, disagreements regarding the management of the plantation would have been the most common influence on overseer disputes with plantation mistresses. But other dynamics were at play, which distinguished aspects of overseer interaction from those that informed dealings with male heads of household. Despite the scarcity of evidence, the similarities between accounts that do survive are noteworthy. Not only was the overseer to George Washington's mother described as a "knave"; it was claimed that dishonest, disloyal, and truculent overseers were the scourge of other southern mistresses. The overseer of Washington's niece Frances B. Washington "refused to be hired" to work on another plantation.[192] One Virginian female slaveholder, Fanny Bland Tucker, complained to her husband at the end of the century that "the overseer has driven off all the most valuable Negroes."[193]

Women employed familiar class-biased rhetoric when criticizing managers, implying that any role that overseers played in separating mistresses from bondpeople merely put women in closer contact with another group of dependents. That same year Tucker's fellow Virginian Lucy Battaille Thornton protested that "the . . .

overseer . . . will not answer my wishes. He has been . . . insolent to me." With her husband recently deceased, this plantation mistress bemoaned her "unhappy fate, [with] no friend near to advise me . . . and a man to superintend my plantation that is scarcely ever sober. He has frightened me almost out of my senses by beating one of the negroes in the most cruel manner." The result was that her "apprehensions [were] so great" that her life had become "a burden" to her. Battaille Thornton felt that men of her overseer's class did not possess the gentility with which elite women were used to being treated. "I thought myself the most forlorn of all creatures," she wrote, "subject to the insults of the unfeeling herd of [mankind] who knows not how to pity the feelings of a helpless woman."[194]

John Steele believed that in his absence, with his wife running the plantation, the overseer would "almost be useless," and his wife's complaints about her managers confirmed his worries.[195] When they resisted women, managers combined an assertion of their authority as males with normative ideas of female subservience: they viewed the relationship through the prism not of societal status, but of gender. In so doing overseers claimed their own adherence to patriarchal ideology, which placed husbands over wives within the family and asserted that women were legally inferior to men, and in which, according to some readings, slave masters colluded to the detriment of their wives' plantation management.[196] While in purely economic terms a male planter might be expected to have superiority over an overseer, the two men had a shared interest in upholding the patriarchal and property relations on which mastery depended.[197] Emboldened to oppose their authority, it is possible that overseers lied to, stole from, and defrauded plantation mistresses more often than they did male employers. And while daily interactions with "brutish" or "roguish" overseers must have distressed elite women, even conscientious managers were in something of a bind about whose orders to follow. Simon Sallard, overseer on John Carter's Virginian plantations in 1737, sought confirmation from his male employer after receiving directions from Carter's wife: "their is four Negro men A Coming Down out of the R. C. Estate Which Mrs· Carter Sayes was yr· Orders I never heard any thing of it before Fryday Last or they should have bin [been] Sowner [sooner]."[198]

Women had their own motivation in highlighting managerial disloyalty: it was a useful device with which to elicit help from male protectors. When combined with legal independence and property, such appeals to "ladyhood" helped widows in particular to stand up to men within and beyond their own families. In conflicts with overseers, slaveholding widows repeatedly defended their interests and actions in terms of their "prerogatives as ladies" and their "duties as loyal wives and devoted mothers." Such a posture often encouraged white men to decide that assisting a widow served "their own financial interests, familial honor, or personal reputation for chivalry."[199] By voicing their despair at indecorous treatment, mistresses reinforced their own femininity against potential disapproval of their involvement in commerce and plantation management. What was more, those women who were married flattered their husbands' patriarchal egos by seeking their wise counsel in directing subordinates. The stereotype of the incompetent overseer, no doubt exacerbated by mistresses' personal experience of individuals, was as useful to women as it was to men.

Overseers were able to carve out for themselves a unique position in plantation society—supervisors but supervised, they were at once autonomous and dependent. In almost every sphere of interaction, their relations with employers show that, far from obsequiously following planters' visions for their slave quarters, managers were anything but deferent. As a consequence slaveholders were even more assured of the relevance of patriarchism as a governing strategy. The more that overseers acted independently, the more their employers were convinced of the dependence of these men. While maintaining the claim to social harmony that William Byrd so admired, the Virginian planter and his counterparts told themselves that this peace was hard-won and exasperating.

There was a further contradiction. Plantation overseers witnessed throughout the eighteenth century an increase in their responsibilities. Particularly after the introduction of new agricultural technologies, slaveholders came to expect greater returns from their lands. But now, often living at increasing distances from slave quarters, patriarchs continued to give overseers "maximum responsibility" with "minimum authority."[200] The stereotype of the unprofessional overseer grew out of this combination of planter concern for their holdings and an attendant lack of confidence in their overseers. One of the most fractious areas of disagreement involved fundamental conceptions about the correct balance of power and how best to delegate authority.[201] Bondpeople were legally dependent on the planter, yet also racially subordinate to the overseer: dominance of black men and women formed such a large part of white independence that overseers held on jealously to their supervisory role. In the struggle between overseer and patriarch for dominion over bondpeople, violent managerial responses contributed too frequently to the best-known aspect of the negative stereotype—the overseer as a brutal injurer of the enslaved.

— *Chapter Five* —

"At their uttermost perils"

Relations among Overseers, Bondpeople, and Servants

Outnumbered by enslaved men and women who were "dead to all," inspired by "desperate fury," and willing to sacrifice everything for their freedom, overseers confronted by organized violent resistance found difficulty in subduing it.[1] A renowned example of insurrection, which occurred in Hanover County, Virginia, at Christmas 1769, was reported in the *Virginia Gazette*.[2] "The Negroes belonging to the plantation having long been treated with too much lenity and indulgence, were grown extremely insolent and unruly; [the owner] therefore had employed a new Steward"; the steward's deputy, "a young man," had struck down a bondman in punishment for giving "most insolent and unruly answers" when asked why he did not rise early each morning to light a fire as instructed. The man responded by striking at the overseer with "an axe (or some such weapon) that was in his hand, but happily missed him."

Other bondmen arrived, and the brawl intensified, with the first man even coming to the assistance of the overseer, who had been "beat[en] . . . very severely." Making his escape the overseer ran off "to procure assistance to quell" the mutinous workforce. In the meantime the bondmen tied up the steward as well as the overseer of a neighboring plantation, whom they "whipped till they were raw from the neck to the waistband." The overseer soon returned with twelve men and two boys, both of whom were armed. They found thirty to fifty bondpeople holed up in a barn, "on whom they tried to prevail with persuasion, but the slaves . . . rushed upon them, armed with clubs and staves; one of them knocked down a white man, and was going to repeat the blow to finish him, which one of the boys seeing, levelled his piece, discharged its contents into the fellow's breast, and brought him to the dust. Another fellow having also knocked down another of the Whites, was, in the same manner, shot by the other boy. In short, the battle continued sometime desperate, but another of the Negroes having his head almost cut off with a broad sword, and five of them being wounded, the rest fled." Three enslaved people were killed. The ringleader, despite earlier having helped the manager to escape his attackers, was one of those slain.[3]

It is noteworthy that the overseer was forced to call on the assistance of other whites in order to put down this uprising, one of the most significant in the eighteenth century. Clearly two unaided men—the overseer and the steward—represented a feeble bulwark against enslaved rebellion. And it was precisely owning to the weakness of the overseer's position that the bondmen were able to prosecute their mutiny. Only once the balance of force had been restored, with the unleashing of firearms against the bondpeople, was the resistance quashed. Force determined the stability of the slave system across both regions, whether it took the form of the overseer's whip, the threat of punishment for violent resistance, or the significant likelihood that a bondperson would face capture and punishment if he or she attempted to escape. Overseers could maintain effective authority only as long as they were believed to possess recourse to such force. Once this was shown to be wanting, the potential for enslaved resistance was greater.

The report highlights a number of further dimensions to the overseer-slave relationship. First, it is revealing that the event appeared in newspapers printed as far distant as New York.[4] Eighteenth-century America feared attacks by bondpeople on their overseers since such assaults represented an affront not only to their supervisor's authority, but by extension to that of white hegemony at large; the legal structures of southern colonies underlined oversight's societal role. Second, the account illuminates how tensions played out on a plantation between an overseer and his enslaved charges. Men and women often reacted strongly when their situation changed—in this case a previous superintendent had granted them more latitude. Successful overseers consistently employed subtlety in their dealings with enslaved people, understanding that negotiation and compromise were often more effective than stern rule. Nonviolent resistance such as running away was relatively common, but small oppositional acts could transform into violence and large scale defiance. Subtlety also meant knowing when to use appropriate positive inducements, and when to use violence: the newspaper article criticized the original overseer's leniency as directly contributing to the uprising. Because violence underpinned order on southern plantations, employers sought to maintain control of its use. Patriarchs' criticism of overseers for misusing violence formed part of the widespread denunciation of managerial competence by the end of the 1700s, while the devolution to managers of the punishment that was integral to slavery represented a central contribution to the stereotype of the brutal overseer.

Violence, however, did not reach the level of stigmatization in the patriarchal era that it would in the years following the Revolutionary War. Of more concern to slave owners was that their authority be felt on the plantation, and that rule by overseers be balanced. In the underinstitutionalized plantation world, patriarchs made up for the lack of centralized authority by effectively claiming judicial power over their dependents. God was the ultimate arbiter of all human actions, but in the absence of His direct intervention, patriarchs assumed the role of judge, jury, and arbiter of punishment with a seriousness that derived from their concern for the maintenance of social order.[5] Within this judicial metaphor patriarchs sought further control over their dependents, especially those on far-flung plantations.

Patriarchs also sought to rationalize further their relationship with the women, children, white men, and enslaved people whom they judged. They told themselves that with great sociopolitical power came great responsibility. Planter correspondence, diaries, and commonplace books are replete with concerns that patriarchs judiciously fulfill their duty to their dependents, as well as the related anxiety that dependents understand their own obligations. Many slaveholders saw the need to employ overseers as representing a barrier to the "continual exercise of . . . Patience and Economy" that successful patriarchism demanded. By appealing to their workforce over the heads of managers, slaveholders began to lay the foundations for the putatively close relationship between bondpeople and owner that planters would cling to after the Revolution.

And yet, however lofty their rhetorical claims, in the patriarchal age slave owners' focus on reason, duty, and responsibility masked the true character of plantation power. Like the exclusively male appellations of "Patriarch" and paterfamilias, the judicial metaphor gave a relationship between super- and subordinates the respectability and honor implied by an ancient pedigree of societal rule by male elites. The reciprocal connection that planters believed that they shared with their dependents hinged not on sentiment, but on a more mundane currency of economic exchange. If planters jarred with overseers owing to ideological considerations regarding the treatment of enslaved people, concerns for their profit margins also stoked their criticism.

Whites everywhere in the South were always conscious of the fragility of their slave systems. In the 1600s, with the continued growth of the black population as a result of slave trading, southern legislatures drew up laws to guard against bondpeople's rebelliousness.[6] By the following century, as enslaved populations began to reproduce naturally, legislation came to reflect enslaved people's capacity for organized revolt.[7] In Virginia unfree blacks or mulattoes had their arms seized, and offenders were whipped.[8] Because bondpeople were less likely than white indentured servants to commit crime, legislation that focused on their putative criminality also reflected a growing awareness of racial distinctions between dependents, as well as a fear of black people.[9] Worries about enslaved revolt became particularly intense during the 1730s, a "decade of rebellion" when increased imports of African men and women created greater fractiousness.[10] Conspiracy among slaves to rebel or murder became a felony without benefit of clergy (which was a process whereby capital sentences were commuted to lesser punishments), while bondpeople could be emancipated for reporting conspiracies.[11]

Similar statutes existed in the Carolinas and Georgia and gained fresh impetus among South Carolinians after the Stono Rebellion of 1739.[12] Although only twenty-five whites were killed in that uprising, "every one that had any tie of Relation, any Tie of Nature; every one that had a Life to lose were in the most sensible Manner shocked at such Danger daily hanging over their Heads."[13] In response the colonial authorities drew up the 1740 Negro Act. Writing to the *South Carolina Gazette* in 1772, one "Stranger" encapsulated the importance placed in these provisions. Bemoaning the lax enforcement of the act, and in particular the clauses regulating slave gatherings, he asked, "whenever or wherever such nocturnal rendezvouses are made, may it not be concluded, that their deliberations are never intended for the advantage of white people?"[14]

Yet large-scale insurrections were almost unknown before Gabriel's Rebellion in Virginia in 1801, and murder of whites by bondpeople was almost as infrequent.[15] Between 1721 and 1776 in Richmond County, Virginia, there were only two reported cases; in the whole of the colony, enslaved men and women committed only one act of violence against whites per county every ten years.[16] Four whites died in the "most serious outbreak of slave violence in the Low Country between 1763 and 1815," in St. Andrew Parish, Georgia, in 1774.[17] The preponderance of legislation in the face of such infrequency is explained by the fact that murders did not have to occur often—"one nearby, perhaps no closer than a neighboring county and perhaps only once in a decade"—to make a deep impression on slave owners and bondpeople.[18]

The fears that these events engendered in the white population translated into a legal recognition of the importance of overseers, and the laws covering oversight form an important subset of wider slavery legislation. These men were the most visible symbol of authority for servants and bondpeople, a symbol not just of the power of their masters and mistresses, but that of the government of the colony.[19] In 1632 statute linked these sources of authority for the first time. No person in the colony of Virginia was to presume to be disobedient to the present government, "nor servants to their private officers, maysters and overseers, at their uttermost perils."[20] From then on Virginian law frequently restated overseers' important role in resisting rebellion. A servant received two years extra on his indenture for laying "violent hands" on his master, mistress, or overseer.[21] In other colonies attacks by bondpeople on overseers were equally serious: one Georgian advert promised that whoever produced the head of the man who killed "Andrew Crawford, Overseer at the plantation of John Milledge Esq." would receive "THIRTY SHILLINGS."[22] After murdering an overseer on a plantation in Darien in the same colony, two enslaved people were burned alive, their execution intended as a deterrent.[23] And the antislavery "American Farmer" J. Hector St. John de Crèvecoeur claimed how in Charleston he had found a bondman left to expire in a cage suspended in a wood, his eyes bitten out by birds, as punishment for "having killed the overseer of the plantation. They told me that the laws of self-preservation rendered such executions necessary."[24]

Legal requirements providing for the supervision of enslaved people reasserted the societal importance of oversight. Fears of slave revolt led some colonies to prohibit the employment of bondpeople without a white superintendent.

As early as 1726, statute enjoined South Carolinian planters to hire one white man for every ten bondpeople, in response to "persistent and vocal" complaints to low-country grand juries about the threat posed by widespread black management.[25] A concern that its population should not be overwhelmingly black like South Carolina's, its northern neighbor, led Georgia, on introducing slavery in 1750, to insist that planters employ one white man for every four enslaved people.[26] Further equivalent legislation meant that by 1771, a South Carolinian advertisement "WANTED . . . [a] MAN, to reside on a Plantation, to comply with the Law."[27] This halfhearted desire to follow prescription reflected a level of nonchalance among some sections of the population regarding the threat of enslaved rebellion. In fact regulations were flouted consistently. By 1755 only eight Georgian planters were complying with the ratio proposed in 1750, and another six with a new ratio of one white to every twenty blacks stipulated by the slave code of that year.[28] One 1742 letter stated that in South Carolina, legislation met with "discouragement" and "various Pretences" aimed at its subversion.[29] The South Carolinian William Hambleton described the plantation of a neighbor as containing "no white man."[30] Because it required no extra expenditure to employ enslaved drivers and managers—in comparison to the costs of recruiting and hiring white overseers—the concern here was for economic efficiency rather than the defense of an abstract racial hierarchy.

Although in 1700 a petition brought by Middlesex County before the Virginian colonial legislature had requested that "Negroes be not kept att Quarters without Overseers," and Landon Carter worried that unattended bondpeople would be prone to rebel, there were never any laws insisting on white supervision in the more northerly colony.[31] Planters including George Washington and Ralph Wormeley employed enslaved overseers, but the practice was discouraged nevertheless: if there was no white overseer on a quarter, the owner was liable for any damage caused by the enslaved people there.[32] Even those planters who left the management of their grounds to bondmen still feared their perceived inherent restiveness. At the end of the century, Washington distinguished a growing tension between economic priorities and the postwar behavior of enslaved people: "the reason why I doubted about employing an Overseer at [Dogue run plantation], is, that as Union and Dogue run Farms are under one Overseer this year, and the latter conducted in a great measure by the foreman, I had some thoughts of entrusting it solely to him next year, under the direction of the Steward, but when I perceive but too clearly that Negros are growing more and more insolent and difficult to govern, I am more inclined to incur the expense of an Overseer than to hazard the management, and peace of the place to a Negro."[33]

Last, since it was considered folly to leave enslaved people unattended, overseers throughout the colonial period were exempted from militia duty across the South.[34] What this meant for overseers, however, was further exclusion from white, property-holding society. The militia was a "school of political democracy" in the years before the war: "militia musters . . . rearticulated social hierarchies by assigning different roles to white men according to their actual position as laborers, masters of householders, property holders, or county officers."[35] Free blacks, mulattoes, and Indians were all permitted to play a role in the Virginian militia; only enslaved people and overseers were excluded.[36] Though militia exemptions put overseers on the front line of the defense of white society, they also excluded these men from its foundational rituals.[37]

Despite southern whites' fears, the infrequency of enslaved violence against their oppressors suggests that the overseer-slave relationship involved, for the most part, nonviolent interaction. Successful overseers could use positive enticements such as the promise of a visit to a family member on another quarter, or negative inducements including the withdrawal of such promises. The overseer Edward Harleston told his employer how, when the enslaved Clarissa had "wanted to Take a Walk[,] . . . if I had any Thoughts to punish her I would not let her go."[38] Josiah Smith believed that "not . . . so much as one Shall Run away" because he had "properly encouragd [the bondpeople] to stand firm to that heavy Part of this work by a Present of Meat & Liquor which I hope has had the good effect of Keeping them at home."[39] Such tactics aimed to render violence needless through the awarding of "petty privileges."[40] Managers also tended to come to some level of agreement with the enslaved people in their charge. An overseer would appreciate laborers who seemed to demonstrate obedience and diligence, while bondpeople preferred a manager who was not quick to anger, and who was just in dividing labor between them. The many recruitment notices asking that overseers be "discreet" in governing enslaved men and women demonstrate the level of subtlety required.[41] Aside from an overseer's ability in crop cultivation, an aptitude for "the Management of negroes" was most highly prized by employers.[42] But as in the Hanover County incident, slaveholders were prone to condemn overseers who they believed yielded too many advantages to their enslaved charges. In 1770 the Virginian steward Charles Dabney described the regime of a former manager: Thomas "Wingfield . . . was so goodnatured to the Negroes under him that he suffered Hands to Impose on him very much & it is well known to every person that was Acquainted with his Management that the . . . years he Lived in the Business the Estates Suffered . . . by his not keeping them to there duty."[43]

Virginia, with smaller plantations than the lowcountry colonies and a roughly equal population of whites and blacks, developed a greater closeness of relations between races than elsewhere (although the flexibility that distinguished the seventeenth century had reduced by the eighteenth).[44] There are a few instances in the records of bondpeople spending their leisure time with plantation managers: one Chesapeake overseer played "at cards with Negroes who had come to the plantation."[45] The medium of this game brought the white manager closer to the black people's level, where on this occasion they could converse almost as equals.

Richard Dozier, Robert Carter of Nomini Hall's overseer at his Northern Neck plantation, recounted how witnessing black people preach changed his perception of their abilities. After seeing "Negro Lewis belonging to Mr. Brockenbrough in Essex . . . [speak] . . . to about 300 people," Dozier concluded that Lewis's gift "exceeded many white preachers."[46] Religious managers were also inspired to evangelize to the enslaved people in their care, despite some planters instructing overseers to prevent black people's contact with "New Light" preachers.[47] John Self, manager for Landon Carter at his Rings Neck plantation, "had turned a Baptist . . . and would not continue in [Carter's] business but to convert [his] people."[48] Such familiar relations must have bolstered the critique that overseers were too close to bondpeople, and were approaching the level of the enslaved themselves.

Trade was a further sphere in which bondpeople gained some level of parity with their supervisors. William Taylor, also overseer to Robert Carter of Nomini Hall, "bought of [Carter's] negro Old Tom about 1 peck of Corn [and] bought of negro Breachy ½ gallon of meal." But Tom had come by these goods deviously. Dozier, Taylor's colleague, complained to Carter how "it appeared [that]t negro Tom had the Key of a Tobacco House, wherein the plantation Corn lies—; that Tom entred in to . . . the said Tobacco house in the night time, & took out 1 peck of Corn, w[hi]ch he delivered to Wm Taylor." Tom was sent to "tryal," after which he was punished with "switches on [his] bare [Back]."[49] There is some indication that other overseers, especially those on meager salaries, were forced to buy items from enslaved people that they had stolen from plantation owners' stores.[50] Although worries for patriarchal control of resources led masters like Carter to disapprove of trade between the two parties, Henry Laurens was more compliant. Lowcountry bondpeople were more likely to own provision grounds than their Virginian counterparts.[51] No doubt mindful of the cost of provisioning overseers, Laurens told an overseer to "purchase of your own Negroes all that you know lawfully belongs to them at the lowest price they will sell it for." His implication was that the bondpeople could bargain with their overseer: momentarily they were in control.[52]

In another area planters sanctioned a degree of parity between overseers and the people whom they supervised. Although some planters worried about overseers "slid[ing] into" African ways (often because managers needed to adapt to enslaved people's established agricultural practices in order to control them better), indigo cultivation was perhaps the most significant matter on which lowcountry bondpeople cooperated with their managers.[53] After the introduction of this staple, the skills needed for its production spread quickly, often passed on to overseers by enslaved people.[54] Thomas Owen and James Barclay could give detailed descriptions of the production process, but as Henry Laurens admitted, "there is something Extremely unaccountable in the working of Indigo."[55] So tricky was the manufacture that it was believed that two people could not make a dye of the same quality.[56] Figure 5 details some of this complexity—it depicts two bondmen skimming water from an indigo vat, leaving the remaining indigo to thicken into a paste for removal; in the foreground of the picture, another bondman is dividing the thickened indigo into blocks for shipment in barrels. Enslaved people were valued highly for their competence: in South Carolina, a "woman named Hagar" was "strongly recommended for . . . her great care of Indigo."[57]

Because cultivation of the crop was so profitable, planters sometimes recognized their bondpeople's greater knowledge ahead of that of their overseers, resulting in an upheaval of the plantation authority structure. Peter Gourdin placed so much value in a gifted bondman that his will insisted that the man never be forced to do fieldwork—or, significantly, be answerable to an overseer. The bondman was also to gain his freedom after the death of Gourdin's son.[58] In this case at least, the commercial value that provided relative autonomy on the plantation away from a manager's gaze might well have translated into real and tangible freedom.[59]

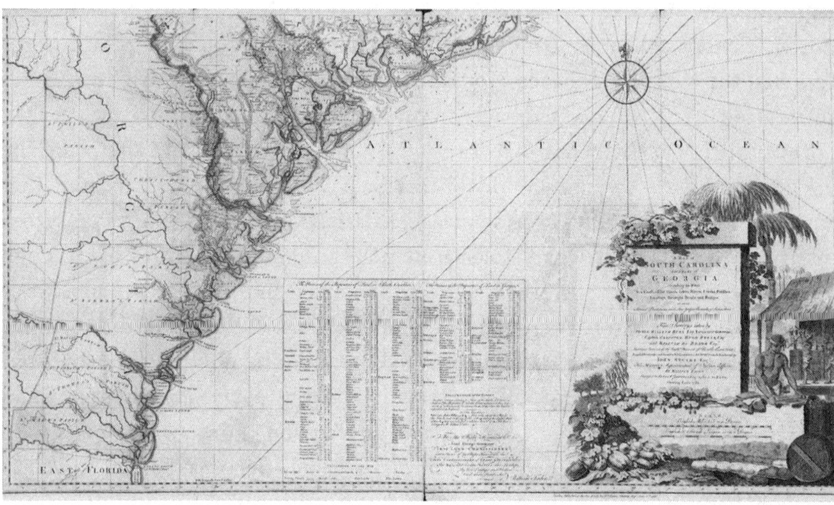

Fig. 5. A Map of South Carolina and a part of Georgia. Containing the whole seacoast; all the islands, inlets, rivers, creeks, parishes, townships, boroughs, roads, and bridges: As also, several plantations, with their proper boundary-lines, their names, and the names of their proprietors. Area Table 75 1780 Faden. Courtesy of Special Collections, University of Virginia, Charlottesville, Virginia.

A far less equal relationship existed between some overseers and the women under their control. Sexual relations between managers and the enslaved were by no means unknown. James Lawrence, overseer to Henry Laurens, was fired for his "familiarity with Hagar which . . . must be very hurtful to my Interest, as it must make a good deal of jealousy and disquiet amongst the Negroes."[60] Such relationships damaged Laurens's "Interest" since they made enslaved people less likely to bow to the overseer's authority, caused the resentment of enslaved men, and, because the discovery of the relationship no doubt caused her distress, in this case threatened to put at risk Hagar's skills in indigo production. Planters knew that any imbalance in plantation stability could weaken their own rule. Abraham Schad's "great partiality shewn . . . to the prejudice of [Elias Ball's] Sisters Negroes" led Ball to "desire . . . the Negroes . . . be separated" in order to curb the disruptive potential of the overseer's actions.[61] Other planters' criticism of sexual relationships revealed even more prosaic concerns. One Georgian slave owner was less perturbed by his manager's relations with bondwomen than by the fact that "he infected every negroe wench on the plantation with a . . . highly virulent disease," which could have rendered them unable to work while they convalesced.[62] Profit, and not propriety, was the watchword for such men.

But sex also provided opportunities for some women, despite the one-sided nature of their relationships with overseers. It enabled them to exploit gaps in the South's racial hierarchy and shift subtly the loci of plantation authority. Low-country jurists denounced interracial sexual relations—or "CRIMINAL CONVERSATIONS"—as evil, their bombastic rhetoric thinly masking a real concern for the stability of slave society.[63] A female bondperson or servant could attempt to ameliorate her individual situation by providing the overseer with sexual gratification.[64] As the courts feared, the emotional attachments that white men formed with black women had the potential to cause slippages in white male dominance. By prosecuting these relationships, overseers demonstrated their inconstant allegiance to this dominance and opened themselves up to further criticism for their closeness to enslaved people.[65]

Now and again it is possible to glimpse in the records instances that suggest a level of solidarity between white and black against the slave system. Managers sometimes aided bondpeople in their attempts at running away, or even fled the plantation with them. These actions added to a long tradition of white servants escaping with black men and women, and poorer whites aiding the flight of enslaved people or servants (black and white laborers were "comrades-in-arms" in Bacon's Rebellion of 1676).[66] Legislation to prevent this collusion peppers seventeenth-century Virginian legal history, when color lines were more fluid. Yet the laws evidently did not work quite as planned, since comparable statutes appeared during the following century to discourage whites from harboring runaway dependents.[67] Later in the 1700s the *Virginia Gazette* printed adverts referencing the phenomenon. "THOMAS WEST," an "Overseer . . . who lived at the Subscriber's plantation about three Years, and just about the time the said three Negroes ran away and left him" was "generally thought" to have "carried them into North Carolina, Virginia, or Maryland."[68]

These acts were not always predicated on equality between the two parties. Punishment for Virginian indentured servants who enticed runaways required the servant to make up to the slave owner any time lost, in recognition that servants might use bondpeople's time for their own purposes.[69] By the eighteenth century, benefit of clergy had been withdrawn for those stealing slaves.[70] Thomas West's motives appear to have been similarly disingenuous—it was widely believed that he would offer his enslaved companions "for sail [sale]." Theft of bondpeople from one's employer represented not only a breach of trust and a betrayal of the authority invested in a manager. It was also an act of subversion against the established social hierarchy, a means by which a white man of relatively lowly status might attempt to expropriate his own small share of the human means of production in the eighteenth-century South.[71]

Enslaved people were no mere pawns in this process. They capitalized on the opportunity to flee their bondage even if managers had dubious motivations. But the majority of runaways left without the sanction of their overseers, and their actions either purposefully or fortuitously undermined managerial authority. Protecting white society from enslaved resistance involved restricting bondpeople's movement, and keeping men and women attached to the plantation cemented a patriarch's feeling of control (once again overseers' duties were therefore vital to the maintenance of plantation norms).[72] From 1680 Virginian law delineated the relationship between flight and rebellion: the crime of running away was linked specifically with revolt by black enslaved people.[73] A number of men and women who had fled their quarters certainly encouraged others to flee. One of John Ewing Colhoun's bondpeople, Will, on trial for poisoning his master, was accused late in the eighteenth century "of attempting to Seduce other Negroes out of State—."[74]

That preventing runaways was a duty that some overseers were unable to shoulder is underlined by adverts that portrayed dependents as having "escaped from [their] overseers," or in reports by supervisors such as Archibald McKewn, who admitted that "Marlborough is Not Come in yet."[75] Owners kept a close eye on news of runaways—a Georgian overseer was told "I hope Boson has Returned or been caught."[76] Enslaved people knew about the popular mistrust in overseers' ability to control their charges, inducing planters to instruct their managers how best to prevent runaways. William Ancrum, a South Carolinian planter and merchant, reflected prejudices about managerial failings in this area when he counseled overseer William Pryor about two runaways who had returned: "I hope your Lenity will not encourage them in such Practices."[77] Ominously nine months earlier Ancrum had commanded Pryor to "use such Means as will prevent ["Negroe Billy"'s] Running away in future."[78]

When running away bondpeople effectively stole from their master or mistress. They removed a slaveholder's human property in themselves so that he or she could no longer use it, and so enslaved men and women could employ their time and labor for their own purposes.[79] They also undermined managerial rule by demonstrating that resources could be used for activities other than plantation work. When an overseer deprived bondpeople of their customary rights to, for example, visit their wives or husbands at another quarter, running away denoted a means by which to avoid these restrictions. William Ancrum admitted to Pryor regarding Billy's whereabouts: "I can hear nothing of Negro Billy, I suspect he is some Way near Town where he has a Bro[ther] whom Mr Kershaw lately hired."[80] Visiting another quarter was the motivation most cited for Chesapeake runaways between 1745 and 1779, while a sixth of Georgian notices between 1783 and 1795 assumed similar destinations.[81]

Other factors in bondpeople's reckoning included geography, and the time of year that they chose. Runaways in the lowcountry took advantage of the smaller white population and greater number of enslaved people to overseers there, recognizing that they had more chance to slip undetected into the backcountry, or across colonial borders.[82] The South Carolinian congressman Jacob Read wrote to Seaborn Jones in Augusta, Georgia, that "Richard Cureton who lives near the big Shoals of Ogeechee . . . is in posesion of a Negro man my property."[83] Toward the end of the century, enslaved people in the Chesapeake were induced to flee by the lure of northern states that, starting with Vermont in 1777 and Pennsylvania in 1780, had begun the process of gradual emancipation. In both regions many men and women left during harvest when work was even harder than usual, and when overseer violence probably rose along with expectations for crop yields.[84] Overseers were obliged to report each runaway; since absent enslaved workers meant financial losses for the planter, managerial testimonies frequently pinned the blame on the runaway. One manager for John Ewing Colhoun implied that a recent absentee was lazy: "Marlbrough is rund away for he was tir[e]d of work—."[85] Another insisted that his own actions were not the impulse that had led a bondman to flee: "Marcus has been a Great Runaway, & is now out for know provocation what ever."[86]

Each of these interactions amounted to a constantly changing, and intricate, network of contacts between managers, servants, and bondpeople. The overseer knew that although it was his duty to uphold plantation discipline and follow his employer's strictures, the autonomy of action that absenteeism yielded meant that it was often in his best interests to interpret and adjust rules according to the temperament of the bondpeople. Enslaved men and women knew this too and discovered that they could test the boundaries of an overseer's authority. In this way both parties changed subtly the structure of power relationships. Despite the formal insistence on social actors having a clearly defined role within the racial hierarchy, all groups found that they could assert some level of independence when an opportunity presented itself. To an extent power was therefore negotiated—when overseers granted rights and privileges to the enslaved people in their command, they legitimated the capacity of the subordinated to exercise a small but important role in the construction of plantation life.[87]

It was an important role because apparently trivial acts of resistance to the subordinating power could from time to time take on broader political meanings, linking them in spirit to overt signs of dissent such as the organized rebellions that southern legislators so feared.[88] Offstage, therefore, and often never meant to be discovered, such resistance communicates a different view from the subalterns' perspective about their assumed devotion to the hierarchical order.[89] Small wonder that George Washington worried about how to control bondpeople. He admonished planters to keep a tight rein: they must "always be with [their] people . . . for when an overseer's back is turned . . . most of [the slaves] will slight in their work, or be idle altogether."[90] Slave owners' misgivings about the ability of their overseers to control enslaved resistance represent one of the primary early tenets of managerial stigmatization.

Everyday resistance presented opportunities to gain concessions outside the arbitrariness of overseer rule, but with less of the risk of overt acts such as running away. Sometimes it was best achieved not by offering direct resistance to managerial diktat but by bending rather than breaking the rules. "Go slow" tactics fell into this category: one of Landon Carter's managers discovered that enslaved people might cause "the loss of a whole day's work of the gang" even if "the most trifling hand is ill but a day or a piece of the day."[91] Because it forced a reevaluation of work patterns, such a tactic enabled the enslaved to define for themselves the makeup of their work gang. On the South Carolinian plantation at Boinneau's Ferry belonging to the lawyer John Ewing Colhoun, the overseer faced a more common problem. As he related late in the century, "the Negroes Wont Eat potatoes not till We[a]t[he]r [is] dry provisions is all most out." Knowing that the overseer could not afford to take chances when it came to food for the labor force, bondpeople were able to have a small say in their diet—the overseer was forced to send to one "Mr Noris" for fifty bushels of corn.[92] Similarly the bondpeople on William Gibbons's Georgian plantations petitioned their overseer for better provisions. John Channing complained that he "gave all the Negroes blankets just before [he] came away, but they are such an unreasonable set of beings that they dont care how much expence a person is put to." It was "a matter of doubt" to Channing if any of the bondpeople "really want[ed]" the blankets.[93] Actions such as these would have created stronger bonds among the enslaved people as they collectively rejected authority.[94]

Other bondpeople found gaps in the organization of the slave system that they could exploit to the detriment of their overseer. Some slaveholders entrusted men and women with the delivery of oral messages to overseers, which (unlike written missives) gave the enslaved person an opportunity to distort the message. One Virginian overseer believed that he was the victim of this strategy. In the earliest days of the Republic he informed his employer, Robert Carter of Nomini Hall, that "Ther may not be any mor messages sent by Tom osterman [because] I have found him to be so treacherous I cannot put any confidence in anything he sais."[95] A South

Carolinian manager would later discover a bondman turning a similar task to his advantage. As he related to John Ewing Colhoun, "you rote me wurd [word] by Mr geneger['s] Boy[,] [C]on . . . he met felop In his returning home wich it seams he informd felop . . . that you Desired he Should be put in the sugar house and remain there till you come down in the cuntry and he said well he would rather go there than be with you and he came straight In to me the next day and said to me that you had rote by Mr g[enege]r['s] boy to put him in the Sugar house and have him w[h]ip[p]ed and he seamed so satisfied to go."

Here the keenness of "Felop" to be punished fired the overseer's suspicions, particularly as the directions had passed through two different enslaved men before reaching him. Perhaps this was an extreme attempt by the bondman to escape the drudgery of fieldwork—the sugar house was a notoriously harsh workhouse for the enslaved—or perhaps moving there was the first stage in an escape attempt. Whatever the motivation, this manager was eager to underline his defense of the employer's interest, and thereby to underline the "voluntary service" that he gave as one free man to another.[96] "I considered yore Intres I asked some of yore best friends and they advised me not to send him by no means but to put him In the field and to kep him tite at work twould be best for him and Les Expence for you wich I have also Done till you . . . make some opportunity to fetch him and there you can take satisfaction without any Expence."[97]

On occasion this overseer's colleagues also protested just a little too much. John Grinninger, seeking to deflect future criticism, told Colhoun that "the Indigo shall be of better Quality—as I mean to . . . go in tierly [entirely] by my direction"—and not allow enslaved people's resistance to have an effect on crop production.[98] Slaveholders were well aware of the methods that bondpeople used to undermine their supervisors. Colhoun deemed it necessary to order another of his overseers to ensure that the "negroes do not steal my Tar in pine land," an expropriation that the bondpeople presumably made to augment their own meager provisions.[99]

Over the course of the 1700s, property in humans increased in value. Since it affected their ability to cultivate crops, one of the major contributory factors to enslaved people's worth was their continued health.[100] A very early letter to the South Carolinian Joseph Morton summarized such thinking: "[bondpeople] are capable of learning anything & I find when they are kindly used & have their belly full of victuals and clothes, they are the truest servants."[101] The botanist William Bartram concurred: "the better they are fed, clothed and treated, the more . . . profit we may expect to derive from their labour."[102] By expressing concern about enslaved people's health, absentee slaveholders also attempted to reestablish the patriarchal dynamic. In 1711 the Virginian Robert Bristow wrote to overseer Thomas Booth that he was "sorry for the loss of 4 of my Negroes & ye mortality which rages so much in ye Country I hope ye will take all ye care imaginable of ye people & [tha]t nothing be wanting to assist them in this distemper."[103] Robert Carter III insisted that some sick people should "drink herb Tea or some water [with] some toast put in it with some salt petre or some sugar put therein" and "that an old Ewe or Wether be killed for them."[104] Joseph Ball demanded in 1743 that his steward "encourage the overseers to make a Good Deal of Corn, and let the folks have their full Shares; and tell ye overseers to keep the keys of the folk's Cornhouses; for else they will Sell it, and Starve themselves; as they did when I was in England before."[105] When he began work as an overseer on the Custis estates in Virginia, Joseph Valentine agreed "to take all the care he can of all the said Custis's Negroes, both old and young, in Sickness & in Health, that are put under his care."[106] In South Carolina William Ancrum urged an overseer that "as I have not been able yet to procure any Clothing for the Negroes ([which] gives me much Uneasiness) you will expose them as little as possible to the Severity of the Weather."[107] Virginian Joseph Ball ordered that bondpeople must "have their clothing in Time; and let them have Good covering to keep them warm at nights: and be sure that they have their due share of Meat."[108] Henry Fitzhugh was not prepared even to take this chance—he suggested that "Mrs Bataille" keep "two new Negros" at "home till March, because the Overseer will not take the Care that is necessary to be taken of them the first Winter."[109]

Owners like Henry Laurens, who had a long-term, proprietorial view of the reproductive capacities of pregnant women, contrasted their own behavior toward pregnant women with that exhibited by their overseers.[110] Laurens advised James Lawrence to "be very careful" with "the Women with Child" owing to the value of their progeny.[111] Virginian planter William Lee warned his overseer that "the Woman with Child shou'd never be hard worked or oppressed in any manner & the Children sh[oul]d always be plentifully fed and have necessary cloathing."[112] Robert Carter III counseled that Criss, who had fallen ill while pregnant, should "take a vomit of Ippacacuena [ipecacuana—a medicinal root] in case She is not near her time of delivery."[113]

Bondpeople fully recognized their innate worth, and incidents abound of enslaved men and women bringing grievances directly to their master or mistress.[114] The English naturalist Thomas Pennant recorded one example from William Byrd's Virginian plantations. He related how "Col. Byrd was formerly obliged in a scarcity of Mayz to feed his slaves with Wheat. They lost their strength to such a degree that they petitiond their master to have their old food restored."[115] Problems arose for overseers when slaveholders heeded bondpeople's complaints against their managers. Partly this was in recognition of enslaved people's value; partly it acknowledged that enslaved men and women remained on plantations for longer periods than supervisors and hence their skills and experience were of greater import. When slaveholders responded to appeals against managers, the well-being of the labor force was more significant to the planter than the social standing and potential shame of the overseer.[116] It also made the overseer's duty to control enslaved people even more difficult and exacerbated his reputation for incompetence. Bondpeople capitalized on the overseer's poor image, knowing that they would find a sympathetic ear with their owner. When an enslaved person's word came up against a manager's, the former often won out.

Talebearing against overseers took a variety of forms, each with a different motive. Bondpeople might complain of mistreatment by the overseer in an effort to get him removed, or at the very least to gain concessions. If they believed that the overseer was guilty of misappropriating plantation resources, men and women feared that his crimes could have material repercussions on their own subsistence.[117] Sam, a bondman on Henry Laurens's Wrights Savannah plantation, informed John Lewis Gervais that seed rice had been used by the overseer William Godfrey for domestic planting, that bondpeople had worked "for Mr. Godfrey," and that the overseer had appropriated a small barrel of rice for his own plantation.[118] Knowing how valuable crops and labor were to Laurens, and recognizing the managerial reputation for theft, Sam was able to construct a persuasive report. Bondpeople also bore tales of how managers transgressed enslaved people's own limited property rights. One of Robert Carter III's workforce complained to the slaveholder in 1781 that his overseer had stolen one of his pots; Carter took the bondman's side.[119] The enslaved also carved for themselves greater agency by building on—and building up—the managerial reputation for incompetence. On one of Landon Carter's plantations, an overseer suggested that a day's cutting would fill a sixty-foot tobacco house. But the "old Stagers in the Gang lookt with some contempt at his saying so." Carter then asked for the longest-standing people's opinion, which they duly gave, in front of their manager.[120] From then on the overseer would have needed to treat the bondpeople more carefully in order to avoid further rebukes and to maintain his professional reputation. Perhaps he also gave them a greater say in crop cultivation. On Landon Carter's Virginian plantations, enslaved women accused an overseer's wife of cruelty against a child in order to try to get the child moved out of the overseer's house where she had been serving.[121]

If economic reasons led in large part to slave owners' concerns for the wellbeing of their human property, why did they undermine their overseers' authority over enslaved people, potentially reducing managerial confidence, and ultimately disrupting long-term efficiency and profitability?[122] Talebearing by bondpeople was viewed as an alternative (and perhaps more reliable) source of information about the management of the plantation. Because talebearing enabled planters both to secure profits and to reestablish patriarchal control over distant quarters, slave owners tended to privilege its immediate benefits above any ultimate problems that it might cause.

The patriarchal cultural metaphor went even further—it positioned slaveholders as the final arbiters of plantation justice. In 1737 a suboverseer who worked under the overseer Simon Sallard faced criticism from his workforce. The enslaved people whom he supervised had "Liv'd So Long" at their quarter that "They would not work but as they Pleasd." The suboverseer therefore gave them "Some . . . Correction." In response the men and women "abusd him Very mutch and after went to Mr Landon Carter to Complain." Carter wrote to Sallard that he should dismiss the suboverseer.[123] Also in Virginia overseer John Blair reported to steward Charles Dabney that "Maximus, one of the fellows under Clackston [an overseer] is just arrived here & complains that his overseer was going to whip him without cause; his story is pretty long, & not worth mentioning to you, as you'll have an opportunity of inquiring into the whole matter your self, which you are desired to do, & have the fellow corrected or excused, as you may judge proper." Cognizant of how Dabney's own pretension to judicious dominance might affect the success of his regime, Blair urged his supervisor to "advise the [other] overseers never to threaten a Negroe but always to punish them at once."[124]

By encouraging enslaved people to look to him for protection from the overseer, a slaveholder could thereby extend his authority over an absentee plantation through his position as judicious conciliator in bondpeople's disputes with their managers.[125] Another advantage was that planters could deflect criticism away from themselves and strive to make enslaved people more dependent (since it was to the Big House that they turned for redress), all the while presenting bondpeople with a facsimile of autonomy.[126] This network of tensions needed a central focus, however; by appealing to the familiar stereotype of managerial incompetence, slave owners could justify selecting the overseer to play this role. Enslaved men and women could also win greater autonomy through referencing patriarchal understandings of black people, not least the idea that called for the promotion of the "degenerate" enslaved to a level of relative civility. Bondpeople were continually aware that a central component of their survival was the ability to gratify, or at least appear to gratify, the innermost wishes of masters and mistresses—such actions representing "clever ploys in an endless war."[127] By working slowly a bondperson could appeal to the stereotype of the lazy slave and toil at an easier rate than otherwise might be permitted.[128] Enslaved people could also play up to a widely held conception of a "child-like" slave, harassed by a bullying overseer.[129]

Evidence suggests that when slave owners attempted to bring order to their quarters, any balance that they thought that they had achieved was often fictional. When planters raised bondpeople to positions of authority, tensions with managers over the locus of power became clear. In 1781 a Georgian planter related to his overseer the positive attributes of the driver whom he was sending: "he is a good planter and I have always found him faithful."[130] Any owner would have expected his overseer to treat such a valued bondperson with care. But whether or not they were so prized, drivers tended to clash with managers. Edward Harleston, overseer at the Moultrie plantations in South Carolina, described one such instance: "when I went in the field . . . I see Samson Cook for the People, and Ratleip at the far end I asked him was not he Afraid that Ratleip would get of[f] he said there was no danger. I Told him that I never see a Driver that would have a Runaway Negroe under his Care. Told him so Careless and further Told him Repeatedly that he would get away from him so if he did not take Act."

Samson paid no heed: the driver rejected Harleston's advice about seating arrangements. Harleston even suspected "a Composition between them all," an indication both of the level of suspicion that many overseers felt toward drivers, and of how drivers could employ other enslaved people in subverting an overseer's position. Later in the letter, Harleston revealed that this was not the only area in which Samson had tested managerial authority: "I never went in the field Where the Negroes Worked, but I would see the One half of them Set down Sculking. I will act as Driver those Two months to come as it is Giving me but very little more Trouble, for I never could depend on Samson he is so Stupid, and must Tell him the Thing Over Many Times before he Will Understand, and is Sure to do the Wrong [thing]."[131]

There is a significant possibility that Harleston, cognizant of drivers' many opportunities to undermine management, was getting his excuses in early for any shortcomings in the running of the plantation. It is also possible that Samson feigned stupidity by incorrectly supervising Ratleip, and in failing to keep his charges to their work.[132] This strategy would have enabled the driver to win a greater degree of freedom to decide the amount and intensity of his fellow bondpeople's labor. In his determining where Ratleip should sit, and allowing bondpeople to shirk at their work, the labor force would have seen Samson as an alternative authority. Since Samson's regime was clearly more favorable than Harleston's, these bondpeople seem to have followed him with greater alacrity. Similar tensions over the positioning of authority arose elsewhere in the lowcountry. Tidal rice cultivation spread during the 1780s and 1790s, resulting in a greater tendency for plantations to have drivers. The value that owners placed in good drivers influenced slaveholders' dealings with their managers. When one of Henry Laurens's overseers refused to take advice from a driver, Cuffy, Laurens fired him.[133]

Though most interactions between supervised and supervisor were peaceable, the interplay of enslaved resistance, contested authority, and demanding profit margins created forceful tensions between overseers and subordinates that did spill over now and again. Uncovering just why day-to-day resistance transformed into full-on violence reveals complex layers of motivation. A Virginian servant at the start of the century violently rebuffed punishment by an overseer because she associated chastisement with the enforced servitude of black people rather than white, voluntary, indenture.[134] This woman's reaction allowed her to reassert a measure of control over the "personal" terrain of her body; there is also the likelihood that the overseer himself was indentured, making his regime the more unbearable.[135]

Violence followed other attempts by managers to transgress subordinates' autonomy. Bondpeople always held time off work dearly since many slaveholders guaranteed it. In particular the lowcountry task system meant that enslaved people had time to cultivate their own crops once their daily tasks were completed—and expand on their meager standard provisions. As the South Carolinian John Lloyd explained (albeit in an apology of slavery sent to a British correspondent, which distorted his conception of the length of the working day), "in working for me [bondpeople] are Tasked so they frequently get done by noon, the remainder of their day is at their disposal. So that they have plenty of time (on which I never trespass) to cultivate their ground without working on the Sabbath." Lloyd also described how the "yards abounded with poultry which [bondpeople] readily sell to persons who go about the country to collect them."[136] Time off work, and the goods that bondpeople produced during that time, were defended with as much spirit as they were enjoyed. In 1781 a group of South Carolinian bondmen attempted to murder their supervisor when he tried to appropriate the corn that they had been trying to sell.[137] This commodity represented not only a means of earning money, but also an opportunity to assert a degree of independence outside the plantation.[138]

In like manner the "extremely insolent and unruly" bondpeople involved in the Hanover County rebellion turned to violence because they saw in the stricter regime of their new steward an attack on their "hard-won customary rights," in this case the "Indulgences" that they had enjoyed during their five-day Christmas break.[139] Contemporary experts on the slave system warned how experience in managing bondpeople was of especial importance "at [the] critical time just when Negroes are beginning to plant," since even "an ordinary Overseer, well acquainted with them, can do more than a good One who happens to be a stranger."[140] The Virginian planter Edward Ambler viewed the problems associated with changing an oversight regime as part of the patriarchal "burden": "it appears to me very Plain, that the changes of Overseer [are] already too heavy upon the Produce of the Land & Negroes and of course the settling another must contribute to increase that weight."[141] The enslaved people who had worked under his "goodnatured" overseer, Thomas Wingfield, attempted to get their new supervisor, John Smith, "turned off," because, according to Ambler's analysis, the bondpeople who had enjoyed Wingfield's leniency believed themselves to be "almost free." As a result they were "very unwilling to give up the privileges they [had been] allowed" and were "determined to Maintain them." The people prevailed on the oldest man on the plantation, George, to visit their owner, believing that "a complaint from him wou'd be listened to."[142]

Because of pressures such as these, the discretion in slave management required by gazette adverts proved elusive. Although a "carrot" approach was often effective, all too frequently overseers resorted to the "stick" (in some cases quite literally, the Georgia slave code permitting "beating with a . . . Cow Skin Switch or Small Stick" among acceptable punishments).[143] Laborers received punishment for any number of misdemeanors, including fleeing the plantation, theft, inebriation, and neglect of work.[144] Since all such infractions slowed down agricultural production, chastisement was designedly severe.[145] Henry Laurens suggested to an overseer that the bondman Big Adam should have been given "a good lining to his Breeches" for having ridden to Charleston without permission.[146] The Englishman James Barclay showed some sympathy for the people who suffered under such regimes: he noted that when work was "not done to the overseer's satisfaction, the poor wretches must undergo a severe lashing."[147] Yet he still saw the efficacy of violence, threatening to lash a bondman for the theft of a stolen pig. Later John C. Grinninger undertook to punish one of John Ewing Colhoun's runaways by combining physical with psychological torture. "I have Cought Mingo and mean to give him wips and Put Iron on his neck—as that may shame him, and perhaps Waring that a wik [week] may keep him home."[148]

Punishment was one of the key reasons why bondpeople were moved to violence—particularly on occasions when, owing to the availability of alternative, positive inducements, men and women deemed managerial violence to be all the more arbitrary and unfair. Enslaved people would tolerate violent discipline to some degree but might turn rebellious under a brutal command. Virginian law throughout the eighteenth century attempted to distinguish between punishment and excessive cruelty, while the Georgian slave code divined a need to "restrain and prevent Barbarity being exercised towards slaves," such as murder, castration, cutting out the tongue, and putting the eyes out.[149] James Barclay gave a very rare, if stylized, account of how bondpeople distinguished between "good" and "bad" supervisors. When the people under his command were "flogged by the overseers . . . they will sob and sigh . . . 'Da buccary no be good fatru;' that is, 'That white man is not "good to be sure".'"[150] As the Hanover County incident demonstrated, overseer violence might itself beget violence, momentarily diluting the force that underpinned plantation hierarchies. When James Barclay threatened his hog-stealing bondman with punishment, the man threatened in turn to stab Barclay.[151] Whether or not they were carried out, actions like these set boundaries that overseers were wary of crossing. It was an effective tactic: a runaway named Ben from King and Queen County, Virginia, had "made several overseers fear him."[152]

There is little doubt that overseeing could from time to time be a dangerous—and even a fatal—occupation. Violence by blacks was rare, not least because simply striking an overseer became a capital offence after the second or third infraction, and managerial murder was delineated everywhere as "petty treason": a crime for which the punishment was execution.[153] Overseers were nevertheless on the very front line in the "endless war" for the defense of white society. In 1733 one of the South Carolinian planter Thomas Fleming's enslaved men "killed [his] overseer with an axe."[154] Another man in Georgia killed his overseer just after the middle of the century.[155] When relating how his bondpeople despised one of their managers, Henry Laurens confessed that he was "afraid of some fatal accident."[156] Some years before, Samuel Huey, another of his overseers, had been murdered by the people that he supervised.[157] Huey oversaw Laurens's new plantations in the undeveloped colony of East Florida, where there was not much in the way of assistance for whites if attacked by bondpeople.[158] In 1744 a Virginian bondman murdered his overseer's wife.[159]

The scattered nature of absentee plantations across the South meant that overseers were in greater danger there than on home quarters. An instance from Georgia illustrates how autonomous overseers responded, devising their own methods for disciplining bondpeople. After a South Carolinian benefactor loaned a group of enslaved people to the Salzburgers, a German Pietist community living in the colony, one of their number, Gronau, complained that he was unsure about the correct punishment for a man who had threatened his supervisor with an axe. He called an overseer "and asked him what was to be done so that the people would not get too much or too little punishment . . . he . . . told the people to go back to work, and he whipped the one that had threatened him."[160] Although it is difficult to establish whether instances of managerial violence rose with the extension of absenteeism, it is probable that to cement their regime many overseers used exemplary violence.[161] Overseer brutality was connoted particularly with the larger plantations of the lowcountry, where Alexander Hewatt found that managers tended to be "ignorant and cruel," especially when their employers had "several settlements at considerable distance" from their homes.[162] The violence that resulted when overseers had free rein to decide on punishment was sometimes grotesque. Philip Vickers Fithian, tutor to the children of the Virginian Robert Carter of Nomini Hall, told how an overseer related a favorite punishment: "Take a Negro, strip him, tie him fast to a post; take then a sharp Curry-comb, & curry him severely til he is well scrap'd."[163]

Absentee plantations were very difficult to police; in addition white people rarely faced prosecution for executing punishment that contravened slave codes. Virginia exonerated the killing of "any Slave . . . in the Act of Resistance to his lawful Owner or Master, or . . . any Slave dying under moderate Correction." And though the colony provided for the execution of bondpeople's murderers, it decided in 1729 against punishing an overseer who had whipped a slave to death as the act would "in all probability stir up the Negro's to a contempt of their Masters and Overseers." South Carolina merely imposed a fine on willful murderers of bondpeople, and Georgia made the first offence subject to benefit of clergy.[164] In the late 1760s and early 1770s such murderers in South Carolina generally received a fine of £350, but if they were unable to pay, half of the fine was suspended.[165] Although "one Marlowe, lately overseer on the plantation of Mr. William Williamson in South Carolina" was "sent to goal . . . on suspicion of having killed a negroe fellow, the property of Messrs. Daniel and Moses Nunez," the murdered man was, significantly, not in Marlowe's charge.[166] There are no known cases of white men being hanged for the murder of enslaved people in South Carolina in the entire eighteenth century.

Planter intervention was similarly ineffective—they had little legal redress against excessive managerial violence other than dismissal, since blacks' testimonies were inadmissible as evidence.[167]

When patriarchs expressed concern for the levels of violence that overseers perpetrated, they demonstrated their anxieties for the value of their investments rather than a human expression of sympathy. Henry Laurens's interventions to protect the well-being of his workforce have led to the suggestion that his concern went beyond mere protection.[168] The reality was probably more mundane; profit motives affected assessments of the overseer-slave dynamic in two ways. First, masters and mistresses were anxious that managerial behavior did not engender discontent. Planters like Joseph Ball expected dependents to be at each others' throats. While he counseled his steward, "let not the overseers abuse my People," he also stressed "nor let them abuse their overseers."[169] Second, mistreatment of enslaved people could endanger their health and render them less productive. This meant that while violent punishment was still deemed very necessary, it was to be used sparingly. The Virginian William Cabell blamed the passionate nature of an overseer for his cruelty and its effect on bondpeople's well-being. On hiring Theodorick Scruggs, Cabell explained that he was "not to correct my slaves immoderately, nor to work them at unseasonable times, such as in the Night, or in Rains or snows."[170] Just one month later, Cabell dismissed Scruggs because he "had heard so shocking Acc[oun]ts of his Cruelty to slaves & his Baseness in other respects that I could not think of Employing him as an Overseer."[171] Henry Laurens suggested to his manager, John Smith, that the most judicious course of action when dealing with a group of unruly bondpeople was to "make choice of the most stubborn one or two & chastise them severely but properly."[172] For Cabell and Laurens, as for the Virginia slave code, whipping should provide an exemplary corrective, and not indulge a penchant for violence.[173] Laurens elsewhere forbade "Acts of Cruelty or unnecessary . . . severity to be exercised against those Poor Wretches," insisting that "there is a Medium which ought to be observed . . . which . . . would produce good effects . . . to Your Plantation Crops . . . [and] the health . . . of the Negroes."[174]

Laurens held firm to the necessity of "proper" punishment because according to the patriarchal managing ethos, relationships between free heads of family and their dependents did not preclude violence. For much of the eighteenth century, control and discipline were planter watchwords. While acknowledging their duties to provide for bondpeople and servants, slaveholders were also quick to judge and punish. In truth they were often brutal, whipping and dismembering slaves "almost at will."[175] Witness William Byrd II, who, toward the beginning of the century, would refer to his enslaved "family," and seems to have developed a real affection for his bondmen, reading them prayers at night.[176] As part of an exculpatory description of Virginia written to an English correspondent, Byrd claimed that there were no "crueltys exercisd upon [enslaved people], unless by great accident, they happen to fall into the Hands of [a] Brute, who always passes here as a Monster."[177] Yet although he chastised himself at times for his actions, he would whip his men and women routinely. And he saw cruel punishments as appropriate if they were effective. When "Eugene pissed abed again," Byrd "made him drink a pint of piss."[178]

In like manner Joseph Ball described the complex mix of violent punishment and psychological inducement of enslaved people that patriarchs clove to. He wrote to his steward, Joseph Chinn, about a bondman whom he was sending from England: "Aron I believe will be too Saucy. If he offer's to be unruly or Strike his Overseer, he must be tyed up and Slasht Severly, and pickled. I suppose if you go to do it he will Resist you; for he Resisted me twice: If you have a reason to Slash him get two or three Good white men to help; & give it him heartily at Once. And if he should Runaway, he must wear a Pothook about his Neck. And if that won't bring him Under, he must wear Iron . . . upon his Legs till you are pretty Sure he will be orderly; for as he is my Slave he must and Shall be obedient but if he be orderly, use him kindly." Aron must have been literate—Ball wrote him a letter directly, and asked Chinn to show it to the bondman. In it Ball reiterated the punishments that he had described to Chinn, and closed the letter as follows, "if you behave yourself well you Shall be used kindly. If I hear a Good Character of you, I will send you some of my best old Cloth[e]s; and other things. Take warning and don't Ruin yourself by your folly. . . . If you will be good I shall be y[ou]r Loving Master."[179]

Violence qua violence was acceptable if used as a means of disciplining: patriarchs viewed it in almost the same light as the far less severe physical punishment that they used to correct their own children. At this stage in the century it was uncertain that planter concerns yet extended "beyond protection." Violence was a key aspect of a reciprocal relationship that lay at patriarchism's core, where the enslaved could expect to avoid punishment and receive food if they behaved themselves. But a notable shift in the rhetoric of slavery was emerging, which would fortify enlightened patriarchal doctrine in the years following the Revolution. Because overseers held an ambiguous position outside the patriarchal unit, their presence enabled planters to employ new language when outlining discipline for bondpeople. Even at an early stage in the century, William Byrd on numerous occasions employed the obliquely passive formulation "I caused [a slave] to be whipped" to describe the violence that he sanctioned.[180] His woolly construction distanced Byrd from the execution of punishment and allowed the conscience of this increasingly sentimental planter to remain clear.

With the construction of absenteeism a framework had developed that at once placed overseers outside the control of plantation owners and left them to their own brutal devices. As much as patriarchs complained that they had thereby devolved too great a responsibility to their managers, as much as they feared that dependent and violent overseers would harm bondpeople physically and injure productivity, they benefited from a system that removed them from the everyday horrors of slavery. If it was the desire to make a return on their investment that had first stoked planter prejudices, by late century this distance would enable American slave societies to delude themselves into considering slavery a positive good for its victims, and slaveholders compassionate, enlightened rulers. While the first stirrings of this sentiment were already beginning to appear before the Revolutionary War, it was the societal and political upheavals of that conflict that brought it out into the open. In the process the southern plantation overseer became a figure of true hate and derision.

— *Chapter Six* —

"Insurgents . . . disappointed in their villainous Stratagems"

Plantation Overseeing during the American Revolutionary War

> A State of ye Crops made on ye late John Ball's plantation in Fauquier County from ye1st of January 1774 to ye1st of January 1782 being yetime it was in possession of Reginald Graham dec[ease]d the average of ye Crops of each year is as followeth:—1200lb Tob[acc]oa share (7 Sharers) amounting to 67,200lb Tobo—
>
> Also 30 barrells of Corn a share on 8 Sharers is 1920 barrells
>
> Also 29 bushells of Wheat a share on 7 Sharers is 1120 bushells— . . .
>
> Harman Utterback came before me Justice of s[ai]d County and made oath that he was an overseer on ye above mentioned plantation during the time above mentioned, and that to ye best of his knowledge the aforesaid state is just and true.
>
> Martin Pickett[1]

The spatially limited nature of the American Revolutionary War permitted those not involved directly in the struggle to continue the jobs that they had performed before 1775. Battles were relatively small in scale—Washington's army usually numbered around five thousand; at one point it dwindled to two thousand.[2] At least in the war's early stages, popular support for it throughout the American colonies was less than unanimous. Intersectional disagreements, particularly those between southern elite Tidewater and lowcountry proponents and smallholding Appalachian opponents of the Revolution, put into question Henry Laurens's early assessment of wartime South Carolina that "in a word the Country [was] Military."[3] But the economic difficulties caused by the British embargo on American trade, and the popularization of Revolutionary debates in newspapers and pamphlets (not least Thomas Paine's *Common Sense,* which sold 120,000 copies), did much to spread the conflict away from the battlefields.[4]

Ordered wartime oversight by men like Harman Utterback certainly proved challenging.[5] Overseers were conferred more responsibility during the seven years of war than in any previous period. On plantations across the South, it fell to them to guarantee continuing returns in the face of wartime deprivation and difficulties of supply. During the war years, normative criticism of overseers' agricultural competences significantly—indeed terminally—intensified. Managerial failures formed one side of the dialogic process that gave birth to these critiques: planters' concerns the other. Revolutionary duties compelled some slaveholders to be absent from their plantations for extended periods; many others suffered disruptions to their communication networks. Still patriarchal anxieties for their distant lands provoked frequent correspondence with overseers in spite of these complications. And plangent slave owners exchanged letters with each other, bemoaning the incurable disorder of their agricultural investments.

Between 1775 and 1782, relations between overseers and bondpeople were more strained than at any other time in the century.[6] Promises of manumission to those bondmen who would join the British ranks proved highly persuasive; overseers were charged with reigning in those enslaved people who, inspired by libertarian rhetoric and encouraged by the tabescence of management structures, sought to resist managerial rule. Worried southern authorities duly restated the importance of oversight to the defense of slavery, and for a short while some continued to prohibit overseer enlistment in the militia. Overseers responded in a variety of ways to bondpeople's oppositional activity during these fractious years, as the "concrete political realities" of slave society power were undermined.[7] Where certain individuals managed capably, many were less successful; some were even murdered. The war played a central role in the development of prejudices against overseers, since the failings of those overseers who struggled to prevent slave rebellion contributed enduringly to the stigmatization of the profession.

This hardening of attitudes was also grounded in a prewar context, a paradigm shaped by the political, ideological, and juridical concerns of the colonial period. There were many continuities with the years before the Revolutionary War for, while revolutionary moments may make "spectacular" breaks with the past, they are also formed by them.[8] Southerners continued to employ a syncretic dynamic in their construction of negative overseer stereotypes. During the Revolutionary period, and with ever-increasing frequency thereafter, prejudices against plantation overseers derived from an interplay between ideology and context, between representation and reality. The Revolutionary War was a crucial phase in the development of such prejudices. Employers' critiques of managerial incompetence, their fears of yielding control over plantations, and their concerns for the stability of their society—each of which influenced slaveholder preconceptions came very much to the fore between 1775 and 1782.

Plantation management involved some of the same routines in wartime as it had done throughout the eighteenth century. Employers continued to recruit overseers in winter, in readiness for the planting season. In February 1776 the Charleston lawyer John Gibbons appointed an supervisor for his home quarter, thereby defraying the indentures by which his new employee "had been bound for four years."[9] The day-to-day tasks of plantation upkeep also helped to sustain managerial recruitment.[10] Most overseers experienced at least some wartime alteration to their responsibilities, however. Marlow Pryor, who worked for the South Carolinian William Ancrum, was a typical example. His employer informed him in 1779 that "the extreme Scarcity & Dearness of provisions in Town oblige me to have Recourse to you for a larger Supply of Hams & Bacon than formerly"; Ancrum therefore asked if Pryor could "cure . . . about Six Hogs." In addition the overseer was urged to be "as frugal as possible" with saltpeter. Unsurprisingly—since it was the chief constituent of gunpowder—"this Article is become so excessive dear."[11] "The unsettled state of our public affairs" meant that Ancrum also suffered from wartime embargoes on rice, indigo, and salt, and iron for mending plantation tools.[12]

Overseers expected to receive compensation in spite of the undeniable financial difficulties that their employers faced. The planters of South Carolina and Georgia, who before the war had raised much of their income in the Atlantic trade, were particularly hard hit by the British blockade. William Ancrum reported to his manager in 1780 that "at present there is an Embargo & likely to be an intense stagnation of Trade."[13] Even so contractual obligations to managers held.[14] Isaac Hayne, a South Carolinian planter, mill owner, and officer of the Revolutionary militia, was scrupulous in his wartime bookkeeping. Right up until his 1781 execution by the British occupiers in Charleston he assiduously noted in his "Memorandoms" the frequent recruitments and dismissals of overseers at his two plantations.[15] In October 1779 he recorded the names of bondpeople to whom his overseer was to give blankets; in November 1780 he did the same for a batch of "London Duffils."[16]

Hayne was an archetypal eighteenth-century planter, his fastidious note taking an indication of the anxieties that he held for the state of his lands. Like his contemporaries, he invested in his acreage not only material wealth, but also social capital: in spite of the deprivations that he faced, his personal reputation was still tied closely to the quality of the rice crop. Hayne was blessed by distance—he could reach his two plantations in St. Paul's Parish easily from Charleston, where he served as both representative and senator. Many of his fellow slaveholders were not so fortunate. The demands of war prevented them from having the same access to their farms that Hayne enjoyed, obliging them to entrust plantation management to stewards and, often reluctantly, to overseers. Henry Laurens, imprisoned by the British in the Tower of London for sixteen months during the conflict, entrusted plantation management to his friend, state senator and member of the Continental Congress John Lewis Gervais, who promised that "my attention to your Interest shall not be wanting."[17]

As he was commander in chief of the Continental Army, George Washington's wartime absences from his plantations were more protracted than those of other slave owners. Yet the frequency of his missives, and the concern that he expressed for his agricultural interests, were characteristic of most itinerant planters. Just as it had for those slaveholders with far-distant plantations, regular wartime communication substituted for impracticable personal visits. Washington's cousin Lund contacted him every month throughout the Revolution, "detailing minutely all the events that occurred on the plantations."[18] Henry Laurens, while in prison, had an equivalent desire for information about the condition of his lands. One Mr. Owen "intended to take up his quarters some Where upon Santi and frequently to visit Mepkin & Mount Tacitus," two of Laurens's Berkeley County plantations.[19] And Laurens depended on overseers for news from the front. In 1776 he recounted (with no little patriotic sarcasm) how "to hear Shubrick's Overse[e]r relate the manner of [the British] firing on the Cattle & the very few of their shot which hit the Mark, is droll enough."[20]

Despite his regular correspondence, Washington's aggravation at being kept away from his plantations manifested itself continually. Crucially his experiences during the war led him to combine criticism of distance with a universal critique of overseers. In a letter of 1782, Washington revealed his desire to appoint a "good steward," "the advantage of which, every person who has had any thing to do with Overseers, and Plantations at a distance, must be amply convinced of."[21] The inference is clear: overseers were incapable of supervising plantations with their employers far removed. Since commitments prevented his personal intervention, Washington wished to send a steward who possessed the aptitude so lacking in his overseers. Furthermore he claimed consensus on this issue: he presented his view as one that "every person" would recognize.

Concern for the profitable administration of his lands again motivated Washington's assessment. But during the Revolution his pecuniary distress, like that of other Virginians, grew deeper than at any previous moment in the eighteenth century. Although the British economic blockade would greatly damage South Carolina and Georgia—planter Margaret Colleton worried that between 1775 and 1778 she had not "receive[d] . . . the smallest remittance" from her lands—Virginian slaveholders were generally less prosperous, more susceptible to cash crop price fluctuations, and more in hock to British creditors, than their counterparts further south.[22] Given that the Revolutionary War stemmed from a quarrel over America's right to economic autonomy, debts to the British proved intensely galling to Virginian pride.

If the Revolution threw up different, if not unprecedented challenges for distant plantation owners who wished to survey their agricultural investments, it also revived ideological concerns surrounding the relationship between planters and their social subordinates. Still powerfully influenced by the notion of personal, face-to-face authority over dependents, many patriarchs found the war years acutely trying. Difficulties of communication and distance created more hurdles to the enacting of their authority than they had yet experienced.[23] Wartime societal dislocation threatened to injure planters' hard-won reputations as patriarchal rulers of dependents. In 1778 condemnation of Alexander Gray's plantation management by Patrick Tonyn, governor of the British colony of Florida, compelled Gray to aver that "the white people as well as the negroes are entirely at my Command."[24]

Bondpeople's oppositional activity was destructive enough in peacetime, but faced with the steady erosion of direct control over their plantations, and apprehensive that the confusion of war would offer novel opportunities for enslaved men and women to escape, southern planters confronted the very real possibility of losing their entire capital investment in humans. Political events honed their fears. In his infamous proclamation of November 1775, John Murray, Lord Dunmore, the royal governor of Virginia, with the sanction of the British government pledged enslaved bondmen belonging to rebel owners their freedom in return for fighting on behalf of the Loyalists.[25] Commanding the American army in Cambridge, Massachusetts, George Washington was alarmed: "if that Man is not crushed before spring, he will become the most formidable Enemy America has—his strength will Increase as a Snow ball by Rolling."[26] In a dramatic enactment of the need that planters felt to intervene at crisis times, Robert Carter III just after the Declaration of Independence "directed Mathew Leonard, overseer to collect together most of [his] slaves" at his Cole's Point plantation "to who [he] made a Speech":

> I observed therein that the King of Great Britain had declared War ag[ain]st the people of the Colony of Virginia [and the other mainland colonies] . . . that Many of the people in Great Britain disapproved of the present Dispute between them and the 13 united Colonies in North America, and had refused to enlist as Soldiers, therefor the King of G.B. had employed foreign Soldiers to fight for him ag[ain]st us; That—Lord Dunmore, had called upon the black people in North America to join him—and he has declared that all white indentured servants & Slaves, who may run away from their masters & enter into the King's service shall be free, & that their masters should have no future claim whatever ag[ain]st them—Question—will [Dunmore] not sell [the Slaves] to white people living in the West Islands?

Carter then moved from stoking his bondpeople's fears to appealing to their better judgment. "Do any of ye dislike y[ou]r present condition of Life, as do wish to enter into L[or]d D[u]n[more's] Service, & trust to the consequences?" The proud patriarch caricatured the people's response as both loyal and patriotic: "we do not wish to enter into L[or]d D[unmore']s [army] to fight ag[ain]st ye white People of the 15 united provinces—but we all fully intend to serve you our master and we do now promise to use our whole might & force to execute your Commands." But soon Carter was back both to threats, and to presenting himself as the enslaved people's salvation: "if any of L[or]d Dunmore's party of men should land on Coles-point, that ye black men, take your wives, children, male & female Acquantances,

Cloths, beding & tools, removing all into private places . . . and send a person off to Nomony Hall, immediately, to advise me w[ha]t Place ye are gotten too and I will then give Directions, tending for your imediate relief."[27]

Despite the entreaties made by people like Carter, close to eight hundred bondpeople were believed to have joined Dunmore's army, confirming the Proclamation's capacity to deprive white Patriots of their livelihood and independence.[28] Landon Carter lost eleven bondpeople to the British ranks; while Carter's exhortation seems to have worked in the short term, thirty-two of his bondpeople fled when the British returned in 1781.[29] Perhaps more cognizant of the threat to property than fearful of rebellion, the Virginian General Convention responded by guaranteeing that "all such [slaves], who have taken this unlawful and wicked step, may return in safety to their duty, and escape the punishment due to their crimes."[30] Whether George Washington's bondman Frederick—and others among his enslaved force—ran away to the British or were removed by them is unclear.[31] Yet the general's financial worries are unmistakable: he records that Frederick was "about 45 years old; an overseer and valuable."[32] Little wonder that Washington, invoking the language of natural jurisprudence prevalent at the time, would condemn Dunmore as "that arch traitor to the rights of humanity."[33] Though a slaveholder himself, for reasons of military expediency the royal governor had mounted an assault on free men's unalienable right to property.[34]

Further south disquiet at the British army's attempts to enlist enslaved men had been voiced as early as 1773. Two years before Concord and Lexington, these actions portended the opportunistic tactics that Loyalists would employ during the Revolutionary War.[35] In 1776 Henry Laurens recounted to his son how the British ship the *Active* landed at "Bull's Island the property of Capt. Shubrick" with "40 White & 20 black Men" before augmenting her "black Guard by stealing Six more Negroes."[36] Laurens decried this "inglorious privilege" and made a similar appeal to his bondpeople's loyalty to that attempted by Robert Carter.[37] John Lewis Gervais, corresponding with Henry Laurens, imagined that the British deeds constituted a personal assault: "I dread at the same time to learn that among others they have carried off all my negros They have a great spleen against me particularly."[38] The Philipsburg Proclamation of 30 June 1779, issued just prior to General Clinton's ill-fated southern campaign, gave this rather extemporaneous policy de facto legitimacy. Clinton advised that all bondpeople taken in rebel service by the British armies would be sold for the benefit of their captors, but promised that those who deserted for Loyalist lines would be awarded "full security to follow within these Lines, any Occupation which [they] shall think proper"; in the same year hundreds of blacks fought in the defense of Savannah against the Americans and French.[39] Overseer William Ancrum was not surprised to discover in 1780 "the Desertion of the Negroes" from Margaret Colleton's quarters, since they had been "so much encourage[d] to."[40]

Though the war did not end happily for Britain, the economic effects of its actions would long resound in America. In 1786, after the dust of revolutionary tumult had settled, Aaron Loocock made an appraisal of John Nassau Colleton's South Carolina plantations. Of fifty-five enslaved people residing at his quarters at the outset of war, one-fifth had been either "carried off" or "enticed away."[41] It is difficult to assess with precision the total number of people who deserted their owners, but estimates, by contemporaries as well as historians, put the figure at between eighty and one hundred thousand men and women.[42] In Georgia Samuel Stiles reckoned at the beginning of 1786 that there were not "enough [bondpeople] left after the war to put them on the Plantation belonging to the Estate, the buildings &ca being destroyed—to rebuild which, pay Overseer &ca was more than the Estate could afford."[43] Georgia saw perhaps as many as 90 percent of its enslaved people either removed by Loyalist owners or the British, stolen, or departed.[44] In South Carolina John Lloyd reported that "the seasons for several years after the peace were entirely unfavourable[;] consequently my estate was not productive. Had not my Creditors been uncommonly lenient my estate would soon have been sold."[45] Not by any means were slaveholders' losses entirely the result of Dunmore and Clinton's proclamations—enslaved people fled in the confusion of war. Yet the generals' actions perhaps had a galvanizing effect on white society. They were of particular importance in convincing wavering backcountry slaveholders to join the Revolutionary cause and underlined the importance of the overseer's wartime role in preventing desertion by the enslaved.[46]

Southerners believed, then, that their apprehension about the British measures was warranted. But perhaps the greatest menace to the order of southern plantation societies emanated from slaveholders themselves. White people's calls for liberty and independence, growing increasingly voluble up to 1775, could take on hazardous connotations when adapted by the South's enslaved laborers. Libertarian rhetoric, once unleashed, respected no class or racial boundary, and astute bondpeople laid claim to its intoxicating promises of freedom. Southerners were alert to the volatility of their republican creed, recognizing that in a world of numerous and daily interracial transactions, its tenets could spread among the enslaved with ease. After all, with colorful demonstrations against British authority taking place on the streets of southern cities, the subversive tone to the Patriot cause was difficult to conceal. John Adams, on a 1775 visit to South Carolina, remarked on the danger of discussing such events within earshot of black people: "the negroes have a wonderful art of communicating intelligence among themselves; it will run several hundreds of miles in a week or fortnight."[47] Bondpeople owned by Patriots had particularly intense exposure to the Revolutionary debates—a conspiracy discovered in July 1775 in Charleston almost exclusively involved people enslaved by prominent revolutionaries.[48]

Libertarian rhetoric emboldened bondpeople to resist those who aspired to command them.[49] Combined with the withering away of traditional structures of patriarchal control, this newfound confidence profoundly shocked those who had come to expect obedience. Ishmael, a bondman belonging to James Laurens, spoke soon after the war to Thomas Owen, an overseer who was engaged in locating the whereabouts of Laurens's enslaved people on behalf of James's father, Henry. "Ishmael," John Lewis Gervais wrote, indignant, "says he will go back to you willingly before the final evacuation of this place but not at present, and I find it is not in my power to compel him."[50] Bondpeople were well aware of the freedoms that accrued to them in the fractured slave society. Without intended irony Lund Washington related to his cousin that among the black people and indentured servants on the Washington plantations there was "not a man of them but would leave us if they believ'd they could make there escape. . . . Liberty is sweet."[51]

Southern authorities responded to these challenges much as they had done before the Revolution, when they faced the related dilemma of upholding order on far-flung absentee plantations. They reemphasized oversight's pivotal role in the containment of enslaved rebellion and, at least in the early stages of war, continued to forbid overseer enlistment in the militia—hence Virginia's 1775 law that retained managerial exemptions for the coming conflict in order to restore order and control on larger plantations where slaves were agitating for their own independence.[52] It is apparent, too, that a small number of overseers avoided mustering by virtue of their advanced age.[53] Whatever their grounds for remaining at their stations, certain overseers carried out a function that would prove integral to the Patriots' victory: Thomas Egan, employed by Margaret Colleton, provided "sundry ferriages" and "Chargo."[54] The enemy needed provisioning too, in which instance Robert Carter urged pragmatism. He directed his overseer to "attend to the growing Crops at Coles point Plantation as usual, keep a constant look out & . . . if any [British soldiers] should land here & demand Provisions, do not refuse, but whatever provisions that may be taken by them, refuse money or any other Consideration, if any may be offered for Provisions."[55] In Georgia William Gibbons's plantations were visited in 1779 by "the Light Dragoons . . . [who] killed seven hoggs and turned their horse in the field," as well as helping themselves to a bushel of potatoes.[56]

Managerial sympathies did not lie uniformly with the rebels. The military records of both sides are too incomplete, and the names of many overseers too commonplace, for any general conclusions to be drawn.[57] Nonetheless contemporary accounts seem to confirm the existence of Loyalist overseers. It must have aggrieved John Lewis Gervais deeply to inform the ardent Patriot Henry Laurens—who went on to represent the new United States at the Paris peace conference—in a letter of 1782 that one of his overseers, Mr. Campbell, had left his post and "was at Charles Town with the Enemy."[58] Yet Laurens was happy to maintain a Loyalist overseer, Andrew Campbell, in his employ although Campbell regularly mustered with the British enemy. Laurens's respect for his managerial qualities in this instance outweighed their political disagreements.[59] Josiah Smith had to contend not only with broken rice dams when he surveyed his Georgia plantation in 1780—Smith's Tory overseer had also taken some of his bondpeople away, as did George Aaron, one of Laurens's overseers.[60] Personal choice, rather than legal restrictions, determined managerial loyalties.

Laws excusing overseers from enlisting in the Revolutionary forces were quickly overturned.[61] Barely four months after the Declaration of Independence, the Virginian slaveholder and Patriot Francis Lightfoot Lee wrote to Landon Carter of the "impropriety of Overseers mustering," prompted by the recent abandonment of Virginia's exemption law.[62] Neither were lowcountry overseers exempt. The managers of Margaret Colleton's lands in Berkeley County, South Carolina, were both "draughted" in January 1779; five of Ralph Izard's six overseers enlisted in the Continental Army in the first year of the war.[63] Supervisors who remained on their plantations might face contact with the British—William Roddick and his wife were threatened and robbed by passing soldiers on Laurens's plantations in 1780.[64]

"Draughting" included no requirement to serve the length of the war, however. Armies did not fight all year round—indeed most battles took place during the summer months, when overseers were least occupied. And militia membership did not lead inevitably to service; it simply entailed the possibility of enlistment into the Continental Army or mobilization for state duty. Archibald McKewn, later overseer for John Ewing Colhoun, performed "28 Days Militia Duty in 1782," for which he received "St[erlin]g £2:11:9"; but he claimed—contrary to the army's opinion—to have "never received any" of his due wages for "twenty nine Days Servis in Genl Marions Brigade as a Sargent."[65] Less grandly William Yates, a Laurens employee, spent "30 days . . . as Private in the Militia," also in 1782.[66] Peter Papot, an overseer in Georgia for William Gibbons, "left the plantation the 9th June, 1778 to go upon the expedition to the Southward. He returnd from the expedition in August."[67]

Why did southerners nullify exemption laws at the outset of the Revolutionary War, even as they confronted the greatest ever threat to their slaveholdings? It seems certain that pragmatism won out in the initial debates over managerial enlistment. Though the Continental Army adopted guerrilla-style tactics against the highly regimented British battalions, legislators in the Chesapeake and lowcountry had scant notion that the conflict would take the limited form that it eventually did. Southern administrations perennially were terrified of Indian raids on their western boundaries and desired to arm all military-age men against a combined offensive by British and Indian forces. The Second Cherokee War of 1776, in which Indians agreed with the British to attack the frontier from Georgia to North Carolina, cemented their worries. Most influential in the decision to overturn the laws were supply concerns. South Carolina and Georgia possessed in Savannah and Charleston two of North America's most accessible ports; Virginia bestrode the equally navigable Chesapeake Bay. When the British armies wheeled south, first on Clinton's campaign, next on Cornwallis's fateful adventure to Yorktown, local militias equipped for their challenge.

At least in Virginia, a further, political imperative appears to have informed the legislators' actions. The state's circumspect gentry looked to garner popular support among citizens who understood the conflict to be primarily a merchants' war, waged for all-too-abstract ideological reasons. Elites aspired to forestall divisions among the white lower classes, for racial solidarity represented a sturdy redoubt against the threat of slave uprising. Small farmers from Lunenburg County in Virginia's southside frontier region identified class privilege in managerial exemptions: they grumbled that wealthy slaveholders "are become Overseers that otherways wou'd not, on purpose to Secure themselves from fighting."[68] More than a quarter of the militia from neighboring Amelia County also complained about the exemption. They felt that there were at least 250 overseers—or another quarter of the whole militia in the county—who were exempted from regular militia service. Petitioners believed that many of these men were "possessed of Considerable Property in Lands and Slaves."[69]

Planters abused the exemption in other ways. Robert Carter requested the militia colonel of Westmoreland County to remove one Robert Mitchell from the list of those required to muster. Mitchell had been employed as a clerk and steward, not as an overseer.[70] And if overseers—most of whom were single men—did not enlist, minor planters feared that the authorities would conscript them instead. With the chief provider absent, their families risked severe economic deprivation.[71] In discarding the 1775 exemption law, Virginian burgesses therefore attempted to show a responsive, judicious face to the populace. South Carolinian grand juries witnessed similar depositions, though overseer involvement in wartime slave patrols exercised plaintiffs there. The residents believed that these supplementary patrollers exploited the slave patrol needs of their state to avoid serving in the militia, at a time when the Revolutionary struggle was going badly.[72]

Debates over managerial exemptions are illustrative of later attitudes toward the overseer profession. While on the one hand legislators acknowledged overseers' vital function in subduing oppositional activity among the enslaved, on the other hand, when Virginia, South Carolina, and Georgia faced the existential threat of a foreign invading force, the requirements of this more precipitate danger superseded oversight's internal defensive role. The small planters' skepticism, furthermore, bespoke a deep-seated and abiding wariness of overseers. Far from trusting in the centrality of oversight, in voicing their suspicions they reemphasized managers' peripheral social standing and reaffirmed the mistrust that dependents inspired in the eighteenth-century Anglo-Saxon world.[73] Elites were the principal originators of negative overseer stereotypes, but their shrewd sensitivity to these more extensively held animosities amounted to a significant juncture in the development of southern prejudices against managers. Because they resulted from comparable dialogic processes, similar prejudices would find a broad and receptive audience in the closing decades of the eighteenth century.

To emphasize the political and ideological climate of white society during the Revolutionary War is, perhaps, to discount bondpeople's own fervent and long-standing yearnings for freedom. So many people heeded Dunmore and Clinton's promises precisely because manumission would fulfill their dearest dreams, and libertarian rhetoric could take root only in already fertile soil. Further still to focus our attention on those who chanced "to make there escape" in pursuit of their "Liberty" as freedpeople is to ignore myriad other acts of resistance by southern enslaved people. A number of these acts—the murder of an overseer for example—were spectacular, both in terms of the gruesome repercussions that faced the people who committed them, and in the horror that they aroused in the white population. Enslaved people who were found guilty of rebellion were hanged, and their bodies often burned.[74] Some acts were more humdrum, drawn from the arsenals of everyday resistance that enslaved populations had stockpiled for a hundred years.

Bondpeople were opportunists. Whether they fought for the Loyalist (or indeed the Patriot) cause, or whether they remained on their quarters, preferring familiarity to a fugitive life, enslaved people strove persistently to benefit from the circumstances in which they found themselves.[75] Others sought the familiarity of their loved ones, and during the war many such bondpeople took themselves off. Often alone, and with little faith in the assistance of slave patrols, overseers suffered the absences of men like William Ancrum's Billy, who was suspected of being "some Way near Town where he has a Bro[ther] whom Mr Kershaw lately hired."[76] Similarly Ned, rented in 1778 to work one of Ancrum's South Carolinian plantations, "two days ago . . . again Decamped." "I have not rec[eive]d any tidings of him," reported Ancrum, concluding that, "as he seemed to be attached to his old Range, he probably has again steered his Course Northwardly."[77]

Billy and Ned's oppositional activity was not strictly equivalent to the actions of those people who sought manumission. Their disappearances were very likely temporary: they were more accurately guilty of "truancy" than flight.[78] William Ancrum expected Ned to come again "into [his] hands," in which instance he promised Ned's owner, Parker Quince, that he would "dispose of him as you direct." In similar fashion some of Henry Laurens's people at Mount Tacitus "emigrated to Mepkin" during the war, a Laurens plantation on the Cooper River.[79] But Billy and Ned comprehended, with so many others across the South, that the Revolution offered them unique and frequent chances to ameliorate in however small a manner their pitiable situation. Prefiguring the "saturnalic claims" of their counterparts in the Civil War, enslaved people made revolutionary claims not only on language and ideas, but on space and time, too: in clear recognition of their managers' impotence, they discovered new opportunities to run away, or shirk at their daily labor.[80] Robert Carter of Nomini Hall noted that over the course of nine days in 1781, thirty-two bondpeople left his plantation.[81] In this way the conflict became an enslaved revolution against white control as much as a free rebellion against British taxation.[82]

White contemporaries fretted about the revolutionary intentions of enslaved people. Rumors of revolts abounded, fuelled by infrequent yet nonetheless terrifying instances of the real thing, in southern cities like Wilmington, North Carolina.[83] Whites gave increasingly weighty credence to the prewar legal notion that blacks were a seditious "enemy within," and Lord Dunmore's deeds put their anxieties into sharp focus. The Virginian governor was rumored to be planning his proclamation as early as March 1775. In June James Madison wrote that Dunmore "has it in contemplation to make great Use of [the slaves] in case of a civil war in this province . . . if we should be subdued, we shall fall like Achilles by the hand of one that knows that secret."[84] Even those bondpeople who resisted Dunmore and Clinton's enticements were viewed in a suspicious light. Envisioning the conclusions reached by modern students of subaltern resistance, overseers (who were charged with the early detection of potential sedition) suspected that small, plantation-level acts of enslaved rebellion presaged larger, and more insidious, political aims.[85] In November 1779 William Ancrum expressed in a letter to the overseer Marlow Pryor his pleasure that "your Insurgents have been disappointed in their villainous Stratagems," adding that he hoped "such Measures will be taken as to secure You from any attempt of the like nature in future."[86]

Ancrum's purple language betrayed his horror of insurrectionary activity as well as his distrust of enslaved people. But he made, albeit indirectly, an accurate evaluation of the resistance that bondpeople offered to overseers. Enslaved resistance gained its greatest meaning in the perpetual battle against white authority. Like all combatants Pryor's "Insurgents" would have rehearsed their "villainous Stratagems" on many previous occasions.[87] Now that war had arrived, time wasting, feigning illness, and truanting not only became more feasible: as long as the Revolution permitted enslaved people "to do visibly what formerly had been cloaked," it also permitted them to make, as part of a large-scale "revolutionary movement," a "political breakthrough."[88] The potentiality of small yet frequent rebellious acts to engender mass resistance finds confirmation in the enslaved response to the Dunmore and Clinton Proclamations. Though many planters would take on the unshakable conviction that their loyal men and women had been "carried away" in British raids, the penchant for absenteeism exhibited by some bondpeople prior to the conflict tells a different tale. It is likely that enslaved people acquired knowledge of their local terrain from acquaintances who had truanted before, or from those bondpeople—boatmen or carriage drivers, for instance—whose occupations permitted them to travel away from the plantation.[89] This, then, was educated flight: the information that they shared empowered bondpeople to steal themselves from their owners.[90] John Lewis Gervais's conversation with Ishmael during the Revolutionary War serves as confirmation that bondpeople assisted each other in running away. Ishmael "pretend[ed] to know nothing of where any of the others [were]."[91]

Clashes between the managerial duty to suppress resistance and bondpeople's newfound confidence proved most cataclysmic when they centered on the established rights of the enslaved. These fall under two broad categories. First, after years of struggle before the war, the enslaved had won their owners' consent for "customary rights."[92] Second, men and women enjoyed what might be called "revolutionary rights"—the "saturnalic" opportunities that many people now regarded as entitlements, and which slaveholders and overseers viewed as anything but. Bondpeople rebuffed this taxonomy, strenuously rejecting attempts to delegitimate the second group. Yet they were quick to invoke the sanctioned legitimacy of their customary rights when it proved useful. Mindful of planter endorsement, bondpeople continued to cultivate and market their own produce throughout the Revolutionary War.[93]

Overseers and enslaved people clashed frequently in the colonial period; where relations between the two parties differed between 1775 and 1782, however, was in the increased volatility of their disagreements. Managers were aware of the need to treat their charges with an especial subtlety to avoid provoking enslaved flight to the British lines. They were aware, too, that the absence of effective support from elsewhere weakened their claims to the monopoly of plantation violence. But rendered ignorant of enslaved people's customary rights by difficulties of communication with their employers, many overseers sternly reemphasized the plantation's rules—with often disastrous consequences. Recall the group of South Carolinian bondpeople who attempted to murder their supervisor in 1781 when he tried to appropriate the corn, grown in their time off, that they had reserved for sale.[94]

Whenever beleaguered wartime managers reinforced spatial strictures, they also made temporal demands. Savannah in 1779 witnessed the overseer Joseph Weatherly violate his workers' "revolutionary rights" both to their autonomy of movement and the ownership of their time. He threatened "to punish any Negroe that refused to go with him to Ogeechee" and further aggravated one bondman, Charles, by "following [and] troubling him." Bondpeople saw with clarity that overseers also worked under restraints (their lack of outside succor being the most pertinent), and some fiercely resisted those managers who transgressed. James Weatherly's miserable fate was to be killed by Charles and another slave whom he had attempted to co-opt.[95]

If fruitless "Stratagems" enlivened white fears of the enslaved, the wartime murder of an overseer generated an even more fervid reaction. Such anxieties reflected a profound concern for the survival of the entire slave system. By blurring the overseer's unique right to violent sanction, even those people who merely attempted violence against their supervisors introduced a corrosive agent to the South's façade of stability. Perhaps worse for white authority, in choosing to resist the delimitations of their everyday lives bondpeople also revealed themselves to be canny political actors. Even men and women who chose not to not make "saturnalic claims" on time and space were taught by their more adventurous counterparts of a "rival geography" that transcended the plantation's borders, an alternative space where enslaved people successfully disputed the restrictions inflicted on them.[96] Like Joseph Weatherly's assailants, many of the bondpeople who did make such claims transformed the mechanisms of spatial and temporal suasion into focal points of violent oppositional activity that threatened to test the plantation power structure to its limits.[97] Made to accompany Joseph Weatherly on a previous visit to the Ogechee River plantation, Charles had noted a propitious topography for the execution of his plan. He tried to convince "the rest of the Negroes" to "go out to Ogechee and kill Mr. Weatherly, by hiding themselves in the Bushes and shooting him as he rode along."[98]

The American Revolution comprised no general enslaved revolt along the lines that white Virginians, South Carolinians, and Georgians had apprehended.[99] But bondpeople's activities during the war would have long-lived consequences for their relations with supervisors. Whether, like Harman Utterback, overseers lingered on the same quarters that they had administered between 1775 and 1782, or whether they moved elsewhere, perhaps establishing plantations of their own, the lessons that they learned during these tumultuous years burned vividly in the collective managerial conscience. Despite the postwar reinvigoration of mechanisms of slave control, overseers would have had to think carefully before transgressing enslaved people's hard-won rights. In their everyday interactions, they must have acknowledged that a greater level of delicacy was now expedient in order to avoid the devastating outcomes that many colleagues had experienced firsthand. George Washington remarked in 1781 on the difficulties of returning escaped men and women to their former subordinated status, while Eliza Lucas Pinckney complained that the war had permitted enslaved men and women to "do as they please anywhere."[100] She claimed that her own workforce "behaved so infamously and even those who remain'd at home [were] so Insolent and quite their own masters."[101] Though overseers and planters offered firm opposition, the Revolution had permitted bondpeople to alter subtly, but in a multiplicity of permanent ways, the boundaries of American slavery.[102]

Whites, then, were avowedly sensitive to the broad spectrum of freedoms that America's Revolution yielded its enslaved captives. Yet it was an ironic, if predictable, result of wartime slave resistance that even as oversight confronted its sternest test, popular criticism of the profession reached a crescendo. Again this stemmed from the anger that many planters felt over the ravages done to their lands and enslaved property. Witnesses linked the dilapidation of outlying quarters to deficient superintendence of the enslaved. Following Margaret Colleton's death in 1779, William Ancrum undertook to manage the sale of her South Carolinian estates. He explained to James Edward Colleton in Berkshire, England, that "Altho' the Seasons have been favourable[,] yet from . . . the small pox Spreading among [the slaves] & their being under little or no Subjection to the Overseers, I am very apprehensive for the Crop now on the Ground."[103] Ishmael, the bondman whom Thomas Owen memorably was unable to "compel" to return to his plantation, had stocked up on confidence in the absence of a resident overseer.

The managers of unsupervised plantations might have been enlisted, or simply might have deserted their posts. But the connection between overseer failings and the incomplete subordination of the enslaved labor force was an important and enduring one. It was also somewhat paradoxical, as demonstrated by the causal logic to which William Ancrum subscribed. Stimulated by traditional prejudices toward dependents, in his letter he damned managerial inconstancy and unreliability. Yet he implicitly acknowledged oversight's integral position by linking the plantation's squalor to overseer disappearances. Akin to those Virginians who petitioned against managerial militia exemptions, Ancrum had bought into a widespread, though antinomic distinction that would become markedly influential in succeeding decades. Precisely because the importance of overseeing had expanded during the Revolution, southerners highlighted the incapacity of overseers to carry out their more extensive responsibilities.

Bondpeople sometimes ended up with no overseer at all not because of managerial desertions but because wartime deprivations made managerial recruitment trying during periods of urgency. John Lewis Gervais had in mind an overseer for Henry Laurens's plantations during Laurens's captivity in the Tower of London, but the overseer died. On inspecting one of Laurens's quarters, Gervais found that "Montezuma," a bondman, "was Commander in Chief, and take it upon the whole I think they have behaved very well, however some of the Negroes had emigrated to [Laurens's home plantation of] Mepkin."[104] Reports like this served to shore up the postwar conviction of some slaveholders that bondpeople were gratifyingly loyal, while the position of overseers was less assured.[105]

Overseer conduct in the Revolutionary War had a substantial impact on how managers were later portrayed. Between 1775 and 1782, the suspicions of critics such as William Ancrum were everywhere borne out. Most real-world overseers lacked the abilities that eighteenth-century laws inferred; few successfully adjusted their management style to bondpeople's magnified opportunities for flight and other forms of resistance. Instead—seeking new ways to assert their supremacy, and under the threat of attack by enslaved men and women—overseers inclined toward the old modes of violent dominance. Whether or not managers employed *more* violence than they had done before the war is difficult to ascertain.[106] But it is probable that they defined their fragile rule with frequent recourse to vicious discipline, much as bondpeople in the Revolution violently repelled their supervisors in an effort to redefine the boundaries of their subjection.

In demanding overseer enlistment during the American Revolutionary War, southerners were forever conscious that they risked compromising their society's internal stability for the benefit of its external security. They were conscious, too, that overseeing would become increasingly untenable with the evanescence of slave patrols and other measures of control. Nevertheless managerial failures to check the wartime flight of human property—combined with their failure to dampen enslaved resistance—served merely to strengthen the popular conception of oversight's importance. This was also the period in which normative critiques of the oversight system came to the fore. Individual mistakes contributed inexorably to the general censure of the managerial profession, but additional condemnation arose from wartime discrepancies between societal imperatives and structural deterioration, between juridical expectations and plantation reality, and between the integral significance of oversight and the liminal social status of its practitioners, critiques that galvanized irreparably during the closing decades of the 1700s.

Epilogue

"Little better . . . than human brutes"— The Consolidation of Anti-overseer Stereotypes

In their memoirs and novels, nineteenth-century abolitionists decried the capricious temper, arbitrariness of judgment, and insatiable sadism that, they believed, characterized plantation overseers. The best-known contemporary account of life under slavery, Frederick Douglass's *My Bondage and My Freedom,* portrayed plantation managers as "little better than . . . human brute[s]," wont to accuse bondpeople of "'impudence,'" "one of the commonest and most indefinite in the whole catalogue of offences usually laid to the charge of slaves."[1] This, Douglass explained, might "mean almost anything, or nothing at all, just according to the caprice of . . . the overseer, at the moment."[2] Douglass's critiques of overseeing feature another motif common in abolitionist writing: in order to present a riposte to southern claims of gallantry and chivalry, he and others exposed the horrendous violence that overseers perpetrated against women. Recounting the arrival of his cousin Milly, Douglass described her neck and shoulders as "covered with scars, newly made; and not content with marring her neck and shoulders, with the cowhide, the cowardly [overseer] had dealt her a blow on the head with a hickory club, which cut a horrible gash, and left her face literally covered with blood."[3]

The twin themes of overseer caprice and violence against women appear in unison in many other abolitionists' works. One enslaved character in an 1857 novel attributed his overseer's violence to an inability to control his emotions, reporting that, "'de oberseer, he dreffful mad . . . an' whip and crack de slaves like ebery ting.'" His friend concurred: "'I hearn im' say . . . dat he'd put 'er in de ground widout nothin' on 'er, an' kick an' break 'er bones, and pull and burn 'er tongue, [because] she hollered de oder night.'"[4] A further fictional bondman upbraided an overseer for attacking his wife without cause and resolved to take physical action. Rushing forward, "and before the overseer was aware, he seized his whip, snatched it from his hand; and demanded what he meant by beating a woman in that way, for no offence whatever."[5] Harriet Beecher Stowe's overseers were the embodiment of antebellum slavery's pernicious cruelty. One of her characters described a manager as a "great, tall, slabsided, two-fisted renegade son of Vermont . . . who had gone through a regular apprenticeship in hardness and brutality and taken his degree to be admitted to practice. . . . [He was] the absolute despot of the estate."[6]

Violence was personified in the overseer, and the overseer was defined by violence. In literature he came to be represented not in person, but by what one historian has called his "badge of office": when some fictional masters attacked the enslaved, they did so armed not with their own but with "the overseer's whip."[7] Pre–Civil War proslavery literature was no more generous in its depiction of overseers and contrasted their violence with the putatively gentler regimes of those with a proprietorial attachment to bondpeople. An anonymous "slave" in an 1857 article described overseers as "those dreaded and despised obstacles between slaves and their owners, who commonly have no bowels of compassion for the slave, and care little for the interests of the master." The owner of the "slave," on the other hand, if he "thought it necessary to reprove [him], 'twas always more in kindness than in anger, and to blows he never resorted."[8] A nineteenth-century tract entitled *Rules for the Government and Management of Slaves, to Be Observed by the Overseer* warned that while "the Proprietor is always ready to excuse such errors as may proceed from want of judgement; . . . he never can or will excuse any cruelty, severity or want of care towards the negroes." An overseer was "to conduct the business steadily and firmly, without weakness on the one hand, or harshness on the other." No abusive language or violence of demeanor was permitted, as "they reduce the man who uses them to a level with the negro."[9] And the Alabama journal *Southern Agriculturist* opined that "the overseer . . . *presses everything at the end of the lash; pays no attention to the sick . . . and drives them out again at the first moment. He has no other interest than to make a big . . . crop.*"[10]

The vitality of this characterization was such that it recurs in the works of later authors. In particular violence and overseeing go hand in hand in the late twentieth-century novels that appeared in the years after the 1960s civil rights movement. In one of the most widely read, Alex Haley's *Roots,* among the first English words that the newly arrived Mandinka bondman Kunta Kinte learns is "oberseer," his lexicon broadened as a result of an attempted escape. Again the overseer drives his point home at the end of a lash that cuts "into the flesh across Kunta's shoulders and back, with the "oberseer" grunting and Kunta shuddering under the force of each blow."[11] Managerial violence against women also features in recent literature. In Toni Morrison's prize-winning work *Beloved,* the overseer "Schoolteacher" takes over the plantation on which the principal character, the bondwoman Sethe, grew up. There he institutes a violent regime that forces Sethe to run away.[12]

The "enlightened patriarchal" era linked the early growth of anti-overseer prejudices among pro- and antislavery voices in the patriarchal era with the consolidation of these ideas in the nineteenth century. Absenteeism already had given overseers a level of responsibility for the instigation of violent punishment that made many planters uneasy; in the years following the Revolution, new ways of understanding violence against enslaved men and women compounded their unease.

Prejudices against overseers due to their position as dependent men went in new directions, too. Southern planters were among some of the most prominent authors of the Constitution of the new Republic. The debates around that document centered on the correct uses and balance of power, and slaveholders posed the same questions in the management of their estates. Mistrust of dependents' abilities to supervise others gained new vitality as Americans strove to construct a new nation that would preserve the independence and freedoms for which they had fought so hard.

The profit motive affected patriarchs' assessment of the overseer-slave dynamic in two significant ways. First, planters were anxious that managers treat bondpeople in a manner that did not engender loss-making discontent; second, they feared for the long-term health of their human property under excessively violent regimes. Yet some of the pronouncements made by slave owners in the closing decades of the eighteenth century suggest that less prosaic concerns were beginning to have sway. Around the time of the Revolution, no doubt under the influence of his antislavery son, John, Henry Laurens seems to have begun to believe that the concern that he expressed for enslaved people's well-being derived from something more than profit. On one occasion, referring to a sick bondman, he urged the overseer of one of his Georgian plantations to "be kind to Berom in his affliction."[13] Some planters believed that this emotional relationship worked in both directions. In 1776, barely a month after the Declaration of Independence, Laurens wrote a letter to his son, who was studying law in England. A notable phrase related Laurens's belief that his enslaved workers "to a man . . . are strongly attached to me," and would not desert him despite the opportunities for flight that the war had brought: "so are all of mine in [South Carolina], hitherto not one of them has attempted to desert on the contrary those who are most exposed hold themselves always ready to fly from the Enemy in case of a sudden descent—."[14] His testimony demonstrates the influence of early enlightened sentiment, which, though more prevalent among planters of the Upper South, was expressed more and more frequently in South Carolina and Georgia by late century.

One of the most influential deconstructions of American slaveholder paternalism, Eugene D. Genovese's *Roll, Jordan, Roll,* traced the development of paternalist ideology to antebellum southern plantations.[15] More recently historians of colonial American slavery have detected in the outlook of planters such as Henry Laurens evidence of an earlier transformation. Philip D. Morgan's account of the growth of prepaternalistic ideas in the eighteenth-century Virginian Chesapeake and South Carolinian lowcountry is especially useful in accounting for changing attitudes toward overseers. Morgan views the emergence of "enlightened patriarchalism" (which, for reasons outlined above, is referred to here as "enlightened patriarchism") as the result of three pivotal alterations to the patriarchal doctrine. First, although slave owners toward the end of the century continued, like their early patriarch forbears, to stress order and authority, they were more inclined to emphasize their generous treatment of the enslaved labor force. Second, as planters came to highlight their kindness toward enslaved men and women, they came also to expect gratitude, and perhaps even love, in return.[16] Third, where early patriarchs rarely boasted of the submissiveness of their bondpeople, being rather more inclined to underline their rebelliousness, "enlightened" planters gradually came to create the fiction of the contented slave.[17]

Enlightened sentiment grew out of new, closer emotional ties between white and black. By this juncture many bondpeople had grown up on home plantations alongside their owners, with the result that late eighteenth-century slaveholders were often more respectful of enslaved family ties than their predecessors had been, often ensuring that people were sold in family units rather than on their own. Planters were also inspired by a growing sentimentalism that vaunted emotional linkages between people, typified best in the Atlantic context by the publication of Adam Smith's *The Theory of Moral Sentiments*.[18] In 1746 Joseph Ball had agreed only grudgingly to allow a bondman, Jo, to visit his wife "once a month," arguing that "if his wife & he are so fond of each other, she must come at other times to him."[19] His fellow Virginian Francis Jerdone willingly broke up enslaved families for sale.[20] Moreover plantation owners saw the enslaved family primarily as a reproductive unit. On another occasion Ball advised a female slaveholder, "and as to the Negro Children . . . I should think, the Calf should go with the Cow."[21] The gravest violation of enslaved bodies lay in patriarchs' manipulation of their reproduction: pairing males and females was less about compassion than social control. Owners wished to sustain a reproducing, biddable, and healthy workforce.[22] William Byrd II proposed in 1729 that planters buy "both sexes, that their breed may supply the loss [because of death]."[23]

This contrasts with Virginian Robert Carter III, who would eventually emancipate his enslaved workforce after embracing Swedenborgianism, deciding that to "retain them in Slavery" was "contrary to the true Principles of Religion and Justice."[24] Carter once sent for sale a "negro woman Mary Anne" who had been "reared in [his] nursery" after she had been accused of beating one of his children. And as a form of punishment, he sold on enslaved people who had deserted him during the Revolution. But he later worried about the consequences of slave marketing for enslaved families and tried to respect bondpeople's familial ties when sending workforces to his various plantations.[25] In 1769 Carter instructed that the "Negroes who have alliances at Bell-air may not be sold . . . & that Negroes be sold with Wife & Husband." Though economic realities constrained his ability to ensure that his wishes were met, he endeavored to influence the sale of bondpeople. Carter reported how "my Wife & I had rather let those Slaves chuse masters in Maryland than send [the]m to Plantations, f[o]r we can not employ [the]m in our Family."[26]

Larger slave units and a higher prevalence of absenteeism than Virginia meant that "the distance between a slave and his master" in the lowcountry was "great."

Lowcountry commentators noted that "a "lack of intimacy" between enslaved people and their owners pertained on large-scale absentee plantations since "many a slave has been born, lived to old age, and died on a plantation, without ever having been within the walls of his master's domicil."[27] Nevertheless enlightened patriarchal statements also appear frequently in southeastern documents. The year 1787 saw sixty residents of Georgetown, South Carolina, petition on behalf of the Cuttino family, who were "very distressed at the prospect of having a [bondperson] executed who has been in the Family a considerable time and for whom they entertain a certain degree of affection."[28] Enslaved family ties were important to certain South Carolinian owners, too: Henry Laurens in 1765 wrote to Elias Ball, son of his late brother-in-law, bemoaning the "division of fathers, mothers, husbands, wives and children who, tho slaves, are still human creatures, and I cannot be deaf to their cries."[29] In Savannah Levi Shefhall rejected a number of offers for a bondman, Ben, but agreed eventually to sell him to Seaborn Jones as "you have his wife and child."[30] An agent to the South Carolinian slaveholder Margaret Colleton reported to her in 1773 that by selling her "Estate . . . [she] would convay away a parcel of old Family Negroes, who being past labour, are supported by you, but would probably be required to work by a less indulgent owner."[31]

As well as the notion that slave sale was undesirable owing to its pernicious effects, explicit in the agent's letter is a further, crucial tenet of enlightened patriarchism: praise for Colleton's benevolence in her treatment of enslaved people. The tendency to appeal to bondpeople ahead of threatening them derived from the unprecedented dislocations of the Revolutionary period. Recalling their losses during the war, when many people fled the plantations (some to Dunmore's army), enlightened patriarchs claimed that they preferred exhortations to violence. A further result of widespread flight was that those who did remain on plantations were considered loyal, a factor in the growing myth of enslaved contentedness.[32] Back in 1754 Joseph Ball had sent a bondwoman, Virginia, to his home plantation from England. Though Ball counseled that "she must be used Tenderly for the first Year at least," Virginia's preferential treatment was not to last. Using her "Tenderly" meant that Ball "would have her put in for half a share"; the year after, having been kept "a little out of Idleness," she would be worked "for a whole share."[33] In marked contrast later slaveholders attempted to convince their correspondents of the benignity of their regimes. Prefiguring defenses of antebellum slavery that stressed slaveholder protection of enslaved people in opposition to the cruelties of capitalistic wage labor, the South Carolinian planter John Lloyd boasted to an English correspondent that "the [European] peasantry are not so happily situated as are the black people in the [United] States."[34]

But in a labor system that centered on force, benevolence conflicted with reality.[35] Many enlightened patriarchs of the late eighteenth century perceived a tension between a continued need to discipline enslaved people, through violence or breaking up families, and the new trend to appear solicitous toward them. Detectable in runaway advertisements from the later part of the 1700s is a tendency for slaveholders publicly to represent themselves as having treated their enslaved people with kindness. Whereas at midcentury a planter noted in a newspaper advert merely that one of his men "ran away without any Cause," by the later 1700s another was moved to declare that he had always been "tender" of his people and "particularly attentive in the good usage of them."[36] John Edmondson reported that a "well made mulatto fellow named Tom" was believed to have run to South Carolina "as his wife was sold to a gentle man there a few months ago, and my refusing to sell him is the only occasion of his running away."[37] Edmondson was prepared to admit to breaking up families, but not to the accusation that he had driven his bondpeople away through force. John Lloyd desired similarly to conceal the more distasteful aspects of slavery. For all his praise for the benevolence of the southern slave system, he advised a correspondent that "concerning the negroes which you have mentioned . . . I think it would be better to sell them in No[rth] Caro[lina] . . . the business I should suppose might be conducted with more privacy in N.C. than in Georgia."[38] And Margaret Colleton had at least considered selling the "parcel of old Family Negroes" along with the land that she wished to dispose of.

As William Byrd had earlier discovered, overseers were of considerable practical use in executing the punishment that remained very necessary to the profitable functioning of the plantation, yet that putatively "loving" owners could not be seen to execute themselves. Almost the epitome of the enlightened slaveholder, Robert Carter of Nomini Hall experienced personally the confusing psychology of the era. On the one hand, he continued to view enslaved people as untrustworthy dependents, worthy of violent punishment; on the other hand, he believed that they were capable of "reform." Fifteen years before his religious conversion he wrote to a supervisor, "I understand that negro David . . . & his wife in W[illiam] sburg have been Saucy to Mrs Crawly who lives att my House there, pray use your Endeavour to reform their behaviour, either by advise, or flogging as you may Judge most likely to affect that purpose."[39] Even when he was just about to emancipate his workforce, an overseer wrote to Carter that "your negroes flushed with notions of freedom particularly at this time will require some vigour."[40] The Virginian steward Charles Dabney advised overseers not to treat bondpeople with more "severity than is Absolutely Necessary to keep them in Subjection. Cruelty to the poor slaves is a thing I always Abhored[;] I should think myself happy cou'd I keep them to there duty without being Obliged to correct them but every person that has had the management of Slaves must know that it is Impossible to manage so large a gang of Negroes without using some severity, it has been my Orders to the Overseers to Overlook small falts in the Negroes under them & to Correct large ones with Moderation."[41] Henry Laurens gave mixed messages too. He advised his overseers that in dealing with enslaved people they should "with the well ones use gentle means . . . mixed with authority at first," while for the more resistant he recommended punishment but with "mercy so that they may be convinced that their end of their correction is to be amendment."[42]

John Steele informed his wife that he had "an affection for [his] black people, and [held] [him]self amenable to heaven for the manner of treating them." His approach to their treatment was detectably a mélange of old patriarchal assumptions and a new expression of some commonality with enslaved people: "if they exercise their duty towards me, you are sure I will act generously and humanely towards them . . . they have most of them sense enough to act in such a manner as will promote their own happiness, and at the same time my interest." Later Steele connoted overseeing with violence. On hiring a new manager, the planter advised that "whipping is disagreeable, and ought not to be resorted to but upon the most urgent necessity."[43] Yet Steele's benevolence—and his criticism of overseers—only extended so far. Because he was away in the then-capital, Philadelphia, Steele left his wife in charge of the plantation. In the same letter, he advised her to order the overseer to deal with a truculent bondman "and have him trounced soundly." Here was the limit of enlightened patriarchism: Steele concluded that "if love for his Master & Mistress will have no influence upon him, perhaps fear may."[44]

The oversight system enabled female planters to employ the same tactic. A Virginian planter, Lucy Thornton, related how her overseer had meted out severe punishment to an enslaved man, her story serving "chiefly to highlight her own sensitivity as a viewer." The bondman recovered "with the loss of three or four days work," but Thornton was so upset by the incident that she recalled that her "life [was] a burden" to her: she believed that the victim had recovered "more quickly and more fully" than herself.[45] By lamenting the violence that they sanctioned and alternating that violence with "little gifts and favors," such women could maintain their self-image as conscientious, restrained, and sensitive planters.[46] Indeed piety did not bar women from calculating how best to use force: their claims of restraint helped "preserve the myth of Christian stewardship."[47]

A second look at Virginian runaway adverts from the later decades of the century reveals how planters abdicated their responsibility for the punishment of enslaved people. Overseers, and not the slaveholders themselves, were to blame for the punishment that had induced men and women to run. The *Virginia Gazette* featured an advertisement for "a Virginia born Negro Woman named BETTY . . . [who] has a Scar on a Breast occasioned by a Stroke from her Overseer."[48] Another suggested that "Phebe" of Essex County, Virginia, "had [a] Propensity for Pleasure in the Night [that] brought a little Punishment from her Overseer, which . . . made her run off."[49] Different sources point to a similar conclusion. George Washington, who by the end of the century was beginning to turn against slavery, in 1795 showed a desire to distance himself from the violence that might accompany a bondperson's arrest.[50] There is some evidence that on occasion Washington had contemplated kidnapping escaped men and women. Yet when one of his people ran away, although he instructed his overseer to take measures to apprehend the fugitive, Washington "would not have [his] name appear in any advertisement, or other measure, leading to it."[51]

Many scholars have underlined the false promises of paternalism, arguing that it was more often a pose that slaveholders put on for one another than a praxis through which they governed their bondpeople.[52] When slaveholders sought to keep families intact, paternalistic sentiment was not necessarily the motivation. Planters recognized that "such relationships [and] especially the sexual order and stability they conferred on the slave quarters . . . were very much to [their] advantage."[53] They "recognized, moreover, the extent to which the enforced separation of black couples, and parents from their children, comprised a powerful motive for running away."[54] Paternalism represented a means through which planters hid their queasy accommodation to the market economy by stressing the mutual obligations that they claimed to hold with their dependents, and by distancing themselves "from the reality of the exploitation that they otherwise encouraged."[55] Indeed the role of violent force was central to the practice of paternalism.[56]

The prejudices leveled at overseers suggest that late eighteenth-century slaveholders sanctioned violence in order to uphold the market profitability of their slaveholdings. But they shifted physical punishment to the periphery of their quarters, into the managerial remit. Because they were dependents, overseers fitted the bill as executors of violence. Crucially slave owners also hid this violence under a rhetorical pall. Unlike Henry Laurens some South Carolinian planters were unmoved by the new enlightened sentiment. John Ewing Colhoun once directed an overseer to "hobble Bella & Marlborough," two known runaways. He would have been under no illusions as to the putative "love" that his people held for him after two of them faced trial for attempting to poison Colhoun and his wife.[57] Yet even this planter was influenced by the rhetoric—if not the practice—of enlightened patriarchism, by the requirement to demonstrate that the lot of his people was a happy, and an explicitly nonviolent one. When his neighbors began a 1798 whispering campaign against him, accusing him of having whipped a bondman to death, his overseer, one J. Greene, signed an affidavit claiming culpability for the incident. Thus "the report of [Colhoun's] having cruelly whipped or punished the s[ai]d fellow in any way previous to the fellows death is utterly false and without foundation"; instead Greene had given "such correction as I thought he diserved & I judged proper."[58] Crucially it was to the overseer that blame for excessive and socially unacceptable violence was apportioned.

This new language influenced another overseer who worked for John Ewing Colhoun, but he turned the violent overseer stereotype on its head in defense of his own position. The presence of a driver enabled John C. Grinninger at Colhoun's St. Stephen's Santee plantation to vaunt his own enlightened credentials, just as the employment of overseers enabled slaveholders to demonstrate their benevolent rule. Grinninger reported in 1795: "I am sorry to here that the negro's look so poor and dejected—I do all in my power in every Resort on the plantation—and do not allow Herty to abuse any of them[.] In report of his pashon [passion] he will never be broke—I believe the Negros have a grate dislikeing to him and tha [they] will never be satisfied wile he is on the Plantation."[59] This manager recognized the utility of using the vocabulary of "passions" when presenting himself as the bondpeople's protector, though he was the same overseer who had promised to "give [Mingo] wips and Put Iron on his neck."

Enlightened slaveholders also claimed a new emphasis on the sanctity of enslaved women's bodies. Partly this still derived from their desire to protect women's reproductive capabilities, as demonstrated by Henry Laurens's condemnation of the overseer who "whip[ped] Wenches till they misscarr[ied]." But it also allowed planters to fashion themselves to their neighbors, as they did to their workforce, as bondwomen's defenders against the sexual violence of slavery. This could well have influenced the Virginian runaway advert's reference to Betty, the woman "[who] had a Scar on a Breast occasioned by a Stroke from her Overseer." Planters also defended enslaved people's right to conduct a family life without interference.[60] Against this background should be viewed Robert Carter of Nomini Hall's advice to the overseer who had whipped two boys. Carter counseled not only "moderate correction in every case," but to "make proper allowance for the feelings of the mother."[61] Fully cognizant of the shift to enlightened patriarchism, enslaved men and women continued to bear tales of cruelty to the more solicitous slaveholders in an attempt to undermine their supervisors. Exaggerated or not their reports reinforced planters' general stereotypes about the managerial profession and underlined the "outsider" nature of overseers. Charles Dabney, a relative of Carter, reported to his steward that "Ben has been with me with a terrible Complaint ag[ains]t his Overseer. I beg that you will enquire into it, & not suffer the Negroes to be abused. I am a stranger to his Overseer, but know very well that few common Overseers are to be trusted."[62]

Late-century visitors to the United States like British envoy David M. Erskine described how southerners hired out black people "much as horses are in England," while the French American Enlightenment author Hector St. John de Crèvecoeur observed that Carolinians looked on their bondpeople "with half the kindness and affection with which they consider their dogs and horses."[63] Yet Carter's emphasis on the enslaved mother's feelings formed part of a new fashion among enlightened owners for stressing the humanity of bondpeople.[64] In 1772 the Virginia House of Burgesses requested that the crown curtail slave imports, a "Trade of great Inhumanity."[65] Henry Laurens balked at the division of enslaved families because they were "still human creatures."[66] Like Robert Carter III, the South Carolinian planter Thomas Wadsworth was inspired by religion (in his case Quakerism) to emancipate his workforce out of "Motives of Humanity."[67] John Channing, a Georgian planter, was prepared to acknowledge enslaved people's rational behavior as a facet of their human personality. When he left his estates in the charge of Edward Telfair in 1786, Channing underlined the importance of slave management: "I wish them to be treated as reasonable creatures, that is, with humanity and kindness."[68]

Most significantly planters drew a distinction between their own humane and enlightened treatment of enslaved men and women, and the bestial supervision offered by overseers.[69] Hugh Washington asserted in 1788 that "very few of the common Overseers . . . have the least feeling of humanity for Slaves."[70] Having warned his supervisor that "the Woman with Child shou'd never be hard worked or oppressed in any manner," William Lee played the loving, dutiful patriarch when explaining how he wished "them all to be treated as human Beings, whom Heaven has placed under my Care, not only to minister to my Luxury, but also to contribute to their happiness, in return for which, I have a right to expect their fruitful, honest & diligent service."[71] Remember that George Washington accused overseers of viewing "a Negro much in the same light as they do the brute beasts, on the farms, and oftentimes treat them as inhumanly."[72] In the same letter, Hugh Washington wrote that overseers treated enslaved people "in general . . . as if they were not of the same species."[73]

The notion that men of overseers' social status would turn to bestial force in asserting their rule was a common patriarchal prejudice against irrational dependents.[74] At midcentury the Virginian Joseph Ball urged his steward not to "let unmerciful Overseers beat, and abuse [bondpeople] inhumanly, and Break their hearts."[75] In 1777 Robert Carter III reported both cruelty and caprice: "Rich[ar]d Bennett . . . now in my Service—beat inhumanly—Negro Will . . . using the Bar of the Kitchen-door . . . Charles Clark . . . saw the whole of Bennett's conduct—who said that Bennett was very blameable, in [thi]s Affair—because Will gave him no provocation."[76] An overseer's wife might face the same charge—Joseph Ball highlighted the "barbarity" of one woman's actions after she was accused of striking an enslaved child and drawing blood.[77] Virginian slave mistress Frances Tucker objected to managerial cruelty because she did not wish her "miserable creatures" to become "a prey to the worst part of mankind."[78] By deferring violence to men, women could protect their self-image as gentlewomen without renouncing violence as a tool of control. Crucially, when they delegated to men such as overseers whom they considered their social inferiors, "it worked a deeper magic: reinforcing class distinctions . . . delegating whippings to an overseer . . . confirmed [a woman's] refinement and his coarseness."[79]

In the lowcountry Georgian Alexander Hewatt linked overseer violence to the requirement for absentee slaveholders to yield supervisory responsibilities: "good masters and mistresses, whose humanity and a sense of interest will not permit them to treat their negroes in a harsh manner, do not always reside at their plantations."[80] And Henry Laurens reminded Abraham Schad that a bondman was "a human Creature whether you like him or not."[81] On another occasion Laurens declared that he preferred an overseer who made "less Rice with more hands but treats my Negroes with Humanity" to "one who should make twice as much Rice and exercise any degree of Cruelty towards those poor Creatures who look up to their Master as their Father, their Guardian, and Protector."[82]

A newly strengthened animus against overseers resulted also from enlightened slave owners' claims, now that they saw enslaved people as human, no longer to view them in animalistic terms.[83] George Washington wrote to Alexander Spotswood that because he was "principled ag[ains]t. selling negros, as you would do cattle in the market," he did not wish, "in twelve months from this date, [to] be possessed of one, as a slave."[84] The humanization of bondpeople also explains the increased focus on managerial attacks on enslaved women. Overseers now were infected even more deeply with the passionate traits—such as lasciviousness—that all dependents formerly were accused of sharing. By underlining overseer violence against females, enlightened owners burnished their credentials as protectors of enslaved women's physical health and sexual propriety and in so doing further attempted to project their beliefs that enslaved people were human rather than reproductive beasts of burden. The presence of overseers, therefore, allowed slaveholders' professions of humanity to be compatible with social control and exploitation.[85]

Presaging the rhetoric of later abolitionists, eighteenth-century antislavery writers focused on the arbitrary and capricious nature of rule by overseers in possession of excessive authority. The Reverend John Newton, one of the founders of Christian Evangelicalism and a mentor to William Wilberforce, wrote how enslaved captives, having endured the horrors of the Middle Passage, then faced "a continual progress from bad to worse."[86] Their future consisted of "excessive toil, hunger, and the excruciating tortures of the cart-whip inflicted at the caprice of an unfeeling overseer, proud of the power allowed him of punishing whom, and when, and how he pleases."[87] Writer Maria Edgeworth echoed the slaveholder tack of blaming overseers for violence when she distinguished "good" from "bad" slaveholders: Mr. Edwards, her "good" planter, kept a close eye on all aspects of estate management, while the indebted, drunken "bad" owner, Mr. Jefferies, devolved too much responsibility to his overseer, whose vicious behavior provoked revolt among the bondpeople.[88] One of the most prominent abolitionists, Thomas Clarkson, likewise repeated the argument that overseers behaved cruelly as they had no proprietorial attachment to the men and women in their charge. "We might perhaps flatter ourselves with saying, that [enslaved people] were subject to the will of Englishmen. But Englishmen were not better than others, when in possession of arbitrary power. The very fairest exercise of it was a never-failing corrupter of the heart. But suppose it were allowed, that self-interest might operate some little against cruelty; yet where was the interest of the overseer or the driver?"[89]

Similarly fearful of irrational managerial tendencies, though Robert Carter III continued to sanction violent punishment in the years before his religious conversion, like other enlightened patriarchs he also set limits. Carter wrote to overseer Thomas Olive during the Revolutionary War: "sir—When you undertook the management of my plantation . . . I submitted the conduct of the negroes, there, to your consideration & empowered you to rebuke and inflict corporal punishment as you might Judge necessary—and the same authority has been continued till now—but I do herein take from you part of the aforesaid power and I do forbid you to correct, in any manner what ever, either old or young negro belonging to me."[90] Robert Carter never used the word "Judge" lightly.[91] Judicious dominance apparently had proved too challenging for Olive: a practiced social contractarian, Carter reset the delicate hierarchical balance by reclaiming some of the authority that wartime absenteeism had required him to cede.

But Carter's rebuke gained strength from newly minted influences as well as traditional prejudices against dependents. As an enlightened citizen of the new Republic, Carter understood the difficulties inherent in the granting and positioning of political authority. The year that the Revolution began, the slaveholder had read "Coke on Littleton"—the treatise by English lawyer Sir Edward Coke that John Rutledge, post-Revolution governor of South Carolina and later Supreme Court chief justice, claimed was "almost the foundation of our law." At the same time, Carter was studying Montesquieu's *Spirit of the Laws* (the Enlightenment tract that held that liberty was only possible through the separation of powers).[92] Stewards bought into the same rhetoric as Carter and set new boundaries. The South Carolinian steward Josiah Smith told George Austin that though a recently arrived overseer knew "there [was] a necessity of much more Patience with the Short Comings of Negroes than with those of his Own colour, a due Attendance on this matter I have very much insisted upon & Shall severely rebuke him whenever I find that he acts out of reasonable bounds."[93] On another occasion Smith summoned the contemporary language of "oppression," writing to his employer that "your expressions of tenderness for your Slaves, added to my own inclination that way, hath always induced me to make their Lives a little comfortable, directing your Overseers, not to overdrive or otherwise oppress them, charging them always to be well-fed, & properly attended to when sick: & of this I believe they can boast, beyond most other Plantation Gangs, this method of treating them."[94]

On the plantation, as in a republic, balance was all. John Adams, by then president, wrote to a group of young Georgians in 1798 that "it is a gratification to my pride to see you boast of a well balanced republic—the essence of a free republic is in the balance—the security of Liberty, property, Character and Life depends every moment upon its preservation, and . . . America will be scourged by the Rods of Vengeance if they will not study and preserve Balance, as the only ark of Safety."[95] Overseer caprice was undesirable partly because it gave the lie to the claimed balance of enlightened patriarchism. In voicing their prejudices against managers, slaveholders delineated "which of the practices that comprise[d] the inevitable dirty work of power must be screened from public view."[96] Thomas Jefferson's assessment of overseers reflected a further vision: the need for balance as a bulwark against overweening corrupting influences. When he described managers as "the most abject, degraded, and unprincipled race," Jefferson added that of all the social ranks in Virginian society, the "last and lowest [is] a seculum of beings called overseers . . . always cap in hand to the Dons who employed them, and furnishing materials for the exercise of their pride, insolence and spirit of domination."[97]

In another statement Jefferson expanded on this association between dependence, tyranny, and corruption. He argued that "dependance begets subservience and venality, suffocates the germ of virtue, and prepares fit tools for the design of ambition."[98] In the lowcountry Henry Laurens worried about the "tyranny and villainy of overseers" and their "vicious designs."[99] Many of the great slaveholders of Virginia, South Carolina, and Georgia had fought against British tyranny and corruption; many were involved in the framing of a Constitution designed to thwart the repeat of such evils, by setting a virtuous citizenship and balanced constitution against the threat of anarchy. On their plantations, and in their opinions of overseers, they posed analogous questions regarding the correct uses of political authority, feared the tyranny and despotism that incorrectly used authority could entrain, and, by establishing overseers as antithetical to free white society, had them play an important scapegoat role as Americans began the political formation of a new country.

The combined force of prejudices against overseers' perceived inhumanity and their notorious caprice posed considerable obstacles to successful management. Solomon Betton's experience demonstrates how enlightened patriarchal sentiment could obstruct the execution of punishment against recalcitrant bondpeople. In September 1791 Betton, who was overseer to John Mercer in Virginia, reported that "Davey has made his escape this Morning." Davey had reacted strongly to Betton's punishment of another bondman, Valentine; when Betton attempted to whip Davey in response, he fled, saying he was heading to Mercer. Davey "perswaded" Valentine to leave with him overnight, but though Valentine returned, Davey failed to show up the following day. Betton acknowledged that it was Mercer's prerogative to decide how best to discipline Davey should he appear but worried about the consequences of Mercer giving too much credence to Davey's tales. The overseer wrote, "you will know what is proper to be done—[i]f one [bondperson] is countenanced, all will expect the same."[100]

Betton understood that the demands of the new tendency to humanize enslaved people had the potential to disrupt his regime. "Countenancing" enslaved criticism put bondpeople's complaints ahead of his right to rule dependents. Planters might make claims to be "enlightened," but overseers like Betton clove to the harsher modalities of patriarchism: "you may rest assured of my humanity toward them, but that they all, shall pay disregard to my orders, and commands, let it be given whenever it may—and that an offence of this kind, shall be punished with many stripes, let him come whenever he may—An oppen opposition to any authority, is such a piece of boldness as cannot be overlooked, and then to run away is equally bad, as one is directly and the other in directly setting my commands and authority at naught."[101] For this overseer, who believed all his charges "to be rogues," enslaved people's discipline rested on an unadorned patriarchal equation: "if they behave well, they will be treated well—If not, their treatment will vary accordingly."[102]

Robert Carter's overseer Thomas Olive also felt that violence was an integral part of management, and the right to punish bondpeople a central plank of his authority. Carter continued to employ Olive for some years after the rebuke outlined above, but his relationships with enslaved men and women did not go smoothly. Carter recounted: "Abraham, foreman, Tom, Tom, boy, Cartman . . . were with me this morning—Mr Tho[ma]s Olive also—he informed me that he lately ordered Vincent to strip himself to be Scourged—Abraham, foreman, did not fall in with the propriety of the whipping intended, therefore he did not aid Mr Olive therein." Olive's petition to Carter suggests he felt shame at his weakened position: "the Overseer asked in the presence of Abraham if he had not full power & Authority to beat strip & whip all the Negroes at Billingsgate Q[uarte]r—I answered Mr Olive that I did not allow him to use his pleasure in such a manner—that I apprehended he was as violent, now, as formerly, when I took the power of Correction from him."[103]

Abraham's resistance gained strength from Carter's newfound "enlightened" stance on plantation justice, and he sought notably to use similar arguments regarding the justness of Olive's planned discipline. Thereafter Carter began to insist that all violent punishment be reported to him so that he could "Interfere" if necessary; Olive left Carter's employ at the end of that year.[104] On another occasion his respect for enslaved family ties led Carter to instruct an overseer that he was wrong to have whipped "Negro Jerry" because the "offense you Charged him with was a matter in his own house"—an argument with other bondmen over "Negro Mary."[105] The difficulties faced by Betton, Olive, and Carter's other overseers derived from their position at the stress point between rhetoric and reality. Their individual struggles to establish authority underlined the limits both of enlightened patriarchism, and of the liberty that, after the Revolution, white men of all classes now had a claim to share.

Jefferson's condemnation of the "unprincipled race" of overseers contained a further, developing ideological assessment: a critique of the slave system itself. That he saw managers as "degraded" points to a growing contemporary belief that the practice of slavery had a debilitating effect on the morality of its practitioners. With the rise of enlightened patriarchism, a number of southerners came to believe that slavery was undermining the new republican civility that they expounded. Jefferson was not alone in believing that "there must doubtless be an unhappy influence on the manners of our people produced by the experience of slavery among us."[106] As early as 1759, in one of the strongest attacks on slavery during the late colonial period, Richard Henry Lee focused largely on questions of morality when arguing for the continuation of colonial duties on slave imports, designed to lessen Virginia's reliance on the institution.[107] Because it removed the need to work, others detected an assault by slavery on "industry . . . frugality and virtue"—the very qualities that were thought to combat widely feared indebtedness.[108] George Mason, Virginian delegate to the Constitutional Convention, opposed new slave imports for moral reasons: "slavery discourages arts & manufactures. The poor despise labor when performed by slaves. They prevent the immigration of Whites, who really enrich & strengthen a Country. They produce the most pernicious effect on manners. Every master of slaves is born a petty tyrant. They bring the judgment of heaven on a Country."[109]

Like these planters early abolitionists such as Arthur Lee rejected the institution on moral grounds, more concerned about its effects on whites than on blacks, whom Lee considered "abominable objects."[110] In a letter to George Washington, the Virginian Jonathon Boucher took the critique to a new metaphorical level. Discussing the improvement of the human spirit, he presented an image of a plantation owner who "will unwillingly apply to any Improvemts. Either in Arts or Sciences." The result of this? "Sunk in unmanly Sloth, his Estate will [be] left to ye. Management of some worthless Overseer." Boucher's tale opposed one of the main ideological focuses of the time—improvement—with a metonymical overseer, the harbinger of moral corruption.[111]

As he did when condemning dependence itself, Jefferson argued that the dependent power relations inherent in slavery were at the root of all its evils and linked the absolute power of slave superintendents with arbitrary and irrational rule. Echoing George Mason, Jefferson opined that "the whole commerce between master and slave is a perpetual exercise of the most boisterous passions, the most unremitting despotism on one part, and degrading submissions on the other," and he concluded that "the man must be a prodigy who can retain his manners and morals undepraved by such circumstances."[112] Jefferson had often decried tobacco culture—and not only because it damaged Virginian soils. He preferred the cultivation of grain, a crop that did not rely on enslaved or dependent labor and allowed all white men a share of independence.[113] He believed, furthermore, that the consequences of not owning land were akin to the consequences of untrammeled rule over dependents. Because "possession of personal independence demonstrated . . . that a gentleman was morally sound" and "independent persons . . . stood above the scramble after power and wealth," in stark contrast to his views on overseers Jefferson idealized the yeoman farmer.[114] For the future president, "those who labour in the earth are the chosen people of God. . . . Corruption of morals in the mass of cultivators is a phenomenon of which no age nor nation has furnished an example."[115]

Later, when discussing the "seculum of beings called overseers," Jefferson compared them unfavorably with this "solid independent yeomanry."[116] Jefferson did not choose to stigmatize labor, as Greek and Roman slaveholders had once done: for him working the ground had become invested with a moral purity. Jefferson's fellow Virginian Robert Carter, son of Charles Carter of Shirley and uncle of Confederate general Robert E. Lee, resurrected the commonly held bucolic ideal in his own condemnation of slavery. He recalled how his "aversion" to the practice did not diminish when he became a "slave-holder and witness[ed] many cruelties." Instead Carter's "short trial of the agricultural line disgusted [him] entirely with the mode practiced in the southern States. Nay, almost obliterated the recollections of those pleasing sensations which most people have experienced upon contemplating the happy husbandman, embosomed in his harvest field, collecting the well earned fruits of his industry."[117]

Though these were familiar eighteenth-century critiques, the Revolution had brought venerable prejudices into sharp relief. Even a conservative like John Adams, who "distrusted the era's democratic pretensions," still believed that "equal liberty" meant enabling "every member of society" to acquire land.[118] At the Constitutional Convention in 1787, the aristocratic South Carolinian delegate Charles Cotesworth Pinckney argued that "the members of the Legislature, the Executive, and the Judges, should be possessed of competent property to make them independent & respectable. It was prudent when such great powers were to be trusted to connect the tie of property with that of reputation in securing a faithful administration. The Legislature would have the fate of the Nation put into their hands."[119]

By the closing decades of the century, some overseers had managed to acquire land and slaveholdings and start their own households.[120] At the time of his death in 1773, William Cantey, who had been overseer to Henry Laurens at his Broughton Island plantation in Georgia, owned five hundred acres of land on Saint Simon's Island and was married with "Several Young Children."[121] John Fairfax, an overseer from a significant Virginian family who left George Washington's service in 1790, settled in Monongalia County on the border with Pennsylvania, where he became a justice of the peace and later represented the county in the Virginia House of Delegates.[122] Yet most were like the Virginian Richard Scammell, overseer to Allen Cockes in 1790s Surry County, whose 1799 will contains no details of lands or bondpeople.[123]

Out of 232 late eighteenth-century Virginian overseers recorded, only twenty-two appeared in tax records for 1782 as heading a household, and thirty-six in 1790.[124] Using the federal population census of 1810, James Baird found that by that year only forty-six out of ninety-eight Virginian men employed as overseers between 1782 and 1810 were listed as independent heads of household. Of those forty-six, just twenty-seven owned bondpeople; none owned more than ten, and two-thirds owned five or fewer.[125] There is some evidence that Virginian overseers looked beyond the state's boundaries to seek a life of independence, as Baird's work on the migratory patterns of dependents would affirm.[126] Seven of 249 late eighteenth-century overseers were tracked to Kentucky in the 1790 and 1800 censuses of that state. Many of these emigrants originated either in Tidewater counties or in counties near the Chesapeake—some of the earliest-settled areas, where aspiring landholders would have found difficulty in purchasing a farm or plantation.[127]

The patchy nature of lowcountry tax and census records makes similar attempts at reconstruction a challenge; but of 141 late eighteenth-century lowcountry overseers that could be traced with any confidence, none appeared in the 1790 South Carolina section of the federal population census, and thirteen appeared as heads of household in the federal census for Georgia in 1820.[128] It is difficult to tell from such data how these levels of achievement compared with other dependent groups. But it seems clear that by late century, overseeing was still associated strongly with dependence, not least because improvements in tidal cultivation and seed selection made both coastal and inland plantations prohibitively expensive for men with modest resources.[129] Solomon Betton outlined the quandary that overseers faced. "I am spending the prime of life in the business of another, and however agre[e]able it may be when there is no alternative it is not agre[e]able when there is and to enable me to fix permanently on my own soil in the shortest time possible will influence me to make use of every exertion to pay for it."[130]

Like other lowly white men, managers "struggled to reconcile their aspirations to independence with the reality of their dependence."[131] Inspired by Revolutionary ideas, they invoked the current language of freedom and despotism with vigor, employing it to support their traditional patriarchal claims to the subordination of enslaved people. John Irby complained to Virginian planter Henry Banks about the "almighty and plenipotentiary . . . Mr John Hargrave," a steward. Hargrave had "accused [Irby] of not having answered his Letters," claiming that the overseer was "wanting of attention to [Banks's] interest, and had "a number of hands not engaged." These suggestions so infuriated the overseer that even though his "sentiments [were] not altogether consistent with the necessary obedience incumbent on me, in my situation, if this should be an objection I can only excuse myself in this way, that it is a fault in my nature, which prompts me to believe, that to be as free as the wind of Heaven is my birth right, and that I will defend and maintain it through out life, is as certen as I now have an existence, this its likely would disconcert the despotic Law of Mr. Hargrave." The overseer warned that if Banks continued to "countenance [the] impudence" of this "bloted and suspicious man," he would "no longer than Christm[a]s continue in [Banks's] service."[132]

Irby's outrage reveals a personal struggle that derived from his wish to be seen as competent and protective of his employer's interests, and to overcome his doubly dependent position. Solomon Betton voiced this confusing mentality in a letter to his employer, the Virginian James Mercer: "altho[ugh] it might be considerably to my Int[erest] to stop at nothing might secure me your permanent fr[ien]dship," he wrote, Betton drew the line at "acting in the Servile character of derogatory to that of a Man of Sentiment and honour."[133] For in the enlightened patriarchs' conception, landless dependence joined in unholy alliance with dependence on another man's will as the ultimate corruptors of humanity. A few years after the conflict, the South Carolinian historian David Ramsay wrote in his *History of the American Revolution* that slavery "nurtured a spirit of liberty among the free inhabitants" since nothing could excite slave owners' opposition to British tyranny more effectively than the fear of being "degraded" to a position akin to that held by their enslaved people.[134] Thomas Jefferson believed that "if a slave is to have a country in this world, it must be any other in preference to that in which he is born to live and labour for another: in which he must lock up the faculties of his nature."[135]

This was something of a departure from the patriarchal age, when most planters believed slavery to be a morally neutral institution, and when overseers' behavioral characteristics were redeemable if managers became independent householders. (Compare the late-century enlightened hope that enslaved people could develop human reason with the hardening conviction that managers shared common, and irreversible, negative character traits). The war with Britain had brought the defamed social status of overseers to the fore. Now whether or not they held land or human capital, in their submission to the will of another—and paradoxically because their role yielded them such capricious powers over bondpeople—managers represented the antithesis of every idea of ordered liberty that Revolutionary Americans held. The deepest irony was that although overseers affronted the moral mission of the late eighteenth-century planter class, they also represented a very necessary part of a slave system that had given planters enough wealth to presume themselves capable of directing the virtues and manners of a new nation. The result of this confluence of ideas about status, authority, and freedom was that overseers would continue to face stigmatization for their dependent position and inherent violence throughout the closing decades of the 1700s and into the fateful nineteenth century.

In the final analysis of eighteenth-century plantation overseers in Virginia, South Carolina, and Georgia, we return to the notion of distance. The stigmatization of oversight resulted in part from an increase in social distance between the overseer and his employer over the course of the 1700s. According to popular conceptions, those one hundred years saw the two parties move ever further to the pinnacle and base of eighteenth-century society. By the turn of the 1800s, overseers were viewed as a dependent, landless class, vilified consistently by those who relied on the overseeing system to accumulate wealth. This status aspect to the negative image of overseeing has not been researched widely before.

The increase in distance that had the biggest effect on southern opinions of overseeing was the growth in physical distance between slaveholders and many of their subordinates. Planters were required to maintain control over plantation management despite the rise of absenteeism. They needed to do so because they had invested significant reserves of financial and emotional capital in their holdings; related social pressures around the requirement for slaveholders to control their subordinates represented a further influence. Planter control left even skilled overseers little room for maneuver, and the proprietorial class came to criticize overseers in general as incompetent and agriculturally inept. Employers made the situation worse because many contracted their overseers for too short a time to render their work profitable.

Despite their pretensions to aristocratic rule over subordinates, the greatest influence on planters' dealings with their overseers was more down-to-earth. When recruiting, owners worried about frugality; when they gave orders to overseers, they feared for their investments; and in demanding good treatment of enslaved people, they endeavored to bring about a relatively happy and productive workforce. In attempting to exert authority over bondpeople after absenteeism had made it more difficult to do so, plantation owners found that they could appeal to nascent prejudices against overseers. Managers became a focus for enslaved people's dissatisfaction with the plantation system itself; as vital scapegoats, overseers—and in particular overseers on absentee plantations—were therefore of central importance in the development of the "enlightened patriarchal" ideas that presaged antebellum paternalism. Some historians of nineteenth-century slavery have suggested that only "close living masters and slaves" could "develop a sense of paternalistic duty." But eighteenth-century planters attempted to compensate for the assault that absenteeism brought to bear on traditional patriarchal relationships and in doing so created many of the rhetorical presuppositions from which antebellum paternalism later developed.[136] Studying overseers therefore adds much to our understanding of the limits and meaning of patriarchal authority, and the meaning and practice of resistance.

In addition, by delegating violent punishment to overseers, planters aided the creation of one of the most enduring facets of the plantation manager's negative image: the overseer as a violent brutalizer of enslaved people. Future research could uncover whether absenteeism led managers to prosecute more violence, or to carry out more visible violence—exemplary, demonstrative acts of punishment—against bondpeople.[137] Also useful would be a wider study into whether slaveholders' attitudes to managerial violence against enslaved people on home plantations differed from the way in which they viewed violence on absentee quarters. Furthermore, how did enlightened planters' opinions of overseers, whom they increasingly despised, diverge from their views of enslaved people, for whom slaveholders claimed increasingly to feel affection. This was a far cry from the patriarchal tendency to see all dependents, white and black, as uniformly untrustworthy and irrational.

There were structural and topographical differences between Virginia, South Carolina and, Georgia, but this book has uncovered many similarities. Understanding the political thinking of all three colonies is central to a complete understanding of oversight. Ideas about overseers showed particularly marked similarities across the Chesapeake and lowcountry, not least because they grew out of an Atlantic substrate of theories about dependence that informed many southern prejudices. Though different Americans experienced the Revolution in different ways, the postwar treatment of managers—as somehow inimical to the ideals of the new Republic—was notably consistent. This is not to argue against analyzing in greater depth differences between the stigmatization of overseers across regions. While it was beyond the scope of this study, further enquiry could reveal much about how far the different speeds of development of plantation societies impacted on the prejudices of colonial and early national southerners (recall how criticism of overseers was already well established by the time of slavery's introduction to Georgia). Varying plantation sizes and the prevalence of absentee versus resident planters; closer working relationships between white and black; varying work patterns, different managerial skill-sets, and relative degrees of professionalism; contrasting prospects for social advancement and levels of societal stratification; and the importance of Evangelical Protestantism each could have played a role in generating distinctive ideas about managers across different regions.[138]

Viewing overseeing in its political totality sheds new light on the study of authority and resistance in colonial and early republican America. There were links between the way that planters viewed social relations on their plantations and the political frameworks that many of them desired to erect in the new Republic. The overseer was in an unusual position because, when pushed, he was able to turn his "outsider" status to his advantage and bargain with his employer for better living or professional conditions, a privilege that was difficult to come by for household dependents. Managers' liminal positions thereby gave them some flexibility to resist the presuppositions of white elites, not least when it came to stressing their professionalism against criticism of their agricultural competence.

But if anything placing overseers at the edge of society was of more benefit to the slaveholding classes. The Revolution let slip countless radical ideas about the ordering of politics and the meaning of liberty. In the South, and particularly the lowcountry, the persistence of slavery meant that little changed for the majority of inhabitants, white or black. There was a marked contradiction between the liberal Revolution and the aristocratic settlement that followed it. Particularly when the likes of Jefferson contrasted overseers with virtuous small landholders, slaveholders attempted a feat similar to the one that they had achieved when depicting managers as implacably violent. It was to overseers that the perniciousness, arbitrariness, and caprice of slavery devolved, characteristics so far removed from the balance, good governance, and virtue of civic republicanism. The presence of overseers helped explain how slaveholders could acknowledge bondpeople's human attributes while treating them as possessions, and how they could defend an exploitative economic arrangement as a societal and governing ideology. Further study might link eighteenth-century thinking about the positioning of authority on the plantation (and the suitability of the individuals who held that authority), with similar dynamics elsewhere in the English-speaking plantation world, as well as with nineteenth-century pro- and antislavery rhetoric about the uses and abuses of plantation power.[139]

The role that overseers played in amending contradictions between the eighteenth-century slave economy and the burgeoning market economy represents another fruitful area of enquiry.[140] Stereotypes help bind societies—by demonstrating what they stand against, stereotypes inversely reflect what societies stand for.[141] It is noteworthy that with the expansion of the southern slave system during the period now known as the "second slavery," prejudices against overseers not only survived but intensified. They were joined by the vitriol heaped on interstate slave traders following the abolition of imports of enslaved people in 1808. There seems to have been a reckoning among southerners about the appropriateness of the nastier aspects of slavery at a time when southern intellectuals were grappling with the meaning of ideas such as progress and modernity in the plantation context.[142] Contemporaries believed that men who entered the slave trade became "debauched, drunken . . . gambling, ruthless swindlers," who "emphasized profit above piety . . . and ruined paternalism."[143] Akin to how planters' negative attention turned to overseers at the time of the expansion of absenteeism, criticisms of slave traders intensified just when the interstate slave trade expanded into a central feature of the political economy of slavery.[144]

Researching overseers and other outsiders sheds light on how the nineteenth-century heirs of the slaveholders who originated anti-overseer prejudices dealt with the glaring contradictions of their own belief systems, and how their prejudices reflected nineteenth-century southerners' worst fears for the survival of their way of life. Outsiders seemed to have enabled elites to account for the cognitive dissonance that resulted not only from owning other human beings, but from the disruptions to the slave system that the nascent global market economy brought about. Considerable changes were in the offing with regard to the technological, financial, geographical, and political character of the slave South. If eighteenth-century plantation economies still operated on a commercial capitalist model, the nineteenth century began to move toward models of industrial capitalism.[145] The experiments with and developments in indigo production that took place before the American Revolution foreshadowed the technological issues raised by the invention of the cotton gin, mechanized rice production, and the industrialization of the production of other staples. To some extent lowcountry rice producers became industrial plant managers, and overseers ideally would have become technocrats as well as managers. Yet enslaved laborers themselves became increasingly restive, especially once they were expected to adapt new skills in order to install, operate, and maintain the new machinery. As had earlier occurred with indigo, overseers might well have been sidelined as bondpeople took on these new responsibilities.

Overseers played an important sociological role in delineating the cultural assumptions of white society. Southerners defined themselves against the various stereotypes that they leveled at overseers, and the stereotypes that they constructed permitted the later establishment of antebellum paternalism. Yet rhetoric could never be divorced entirely from reality. Frederick Douglass's testimony of managerial violence shows that the relationship between individual whippings and overseers' general reputation for brutality was emotionally as well as rhetorically dialogic: bondpeople's "dark fears" were only confirmed by "darker realities."[146] Betty still had a scar on her breast; the women under Frederick Wiggins's supervision still miscarried. Disciplinary violence was sometimes so grotesque that it resonated long after the event. Josiah Henson as a very young boy witnessed his father "with his head bloodied and his back lacerated" after receiving one hundred lashes, and having had his right ear cut off, for beating an overseer who had brutally assaulted Josiah's mother in the late eighteenth-century Chesapeake. Sixty years later Henson recounted the incident in his 1849 autobiography, on which Harriet Beecher Stowe based her famous novel.[147] Henson's experience is a salutary reminder that while wounds might have repaired over time, memories of overseer brutality took much longer to heal.

Notes

Abbreviations

CWF	John D. Rockefeller Library, Colonial Williamsburg Foundation, Williamsburg, Virginia
Duke	Duke University Perkins Special Collections Library, Durham, North Carolina
GDAH	Georgia Department of Archives and History, Atlanta, Georgia
GG	*Georgia Gazette*
GHS	Georgia Historical Society, Savannah, Georgia
HL Papers	*The Papers of Henry Laurens*
L. of Va.	Library of Virginia, Richmond, Virginia
SCDAH	South Carolina Department of Archives and History, Columbia, South Carolina
SCG	*South Carolina Gazette*
SCHS	South Carolina Historical Society, Charleston, South Carolina
SCL, USC	South Caroliniana Library, University of South Carolina, Columbia, South Carolina
Swem	Manuscripts Department, Earl Gregg Swem Library, College of William and Mary, Williamsburg, Virginia
U. of Va.	Alderman Library, Special Collections, University of Virginia, Charlottesville, Virginia
UNC	Manuscripts Department, Southern Historical Collection, University of North Carolina, Chapel Hill, North Carolina
VG	*Virginia Gazette*
VHS	Virginia Historical Society, Richmond, Virginia

A Note on Terminology

1. See, for example, H. Jones, *Present State of Virginia,* 36.
2. *GG,* 18 October 1764, 3.
3. *SCG,* 19 January to 2 February 1767, 2.
4. *SCG,* 1 December 1768, 3.
5. Scarborough, *Overseer,* 23.
6. See, for example, *VG* (Purdie and Dixon), 15 October 1767, 2.
7. See, for example, L. Carter, *Diary of Colonel Landon Carter,* 1:389; Jefferson to Thomas Mann Randolph Jr., 2 November 1793, Jefferson, *Works of Thomas Jefferson in Twelve Volumes,* http://hdl.loc.gov/loc.mss/mtj.mtjbib008131 (accessed 30 April 2015).
8. See Edward Snickers Account, 10 January 1774–20 June 1776; 9 April 1785 to Earl of Dunmore, Swem.
9. Robert Carter III to John Ridout, 18 September 1769, Letterbook of Robert Carter III of Nominy Hall, 1769, viewed in typescript at CWF.
10. *VG* (Purdie), 28 June 1776, 3.
11. In fact, in one of the few instances where the term "steward" is used, it has a different meaning. Martha Washington in 1797 wrote to a female acquaintance to solicit her assistance in finding "a Steward—or Cook"—an enslaved man skilled enough to take over her kitchen. Martha Washington to Mrs. Powell, 1 May 1797, L. of Va. For "manager" used as a term to describe

a steward, see Burwell Bassett to George Washington, 25 December 1771, in Hamilton, *Letters to Washington and Accompanying Papers,* http://memory.loc.gov/cgi-bin/query/r?ammem/mgw:@field(DOCID+@lit(lw040062)) (accessed 13 November 2014).

12. *VG* (Rind), 25 January 1770.

13. See, for example, George Washington to William Tilghman, 21 July 1793, in Washington, *Writings of Washington from the Original Manuscript Sources,* http://memory.loc.gov/cgi-bin/query/r?ammem/mgw:@field(DOCID+@lit(gw330024)) (accessed 30 April 2015); Robert Carter III to Edward Hunt and Son, 13 May 1765; Robert Carter to Benjamin Tasker, n.d., Letterbook of Robert Carter III of Nominy Hall, 1760–64, CWF.

14. Henry Laurens to Richard Oswald, 12 August 1766, in Laurens, *HL Papers,* ed. Chesnutt and Rogers, 5:159.

15. William Cash to [Edward Telfair], 13 July 1789, Edward Telfair Papers, 1761–1847, 1787–90 folder, box 3, Duke.

16. Cf. Joseph Ball to Joseph Chinn, 11 April 1748, Joseph Ball Letterbook, CWF; Robert Bristow to Thomas Booth, 30 September 1719, Robert Bristow Copybook, L. of Va., 758.

17. See Baird, "Between Slavery and Independence."

18. See, for example, Joseph Ball to Joseph Chinn, 11 April 1748, Joseph Ball Letterbook, CWF.

19. Robert Carter of Nomini Hall Letterbook, 9 vols., Chauvenet Collection, viewed in typescript at CWF, 6:219.

20. I am grateful to Professor Allan Kulikoff for sharing this analogy.

21. George Washington to Frances B. Washington, 18 August 1793, in Washington, *Writings of Washington from the Original Manuscript Sources,* http://memory.loc.gov/cgi-bin/query/r?ammem/mgw:@field(DOCID+@lit(gw330052)) (accessed 2 May 2015).

22. Henry Laurens to Richard Oswald, 12 August 1766, in Laurens, *HL Papers,* ed. Chesnutt and Rogers, 5:159.

23. Pinckney, *Letterbook of Eliza Lucas Pinckney,* 144.

24. Josiah Smith to George Austin, 30 July 1772, Josiah Smith Jr. Lettercopy Book, 1771–84, UNC, 105.

25. See, for example, L. Carter, "Diary of Col. Landon Carter," 39; Robert Carter to Edward Ransdale, 24 June 1767, Robert Carter of Nomini Hall Letterbook, 9 vols., CWF, 63.

26. Cf. Sandy, "Homemakers, Supervisors and Peach Stealing Bitches," 475.

27. Entry for 20 August 1762, Francis Jerdone Memorandum Book, Swem.

Introduction

1. This book prefers the terms "enslaved people" and "bondpeople" to "slave." Stephanie Camp remarked that "slave" "risks flattening the complex history of slavery and essentializing the personhood of bondpeople." Camp, *Closer to Freedom,* 144n2.

2. P. Morgan, *Slave Counterpoint,* 166–70.

3. See for example John Couturier to John Ewing Colhoun, 14 January 1793, John Ewing Colhoun Papers, viewed on microfilm at SCL, USC.

4. See Stubbs, "Rice"; P. Morgan, *Slave Counterpoint,* 149–53; Trinkley et al., *Liberty Hall,* 13–41.

5. For shifts in the two regions' enslaved populations over time, see P. Morgan, *Slave Counterpoint,* 95.

6. *VG* (Rind), 25 January 1770. W. Parks first published the *Virginia Gazette,* but the paper was discontinued temporarily after his death in 1750. William Hunter, who died in 1761, reestablished the *Gazette* in February 1751. J. Royle next published the newspaper; after his death Purdie and Dixon continued its publication until the opening of the Revolutionary War. During a portion of the war Purdie published it alone. In May 1766, through the influence of Thomas

Jefferson, William Rind established a second paper (also called the *Virginia Gazette*). J. Clarkson and A. Davis started still another *Virginia Gazette* in 1775, which they continued, weekly, for several years. Whenever an issue of the *Virginia Gazette* is cited below therefore, the name of the publisher appears.

7. A number of sources outline the importance of the spatial and temporal dimensions to the control of bondpeople, especially Camp, *Closer to Freedom;* Isaac, *Transformation of Virginia,* 52–53; Berlin, "Time, Space and the Evolution of Afro-American Society on British Mainland North America"; Mark Smith, *Mastered by the Clock;* and Mark Smith, "Old South Time in Comparative Perspective." See also Stubbs, "Space, Time and Female Resistance to Slavery on Antebellum Plantations."

8. Cf. Baird, "Between Slavery and Independence," 157.

9. Robert Carter, cited in Mullin, *Flight and Rebellion,* 71.

10. Or, to apply colonial theorist Frantz Fanon's phrase, bondpeople were "surrounded by an atmosphere of certain uncertainty." Fanon cited in Camp, *Closer to Freedom,* 67.

11. John C. Grinninger to John Ewing Colhoun, 22 August 1795, John Ewing Colhoun Papers, SCL, USC.

12. Cf. R. Brown and B. Brown, *Virginia 1705–1786,* 50. Though the salt was intended as an antiseptic, and the tar as a suture, both methods were naturally more painful than they were palliative.

13. Carter cited in Mullin, *Flight and Rebellion,* 71.

14. *VG* (Purdie and Dixon), 6 August 1772.

15. Henry Laurens to John Jackson, 2 April 1766, in Laurens, *HL Papers,* ed. Chesnutt and Rogers, 5:96.

16. Hewatt, *Historical Account of the Rise and Progress of the Colonies of South Carolina and Georgia;* Hewatt cited in B. Wood, *Slavery in Colonial Georgia,* 141.

17. Thomas Jefferson to William Wirt, 5 August 1815, in Jefferson, *Works of Thomas Jefferson in Twelve Volumes,* vol. 11, http://hdl.loc.gov/loc.mss/mtj.mtjbib022119 (accessed 8 May 2015); Washington cited in Scarborough, Overseer, 94–95. The Thomas Jefferson and George Washington papers were both consulted online; the websites that display these holdings often do not give page numbers from the original printed works.

18. Kolchin, *American Slavery 1619–1877,* 60.

19. B. Wood, *Slavery in Colonial Georgia,* 142.

20. Simpson and Weiner, *Oxford English Dictionary,* 16:651.

21. Traditional theories of slaveholder paternalism such as those expounded by U. B. Phillips and, more recently, by Eugene Genovese, have tended to ignore the determining role of force in limiting oppositional activity, proposing instead a formidable degree of psychological suasion that encouraged accommodation, event consent, among the enslaved. Camp, *Closer to Freedom,* 3; 144; see also Stubbs, "Space, Time and Female Resistance to Slavery on Antebellum Plantations."

22. George Washington to Bartholomew Dandridge, 5 June 1782, in Washington, *Writings of Washington from the Original Manuscript Sources,* Series 3H, Letterbook 2, 319.

23. Thomas Jefferson to George Washington, 14 May 1794, Notes, in Jefferson, *Works of Thomas Jefferson in Twelve Volumes,* http://hdl.loc.gov/loc.mss/mtj.mtjbib008396 (accessed 8 May 2015).

24. George Washington to Arthur Young, 18 June 1792, in Washington, *Writings of Washington from the Original Manuscript Sources,* http://memory.loc.gov/cgi-bin/ampage?collId=mgw4&fileName=gwpage102.db&recNum=84&tempFile=./temp/~ammem_5d1g&filecode=mgw&next_filecode=mgw&itemnum=1&ndocs=100 (accessed 8 May 2015).

25. Thomas Jefferson to William Wirt, 5 August 1815, in Jefferson, *Works of Thomas Jefferson in Twelve Volumes,* vol. 11, http://hdl.loc.gov/loc.mss/mtj.mtjbib022119 (accessed 8 May 2015).

26. George Washington to James Mercer, 12 December 1774, Account book 2, in Washington, *Writings of Washington from the Original Manuscript Sources,* http://memory.loc.gov/cgi-bin/query/r?ammem/mgw:@field(DOCID+@lit(gw030179)) (accessed 8 May 2015).

27. Pinckney, *Letterbook of Eliza Lucas Pinckney,* 144.

28. *VG* (Purdie), 2 February 1776 (italics in the original).

29. George Washington to Frances B. Washington, 18 August 1793, in Washington, *Writings of Washington from the Original Manuscript Sources,* http://memory.loc.gov/cgi-bin/query/r?ammem/mgw:@field(DOCID+@lit(gw330052)) (accessed 8 May 2015).

30. *VG* (Purdie), 5 April 1776 (italics in the original).

31. The nineteenth-century salience of overseers' reputation for incompetence is evidenced by the large number of times this prejudice appeared in industrial lawsuits. See Schmidt, "Overseers and the Nature of Southern Labor Contracts."

32. Beverley, *History and Present State of Virginia,* 272.

33. H. Jones, *Present State of Virginia,* 54.

34. George Washington always stressed that his lack of faith in the ability of the managerial class derived from unhappy experience. George Washington to Bartholomew Dandridge, 5 June 1782, in Washington, *Writings of Washington from the Original Manuscript Sources,* Series 3H, Letterbook 2, 319, http://memory.loc.gov/ammem/gwhtml/gwhome.html (accessed 8 May 2015).

35. See Baird, "Between Slavery and Independence," 54–56.

36. Cf. ibid.

37. While as early as 1774 the term "race" denoted "one of the great divisions of mankind, having certain physical peculiarities in common," in the eighteenth century it more commonly connoted a "group or class of persons . . . having some common feature or features." Cf. Simpson and Weiner, *Oxford English Dictionary,* 13:69. Today "'racial'" distinctions are "predicated on the belief in inherent and immutable differences rather than in distinctions based on particular social . . . conditions." Kolchin, *Unfree Labor,* 170.

38. *VG* (Purdie), 5 April 1776 (italics in the original).

39. Planters often wrote to young, nonhouseholding sons about the importance of controlling their passions. But although they were concerned with the momentary behavioral ramifications of dependence, they knew that landed independence would await their offspring in the future. Cf. Baird, "Between Slavery and Independence," 3.

40. Stampp, *Peculiar Institution,* 40.

41. James Benson Sellers and Kenneth M. Stampp both stressed the need to reappraise the overseer, terming him "neglected." Sellers and Stampp cited in ibid., xii. Only a few monographs discuss oversight at any great length; all focus on the nineteenth century, and two are now well over forty years old. John Spencer Bassett's *Southern Plantation Overseer as Revealed in His Letters* takes as its source material the letters of antebellum slaveholder president James K. Polk to his plantations in Tennessee and describes in detail the routine of the overseer, his relations with his employer, and his dealings with enslaved people. While the work stands up well as a description of overseeing, it is limited by its narrow geographical and chronological focus. Bassett, *Southern Plantation Overseer as Revealed in His Letters.*

42. Scarborough, *Overseer.* Structurally the work is similar to this book. It considers every aspect of overseeing, from recruitment to dismissal, and includes welcome discussions of plantation stewards and the so-called overseer elite—those most skilled in agriculture. Its greatest contribution is its statistical survey of overseers—based on the 1860 federal census—which describes their distribution on southern plantations and their limited social advancement. Scarborough's intention was to reassert the importance of oversight; through in its sheer depth, his study goes a long way to achieving that aim.

43. Wiethoff, *Crafting the Overseer's Image,* ix. Cf. Wiethoff, "Enslaved Africans' Rivalry with White Overseers in Plantation Culture."

44. See, for example, R. Brown and B. Brown, *Virginia 1705–1786,* 50; Clinton, *"Plantation Mistress,"* 191; Lockley, *Lines in the Sand,* 13; 33–34; 66; Mullin, *Flight and Rebellion,* 29–30; 50–53; 71; 140–44; Olwell, *Masters, Slaves and Subjects,* 155; Sidbury, *Ploughshares into Swords,* 25; Sobel, *World They Made Together,* ix; 32; 41–42; 47–49; 51; 94; 105; 109; 111–13; 136; 146; 198–99; 211; Browne, "Reverend Dr. John Clayton and His Early Map of Jamestown," 1–7; B. Wood, *Slavery in Colonial Georgia,* 138–42; Young, *Domesticating Slavery,* 47; Edelson, *Plantation Enterprise in Colonial South Carolina,* 200–254.

45. This is also true of many other nonelite whites. Since very few nonslaveholders wrote letters or kept diaries, what little is known of them is often filtered through elite sources. Lockley, *Lines in the Sand,* 2. Still the best published account of eighteenth-century overseers, and especially of the dynamics of their relations with bondpeople and planters, appears in a wider study of slavery. Philip D. Morgan's *Slave Counterpoint* details many of the themes that appear below—including slaveholder intervention on behalf of their slave workforce; bondpeople bearing tales against their overseer; tension between enslaved people and their overseer; violence between the two parties; and last, amicable relations between the two parties. P. Morgan, *Slave Counterpoint,* 326–34.

46. In a study of Georgia between the mid-eighteenth century and the Civil War, Tim Lockley has covered overseers' relations with other whites, and with black people away from the plantation. Lockley, *Lines in the Sand,* 33. Managerial involvement in agriculture has received scant attention, although Lorena S. Walsh has produced a worthy exception. Walsh, *From Calabar to Carter's Grove.* Archaeologists have made efforts to adjudge the social status of overseers, most recently on an overseer site in Christ Church Parish, Charleston County, South Carolina. Trinkley et al., *Investigation of an Eighteenth Century Overseer Site (38CH1278), Christ Church Parish, Charleston County, South Carolina.*

47. Baird considers contemporary Virginian attitudes to dependents by focusing on overseers. As part of his argument, he presents invaluable quantitative findings on the preponderance of oversight across time and space, the social advancement—or otherwise—of overseers, and their age. Baird, "Between Slavery and Independence." Baird's prime concern is with the meanings of dependence and authority in eighteenth- and early nineteenth-century Virginia; usefully he also discusses the role of other managerial figures such as agents and stewards. Though traditionally historians have viewed overseers as young, landless men without a family, Baird is the first scholar to attempt to divine the truth of many of these assumptions. See also Baird, "Paternalism and Profits."

48. Sandy, "Role of Overseers in the Management of Slave Plantations in Virginia and South Carolina, 1740–1800." Like Baird, Sandy uses statistical and quantitative analyses in her effort to plug the gap in the historiographical depiction of overseers. Where this book uses quantitative methods, they support analysis of qualitative ideological and intellectual paradigms.

49. Since in Scarborough's opinion the profession changed little in form between the late eighteenth century and the Civil War, his emphasis falls on regional differences between systems of oversight. Scarborough, *Overseer,* xiv.

50. Davis, "Looking at Slavery from Broader Perspectives."

51. The formerly enslaved abolitionist Frederick Douglass described how bondpeople sometimes complained to their owners about their overseers' violence: their "complaining [was], generally, vindicated by the relaxed rigor of the overseer's treatment." Douglass, *My Bondage and My Freedom,* 65. Enslaved people adopted exactly the same tactic in the eighteenth century.

52. Resistance by the enslaved is in itself a very "necessary point of historical inquiry," one that has inspired many studies. Camp, *Closer to Freedom,* 2. But no previous study has specifically researched enslaved resistance to overseers in eighteenth-century Virginia, South Carolina, and Georgia.

53. See, especially, Genovese, *Roll, Jordan, Roll.*

54. The first comprehensive exposition of how elites self-fashioned in early modern literature was Greenblatt, *Renaissance Self-Fashioning.* For American examples see Lockridge, *Diary, and Life, of William Byrd II of Virginia, 1674–1744;* Wolf, "Elite Male Self-Fashioning in Colonial Virginia"; Isaac, *Landon Carter's Uneasy Kingdom;* Massey, *John Laurens and the American Revolution.*

Chapter 1: A "continual exercise of our Patience and Economy"

1. Byrd, William Byrd II to Charles, Earl of Orrery, 5 July 1726.

2. This book uses "patriarchism" ahead of "patriarchalism" for the reasons outlined by Anthony Parent: "*patriarchism,* a term that first appeared in print in 1666, can be defined as an organizational belief system in which society is structured around the supremacy of the patriarch, or father. Its emphasis on organization more aptly describes the formative nature of this type of society in early-eighteenth-century Virginia than the more commonly used *patriarchalism,* a word dating from 1847 and that suggests an established patriarchal social hierarchy and government." Parent, *Foul Means,* 199 (italics in the original). For Ira Berlin the moment when "the master-slave relationship provided the model for all social relations" was a signal of the transition from a "society with slaves" to a "slave society." Berlin, *Many Thousands Gone,* 9–10.

3. Stampp, *Peculiar Institution,* 40.

4. Cf. P. Morgan, *Slave Counterpoint,* 268.

5. P. Morgan, *Slave Counterpoint,* 275.

6. G. Wood, *Radicalism of the American Revolution,* 44; Camp, *Closer to Freedom,* 3.

7. Kulikoff, *Tobacco and Slaves,* 9.

8. Beeman, *Evolution of the Southern Backcountry,* 77.

9. Cf. Kathleen Brown, *Good Wives, Nasty Wenches, and Anxious Patriarchs.* For an equivalent picture drawn three decades later, see Peter Fontaine Jr. to John Fontaine, 9 July 1752, Fontaine-Maury Papers, folder 3, "part 2," 1737–49, Manuscripts Department, Swem.

10. P. Morgan, *Slave Counterpoint,* 296–97.

11. Fernando Ortiz cited in ibid., 298.

12. Ibid., 316.

13. George Lockey cited in ibid., 274.

14. Ibid., 275.

15. Cf. entry for 7 November 1782, Sarah Fouace Nourse Diary, 1781–82, Nourse and Morris Family Papers, Alderman Library, U. of Va., viewed at Swem.

16. For a recent treatment of these themes, see Shalev, *Rome Reborn on Western Shores.*

17. Peter Fontaine to John and Moses Fontaine, 15 April 1754, Fontaine-Maury Papers, "part 2," 1737–49, folder 3, Swem.

18. Haaksonssen, *Adam Smith.*

19. Entry for 8 March 1773, Cabell Commonplace Book, Cabell Commonplace Books, 1769–95, VHS, vol. 4.

20. Eustace, *Passion Is the Gale,* 79. See Baird, "Between Slavery and Independence."

21. Cf. Eustace, *Passion Is the Gale,* 360.

22. Printed text near entry for 20 August 1762, Francis Jerdone Memorandum Book, Swem (italics in the original).

23. The Virginia Almanack for the Year of Our Lord God, 1776, John Page Diary, Swem (italics in the original).

24. Skinner, "Place of History in Public Life."

25. Foner, *Story of American Freedom,* 8.

26. Skinner, "Place of History in Public Life."

27. *Encyclopaedia Britannica,* 2:973; 631.

28. Ibid., 3:605.

29. Catalogue of books ordered, 1755, Joseph Ball Letterbook, CWF, 148.

30. Kulikoff, *Tobacco and Slaves,* 200.

31. John Spotswood to Alexander Spotswood, 29 November 1722, Alexander Spotswood Papers.

32. Peter Fontaine to John and Moses Fontaine, 15 April 1754, Fontaine-Maury Papers, "part 2," 1737–49, folder 3, Swem.

33. Carter cited in Breen, *Tobacco Culture,* 89 (italics in the original).

34. Entry for October, Virginia Almanack for the Year of Our Lord God, 1776, John Page Diary, Swem.

35. Scarborough, *Overseer,* xiv. For the introduction and cultivation of indigo and cotton, see Chaplin, *Anxious Pursuit.*

36. P. Morgan, *Slave Counterpoint,* 194. Cf. Edelson, *Plantation Enterprise in Colonial South Carolina,* 3.

37. P. Morgan, *Slave Counterpoint,* xvii. See also ibid., 38–39; Camp, *Closer to Freedom,* 9.

38. P. Morgan, *Slave Counterpoint,* xviii.

39. Cf. Sandy, "Divided Loyalties in a 'Predatory War,'" 365. Sandy comes to the same conclusion in a study that also focuses on overseers in the Chesapeake and lowcountry.

40. Greene, "Independence and Dependence," in Greene, *Imperatives, Behaviors and Identities,* 175.

41. M. Jones, *Limits of Liberty,* 6; cf. Kulikoff, *Tobacco and Slaves,* 42.

42. Kulikoff, *Tobacco and Slaves,* 81.

43. Joseph Ball to Joseph Chinn, 4 April 1755, Joseph Ball Letterbook, Library of Congress, viewed in typescript at CWF.

44. The area comprised the counties of Essex, Gloucester, King and Queen, King William, Mathews, and Middlesex.

45. Kulikoff, *Tobacco and Slaves,* 13.

46. Ibid., 4–10.

47. This region comprised the counties and parishes of Augusta, Boutetourt, Frederick, Rockbridge, Rockingham, and Shenandoah.

48. Kulikoff, *Tobacco and Slaves,* 79–81.

49. See P. Morgan, *Slave Counterpoint,* 259. Large slaveholdings, however, were more the exception than the rule. In Middlesex County, where Ralph Wormeley's holdings alone embraced just under 20 percent of the county's black population, only one-fifth of male heads of households owned one bondperson or more. Rutman and Rutman, *Place in Time,* 166.

50. Kulikoff, *Tobacco and Slaves,* 4–10; 93.

51. Ibid., 399.

52. See, for example, Bradburn and Coombs, "Smoke and Mirrors," 150.

53. Kulikoff, *Tobacco and Slaves,* 119; 131–41. Puglisi, *Diversity and Accommodation,* is a helpful summary of the eighteenth-century development of societies on Virginia's western frontier.

54. Cf. Clayton, "Letter from Mr. John Clayton."

55. Robert Bristow to Thomas Booth, October 1714, Robert Bristow Copybook, L. of Va., 578.

56. Scarborough, *Overseer,* 3.

57. Cf. E. Morgan, *American Slavery, American Freedom,* 308.

58. Scarborough, *Overseer,* 3.

59. John Buckles oversaw indentured servants for Carter in 1723. See Katharine Brown and Sorrells, *People in Profile,* 113.

60. E. Morgan, *American Slavery, American Freedom,* 308. Those run by plantation mistresses were even more likely to employ overseers, since southerners believed that fieldwork was inappropriate for white women.

61. Entry for 18 June 1757, Francis Jerdone Memorandum Book, Swem.

62. 28 November 1760, Colonel Dudley Digge's plantations in Louisa. Overseer's Reports, 1760–65, Charles William Dabney Papers 1715–1845, vol. 3, folder 404, UNC.

63. Francis Jerdone Memorandum Book, L. of Va., 2–15.

64. List of taxables given in by Mrs. Sarah Fitzhugh, Stafford, April 1772, Henry Fitzhugh Papers, 1746–69, Duke; Articles of Agreement between Charles Dabney and Charles Nicholls, 21 August 1772, Charles William Dabney Papers, 1715–1845, subseries 1.1: 1716–75, box 1, folder 13, UNC; entries for 23 April and November 1776, John Page Diary, Swem.

65. Entry for 2 August 1791, Cabell Commonplace Book, Cabell Commonplace Books, 1769–95, VHS, 9; Mullin, *Flight and Rebellion,* 49–50.

66. Entry for 18 July 1773, Cabell Commonplace Book, Cabell Commonplace Books, 1769–95, VHS, IV.

67. P. Morgan, *Slave Counterpoint,* 326.

68. Berkeley, "Notes on Often-Cited Persons, Places and Things in Robert Carter's Diary and Letters."

69. Francis Jerdone Memorandum Book, L. of Va., 2–3.

70. Ibid., 5.

71. Kulikoff, *Tobacco and Slaves,* 276.

72. Baird, "Between Slavery and Independence," 50.

73. P. Morgan, *Slave Counterpoint,* 326.

74. Baird, "Paternalism and Profits," 157.

75. Kulikoff, *Tobacco and Slaves,* 97.

76. See, for example, Joseph Ball to Joseph Chinn, 14 February 1744, Joseph Ball Letterbook, Library of Congress, viewed in typescript at CWF. Ball wrote to Chinn, his steward, from Stratford-by-Bow, to the east of London.

77. Baird, "Between Slavery and Independence," 192–93.

78. Cf. Nash, "South Carolina and the Atlantic Economy in the Late Seventeenth and Eighteenth Centuries," 679; Nash, "South Carolina Indigo, European Textiles, and the British Atlantic Economy in the Eighteenth Century," 363; 378.

79. Stubbs, "Rice."

80. Nash, "South Carolina and the Atlantic Economy in the Late Seventeenth and Eighteenth Centuries," 680. Edelson, *Plantation Enterprise in Colonial South Carolina,* 5–6, is a useful summary of the development of staple agriculture in South Carolina.

81. Cf. Nash, "South Carolina and the Atlantic Economy in the Late Seventeenth and Eighteenth Centuries," 679.

82. Cf. Greene, "Colonial South Carolina and the Caribbean Connection," in Greene, *Imperatives, Behaviors and Identities,* 72–75.

83. Stubbs, "Rice."

84. Mancall, Rosenbloom, and Weiss, "Slave Prices and the South Carolina Economy, 1722–1809," 629.

85. Nash, "South Carolina and the Atlantic Economy in the Late Seventeenth and Eighteenth Centuries," 692; 694; Nash, "South Carolina Indigo, European Textiles, and the British Atlantic Economy in the Eighteenth Century," 380.

86. Stubbs, "Rice."

87. With her father called to military duty in Antigua in 1739, Eliza took over management of his three South Carolina plantations. There she experimented with various plants and three years later successfully marketed the colony's first crop of indigo. Cf. Klingsberg, *Appraisal of the Negro in Colonial South Carolina,* 90; Chaplin, *Anxious Pursuit,* 152; Stubbs, "Indigo."

88. William Middleton to John Mucklow, 1 February 1748, Zachary Lloyd Collection, folder 54/12, Birmingham Central Library, England; Josiah Smith to William Manning, 13 May 1772, Josiah Smith Jr. Lettercopy Book, UNC, 83.

89. P. Morgan, *Slave Counterpoint,* 159; Nash, "South Carolina Indigo, European Textiles, and the British Atlantic Economy in the Eighteenth Century," 372.

90. Stubbs, "Indigo." See also Greene, "Travails of an Infant Colony," in Greene, *Imperatives, Behaviors and Identities,* 133. For a discussion of the relative importance of the subsidy and other exogenous effects on indigo demand and supply, see Nash, "South Carolina Indigo, European Textiles, and the British Atlantic Economy in the Eighteenth Century," 363; 372; 376.

91. See William Ancrum Account Book and Letterbook, SCL, USC.

92. One hundred and forty adverts were recorded, including those that explicitly referred to overseers (the vast majority), as well as those requiring farm managers, plantation managers, and applicants to other positions that correlated to overseeing. This figure does not include repeats of advertisements. Journals consulted were the *SCG,* the *GG,* and a number of minor publications including the *South Carolina Gazette and Country Journal,* an unstamped journal that ran concurrently with the *SCG* between 1765 and 1768. All journals viewed on microfilm at Cambridge University Library. Nash, "South Carolina and the Atlantic Economy in the Late Seventeenth and Eighteenth Centuries," 695; Nash, "South Carolina Indigo, European Textiles, and the British Atlantic Economy in the Eighteenth Century," 379; 381.

93. Nash, "South Carolina and the Atlantic Economy in the Late Seventeenth and Eighteenth Centuries," 679; Nash, "South Carolina Indigo, European Textiles, and the British Atlantic Economy in the Eighteenth Century," 365.

94. Sarson, *British America 1500–1800,* 178–80. See also B. Wood, *Slavery in Colonial Georgia.*

95. See, for example, P. Morgan, *Slave Counterpoint,* xviii; 38–39; Camp, *Closer to Freedom,* 4–6.

96. Lockley, *Lines in the Sand,* 1.

97. See B. Wood, *Slavery in Colonial Georgia,* 43–46; and Lockley, *Lines in the Sand.*

98. Edelson, *Plantation Enterprise in Colonial South Carolina,* 6.

99. Stubbs, "Rice."

100. Sylvia Frey cited in B. Wood, "Some Aspects of Female Resistance to Chattel Slavery in Low Country Georgia," 605.

101. P. Wood, *Black Majority,* 20.

102. See Chaplin, "Tidal Rice Cultivation and the Problem of Slavery in South Carolina, 1760–1815," for a description of the growth in cultivation of this crop.

103. B. Wood, *Slavery in Colonial Georgia,* 138; Berlin, "Time, Space and the Evolution of Afro-American Society on British Mainland North America," 56.

104. Sandy, "Mary-Anne Schad and Mrs. Brown," 63; P. Morgan, *Slave Counterpoint,* 39–41; Nash, "South Carolina and the Atlantic Economy in the Late Seventeenth and Eighteenth Centuries," 696.

105. See P. Morgan, *Slave Counterpoint,* xviii; 38–39; Camp, *Closer to Freedom,* 9.

106. George Lockey cited in P. Morgan, *Slave Counterpoint,* 298.

107. The names of 164 Virginian overseers were checked against the index: American Council of Learned Societies, *Surnames in the United States Census of 1790.*

108. Isaac Hayne Ledger, 1765–81, viewed on microform at SCHS, 135–37.

109. The names of 143 South Carolinian and Georgian overseers were checked against the index: American Council of Learned Societies, *Surnames in the United States Census of 1790.*

110. Harrower, "Diary of John Harrower, 1773–1776," 67. See Sobel, *World They Made Together,* 49, for Harrower's experience as an overseer.

111. Louis Kelly Crowder Genealogical Collection, SCL, USC.

112. *VG* (Hunter), 30 January 1752.

113. See Kathleen Brown, *Good Wives, Nasty Wenches, and Anxious Patriarchs,* 34; 65; 114.

114. Barclay, *Voyages and Travels of James Barclay,* 3.

115. *SCG,* 26 December 1754, 3.

116. Burgess Mitchell and George Washington, contract for overseer, 1 May 1762, in Washington, *Writings of Washington from the Original Manuscript Sources,* http://memory.loc.gov/cgi-bin/query/P?mgw:1:./temp/~ammem_1gk6:: (accessed 2 May 2015); Clark, *Colonial Soldiers of the South, 1732–1774,* 614.

117. *SCG,* 19 December 1754, 2.

118. Henry Laurens to Richard Oswald and Co., 26 May 1756, in Laurens, *HL Papers,* ed. Hamer, 2:203.

119. The Carolinas and Virginia contained until the nineteenth century the most number of locally born overseers. See Scarborough, *Overseer,* 42.

120. Cf. *VG* (Rind), 10 December 1772; Rutman and Rutman, *Place in Time,* 162.

121. Beverley, *History and Present State of Virginia,* 272. In the first two centuries of British North America, the status of the "vast majority" of immigrants was one of servitude. Aaron S. Fogelman, "From Slaves, Convicts and Servants to Free Passengers," 43.

122. *VG* (Hunter), 30 January 1752. Cf. *VG* (Purdie and Dixon), 17 October 1755, 2. See also "Concerns of a Tobacco Planter 1762," in Washington, *Diaries of George Washington,* 1:296, http://memory.loc.gov/cgi-bin/query/P?mgw:2:./temp/~ammem_kddY:: (accessed 30 April 2015). Given his Virginian birth, Griffin must have indentured himself to Barton in the colony. This makes him distinct from other examples cited here, where overseers took on an indenture before crossing the Atlantic.

123. For Harrower's experience as a manager, see Harrower, "Diary of John Harrower," 66; 78; and Sobel, *World They Made Together,* 9; Harrower cited in ibid., 94. There was no mention of the oversight of convict servants in the sources consulted for this work, nor indeed of current or former convict servants acting as overseer to enslaved people or other servants. Yet the number of convicts imported to the colonies was sizeable. Sixty thousand arrived in the mainland British colonies from 1718 onward, with perhaps twenty thousand ending up in Virginia. Roger Ekirch suggested that fifty thousand convicts were transported during the course of the eighteenth century, "including over two-thirds of all felons convicted at the Old Bailey, London's chief criminal court." Ekirch, *Bound for America,* 1. Around one-third of immigrants before the American Revolution were convicts. Fogelman, "From Slaves, Convicts and Servants to Free Passengers," 44. Most of Virginia's convicts landed at the Northern Neck ports along the Potomac and Rappahannock Rivers, especially at private plantations (in 1774 George Washington purchased some convicts for his Mount Vernon plantation). See Salmon, "Convict Labor during the Colonial Period." Lowcountry planters employed very few indentured servants, but those that did often put them to work in a supervisory capacity. Nash, "South Carolina and the Atlantic Economy in the Late Seventeenth and Eighteenth Centuries," 698. Yet, despite the fact that "planters in the Chesapeake found [convicts] desirable because they were much cheaper than slaves, served longer terms than indentured servants, and received no freedom dues," "Americans in general did not want convicts and often protested to the British authorities for sending so many." Fogelman, "From Slaves, Convicts and Servants to Free Passengers," 49; 56. Given the significant political responsibility that devolved to overseers, perhaps slave owners dismissed lowly convicts as incapable of shouldering the responsibility of managing other dependents.

124. B. Wood, *Slavery in Colonial Georgia,* 140.

125. 21 February 1776, John Gibbons Papers, 1758–89, 1775–79 file, Duke.

126. *SCG,* 21 November 1774, 4.

127. George Keckley, who oversaw for John Ewing Colhoun in 1795, had previously been a blacksmith. George Keckley to John Ewing Colhoun, 13 September 1795, John Ewing Colhoun Papers, SCL, USC. Cf. Letters of Administration 1775–85, SCDAH, 00, 392; *VG* (Dixon), 25 September 1775, 3; entry for 1 November 1777, daybook, XIC:124, Robert Carter Papers, 1772–94, Duke.

128. Laurens cited in B. Wood, *Slavery in Colonial Georgia,* 140.

129. Josiah Smith to George Austin, 30 January 1770, Josiah Smith Jr. Lettercopy Book, 1771–84, UNC, 56.

130. B. Wood, *Slavery in Colonial Georgia,* 139.

131. Cf. Scarborough, *Overseer,* 42–43; Sandy, "Divided Loyalties in a 'Predatory War,'" 391.

132. Cited in R. Brown and B. Brown, *Virginia 1705–1786,* 50.

133. L. Carter, "Will of Landon Carter (1770/1779) of Sabine Hall, Richmond County, Virginia"; Morton, "Robert Wormeley Carter of Sabine Hall."

134. Cf. Scarborough, *Overseer,* 5–6.

135. See Lawrence, "Descendants of Daniel Couturier in South Carolina."

136. Laurens, *HL Papers,* ed. Hamer, 4:503.

137. Ibid., 4:xviii; Henry Laurens to Richard Oswald, 7 July 1764, in ibid., 4:339.

138. See ibid., 4:575n4; Sandy, "Divided Loyalties in a 'Predatory War,'" 370–71.

139. Laurens cited in Lockley, *Lines in the Sand,* 13; George Washington to Arthur Young, 18 June 1792, in Washington, *Writings of Washington from the Original Manuscript Sources,* http://memory.loc.gov/cgi-bin/ampage?collId=mgw4&fileName=gwpage102.db&recNum=84&tempFile=./temp/~ammem_5d1g&filecode=mgw&next_filecode=mgw&itemnum=1&ndocs=100 (accessed 2 May 2015).

140. Cited in Chaplin, "Tidal Rice Cultivation and the Problem of Slavery in South Carolina, 1760–1815," 47.

141. Kulikoff, *Tobacco and Slaves,* 410; cf. Scarborough, *Overseer,* 5.

142. L. Carter, *Diary of Colonel Landon Carter,* 1:461n73.

143. Ibid., 1:489n87. Cf. Jno. Fox to Francis Jerdone, 22 July 1796, Jerdone Family Papers, folder 1, box 3, Swem.

144. Entry for 2 August 1791, Cabell Commonplace Book, Cabell Commonplace Books, 1769–95, VHS, 9.

145. Jno. Fox to Francis Jerdone, 22 July 1796, Jerdone Family Papers, folder 1, box 3, Swem.

146. 15 March 1760, William Gibbons Jr. Papers, 1760–64 file, 1728–71 box, Duke.

147. Entry for 28 April 1797, account between Gideon Denison and Bennet Wheeler, account book 1796–99, folder 3, box 1, Gideon Denison Family Papers, Hargrett Rare Book and Manuscript Library, University of Georgia, Athens, Georgia, 36.

148. Thomas Jefferson to Thomas Mann Randolph Jr., 24 June 1793, in Jefferson, *Works of Thomas Jefferson in Twelve Volumes,* http://www.loc.gov/resource/mtj1.018_0903_0907/ (accessed 30 April 2015).

149. Kulikoff, *Tobacco and Slaves,* 410.

150. Lawrence, "Descendants of Daniel Couturier in South Carolina."

151. Josiah Smith to George Austin, 20 January 1770, Josiah Smith Jr. Lettercopy Book, 1771–84, UNC, 156.

152. Scarborough, *Overseer,* 183.

153. Agreement between Daniel Parke Custis and Joseph Valentine, 14 November 1755, Custis Family Papers, 1683–1858, VHS; *VG* (Rind), 18 July 1771.

154. Washington cited in Mullin, *Flight and Rebellion,* 29.

155. *VG* (Rind), 9 March 1769.

156. P. Morgan, *Slave Counterpoint,* 220.

157. Washington cited in ibid., 220.

158. Owners were to be punished if six slaves were employed "without one or more white person living and residing on the same plantation." Cooper and McCord, *Statutes at Large of South Carolina,* 2:363; 3, 193, 272; 97, 175.

159. Rutman and Rutman, *Place in Time,* 187.

160. Washington, *Diaries of George Washington,* 5:356.

161. Sobel, *World They Made Together,* 32; Carter cited in ibid., 42.

162. Carter cited in ibid., 42.

163. P. Morgan, *Slave Counterpoint,* 221.

164. Bolzius cited in B. Wood, *Slavery in Colonial Georgia,* 67; P. Morgan, *Slave Counterpoint,* 344.

165. Barclay, *Voyages and Travels of James Barclay,* 25–27.

166. B. Wood, *Slavery in Colonial Georgia,* 140.

167. Thomas Owen to Francis Owen, Zachary Lloyd Collection, folder 55/26, Birmingham Central Library, England.

168. Cf. Sandy, "Divided Loyalties in a 'Predatory War,'" 373.

169. Cited in Chaplin, *Anxious Pursuit,* 268.

170. John Couturier to John Ewing Colhoun, 14 January 1793, John Ewing Colhoun Papers, SCL, USC.

171. P. Morgan, *Slave Counterpoint,* 219–20.

172. Ibid., 221.

173. See, for example, Henry Laurens to Peter Horlbeck, 6 April 1765, in Laurens, *HL Papers,* ed. Hamer, 4:602.

174. Henry Laurens to James Grant, 30 January 1767, in Laurens, *HL Papers,* ed. Chesnutt and Rogers, 5:227. Cf. Young, *Domesticating Slavery,* 47.

175. Herbert Gutman refutes Fogel and Engelman's assertion that there were four thousand enslaved (as opposed to black) overseers in the antebellum South. Herbert Gutman, "World Two Cliometricians Made." These discrepancies were the result of a confusion between the terms "slave overseer" and "driver."

176. P. Morgan, *Slave Counterpoint,* 220.

177. Young, *Domesticating Slavery,* 67.

178. Joseph Habersham to Bella Habersham, 5 July 1778, Habersham Family Papers, University of Georgia, cited in ibid., 67.

179. Katharine Brown and Sorrells, *People in Profile,* 113.

180. The inventory of the estate of Timothy Stamps, King George County Inventories 1721–44, viewed on microfilm at CWF.

181. Inventory of the Estate of Charles Stagg, York County, 17 May 1736, viewed on microfilm at CWF.

182. Beeman, *Evolution of the Southern Backcountry,* 294.

183. Beeman, *Evolution of the Southern Backcountry,* 294.

184. Baird, "Between Slavery and Independence," 15.

185. See ibid.

186. Baird, "Between Slavery and Independence," 234.

187. Joseph Davenport to Lund Washington, September 1765, in Washington, *Writings of Washington from the Original Manuscript Sources,* http://memory.loc.gov/cgi-bin/query/r?ammem/mgw:@field(DOCID+@lit(lw030135)) (accessed 2 May 2015).

188. Kulikoff, *Tobacco and Slaves,* 410; cf. Scarborough, *Overseer,* 5; "Concerns of a Tobacco Planter 1762," in Washington, *Diaries of George Washington,* 1:296, http://memory.loc.gov/cgi-bin/query/P?mgw:2:./temp/~ammem_kddY:: (accessed 30 April 2015).

189. Scarborough, *Overseer,* 41.

190. Josiah Smith to George Austin, 30 January 1770, Josiah Smith Jr. Lettercopy Book, 1771–84, UNC, 156.

191. Entry for 27 July 1774, daybook, 13:34; entry for 9 March 1777, daybook, 23:34, Robert Carter Papers, 1772–94, viewed in typescript at Duke.

192. R. Brown and B. Brown, *Virginia 1705–1786,* 50; Baird, "Between Slavery and Independence," 216; 20.

193. Olwell, *Masters, Slaves and Subjects,* 44.

194. Account between James Harrison and Robert Carter, Robert Carter Account Book, 1785–92, Robert Carter Papers, 1760–1815, VHS.

195. Laurens, *HL Papers*, ed. Hamer, 3:628n5; Sandy, "Divided Loyalties in a 'Predatory War,'" 372.

196. Barclay, *Voyages and Travels of James Barclay*, 33.

197. Inventory of estate of Joseph Valentine, 13 February 1773, York County Wills and Inventories 22, 1771–83, viewed on microfilm at CWF, 149; cf. Jacob Fendin to Edward Telfair, 20 March 1774, Edward Telfair Papers, 1761–1847, Duke.

198. See, for example, entry for 18 June 1757, Francis Jerdone Memorandum Book, Swem; contract between John Ewing Colhoun and Michael Boinneau, 11 January 1799, John Ewing Colhoun Papers, SCL, USC.

199. Josiah Smith to George Austin, 22 July 1773, Josiah Smith Jr. Lettercopy Book, 1771–84, UNC, 201.

200. John Ewing Colhoun account with Michael Boinneau, 10 January 1799, John Ewing Colhoun Papers, SCL, USC.

201. Byrd cited in Hast, "Legal Status of the Negro in Virginia 1705–1765," 217–39, 222.

202. Rutman and Rutman, *Place in Time*, 142–43.

203. Tucker cited in "Society in East Virginia."

204. Randolph cited in Brewer, "Entailing Aristocracy in Colonial Virginia," 346.

205. B. Wood, *Slavery in Colonial Georgia*, 43 and 46; cf. Lockley, *Lines in the Sand*, 5. See also ibid., 3, for a further description of slavery's introduction to Georgia.

206. Dornan, "Women Slaveholders in the Georgia and South Carolina Low Country," 197–205.

Chapter 2: "Douptfull of my Diligence"

1. Beeman, *Evolution of the Southern Backcountry*, 77.

2. See, for example, Oakeshott, "The Early Polis," in Oakeshott, *Lectures in the History of Political Thought*; Sadlek, "Otium, Negotium and the Fear of Acedia," 21.

3. Aristotle, *Politics*, 1:24–54.

4. Arendt, *Human Condition*, 9; d'Entrèves, *Political Philosophy of Hannah Arendt*, 58.

5. Kulikoff, *Tobacco and Slaves*, 176. Cf. Dornan, "Women Slaveholders in the Georgia and South Carolina Low Country."

6. Scarborough, *Overseer*, 20.

7. George Washington to George William Fairfax, 30 June 1785, in Washington, *Writings of Washington from the Original Manuscript Sources*, http://memory.loc.gov/cgi-bin/query/r?ammem/mgw:@field(DOCID+@lit(gw280139)) (accessed 2 May 2015).

8. Rutman and Rutman, *Place in Time*, 42.

9. Joseph Ball to Joseph Chinn, 23 January 1755, Joseph Ball Letterbook, CWF; Rutman and Rutman, *Place in Time*, 42.

10. Minor publications include the *South Carolina Gazette and Country Journal*, viewed on microfilm at Cambridge University Library, an unstamped journal that ran concurrently between 1765 and 1768 with the *SCG*.

11. Archibald McKewn to John Ewing Colhoun, 14 September 1792, John Ewing Colhoun Papers, SCL, USC. Cf. Edward Ambler to Charles Dabney, 7 December 1767, Charles William Dabney Papers, 1715–1845, folder 9, box 1, subseries 1.1: 1716–75, UNC; agreement between Edward Telfair and Sherwood Henderson, 5 February 1798, Seaborn Jones Sr. Papers, 1761–1847, Duke.

12. Supplement to *SCG*, 25 September 1752 to 2 October 1752, 4; *SCG*, 19 January 1765 to 26 January 1765, 3; *SCG*, 17 May 1773, 1.

13. See Scarborough, *Overseer*, 23.

14. The figure of 140 includes those that explicitly referred to overseers (the vast majority), as well as those requiring farm managers, plantation managers, and applicants to other positions that correlated to overseeing. This figure does not include repeats of advertisements. See for

example *SCG,* 2 October 1762 to 9 October 1762, 1; *SCG,* 29 October 1764 to 5 November 1764, 1; *SCG,* 30 June 1766 to 7 July 1766, 2; *SCG,* 14 November 1766 to 1 December 1766, 2.

15. Indeed owning sufficient wealth to avoid having to spend too much time in malaria-infested areas represented a form of prestige in itself. The very presence of overseers meant that planters did not need to risk their health, while "overseers and poorer whites . . . could not flee the countryside as easily as members of the planter elite." Chaplin, *Anxious Pursuit,* 97.

16. *SCG,* 29 October 1764 to 5 November 1764, 1; *SCG,* 6 December 1760 to 16 December 1760, 1.

17. De Crèvecoeur, *Letters from an American Farmer,* ix.

18. *GG,* 20 August 1766, 3.

19. *SCG,* 26 December 1774, 2.

20. Vergil is quoted in the original Latin in *SCG,* 1 January 1754, 1.

21. *SCG,* 31 October 1754, 3.

22. Kulikoff, *Tobacco and Slaves,* 198; 227. Ancel Clarkson signed with a mark on his contract with Charles Dabney. Articles of agreement between Charles Dabney and Ancel Clarkson, 21 August 1772, Charles William Dabney Papers, 1715–1845, folder 13, box 1, subseries 1.1: 1716–75, UNC; cf. Agreement between William Gibbons and William May, William Gibbons Jr. Papers, 1769–71 file, 1728–71 box, Duke. Cf. Lockley, *Lines in the Sand,* 2: "the ultimate problem faced by social historians of the plain folk in colonial and antebellum Georgia is the high level of illiteracy among non-slaveholding whites." Laura Sandy has suggested that overseers were "mostly illiterate," though the demands of their day-to-days tasks would have made widespread illiteracy unlikely. Sandy, "Divided Loyalties in a 'Predatory War,'" 361.

23. *SCG,* 11 June 1772, 2.

24. *SCG,* 22 May 1762 to 29 May 1762, 2.

25. See for example Hening, *Statutes at Large,* 6:42; L. Carter, *Diary of Colonel Landon Carter,* 2:717. Cf. Parent, *Foul Means,* 207n17; 219.

26. Cf. Scarborough, *Overseer,* 22. Scarborough noted how, once the knowledge spread that a planter was seeking a new overseer, he would often receive applications from aspirants.

27. There were "roughly one in ten households purchasing newspapers in the late 1700s." Prude, "To Look upon the 'Lower Sort,'" 129. For similar reasons overseer recruitment adverts were seldom used in the antebellum period. As in the eighteenth century, most overseers were secured through correspondence between proprietors or through direct application to prospective employers. Scarborough, *Overseer,* 23.

28. *VG* (Rind), 11 October 1770, 3 (italics in the original).

29. Isaac, *Transformation of Virginia,* 245.

30. Robert Carter to John Pinkey, 18 July 1775, Robert Carter of Nomini Hall Letterbook, Chauvenet Collection, CWF, 3; cf. Robert Carter to A. Purdie, 24 December 1775, Robert Carter of Nomini Hall Letterbook, Chauvenet Collection, CWF, 3:49 and 51.

31. Supplement to *SCG,* 3 November 1766 to 10 November 1766, 1.

32. Supplement to *SCG,* 31 January 1771, 3.

33. *SCG,* 29 November 1760 to 6 December 1760, 4.

34. Cf. *VG* (Purdie and Dixon), 5 May 1765, 3; *VG* (Rind), 21 November 1771, 4; *VG* (Purdie and Dixon), 22 July 1773, 3.

35. Supplement to *SCG,* 7 January 1765, 1.

36. George Washington to Frances B. Washington, 18 August 1793, in Washington, *Writings of Washington from the Original Manuscript Sources,* http://memory.loc.gov/cgi-bin/query/r?ammem/mgw:@field(DOCID+@lit(gw330052)) (accessed 2 May 2015).

37. William Scarborough suggested that planters only "infrequently" advertised for overseers in newspapers. Scarborough, *Overseer,* 23.

38. On his friend John Coming Ball's death, Henry Laurens acquired part of Broughton Island plantation; he elected to continue to employ Frederick Wiggins as overseer rather than

seek a new manager. Henry Laurens to Frederick Wiggins, 1 October 1765, in Laurens, *HL Papers*, ed. Chesnutt and Rogers, 5:10.

39. *SCG*, 14 November 1766 to 1 December 1766; see also *SCG*, 29 August 1768; *SCG*, 23 August 1770; and *GG*, 11 October 1764.

40. *SCG*, 29 October 1764 to 5 November 1764, 1, to Supplement to *SCG*, 11 March 1765, 1. Kenneth Baillie advertised a position eight times in *GG* between 3 January 1765 and 21 March 1766.

41. Account between the estate of William Gibbons and James Johnston, William Gibbons Jr. Papers, 1772–73 file, box 2, Duke.

42. *SCG*, 15 October 1764 to 22 October 1764, 3 and 2 February 1765 to 9 February 1765, 3. See also the advert by Mrs. Beresford, *SCG*, 26 December 1754, 2; and 27 March to 23 April, 1755, 3.

43. *SCG*, 5 January 1759 to 12 January 1759.

44. Henry Laurens to James Grant, 22 April 1766, in Laurens, *HL Papers*, ed. Chesnutt and Rogers, 5:108.

45. *SCG*, 9 March 1765 to 16 March 1765, 4. William Scarborough suggested that nineteenth-century planters tried to counteract the inefficiencies of recruitment adverts by interviewing applicants and corresponding with other slave owners. Scarborough, *Overseer*, 21. Slaveholders themselves brought letters of introduction to local notables when they moved to a new area. See Jacob Read to Thomas Rede, 20 February 1784, folder 1, Jacob Read Papers, SCL, USC.

46. *VG* (Rind), 11 October 1770, 3.

47. *VG* (Purdie), 29 August 1777, 1; cf. *VG* (Purdie), 13 September 1776, 3; *VG* (Dixon), 14 September 1776, 7.

48. *SCG*, 11 May 1765 to 18 May 1765.

49. Recommendation by James Burk, John Fryer, John Kinchelse, William Montgomery, and Benjamin Wigginton, 21 January 1788, Carter Family Papers, 1651–1861, part 3, VHS.

50. Trinkley et al., *Investigation of an Eighteenth Century Overseer Site (38CH1278), Christ Church Parish, Charleston County, South Carolina*, 30.

51. *SCG*, 22 January 1754 to 29 January 1754 (italics in the original).

52. *SCG*, 6 August 1750 to 13 August 1750 (italics in the original).

53. Henry Laurens to James Grant, 30 January 1767, in Laurens, *HL Papers*, 5:227.

54. George Washington to George William Fairfax, 30 June 1785, in Washington, *Writings of Washington*, http://memory.loc.gov/cgi-bin/query/r?ammem/mgw:@field(DOCID+@lit(gw28 0139)) (accessed 2 May 2015).

55. Cited in P. Morgan, *Slave Counterpoint*, 221.

56. Henry Laurens to James Grant, 22 April 1766, in, Laurens, *HL Papers*, 5:108.

57. Barclay, *Voyages and Travels of James Barclay*, 24–25.

58. Henry Laurens to Joseph Brown, 16 September 1765, in Laurens, *HL Papers*, ed. Chesnutt and Rogers, 5:6.

59. Joseph Ball to Joseph Chinn, 30 June 1749, Joseph Ball Letterbook, CWF.

60. Henry Laurens to James Marion, 20 May 1765, in Laurens, *HL Papers*, ed. Hamer, 4:627.

61. Ibid., 4:583n7; Henry Laurens to Joseph Brown, 21 February 1765, in ibid., 4:583.

62. Henry Laurens to Joseph Brown, 2 October 1765, in Laurens, *HL Papers*, ed. Chesnutt and Rogers, 5:27.

63. Pinckney, *Letterbook of Eliza Lucas Pinckney*, 144.

64. Henry Laurens to James Brenard, 14 February 1765, in Laurens, *HL Papers*, ed. Hamer, 4:579.

65. Laurens, *HL Papers*, ed. Chesnutt and Rogers, 5:10n2; Henry Laurens to Frederick Wiggins, 31 July 1766, in ibid., 145.

66. Henry Laurens to Edward Graham, 31 March 1766, in ibid., 96.

67. Ibid., 10n2; Henry Laurens to Frederick Wiggins, 31 July 1766, in ibid., 145.

68. Scarborough, *Overseer*, 73.

69. Kathleen Brown, *Good Wives, Nasty Wenches, and Anxious Patriarchs,* 319–20.

70. *SCG,* 15 December 1758 to 22 January 1759, 4.

71. *SCG,* 5 April 1775, 1.

72. *SCG,* 2 January 1775, 3.

73. *SCG,* 11 June 1772, 2, and 18 June 1772, 4.

74. *SCG,* 17 December to 24 December 1764, 4.

75. P. Morgan, *Slave Counterpoint,* 327; see Henry Laurens to Abraham Schad, 1 March 1766, in Laurens, *HL Papers,* ed. Chesnutt and Rogers, 5:83.

76. *SCG,* 27 September to 2 October 1758, 3.

77. *SCG,* 10 March 1757, 3.

78. Entry for 18 August 1775, daybook, 13:75, Robert Carter Papers, 1772–94, Duke.

79. Laurens cited in B. Wood, *Slavery in Colonial Georgia,* 140.

80. L. Carter, "Landon Carter's Crop Book," 281.

81. Cf. Edelson, *Plantation Enterprise in Colonial South Carolina,* 12; 66–99.

82. Breen, *Tobacco Culture,* xii.

83. Ragsdale, *Planters' Republic,* 24.

84. Breen, *Tobacco Culture,* xii.

85. Ragsdale, *Planters' Republic,* 24.

86. Sarson, *British America 1500–1800,* 227–28.

87. *Boston Chronicle* 1, no. 42, 26 September to 3 October 1768, in South Carolina Regulators: 2 MPs, SCL, USC, 26 September to 3 October and 3 October to 10 October 1768 file, 381.

88. Breen, *Tobacco Culture,* 147–50.

89. See for example Burgess Mitchell and George Washington, contract for overseer, 1 May 1762, in Washington, *Writings of Washington from the Original Manuscript Sources,* http://memory.loc.gov/cgi-bin/query/P?mgw:1:./temp/~ammem_xjoY:: (accessed 2 May 2015).

90. Breen, *Tobacco Culture,* xxvi.

91. Poovey, "Liberal Civil Subject and the Social in Eighteenth-Century British Moral Philosophy," 55.

92. Cf. Baird, "Between Slavery and Independence," 232; Pearsall, *Atlantic Families,* 115–16.

93. Humphrey Knight to George Washington, 16 June 1758, in Washington, *Writings of Washington from the Original Manuscript Sources,* http://memory.loc.gov/cgi-bin/query/r?ammem/mgw:@field(DOCID+@lit(lw020210)) (accessed 2 May 2015).

94. Henry Laurens to Joseph Brown, 13 January 1766, in Laurens, *HL Papers,* ed. Chesnutt and Rogers, 5:48.

95. Isaac, *Transformation of Virginia,* 251.

96. Edward Violet and George Washington, contract for overseer, 5 August 1762, in Washington, *Writings of Washington from the Original Manuscript Sources,* http://memory.loc.gov/cgi-bin/ampage?collId=mgw4&fileName=gwpage032.db&recNum=214&tempFile=./temp/~ammem_dl9d&filecode=mgw&next_filecode=mgw&itemnum=1&ndocs=100 (accessed 2 May 2015); Burgess Mitchell and George Washington, contract for overseer, 1 May 1762, in Washington, *Writings of Washington from the Original Manuscript Sources,* http://memory.loc.gov/cgi-bin/query/P?mgw:1:./temp/~ammem_1gk6:: (accessed 2 May 2015).

97. *SCG,* 29 August 1768, 4; *SCG,* 21 April to 28 April 1759, 4. Cf. Agreement between Samuel Hammond and John Hume, 17 June 1785, folder 1, 1761–93, Seaborn Jones Sr. Papers, Duke.

98. Osborne, *Williamsburg in Colonial Times,* 140.

99. *VG* (Dixon), 18 November 1775, 3; cf. *VG* (Purdie and Dixon), 30 October 1766, 3.

100. Supplement to *SCG,* 4 June 1772, 1.

101. P. V. B. Livingston to Othniel Beale, 1 December 1750, Othniel Beale Papers, SCL, USC.

102. Henry Laurens to Edward Graham, 31 March 1766, in Laurens, *HL Papers,* ed. Chesnutt and Rogers, 5:96.

103. Henry Laurens to Joseph Brown, 16 September 1765, in ibid., 5:6.
104. *SCG,* 23 June 1758, 1.
105. *SCG,* 22 December to 29 December 1766, 2.
106. Washington, "View of the Work at the Several Plantations in the Year 1789 and General Directions for the Execution of It," VHS.
107. Trinkley et al., *Investigation of an Eighteenth Century Overseer Site (38CH1278), Christ Church Parish, Charleston County, South Carolina,* 30–31.
108. All percentages are rounded up or down to the nearest whole number. Studying adverts represents one of the best ways to divine the desired marital status of overseers. Other records tend to be patchy. In colonial South Carolina, for example, there was no systematic procedure for recording marriage licenses issued, and for areas outside coastal South Carolina, marriage records are practically nonexistent. See Holcomb, *South Carolina Marriages 1688–1799,* iii.
109. Cf. Kulikoff, *Tobacco and Slaves,* 86.
110. Holcomb, *South Carolina Marriages 1688–1799,* 158; 55; cf. Holcomb, *Supplement to South Carolina Marriages 1688–1820.*
111. *SCG,* 12 February to 19 February 1763, 3.
112. 17 July 1745, Joseph Ball Letterbook, CWF.
113. George Washington to Burgess Ball, 21 July 1793, in Washington, *Writings of Washington from the Original Manuscript Sources,* http://memory.loc.gov/cgi-bin/ampage?collId=mgw4&-fileName=gwpage104.db&recNum=46&tempFile=./temp/~ammem_gMCf&filecode=mgw&next_filecode=mgw&itemnum=1&ndocs=100 (accessed 2 May 2015). Cf. George Washington to Alexander Spotswood, 14 September 1798, in Washington, *Writings of Washington from the Original Manuscript Sources,* http://memory.loc.gov/cgi-bin/query/r?ammem/mgw:@field(DOCID+@lit(gw360340)) (accessed 2 May 2015).
114. Thomas Jefferson to Thomas Mann Randolph Jr., 24 June 1793, in Jefferson, *Works of Thomas Jefferson in Twelve Volumes,* vol. 11, http://memory.loc.gov/cgi-bin/query/r?ammem/mtj:@field(DOCID+@lit(tj070172)) (accessed 30 April 2015).
115. B. Wood, *Slavery in Colonial Georgia,* 139.
116. Supplement to *SCG,* 3 November to 10 November 1766, 2; *SCG,* 10 November to 17 November, 1766, 1.
117. L. Carter, "Landon Carter's Crop Book," 281.
118. Henry Laurens to James Lawrence, 12 February 1763, in Laurens, *HL Papers,* ed. Hamer, 3:248.
119. Ibid., 3:426.
120. Sandy, "Mary-Anne Schad and Mrs. Brown," 66.
121. Cf. McCurdy, *Citizen Bachelors.*
122. Mercer cited in Baird, "Between Slavery and Independence," 114.
123. Henry Laurens to Abraham Schad, 1 April 1765, in Laurens, *HL Papers,* ed. Hamer, 4:598.
124. Henry Laurens to Abraham Schad, 23 August 1765, in ibid., 665.
125. Henry Laurens to Timothy Creamer, 18 August 1764, in ibid., 369.
126. *GG,* 17 September 1759, 3
127. *SCG,* 23 August 1770, 3.
128. *VG* (Purdie), 29 August 1777, 1; cf. *VG* (Purdie), 13 September 1776, 3; *VG* (Dixon), 14 September 1776, 7.
129. Sandy, "Homemakers, Supervisors and Peach Stealing Bitches," 486–87.
130. Berkin, "Clio's Daughters," 17.
131. Dornan, "Women Slaveholders in the Georgia and South Carolina Low Country," 180.
132. Kimber cited in Kulikoff, *Tobacco and Slaves,* 217.
133. Berkin, "Clio's Daughters," 20.
134. See Pinckney, *Letterbook of Eliza Lucas Pinckney.*

135. Dornan, "Women Slaveholders in the Georgia and South Carolina Low Country," 198. It is important to recognize that though Pinckney stressed her femininity and domesticity, she and other South Carolinian plantation mistresses enjoyed significant economic autonomy in comparison to women in other colonies and of other social classes. The demographic context outlined in the previous paragraph yielded to some South Carolinian women commercial opportunities that, for reasons of propriety, Pinckney's rhetoric attempted to occlude. See, for example, Anzilotti, *Affairs of the World.*

136. Maryann Maury to John Fontaine, 20 July 1753, Fontaine-Maury Papers, folder 3, "part 2," 1737–49, Swem.

137. *SCG,* 21 November 1774, 4. Testimony to the idea that tasks like these generally were assigned to women is that a "SINGLE woman, with a child" placed an advert in South Carolina, declaring herself suitable for similar work. *SCG,* 29 October to 5 November 1764, 1.

138. *SCG,* 11 June 1772, 2.

139. Dornan, "Women Slaveholders in the Georgia and South Carolina Low Country," 194.

140. *SCG,* 11 June 1772, 2.

141. *SCG,* 18 June 1772, 4. Single men were sometimes given teaching jobs, indicating that an unmarried status did not necessarily preclude rational superintendence of dependents. More salient factors in cases like these would have been family background, economic independence, and the need to fill the position. See, for example, *SCG,* 24 April to 11 May 1767, 3.

142. Pinckney, *Letterbook of Eliza Lucas Pinckney,* 144.

143. Dornan, "Women Slaveholders in the Georgia and South Carolina Low Country," 194.

144. George Washington to John Augustine Washington, 16 January 1783, in Washington, *Writings of Washington from the Original Manuscript Sources,* http://memory.loc.gov/cgi-bin/query/r?ammem/mgw:@field(DOCID+@lit(gw260062)) (accessed 2 May 2015).

145. The figure used here is twenty-five since the two adverts placed by overseers themselves are not counted.

146. *SCG,* 24 October 1774, 3.

147. *SCG,* 3 December to 10 December, 1764, 2.

148. *SCG,* 26 December 1754, 2.

149. Mrs. Beresford, *SCG,* 26 December 1754, 2; Martha Williamson, *SCG,* 23 June 1758, 1; Martha Woodcraft, *SCG,* 25 September to 2 October 1762, 4.

150. Dornan, "Women Slaveholders in the Georgia and South Carolina Low Country," 192.

151. *VG* (Purdie and Dixon), 26 August 1773, 3.

Chapter 3: "Nothing pleases me better than to see them in good order"

1. Scarborough, *Overseer,* 68.
2. Cf. B. Wood, *Slavery in Colonial Georgia,* 139.
3. Cf. P. Morgan, *Slave Counterpoint,* 259.
4. See Isaac, *Landon Carter's Uneasy Kingdom,* 88; 173–74.
5. See, for example, entry for 1761, James Glen rice account with John Drayton, 1761–66, James Glen Papers, SCL, USC, for overseers who received both wages and a share of the crop.
6. Kulikoff cited in P. Morgan, *Slave Counterpoint,* 327.
7. Washington, *Diaries of George Washington,* 4:244.
8. *SCG,* 31 January 1771, 3; *Butler Plantation Papers,* University Library, University of Cambridge, 9.
9. Henry Laurens to Frederick Wiggins, 1 October 1765, in Laurens, *HL Papers,* ed. Chesnutt and Rogers, 5:10.
10. Kenneth M. Stampp found that on the South Carolina rice coast during the antebellum period, overseers' terms lasted on average three to six years. Stampp cited in Scarborough, *Overseer,* 39; Joseph Manigault cited in Phillips, *Slave Economy of the Old South,* 105n14.

11. Kulikoff, *Tobacco and Slaves,* 410n54; cf. P. Morgan, *Slave Counterpoint,* 327.

12. Jerdone Family Papers, L. of Va.

13. Hayne, "Records Kept by Colonel Isaac Hayne," 21–23.

14. *VG* (Purdie), 30 August 1776, 4; *VG* (Purdie), 19 September 1777, 1.

15. Scarborough, *Overseer,* 9.

16. Isaac Mims receipt, 1771, John Gibbons Papers, file 1, Duke; B. Wood, *Slavery in Colonial Georgia,* 139.

17. Supplement to *SCG,* 7 January 1765, 1.

18. William Gibbons and Thomas Moore, contract for overseer, 30 November 1769, William Gibbons Papers, 1769–71 file, 1728–71 box, Duke.

19. B. Wood, *Slavery in Colonial Georgia,* 139.

20. See for example Edward Violet and George Washington, contract for overseer, 5 August 1762, in Washington, *Writings of Washington from the Original Manuscript Sources,* http://memory.loc.gov/cgi-bin/ampage?collId=mgw4&fileName=gwpage032.db&recNum=214&tempFile=./temp/~ammem_dl9d&filecode=mgw&next_filecode=mgw&itemnum=1&ndocs=100 (accessed 2 May 2015); Burgess Mitchell and George Washington, contract for overseer, 1 May 1762, in Washington, *Writings of Washington from the Original Manuscript Sources,* http://memory.loc.gov/cgi-bin/query/P?mgw:1:./temp/~ammem_1gk6:: (accessed 2 May 2015); cf. Scarborough, *Overseer,* 23.

21. Henry Laurens to Joseph Brown, 22 October 1765, in Laurens, *HL Papers,* ed. Chesnutt and Rogers, 5:26.

22. Henry Laurens to James Lawrence, 12 February 1763, in Laurens, *HL Papers,* ed. Hamer, 3:248.

23. Articles of agreement between Charles Dabney and Charles Nicholls, 21 August 1772, Charles William Dabney Papers, 1715–1845, folder 13, box 1, subseries 1.1: 1716–75, UNC; cf. Articles of Agreement between Charles Dabney and Ancel Clarkson, 21 August 1772, Charles William Dabney Papers, 1715–1845, folder 13, box 1, subseries 1.1: 1716–75, UNC; memorandum of agreement between John Hall and John Williams, December 1764, William Henry Hall Papers, 1736–1862, Duke.

24. Henry Laurens to Joseph Brown, 16 September 1765, in Laurens, *HL Papers,* ed. Chesnutt and Rogers, 5:6.

25. P. Morgan, *Slave Counterpoint,* 327.

26. Schmidt, "Overseers and the Nature of Southern Labor Contracts."

27. Ibid., 95.

28. Ibid., 90

29. Scarborough, *Overseer,* 39.

30. Ibid., 40.

31. George Washington to Frances B. Washington, 18 August 1793, in Washington, *Writings of Washington from the Original Manuscript Sources,* http://memory.loc.gov/cgi-bin/query/r?ammem/mgw:@field(DOCID+@lit(gw330052)) (accessed 2 May 2015) (italics in the original); cf. George Washington to Alexander Spotswood, 14 September 1798, in ibid., http://memory.loc.gov/cgi-bin/query/r?ammem/mgw:@field(DOCID+@lit(gw360340)) (accessed 2 May 2015).

32. *VG* (Rind), 25 January 1770.

33. See Baird, "Between Slavery and Independence."

34. *VG* (Rind), 26 April 1770, 1 (italics in the original).

35. Francis Jerdone Memorandum Book, L. of Va., 2–3.

36. Ibid., 12; cf. 13.

37. Cf. Scarborough, *Overseer,* 12.

38. Francis Jerdone Memorandum Book, L. of Va., 5.

39. Cf. Scarborough, *Overseer,* 12.

40. *SCG,* 15 March 1773, 2 (italics in the original).

41. B. Wood, *Slavery in Colonial Georgia,* 140.

42. *SCG,* 19 September 1774, 3; cf. *SCG,* 26 September 1774, 3.

43. *SCG,* 26 September 1774, 3.

44. *SCG,* 18 October to October 25 1760, 3; 22 May to 29 May 1762, 2; 23 October to 30 October 1762, 1; additional supplement to *SCG,* 18 July 1768, 2; continuation of *SCG,* 16 August 1770, 4.

45. Entry for 4 May 1776, John Page Diary, Swem.

46. William Gibbons and Peter Papot, contract for overseer, 1776?, William Gibbons Jr. Papers, 1774–84 file, 1728–71 box, Duke.

47. William Gibbons and James Guinn, contract for overseer, 24 February 1770, William Gibbons Jr. Papers, 1774–84 file, 1728–71 box, Duke.

48. *GG,* 17 September 1766, 3.

49. Henry Laurens to Joseph Brown, 16 September 1765, in Laurens, *HL Papers,* ed. Chesnutt and Rogers, 5:6; *SCG,* 23 August to 30 August 1760, 3. This was at a time when irrigation became very important for the production of rice. See Stubbs, "Rice."

50. Mullin, *Flight and Rebellion,* 52.

51. *SCG,* 15 October to 22 October 1764, 3; *GG,* 19 July 1764, 4; 18 October 1764, 3.

52. *SCG,* 29 October to 5 November 1764, 1; cf. 15 October to 22 October 1764, 3; *SCG,* 22 December to 29 December 1766, 2; *SCG,* 20 October to 27 October 1766, 2.

53. Entry for 2 August 1791, Cabell Commonplace Book, Cabell Commonplace Books, 1769–95, VHS, 9; entry for 24 September 1791, ibid., 10.

54. Continuation of *SCG,* 16 August 1770, 4.

55. *SCG,* 25 September to 2 October 1762, 4.

56. Mullin, *Flight and Rebellion,* 26; Valentine Crawford and George Washington, contract for overseer, 20 March 1774, in Washington, *Writings of Washington from the Original Manuscript Sources,* http://memory.loc.gov/cgi-bin/ampage?collId=mgw4&fileName=gwpage033.db&recNum=148&tempFile=./temp/~ammem_jh3W&filecode=mgw&next_filecode=mgw&itemnum=1&ndocs=100 (accessed 2 May 2015); Robert Carter, *The Diary, Correspondence, and Papers of Robert "King" Carter of Virginia, 1701–1732,* ed. Edmund Berkeley Jr., http://carter.lib.virginia.edu/public/ (accessed 6 May 2015); Thomas Jefferson to Thomas Mann Randolph Jr., 15 May 1791, Jefferson, *Works of Thomas Jefferson in Twelve Volumes,* vol. 11, http://memory.loc.gov/cgi-bin/query/r?ammem/mtj:@field(DOCID+@lit(tj060122)) (accessed 30 April 2015). For marketing products see *SCG,* 20 to 27 October 1766, 2. For buying provisions see entries for 19 April, 4 May, and 22 July? 1777, John Page Diary, Swem.

57. Cf. Scarborough, *Overseer,* 67–70.

58. Cf. ibid., 70.

59. See for example Agreement between Daniel Parke Custis and Joseph Valentine, 14 November 1755, Custis Family Papers, 1683–1858, VHS; cf. Scarborough, *Overseer,* 46.

60. Peter Montague cited in Rutman and Rutman, *Place in Time,* 42–43.

61. Entry for 21 June 1781, Sarah Fouace Nourse Diary, 1781–82, Nourse and Morris Family Papers, Swem.

62. Francis Jerdone Memorandum Book, L. of Va., 14.

63. Rutman and Rutman, *Place in Time,* 43; Mullin, *Flight and Rebellion,* 50.

64. Kulikoff, *Tobacco and Slaves,* 100.

65. Hening, *Statutes at Large,* 1:125–6; 152; 166; 344; 347; 419; 2:123, 262, 338; Kulikoff, *Tobacco and Slaves,* 120.

66. Kulikoff, *Tobacco and Slaves,* 157; 429.

67. Hening, *Statutes at Large,* 1:218; 2:120; 306; 3:81; 4:96–7; 136. Cf. *VG* (Purdie and Dixon), 14 January 1768, 3.

68. Manuscript book 13, 1773–76, Robert Carter of Nomini Hall Letterbook, Chauvenet Collection, CWF, 12–13.

69. Agreement between Daniel Parke Custis and Joseph Valentine, 14 November 1755, Custis Family Papers, 1683–1858, VHS.

70. Entry for March 1776, John Page Diary, Swem. See also entries for April, May, June, August, September, October, and November 1776.

71. Thomas Jefferson to George Washington, 14 May 1794, in Jefferson, *Works of Thomas Jefferson,* http://hdl.loc.gov/loc.mss/mtj.mtjbib008396 (accessed 30 April 2015); entry for 2 August 1762, in Washington, *Diaries of George Washington,* 1:304; Thomas Jefferson to George Washington, 18 June 1792, in Jefferson, *Works of Thomas Jefferson,* http://hdl.loc.gov/loc.mss/mtj.mtjbib006309 (accessed 30 April 2015).

72. Washington, *Diaries of George Washington,* 1:xviii; Tobias Lear to Alexander Robertson, 16 December 1792, in Washington, *Writings of Washington from the Original Manuscript Sources,* http://memory.loc.gov/cgi-bin/query/r?ammem/mgw:@field(DOCID+@lit(gw320204)) (accessed 6 February 2015).

73. Washington, *Diaries of George Washington,* 1:xviii. Cf. Washington's frequent and detailed annotations in M. Duhamel du Monceau, *Practical Treatise on Husbandry* (London, 1762), kept at VHS, in which he calculated the value of the greater yields that the "new husbandry" promised. See also Washington's notes from a book on agriculture, Sol Feinstone Collection, CWF.

74. Thomas Jefferson to George Washington, 14 May 1794, in Jefferson, *Works of Thomas Jefferson,* http://hdl.loc.gov/loc.mss/mtj.mtjbib008396 (accessed 30 April 2015); entry for 2 August 1762, in Washington, *Diaries of George Washington,* 1:304; Thomas Jefferson to George Washington, 18 June 1792, in Jefferson, *Works of Thomas Jefferson,* http://hdl.loc.gov/loc.mss/mtj.mtjbib006309 (accessed 30 April 2015); L. Carter, "Landon Carter's Crop Book," 282; Thomas Jefferson to William Pearce, 15 December 1792, in Jefferson, *Works of Thomas Jefferson,* http://hdl.loc.gov/loc.mss/mtj.mtjbib006702 (accessed 30 April 2015).

75. Washington, *Diaries of George Washington,* 1:xxx–xxxiii.

76. Henry Laurens to Richard Oswald and Co., 26 May 1756, in Laurens, *HL Papers,* ed. Hamer, 2:203.

77. Entry for 3 February 1777, Margaret Colleton account, 25 September 1776 to 28 August 1780, Margaret Colleton Papers, folder 5, SCL, USC; Chaplin, "Tidal Rice Cultivation and the Problem of Slavery in South Carolina, 1760–1815," 48; 49.

78. Edelson, *Plantation Enterprise in Colonial South Carolina,* 4.

79. Stubbs, "Indigo"; John Hampton to John Bynum, Richard Hampton Papers, folder: Major John Hampton, 1743–1808, SCL, USC; John Couturier to John Ewing Colhoun, 17 April 1792, John Ewing Colhoun Papers, SCL, USC.

80. Hening, *Statutes at Large,* 6:133.

81. *SCG,* 18 October 1770, 2.

82. See, for example, *VG* (Rind), 8 November 1770; cf. 4 August 1768. For servants see *VG* (Purdie and Dixon), 13 August 1772, 2; *VG* (Rind), 10 August 1772, 4. See also Betty Wood's description of overseer involvement in advertising female runaways. B. Wood, *Slavery in Colonial Georgia,* 172.

83. *Supplement to SCG,* 24 May 1773, 4.

84. See Hadden, *Slave Patrols.*

85. Cf. Lockley, *Lines in the Sand,* 40–41.

86. Cf. ibid., 38–39.

87. Laurens, *HL Papers,* ed. Hamer, 4:2n1.

88. Ibid., 4:628n5.

89. Henry Laurens to John Smith, 30 August 1766, in Laurens, *HL Papers,* ed. Chesnutt and Rogers, 5:175.

90. Henry Laurens to James Cordes Jr., 30 August 1765, in Laurens, *HL Papers,* ed. Hamer, 4:670.

91. Cf. Lockley, *Lines in the Sand,* 40–41.

92. See entry for 23 April 1777, John Page Diary, Swem. Cf. Scarborough, *Overseer,* 28.

93. Robert Carter to John Goodwin, 20 August 1706, in R. Carter, *Diary, Correspondence, and Papers of Robert "King" Carter of Virginia;* John Walker account 1763, Henry Fitzhugh Papers, 1746–49, Duke, 111; Edward Snickers Account, 10 January 1774–20 June 1776; 9 April 1785, to Earl of Dunmore, Swem; *VG* (Purdie), 30 October 1778, 3; Washington, *Diaries of George Washington,* 4:142; L. Carter, "Landon Carter's Crop Book," 281; Mary Douglass to Francis Jerdone, 10 January 1797, Jerdone Family Papers, folder 2, box 3, Swem.

94. *VG* (Purdie), 14 November 1774, 3.

95. Edward Snickers Account, 10 January 1774–20 June 1776; 9 April 1785, to Earl of Dunmore, Swem.

96. Cf. Scarborough, *Overseer,* 27. John J. McCusker is the standard authority on comparative exchange rates in the Anglophone Atlantic world. See McCusker, *Money and Exchange in Europe and America, 1600–1775.*

97. Mullin, *Flight and Rebellion,* 52.

98. Cf. Scarborough, *Overseer,* 27.

99. George Washington to George William Fairfax, 30 June 1785, in Washington, *Writings of Washington from the Original Manuscript Sources,* http://memory.loc.gov/cgi-bin/query/r?ammem/mgw:@field(DOCID+@lit(gw280139)) (accessed 2 May 2015).

100. Tobias Lear to Alexander Robertson, 16 December 1792, in Washington, *Writings of Washington from the Original Manuscript Sources,* http://memory.loc.gov/cgi-bin/query/r?ammem/mgw:@field(DOCID+@lit(gw320204)) (accessed 6 February 2015).

101. Entry for 23 September 1771, miscellaneous notes, Bluff plantation book, John Harleston Papers, ca. 1759–74, SCL, USC, 82.

102. Trinkley et al., *Investigation of an Eighteenth Century Overseer Site (38CH1278), Christ Church Parish, Charleston County, South Carolina,* 41.

103. B. Wood, *Slavery in Colonial Georgia,* 139.

104. 28 January 1769; 30 November 1769; 24 February 1770, 1769–71 file; William Gibbons and Peter Papot, contract for overseer 1776?, 1774–84 file, 1728–71 box, William Gibbons Jr. Papers, Duke. The difference in Papot's annuity possibly also resulted from currency fluctuations at the beginning of the Revolution.

105. *SCG,* 30 January 1775, 3; *SCG,* 19 January to 26 January 1765, 3.

106. *SCG,* 31 December 1772, 2.

107. Henry Laurens to Paul Trapier, 21 August 1766, in Laurens, *HL Papers,* ed. Chesnutt and Rogers, 5:172.

108. Henry Laurens to Edward Graham, 31 March 1766, in ibid., 5:96; Henry Laurens to Joseph Brown, 13 January 1766, in ibid., 5:48.

109. Cf. Scarborough, *Overseer,* 27.

110. R. Brown and B. Brown, *Virginia 1705–1786,* 50. Cf. Washington, *Diaries of George Washington,* 4:142.

111. Washington, *Diaries of George Washington,* 1:xviii. Cf. Scarborough, *Overseer,* 27. Overseer wages may well have risen commensurate with the increase in responsibility engendered by absenteeism, or by the introduction of agricultural innovation over the course of the century.

112. B. Wood, *Slavery in Colonial Georgia,* 139.

113. Henry Laurens to John Smith, 4 February 1766, in Laurens, *HL Papers,* ed. Chesnutt and Rogers, 5:67.

114. Entry for 20 August 1762, Francis Jerdone Memorandum Book, Swem.

115. Scarborough, *Overseer,* 34–35.

116. ibid., 30.

117. Cf. ibid., 40.

118. Some planters offered overseers a choice between payment in shares or a salary. See, for example, *VG* (Purdie), 29 August 1777, 1.

119. H. Jones, *Present State of Virginia,* 36; cf. Scarborough, *Overseer,* 31.

120. Tobias Lear to Alexander Robertson, 16 December 1792, in Washington, *Writings of Washington from the Original Manuscript Sources,* http://memory.loc.gov/cgi-bin/query/r?ammem/mgw:@field(DOCID+@lit(gw320204)) (accessed 6 February 2015).

121. L. Carter, *Diary of Colonel Landon Carter,* 1:585; L. Carter, "Landon Carter's Crop Book," 281.

122. Entry for 23 April 1776, John Page Diary, Swem.

123. Entry for 2 August 1792, Cabell Commonplace Book, Cabell Commonplace Books, 1769–95, VHS, 14.

124. 15 March 1760, William Gibbons Jr. Papers, 1760–64 file, 1728–71 box, Duke.

125. Henry Laurens to James Brenard, 6 January 1764, in Laurens, *HL Papers,* ed. Hamer, 4:121.

126. Scarborough, *Overseer,* 4.

127. Henry Fitzhugh account with William Payne, Henry Fitzhugh Ledger, Duke.

128. Henry Laurens to John Coming Ball, 29 November 1763, in Laurens, *HL Papers,* ed. Hamer, 4:59.

129. Cf. *GG,* 3 January 1765, 3. One study of South Carolinian overseer adverts between 1734 and 1768 found only three references to shares and concluded that the share system was not as prevalent as a means of payment for overseers as other historians had suggested. The analysis carried out for this book found more mentions of shares, particularly when overseers were employed with their own bondpeople. The nature of newspaper recruitment must also be taken into account. When employers recruited unknown overseers, they were largely unaware of these men's agricultural capacities: wages were a safer option. In this sense employing overseers who owned their own enslaved labor force represented more of a surety that candidates could cope with the demands of plantation management. See Trinkley et al., *Investigation of an Eighteenth Century Overseer Site (38CH1278), Christ Church Parish, Charleston County, South Carolina,* 41.

130. Entries for 1762 to 1766, James Glen rice account with John Drayton, 1761–66, James Glen Papers, SCL, USC.

131. *SCG,* 1 December 1768, 3.

132. *SCG,* 23 October to 20 October 1762, 1; *SCG,* 19 January to 26 January 1765, 3.

133. See E. Jones, *Agriculture and the Industrial Revolution.*

134. Cf. Kulikoff, *Tobacco and Slaves,* 429.

135. Moreau de St. Mery cited in Baird, "Between Slavery and Independence," 140.

136. George Washington to George William Fairfax, 30 June 1785, in Washington, *Writings of Washington from the Original Manuscript Sources,* http://memory.loc.gov/cgi-bin/query/r?ammem/mgw:@field(DOCID+@lit(gw280139)) (accessed 2 May 2015); cf. Gilbert Simpson to George Washington, July 1773, in Washington, *Writings of Washington from the Original Manuscript Sources,* http://memory.loc.gov/cgi-bin/query/r?ammem/mgw:@field(DOCID+@lit(lw040128)) (accessed 2 June 2015); Baird, "Paternalism and Profits," 160; Baird, "Between Slavery and Independence," 140.

137. Entry for 26 August 1776, daybook, 13:201, Robert Carter Papers, 1772–94, viewed in typescript at Duke.

138. Scarborough, *Overseer,* 31.

139. Baird, "Between Slavery and Independence."

140. See C. Scott, *Domination and the Arts of Resistance,* 70–107.

141. Entry for 20 August 1762, Francis Jerdone Memorandum Book, Swem.

142. Entry for 6 January 1757, ibid.

143. Entry for 17 July 1757, ibid.

144. Entry for 18 June 1761, ibid. A List of the Crop of Tob[acc]o—made by John Higgason the year 1760, in Colonel Dudley Digge's plantations in Louisa. Overseer's Reports, Charles William Dabney Papers, 1715–1845, vol. 3, folder 404, UNC.

145. *VG* (Rind), 15 July 1773, 4; William Gibbons Jr. Papers, 1776–84 file, box 2, Duke.

146. Baird, "Between Slavery and Independence," 12; entry for 23 September 1771, miscellaneous notes, Bluff plantation book, John Harleston Papers, ca. 1759–74, SCL, USC, 82; William Ancrum to Marlow Pryor, 1 March 1776, William Ancrum Account Book and Letterbook, SCL, USC; shoes bought of Mr. Alexander Watt and to whom delivered, William Gibbons Jr. Papers, 1790–1803 and n.d. file, box 2, Duke; entry for 31 December 1786, Samuel Stiles' Account Book 1783–1803, Colonial Dames Collection, GHS, 2.

147. Francis Jerdone Memorandum Book, L. of Va., 14.

148. Joseph Ball to Joseph Chinn, 13 November 1746, Joseph Ball Letterbook, CWF; Joseph Ball to Joseph Chinn, 11 April 1748, Joseph Ball Letterbook, CWF.

149. Cf. P. Morgan, *Slave Counterpoint,* 276.

150. Max Edelson has argued that by encouraging overseers to purchase goods produced on their plantations, slaveholders in fact yielded them autonomy by permitting them access to a world of material consumption. Edelson, *Plantation Enterprise in Colonial South Carolina,* 209; 216; 231; 236. The suggestion here is that while managers gained significant material benefits from their arrangement with planters, the calumny associated with being dependent on others for an adequate livelihood substantially offset these benefits.

151. Mullin, *Flight and Rebellion,* 50; 29.

152. Joseph Ball to Joseph Chinn, 22 October 1756, Joseph Ball Letterbook, CWF.

153. 15 March 1760, William Gibbons Jr. Papers, 1760–64 file, 1728–71 box, Duke.

154. 28 January 1769; 30 November 1769; 24 February 1770, William Gibbons Jr. Papers, 1769–71 file, 1728–71 box, Duke.

155. Henry Laurens to John Smith, 23 December 1765, in Laurens, *HL Papers,* ed. Chesnutt and Rogers, 5:47; Henry Laurens to Joseph Brown, 13 January 1766, in ibid., 5:48.

156. 12 June 1760, Miscellaneous Bonds, Book O, GDAH, 151–52.

157. Isaac Hayne Ledger, SCHS, 40 and 70.

158. Entry for 13 August 1785, in Washington, *Diaries of George Washington,* 4:182. Cf. Simon Sallard to John Carter, 4 November 1736, Carter Family Papers, 1651–1861, part 3, VHS.

159. Agreement between Daniel Parke Custis and Joseph Valentine, 14 November 1755, Custis Family Papers, 1683–1858, VHS.

160. Carter cited in Mullin, *Flight and Rebellion,* 53. Cf. Entry for 7 August 1762, Francis Jerdone Memorandum Book, Swem.

161. Cf. George Washington to Burgess Ball, 21 July 1793, in Washington, *Writings of Washington from the Original Manuscript Sources,* http://memory.loc.gov/cgi-bin/ampage?collId=mgw4&fileName=gwpage104.db&recNum=46&tempFile=./temp/~ammem_gMCf&filecode=mgw&next_filecode=mgw&itemnum=1&ndocs=100 (accessed 2 May 2015). Cf. Scarborough, *Overseer,* 36; Camp, *Closer to Freedom,* 16–20.

162. Walsh, *From Calabar to Carter's Grove,* 91.

163. Ibid., 181.

164. *VG* (supplement), 25 October 1765, 4.

165. Tobias Lear to Alexander Robertson, 16 December 1792, in Washington, *Writings of Washington from the Original Manuscript Sources,* http://memory.loc.gov/cgi-bin/query/r?ammem/mgw:@field(DOCID+@lit(gw320204)) (accessed 6 February 2015).

166. Henry Laurens to Richard Oswald, 12 August 1766, in Laurens, *HL Papers,* ed. Chesnutt and Rogers, 5:157.

167. Joseph Ball to Joseph Chinn, 14 February 1744, Joseph Ball Letterbook, CWF.

168. James Jones to William Belcher, 13 May 1797, Josiah Tatnall Sr. Papers, folder: financial papers 1797–1803, Duke.

169. Peter Papot account, 26 March 1779, William Gibbons Jr. Papers, 1774–84 file, 1728–71 box, Duke.

170. Henry Laurens to Joseph Brown, 13 January 1766, in Laurens, *HL Papers,* ed. Chesnutt and Rogers, 5:48.

171. Henry Laurens to Joseph Brown, 25 April 1766, in ibid., 5:120.

172. Henry Laurens to John Coming Ball, 27 December 1763, in ibid., 5:120.

173. George Washington to Alexander Spotswood, 14 September 1798, in Washington, *Writings of Washington from the Original Manuscript Sources,* http://memory.loc.gov/cgi-bin/query/r?ammem/mgw:@field(DOCID+@lit(gw360340)) (accessed 2 May 2015) (italics in the original).

174. ? to Robert Carter, 16 November 1793, correspondence of Robert Carter III, Carter Family Papers, 1651–1861, folder 4, section 22, VHS.

175. Joseph Ball to Joseph Chinn, 17 July 1745, Joseph Ball Letterbook, CWF.

176. *SCG,* 2 January 1775, 3.

177. John Houstoun to ?, 17 March 1792, Houstoun Collection, Colonial Dames Collection, folder 5A/4, box 2, GHS.

Chapter 4: "Under the shadow of my own Vine & my own Fig-tree"

1. "Interest (n.)." in *Oxford English Dictionary,* http://www.oed.com/view/Entry/97735 (accessed 13 February 2015), 3.

2. Henry Laurens to Peter Horlbeck, 15 May 1765, in Laurens, *HL Papers,* ed. Hamer, 4:624.

3. Henry Laurens to Thomas Martin, 7 February 1763, in Laurens, *HL Papers,* ed. Hamer, 3:237.

4. Robert Carter to Newyear Branson, 21 January 1768, Robert Carter of Nomini Hall Letterbook, Chauvenet Collection, CWF, 6:66. Cf. Entry for 23 June 1777, Margaret Colleton account, 25 September 1776 to 28 August 1780, Margaret Colleton Papers, folder 5, SCL, USC.

5. P. Morgan, *Slave Counterpoint,* 322.

6. Sarson, *British America 1500–1800,* 213; 227.

7. For the influence of the country ideology in eighteenth-century South Carolina, see Weir, *"Last of American Freemen,"* 1–27.

8. See especially Pocock, *Machiavellian Moment.*

9. Greene, "The Concept of Virtue in Late Colonial British America," in Greene, *Imperatives, Behaviors and Identities,* 226.

10. Ibid., 227. See also Rebecca Starr, *School for Politics.*

11. Greene, "Early South Carolina and the Psychology of British Colonization," in Greene, *Imperatives, Behaviors and Identities,* 108. See also Eustace, *Passion Is the Gale,* 35–36; 56.

12. Hirschman, *Passions and the Interests,* 41.

13. Mandeville, *Fable of the Bees and Other Writings;* A. Smith, *Wealth of Nations, Books 1–3,* book 1, chapter 2, 1.2.2.

14. Greene, "Concept of Virtue in Late Colonial British America," 228–29.

15. Lockey cited in P. Morgan, *Slave Counterpoint,* 298.

16. Beeman, *Evolution of the Southern Backcountry,* 43; Isaac, *Transformation of Virginia,* 39–42.

17. Printed text near entry for 20 August 1762, Francis Jerdone Memorandum Book, Swem.

18. P. V. B. Livingston to Othniel Beale, 1 December 1750, Othniel Beale Papers, SCL, USC.

19. Cf. G. Wood, *Radicalism of the American Revolution,* 17–18; 20–1; 26.

20. Breen, *Tobacco Culture,* 65–69.

21. Robert Bristow to Thomas Booth, 30 September 1719, Robert Bristow Copybook, L. of Va., 758.

22. Joseph Ball to Joseph Chinn, 15 March 1755, Joseph Ball Letterbook, CWF.

23. Breen, *Tobacco Culture,* 16.

24. Edward Ambler to Charles Dabney, 14 July 1767, Charles William Dabney Papers, 1715–1845, folder 9, box 1, subseries 1.1:1716–75, UNC.

25. Pierce Butler to Messrs Thomas Fraser and Co., 13 April 1787, *Butler Plantation Papers,* University Library, University of Cambridge, folder 9, box 2, collection 1447; Pierce Butler to Messrs Simpson and Davison, 14 July 1787, *Butler Plantation Papers,* University Library, University of Cambridge, folder 9, box 2, collection 1447.

26. John Lloyd to George Champion, 28 September 1796, John Lloyd Papers, folder 1, SCL, USC.

27. Nash, "South Carolina Indigo, European Textiles, and the British Atlantic Economy in the Eighteenth Century," 363; 372; 383–84.

28. Greene, "Concept of Virtue in Late Colonial British America," 228–29.

29. Joseph Ball to Anne Dickie, 19 May 1747, Joseph Ball Letterbook, CWF.

30. Robert Carter to Robert B. Carter, 23 April 1783, Robert Carter of Nomini Hall Letterbook, Chauvenet Collection, CWF, 5:128.

31. 5. May 1793, Robert Carter of Nomini Hall Letterbook, Chauvenet Collection, CWF, 13:5.

32. Sarson, *British America 1500–1800,* 243–44.

33. P. Morgan, *Slave Counterpoint,* 35–39.

34. George Washington to Marie Joseph Paul Yves Roch Gilbert du Motier, Marquis de Lafayette, 1 February 1784, Washington, *Writings of Washington from the Original Manuscript Sources,* http://memory.loc.gov/cgi-bin/query/r?ammem/mgw:@field(DOCID+@lit(gw270361)) (accessed 2 May 2015). Cf. "And Judah and Israel dwelt safely, every man under his vine and under his fig tree," 1 Kings 4:25. Washington, *Diaries of George Washington,* 1:xxvi. In 1779 Washington invoked the same verse to demonstrate his affection for the nascent United States. See George Washington to George Mason, 27 March 1779, in Washington, *Writings of Washington from the Original Manuscript Sources,* http://memory.loc.gov/cgi-bin/query/r?ammem/mgw:@field(DOCID+@lit(gw140294)) (accessed 2 May 2015).

35. William Moultrie to Major General Nathaniel Greene, 5 May 1783, William Moultrie Papers, folder 2, box 2, SCL, USC.

36. John Lloyd to E. H. Champion, 14 June 1796, folder 1, John Lloyd Papers, SCL, USC.

37. P. Morgan, *Slave Counterpoint,* 276.

38. Breen, *Tobacco Culture,* 65–69; Mullin, *Flight and Rebellion,* 25.

39. Henry Fitzhugh to James Buchanan, 22 April 1755, Henry Fitzhugh Papers, 1746–69, Duke.

40. Thomas Jefferson to Thomas Mann Randolph Jr., 24 June 1793, Notes, in Jefferson, *Works of Thomas Jefferson in Twelve Volumes,* vol. 11, http://memory.loc.gov/cgi-bin/query/r?ammem/mtj:@field(DOCID+@lit(tj070172)) (accessed 30 April 2015).

41. Scarborough, *Overseer,* 4.

42. Carter cited in Baird, "Between Slavery and Independence," 199–200.

43. Byrd, *Secret Diary of William Byrd of Westover, 1709–1712,* xv.

44. Lockridge, *Diary, and Life, of William Byrd II of Virginia, 1674–1744,* 69.

45. Carter cited in Mullin, *Flight and Rebellion,* 20.

46. Peter Fontaine to Moses Fontaine, 4 September 1749, Fontaine-Maury Papers, folder 1, "part 2," 1737–49, Swem; Mullin, *Flight and Rebellion,* 20.

47. Washington, *Diaries of George Washington,* 1:xviii.

48. Thomas Jefferson to Samuel Biddle, 30 August 1793, in Jefferson, *Works of Thomas Jefferson,* http://hdl.loc.gov/loc.mss/mtj.mtjbib007943 (30 April 2015).

49. Agreement between Daniel Parke Custis and Joseph Valentine, 14 November 1755, Custis Family Papers, 1683–1858, VHS.

50. Washington cited in Baird, "Between Slavery and Independence," 117.

51. Pennant, "Thomas Pennant's Notebook about America," Warwickshire County Record Office, Warwickshire, U.K.; see for example 29 December 1786, in Washington, *Diaries of George Washington,* 5:85. Planters would not have written down a large proportion of the instructions

that they gave to overseers on their home plantations; as a result the records that survive must overrepresent overseers on absentee plantations as well as those slave owners who could afford to own multiple quarters.

52. See, for example, William Ancrum to Marlow Pryor, 4 October 1776; William Ancrum to Marlow Pryor, 15 August 1777, William Ancrum Account Book and Letterbook, SCL, USC.

53. Robert Carter, *The Diary, Correspondence, and Papers of Robert "King" Carter of Virginia, 1701–1732,* ed. Edmund Berkeley Jr., http://carter.lib.virginia.edu/public/ (accessed 6 May 2015).

54. L. Carter, *Diary of Colonel Landon Carter,* 1:461n73.

55. William Lee to Mr. Ellis, 24 June 1778, William Lee's letterbook, 1769–93, Lee Family Papers, 1638–1867, section 115, VHS, 265.

56. Habersham cited in B. Wood, *Slavery in Colonial Georgia,* 138.

57. Josiah Smith to George Austin, 30 July 1772, Josiah Smith Jr. Lettercopy Book, 1771–84, UNC, 105.

58. Josiah Smith to George Austin, 22 July 1773, ibid., 227.

59. George Washington to Lund Washington, 26 November 1775, in Washington, *Writings of Washington from the Original Manuscript Sources,* http://memory.loc.gov/cgi-bin/query/r?ammem/mgw:@field(DOCID+@lit(gw040113)) (accessed 30 April 2015), n18.

60. Washington, "View of the Work at the Several Plantations in the Year 1789 and General Directions for the Execution of It," VHS.

61. Mullin, *Flight and Rebellion,* 22.

62. Robert Carter III to Edward Hunt and Son, 13 May 1765, Letterbook of Robert Carter III of Nominy Hall, 1760–64, CWF.

63. Joseph Ball to Joseph Chinn, 30 June 1749, Joseph Ball Letterbook, CWF.

64. Robert Carter to Edward Ransdale, 24 June 1767, Robert Carter of Nomini Hall Letterbook, 9 vols., Chauvenet Collection, CWF, 63.

65. Henry Laurens to Abraham Schad, 18 April 1766, in Laurens, *HL Papers,* ed. Chesnutt and Rogers, 5:101.

66. William Ancrum to Mr. Geeving, 17 October 1778, William Ancrum Account Book and Letterbook, SCL, USC.

67. See Kulikoff, *Tobacco and Slaves,* 409–10.

68. Scarborough, *Overseer,* 96; B. Wood, *Slavery in Colonial Georgia,* 142.

69. George Washington to William Drayton, 20 November 1786, in Washington, *Writings of Washington from the Original Manuscript Sources,* http://memory.loc.gov/cgi-bin/query/r?ammem/mgw:@field(DOCID+@lit(gw290053)) (accessed 30 April 2015); Washington, *Diaries of George Washington,* http://memory.loc.gov/cgi-bin/query/P?mgw:11:./temp/~ammem_R8lS::, IV, 142, (accessed 30 April 2015).

70. Henry Fitzhugh to James Russel, 29 November 1760; cf. Henry Fitzhugh to James Russel, 11 May 1761, Henry Fitzhugh Papers, 1746–69, Duke.

71. Henry Fitzhugh to John Bland, 11 August 1768, Henry Fitzhugh Papers, 1746–69, Duke; cf. Henry Fitzhugh to John Bland, October 1763, Henry Fitzhugh Papers, 1746–69, Duke.

72. John Palmer to John Ewing Colhoun, 23 May 1792, John Ewing Colhoun Papers, SCL, USC.

73. Henry Laurens to James Grant, 31 January 1766, in Laurens, *HL Papers,* ed. Chesnutt and Rogers, 5:59.

74. Henry Laurens to Richard Oswald, 7 July 1764, in Laurens, *HL Papers,* ed. Hamer, 4:339

75. Henry Laurens to John Smith, 17 September 1765, in Laurens, *HL Papers,* ed. Chesnutt and Rogers, 5:6.

76. Henry Laurens to James Brenard, 14 February 1765, in Laurens, *HL Papers,* ed. Hamer, 4:579.

77. Laurens cited in Lockley, *Lines in the Sand,* 13.

78. Henry Laurens to James Wright, 25 January 1768, in Laurens, *HL Papers,* ed. Chesnutt and Rogers, 5:562.

79. Henry Laurens to James Wright, 27 January 1768, in ibid., 5:608; cf. Henry Laurens to Peter Bachop, 30 March 1768, in ibid., 5:642.

80. Henry Laurens to James Marion, 25 February 1765, in Laurens, *HL Papers,* ed. Hamer, 4:585.

81. Laurens, *HL Papers,* ed. Chesnutt and Rogers, 5:331n3; Henry Laurens to Edward Graham, 31 March 1765, in ibid., 5:96; Henry Laurens to Zachary Villepontoux, 13 February 1765, in Laurens, *HL Papers,* ed. Hamer, 4:578.

82. Henry Laurens to James Theodore Rossel, 8 April 1766, in Laurens, *HL Papers,* ed. Chesnutt and Rogers, 5:100.

83. Cf. Scarborough, *Overseer,* 44.

84. Ibid., 69.

85. Robert Carter, *The Diary, Correspondence, and Papers of Robert "King" Carter of Virginia, 1701–1732,* ed. Edmund Berkeley Jr., http://carter.lib.virginia.edu/public/ (accessed 6 May 2015).

86. 17 July 1745, Joseph Ball Letterbook, CWF.

87. Harrower, "Diary of John Harrower, 1773–1776," 92.

88. Henry Laurens cited in B. Wood, *Slavery in Colonial Georgia,* 140.

89. A. Norris to H. Keylor, 23 January 1795, John Ewing Colhoun Papers, SCL, USC.

90. George Washington to Hertford, Connecticut, Citizens, 2 August 1793, in Washington, *Writings of Washington from the Original Manuscript Sources,* http://memory.loc.gov/cgi-bin/query/r?ammem/mgw:@field(DOCID+@lit(gw330040)) (accessed 30 April 2015). Cf. Washington to ?, 8 January 1774, Sol Feinstone Collection, viewed on microfilm at CWF.

91. 17 July 1745; 2 May 1745, Joseph Ball Letterbook, CWF. Cf. Josiah Smith to George Austin, 22 July 1773, Josiah Smith Jr. Lettercopy Book, 1771–84, UNC, 230.

92. Robert Bristow to Thomas Booth, 5 September 1711, Robert Bristow Copybook, L. of Va., 496.

93. William Lee letterbook, 5 August 1783 to 1 April 1787, Lee Family Papers, 1638–1867, VHS, 295.

94. Henry Laurens to James Lawrence, 1 January 1763, in Laurens, *HL Papers,* ed. Hamer, 3:203.

95. William Ancrum to Marlow Pryor, 30 October 1776; cf. William Ancrum to Marlow Pryor, 4 October 1776, William Ancrum Account Book and Letterbook, SCL, USC.

96. Henry Laurens to Timothy Creamer, 25 January 1765, Laurens, *HL Papers,* ed. Hamer, 4:570.

97. Cf. Greene, "Independence and Dependence," 174; Greene, "Early South Carolina and the Psychology of British Colonization," 104–5; Greene, "Travails of an Infant Colony," 132; Chaplin, "Tidal Rice Cultivation and the Problem of Slavery in South Carolina, 1760–1815," 35.

98. Edelson, *Plantation Enterprise in Colonial South Carolina,* 7.

99. Robert Carter to Robert Rogers, Robert Carter of Nomini Hall Letterbook, Chauvenet Collection, CWF, 8:48.

100. Laurens, *Letter from Henry Laurens to His Son John Laurens August 14, 1776,* 30.

101. George Walton to Seaborn Jones Jr., 18 May 1782, Seaborn Jones Sr. Papers, folder 1, 1761–93, Duke.

102. Chaplin, "Tidal Rice Cultivation and the Problem of Slavery in South Carolina, 1760–1815," 60–61.

103. L. Carter, *Diary of Colonel Landon Carter,* 1:21.

104. Walsh, "Plantation Management in the Chesapeake, 1620–1820," 393.

105. See E. Jones, *Agriculture and the Industrial Revolution.*

106. George Washington to Arthur Young, 18 June 1792, in Washington, *Writings of Washington from the Original Manuscript Sources,* http://memory.loc.gov/cgi-bin/ampage?collId=mgw4&fileName=gwpage102.db&recNum=84&tempFile=./temp/~ammem_5d1g&filecode=mgw&next_filecode=mgw&itemnum=1&ndocs=100 (accessed 2 May 2015).

107. George Washington to Henry Lee, 16 October 1793, in Washington, *Writings of Washington from the Original Manuscript Sources,* http://memory.loc.gov/cgi-bin/ampage?collId=mgw4&fileName=gwpage104.db&recNum=625&tempFile=./temp/~ammem_AO9x&filecode=mgw&next_filecode=mgw&prev_filecode=mgw&itemnum=2&ndocs=100 (accessed 2 May 2015).

108. George Washington to Arthur Young, 18 June 1792, in Washington, *Writings of Washington from the Original Manuscript Sources,* http://memory.loc.gov/cgi-bin/ampage?collId=mgw4&fileName=gwpage102.db&recNum=84&tempFile=./temp/~ammem_5d1g&filecode=mgw&next_filecode=mgw&itemnum=1&ndocs=100 (accessed 2 May 2015).

109. *VG* (Purdie and Dixon), 2 December 1773, 2; cf. *VG* (Rind), 2 December 1773.

110. Cf. B. Wood, *Slavery in Colonial Georgia,* 142.

111. Henry Laurens to John Jackson, 19 March 1766, in Laurens, *HL Papers,* ed. Chesnutt and Rogers, 5:90.

112. Josiah Smith to George Austin, 30 January 1770, Josiah Smith Jr. Lettercopy Book, 1771–84, UNC, 195.

113. John Ewing Colhoun account with Michael Boinneau, 10 January 1799, John Ewing Colhoun Papers, SCL, USC.

114. Entry for 11 December 1791, Cabell Commonplace Book, Cabell Commonplace Books, 1769–95, VHS, 11. See also Ralph Wormeley Account Book, 1773–84, Duke.

115. Henry Laurens to John Smith, 4 October 1765, in Laurens, *HL Papers,* ed. Chesnutt and Rogers, 5:16.

116. Cf. Thomas Bailey to William Gibbons, 25 February 1770, William Gibbons Jr. Papers, 1769–71 file, 1728–71 box, Duke.

117. Henry Laurens to Martha Brown, 29 January 1766, in Laurens, *HL Papers,* ed. Chesnutt and Rogers, 5:50.

118. Henry Laurens to John Coming Ball, 26 June 1764, in Laurens, *HL Papers,* ed. Hamer, 4:298; Henry Laurens to Timothy Creamer, 31 July 1764, in ibid., 4:298; Henry Laurens to Timothy Creamer, 25 January 1765, in ibid., 4:570.

119. Henry Laurens to Timothy Creamer, 25 January 1765, in ibid., 4:570.

120. Henry Laurens to John Smith, 17 September 1765, in Laurens, *HL Papers,* ed. Chesnutt and Rogers, 5:6.

121. Izard cited in P. Morgan, *Slave Counterpoint,* 344; Chaplin, "Tidal Rice Cultivation and the Problem of Slavery in South Carolina, 1760–1815," 57.

122. Mullin, *Flight and Rebellion,* 29–30.

123. Joseph Ball to Joseph Chinn, 18 February 1744, Joseph Ball Letterbook, CWF. Cf. *VG* (Purdie and Dixon), 6 May 1773, 2.

124. Joseph Ball to Joseph Chinn, 18 November 1744, Joseph Ball Letterbook, viewed on microfilm at CWF.

125. Robert Carter to George Newman, 23 May 1786, daybook, 7:143, Robert Carter Papers, 1772–94, Duke; Henry Fitzhugh account with Thomas West, Henry Fitzhugh Ledger, 152, Duke.

126. George Washington to Betty Lewis, 13 September 1789, in Washington, *Writings of Washington from the Original Manuscript Sources,* http://memory.loc.gov/cgi-bin/query/r?ammem/mgw:@field(DOCID+@lit(gw300358)) (accessed 2 May 2015).

127. George Washington to James Mercer, 12 December 1774, Account book 2, in Washington, *Writings of Washington from the Original Manuscript Sources,* http://memory.loc.gov/cgi-bin/query/r?ammem/mgw:@field(DOCID+@lit(gw030179)) (accessed 2 May 2015).

128. George Washington to John Augustine Washington, 16 January 1783, in Washington, *Writings of Washington from the Original Manuscript Sources,* http://memory.loc.gov/cgi-bin/query/r?ammem/mgw:@field(DOCID+@lit(gw260062)) (accessed 2 May 2015).

129. L. Carter, "Diary of Col. Landon Carter," 39.

130. John Steele to Polly Steele, 15 December 1762, John Steele Papers, folder 3, SCL, USC, 2.

131. L. Carter, *Diary of Colonel Landon Carter,* 1:585.

132. Articles of agreement between Charles Dabney and Charles Nicholls, 21 August 1772; cf. Articles of Agreement between Charles Dabney and Ancel Clarkson, 21 August 1772, Charles William Dabney Papers, 1715–1845, folder 13, box 1, subseries 1.1: 1716–75, UNC.

133. Henry Laurens to John Smith, 15 August 1765, in Laurens, *HL Papers,* ed. Hamer, 4:661.

134. P. Morgan, *Slave Counterpoint,* 278.

135. Pinckney, *Letterbook of Eliza Lucas Pinckney,* 144.

136. Henry Laurens to William Mayne, 20 August 1766, in Laurens, *HL Papers,* ed. Chesnutt and Rogers, 5:169.

137. Baird, "Between Slavery and Independence," 120–38.

138. *VG* (Hunter), 12 December 1755, 4.

139. Henry Laurens to Timothy Creamer, 25 January 1765, in Laurens, *HL Papers,* ed. Hamer, 4:570.

140. Printed text near entry for 20 August 1762, Francis Jerdone Memorandum Book, Swem.

141. Cf. B. Wood, *Slavery in Colonial Georgia,* 140.

142. William Byrd to Mr. Proctor, 18 November 1740, Byrd Family Papers, 1684–1842, bound volume: copy made by Elizabeth Byrd Nicholas in 1876, VHS, 142.

143. Baird, "Between Slavery and Independence," 120.

144. Henry Laurens to John Smith, 15 August 1765, in Laurens, *HL Papers,* ed. Hamer, 4:661.

145. Scott, *Domination and the Arts of Resistance,* 202–3; 223.

146. Kulikoff, *Tobacco and Slaves,* 9.

147. Baird, "Between Slavery and Independence," 21–22.

148. Cf. E. Morgan, *American Slavery, American Freedom.*

149. Cf. Kulikoff, *Tobacco and Slaves,* 9.

150. Baird, "Between Slavery and Independence."

151. Cf. Sandy, "Divided Loyalties in a 'Predatory War,'" 363.

152. Cf. Baird, "Between Slavery and Independence," 29.

153. Parent, *Foul Means,* 25–29.

154. Morgan, *American Slavery.* Cf. Parent, *Foul Means,* 105–96.

155. Cf. Baird, "Between Slavery and Independence," 25.

156. Owen Griffith to Landon Carter, 21 December 1771, Sabine Hall Papers, 1650–1779, folder 10, box 1, U. of Va.

157. Cf. Baird, "Between Dependence and Independence," 120–28.

158. Scarborough, *Overseer,* 72. Henry Laurens's experiences with Abraham Schad suggest that long periods of employment could also induce managers to complacency about following the plantation's rules.

159. Ibid., 39–40; cf. Baird, "Between Dependence and Independence," 120–28.

160. Browne, "Reverend Dr. John Clayton and His Early Map of Jamestown," 22.

161. Harrower, *Journal of John Harrower,* 84.

162. Henry Laurens to John Jackson, 19 March 1766, in Laurens, *HL Papers,* ed. Chesnutt and Rogers, 5:90.

163. One scholar has posited that in the antebellum period, employer-overseer tensions often arose because antebellum overseers saw themselves as professionals and desired an apposite influence in decision making. Schmidt, "Overseers and the Nature of Southern Labor Contracts," 92.

William Scarborough highlighted the important role that overseers played in agricultural reform in the antebellum South. This "overseer elite," to which he devoted an entire chapter, engaged in debates on the pages of the agricultural journals that began to appear in the 1820s and 1830s. Interested in the advances of the "manurial revolution," in crop rotation and selective stockbreeding, these individuals were far removed from the overseers of "the meaner sort" on which the negative stereotype was based. Scarborough, *Overseer.*

164. Jacob Fendin to Edward Telfair, 20 March 1774, Edward Telfair Papers, 1761–1847, Duke.

165. Thomas Mitchell to Francis Jerdone, 9 July 1789, Jerdone Family Papers, folder 2, box 2, Swem.

166. William Ancrum to Marlow Pryor, 27 March 1776, William Ancrum Account Book and Letterbook, SCL, USC. Cf. Josiah Smith to George Austin, 20 September 1771, Josiah Smith Jr. Lettercopy Book, UNC, 25; Josiah Smith to James Poyas, 3 September 1779, ibid., 115.

167. Cf. Baird, "Between Slavery and Independence," 20.

168. John Lee to George Lewis, 29 May 1797, VHS.

169. Simon Sallard to John Carter, 4 November 1736, Carter Family Papers, 1651–1861, part 3, VHS.

170. Articles of agreement between Charles Dabney and Ancel Clarkson, 21 August 1772; cf. Articles of Agreement between Charles Dabney and Charles Nicholls, 21 August 1772, Charles William Dabney Papers, 1715–1845, folder 13, box 1, subseries 1.1: 1716–75, UNC.

171. L. Carter, *Diary of Colonel Landon Carter,* 1:330.

172. Laurens cited in B. Wood, *Slavery in Colonial Georgia,* 140.

173. In the nineteenth century, tensions "between employer and employee" often led to "contests about personal honor that ended in violence." Since a penchant for a violent defense of personal honor prevailed in the South both before and after the antebellum period, similar altercations might well have occurred in the eighteenth century. Violence could have been underreported as patriarchs sought to maintain their reputation for plantation control. Schmidt, "Overseers and the Nature of Southern Labor Contracts," 94.

174. Laurens cited in B. Wood, *Slavery in Colonial Georgia,* 141.

175. Lockley, "Crossing the Race Divide," 162.

176. Carter cited in Mullin, *Flight and Rebellion,* 29.

177. Henry Laurens to James Brenard, 7 March 1765, in Laurens, *HL Papers,* ed. Hamer, 4:588.

178. Carter cited in R. Brown and B. Brown, *Virginia 1705–1786,* 50–51.

179. Henry Laurens to Lachlan McIntosh, 25 November 1767, in Laurens, *HL Papers,* ed. Chesnutt and Rogers, 5:484.

180. Cf. Kulikoff, *Tobacco and Slaves,* 167.

181. Trevor Burnard has demonstrated how in the roughly comparable Jamaican plantation world, a maturation of the slave economy (and the attendant employment of overseers) created a link between assumptions of female nonparticipation in labor and women's morality. Eventually all but the poorest women were "seen as icons of propriety." Burnard, "Sexual Life of an Eighteenth-Century Jamaican Slave Overseer," 174; Burnard, *Mastery, Tyranny and Desire.*

182. Fithian cited in Young, *Domesticating Slavery,* 67–68.

183. Tonyn cited in ibid., 68. For an example of the "tyranny" that was believed to result when a woman usurped her natural position in the patriarchal unit, see Maryann Maury to Elizabeth Torin, 2 September 1745, Fontaine-Maury Papers, folder 1, "part 2," 1737–49, Swem.

184. Cf. Kulikoff, *Tobacco and Slaves,* 183; 230–31.

185. Cf. Anzilotti, *Affairs of the World.*

186. Pinckney, *Letterbook of Eliza Lucas Pinckney,* 56.

187. John Steele to Mary (Polly) Steele, 7 August 1796, John Steele Papers, folder 2, SCL, USC.

188. Pinckney, *Letterbook of Eliza Lucas Pinckney,* 144.

189. Dornan, "Women Slaveholders in the Georgia and South Carolina Low Country," 200. Similarly, social constraints meant that for Pinckney the factors who sold her products were "vital"; for male planters they were merely beneficial. Ibid., 197–205; K. Wood, *Masterful Women*, 6–7.

190. K. Wood, *Masterful Women*, 6–7.

191. Somerville, "Rape, Race, and Castration in Slave Law in the Colonial and Early South," 83.

192. George Washington to Frances B. Washington, 18 August 1793, in Washington, *Writings of Washington from the Original Manuscript Sources*, http://memory.loc.gov/cgi-bin/query/r?ammem/mgw:@field(DOCID+@lit(gw330052)) (accessed 2 May 2015).

193. Bland cited in Clinton, *"Plantation Mistress,"* 191.

194. Ibid., 191; Lucy Battaille Thornton to Mary Robinson, 15 November 1799, Lucy Battaille Thornton Papers, 1798–1862, viewed in typescript at VHS.

195. John Steele to Polly Steele, 15 December 1796, John Steele Papers, folder 3, 2; John Steele to Polly Steele, 3 February 1797, John Steele Papers, folder 3, SCL, USC.

196. Kulikoff, *Tobacco and Slaves*, 166.

197. K. Wood, *Masterful Women*, 116.

198. Simon Sallard to John Carter, 9 October 1737, Simon Sallard Papers, 1732–37 folder, U. of Va.

199. K. Wood, *Masterful Women*, 10.

200. Scarborough, *Overseer*, 6.

201. Mullin, *Flight and Rebellion*, 30.

Chapter 5: "At their uttermost perils"

1. *VG* (Rind), 25 January 1770.

2. That this is a well-known example of slave rebellion in Virginia is suggested by its inclusion in the narrative of Alex Haley's *Roots*, 351.

3. *VG* (Rind), 25 January 1770.

4. The incident was also reported in the *New York Journal; or, General Advertiser*, 15 February 1770, supplement. Because of the serious nature of this event, and in order to sell newspapers, the account might have been exaggerated. Yet the report acknowledges its own limits, describing how "the accounts vary; some say three [bondpeople were] killed upon the spot, and five wounded, others that two were killed, and five wounded, one of whom died soon after." The importance for the present study is how southerners perceived such incidents, and what this perception meant for the position of overseers.

5. Cf. Parent, *Foul Means*, 208; P. Morgan, *Slave Counterpoint*, 276–78.

6. A Virginian act as early as 1639—well before the end of the century, when bondpeople began to arrive in large numbers—prohibited the arming of blacks. Meetings of enslaved people under the "pretence" of feasts and burials were made illegal from 1680, for fear of insurrection. Lifting a hand against any "Christian" warranted a punishment of thirty lashes, and if a bondperson chose "to resist any person or persons that shalby any lawfull authority be imployed to apprehend and take the said negroe," he or she could be killed. Such harsh punishment was designed for enslaved people alone; the strongest sanctions placed on white indentured servants were equivalent to those that they received for fleeing their masters and mistresses. By the late seventeenth century, then, enslaved people already were seen as a separate, rebellious entity within Virginian society. Hening, *Statutes at Large*, 2:481; cf. 4:128–30; 1:481–82; cf. 3:336; 460; 5:22; 29; 6:111; 538. Cf. Jordan, *White over Black*.

7. The eighteenth century also saw punishment for slave outlawry that included dismemberment. Hening, *Statutes at Large*, 3:461; 4:132; 6:111. For striking a white man in Virginia, a bondperson received thirty-nine lashes in 1705, reduced to thirty lashes forty years later. P. Morgan, *Slave Counterpoint*, 264.

8. Hening, *Statutes at Large,* 4:131; 5:17; 6:109–10.

9. See Rutman and Rutman, *Place in Time,* 175.

10. Parent, *Foul Means,* 159.

11. Hening, *Statutes at Large,* 3:536; 4:126; 6:105; 109; 3:536.

12. Wicek, "Statutory Law of Slavery and Race in the Thirteen Mainland Colonies of British America," 274. For the Stono Rebellion, see Hoffer, *Cry Liberty;* Shuler, *Calling Out Liberty.*

13. P. Wood, *Black Majority,* 308.

14. Ibid., 343.

15. Wicek, "Statutory Law of Slavery and Race in the Thirteen Mainland Colonies of British America," 274.

16. P. Morgan, *Slave Counterpoint,* 394; Kulikoff, *Tobacco and Slaves,* 390.

17. B. Wood, "Some Aspects of Female Resistance to Chattel Slavery in Low Country Georgia," 611.

18. Genovese cited in P. Morgan, *Slave Counterpoint,* 395.

19. Scarborough, *Overseer,* 68; see also Hening, *Statutes at Large,* 3:447–52; 5:551; 6:360, for the importance of overseers in preventing resistance by indentured servants.

20. Hening, *Statutes at Large,* 1:174; cf. 198.

21. Ibid., 1:538.

22. *GG,* 7 June 1763.

23. Lockley, *Lines in the Sand,* 33.

24. De Crèvecoeur, *Letters from an American Farmer,* ix.

25. P. Morgan, *Slave Counterpoint,* 221.

26. Lockley, *Lines in the Sand,* 6.

27. *SCG,* 9 May 1771, 1.

28. Lockley, *Lines in the Sand,* 6.

29. Letter to *SCG,* 8 November 1742, cited in P. Morgan, *Slave Counterpoint,* 221.

30. Hambleton cited in ibid., 221.

31. Petition cited in Rutman and Rutman, *Place in Time,* 175; Landon Carter to *Virginia Gazette,* 1771, Sabine Hall Papers, 1650–1779, folder 10, box 1, U. of Va.

32. Hening, *Statutes at Large,* 3:103; 460. Ralph Wormeley employed his bondman "Captain" as overseer of his Rosegill estate in Middlesex County. Rutman and Rutman, *Place in Time,* 187.

33. George Washington to Alexander Spotswood, 14 September 1798, in Washington, *Writings of Washington from the Original Manuscript Sources,* http://memory.loc.gov/cgi-bin/query/r?ammem/mgw:@field(DOCID+@lit(gw360340)) (accessed 2 May 2015).

34. Wicek, "Statutory Law of Slavery and Race in the Thirteen Mainland Colonies of British America," 272; Hening, *Statutes at Large,* 2:481–82; 3:336; 5:22; 29; 6:538; cf. 5:24; 99; 228; 6:350. Allan Kulikoff has contended that this measure was introduced only at the time of the Revolution. As such it forms part of his general argument regarding social control of lower classes in the Chesapeake. Hening's *Statutes* shows, however, that overseers were exempt from militia duty across the whole century, with the exception of the Revolution. Kulikoff, *Tobacco and Slaves,* 311.

35. Foner, *Tom Paine and Revolutionary America,* 63–64; Kathleen Brown, *Good Wives, Nasty Wenches, and Anxious Patriarchs,* 277.

36. Wicek, "Statutory Law of Slavery and Race in the Thirteen Mainland Colonies of British America," 268.

37. Foner, *Tom Paine and Revolutionary America,* 63–64; Kathleen Brown, *Good Wives, Nasty Wenches, and Anxious Patriarchs,* 277.

38. Edward Harleston to ?, 30 October 1801, William Moultrie Papers, folder 24, box 2, SCL, USC.

39. Josiah Smith to George Austin, 30 July 1772, Josiah Smith Jr. Lettercopy Book, 1771–84, UNC, 106.

40. Kolchin, *American Slavery 1619–1877,* 60. Cf. Chaplin, *Anxious Pursuit,* 230.

41. See, for example, *SCG,* 7 January to 12 January 1770, 4.

42. Cf. *SCG,* 2 January 1775, 3.

43. Charles Dabney to ?, 1770, Charles William Dabney Papers, 1715–45, UNC.

44. Similar proportions continued in piedmont Virginia throughout the century, where, in some counties in 1775 the number of enslaved people in the total population was around half of the number in some Tidewater counties. Kulikoff, *Tobacco and Slaves,* 276. See also P. Morgan, *Slave Counterpoint,* 296–97.

45. Ibid., 416–17.

46. Dozier cited in Sobel, *World They Made Together,* 211.

47. Ibid., 199.

48. Carter cited in ibid., 198.

49. Entry for 9 March 1777, daybook, 23:34–35, Robert Carter Papers, 1772–94, Duke.

50. Sobel, *World They Made Together,* 259.

51. Baird, "Between Slavery and Independence," 184.

52. Laurens cited in Olwell, *Masters, Slaves and Subjects,* 155.

53. Sobel, *World They Made Together,* 47.

54. Klingsberg, *Appraisal of the Negro in Colonial South Carolina,* 90. Cf. Berlin, "Time, Space and the Evolution of Afro-American Society on British Mainland North America," 56.

55. Laurens cited in P. Morgan, *Slave Counterpoint,* 163.

56. Barclay, *Voyages and Travels of James Barclay,* 29; Thomas Owen to John Zachary, 24 January 1735, folder 55/26, Zachary Lloyd Collection, Birmingham Central Library, England.

57. Henry Laurens to John Smith, 9 May 1766, in Laurens, *HL Papers,* ed. Chesnutt and Rogers, 5:125.

58. P. Morgan, *Slave Counterpoint,* 164.

59. There is also a significant amount of evidence that enslaved people passed on African knowledge that improved the cultivation of rice in the lowcountry. Bondpeople from rice-growing regions of Africa such as the Senegambia fetched a premium in South Carolina and Georgia. See Littlefield, *Rice and Slaves,* 76–77. Cf. P. Wood, *Black Majority,* 34–62; Stubbs, "Rice."

60. Henry Laurens to James Lawrence, 12 February 1763, in Laurens, *HL Papers,* ed. Hamer, 3:248.

61. Henry Laurens to Abraham Schad, 1 March 1766, in Laurens, *HL Papers,* ed. Chesnutt and Rogers, 5:83.

62. *GG,* 26 September 1765, cited in P. Morgan, *Slave Counterpoint,* 406.

63. *SCG,* 28 March 1743, cited in ibid., 406.

64. Ibid., 326.

65. Cf. Burnard, "Sexual Life of an Eighteenth-Century Jamaican Slave Overseer," 183; 179.

66. Parent, *Foul Means,* 267; Hening, *Statutes at Large,* 5:551–52.

67. As early as 1632, an act was passed to prevent servants from running away from their quarters to people who had entered into a covenant with them. Hening, *Statutes at Large,* 5:551–52.

68. *VG* (Purdie and Dixon), 14 January 1773.

69. Cf. Hening, *Statutes at Large,* 5:551–52.

70. Hening, *Statutes at Large,* 4:325–26; 5:558; 6:369; cf. 3:459.

71. Cf. Kulikoff, *Tobacco and Slaves,* 9.

72. Cf. Camp, *Closer to Freedom,* 13–14.

73. Hening, *Statutes at Large,* 2:481–82.

74. Report of trial at John Ewing Colhoun's plantation at 12 Mile River, 29 August 1798, John Ewing Colhoun Papers, SCL, USC.

75. Archibald McKewn to John Ewing Colhoun, 14 September 1792, John Ewing Colhoun Papers, SCL, USC. Cf. *VG* (Rind), 18 July 1771; *VG* (Rind), 1 September 1774, 3.

76. John Houstoun to William Steven, 7 April 1781, Houstoun Collection, folder 5A/4, box 2, GHS. Cf. William Lee to Charles Lee, 11 August 1779, Lee Family Papers, 1638–1867, section 133, VHS.

77. William Ancrum to Marlow Pryor, 23 December 1776, William Ancrum Account Book and Letterbook, SCL, USC.

78. William Ancrum to Marlow Pryor, 23 March 1776, William Ancrum Account Book and Letterbook, SCL, USC.

79. Camp, *Closer to Freedom,* 58. Cf. Hendrich Keylor to John Ewing Colhoun, 13 August 1794, John Ewing Colhoun Papers. Some overseers used enslaved flight as an excuse for worsened performance. Another of Colhoun's overseers reported that his crop "would have Been better But Markes Rund away from us the first day of July and we . . . fell Back in our work." Peter Bradhimer to John Ewing Colhoun, 8 September 1796, John Ewing Colhoun Papers, SCL, USC.

80. William Ancrum to Marlow Pryor, 1 March 1776, William Ancrum Account Book and Letterbook, SCL, USC. Similar problems beset Ancrum's fellow planters. Cf. William Ancrum to Parker Quince, 5 September 1778, William Ancrum Account Book and Letterbook, SCL, USC.

81. Kulikoff, *Tobacco and Slaves,* 345; B. Wood, "Some Aspects of Female Resistance to Chattel Slavery in Low Country Georgia," 614.

82. Cf. P. Morgan, *Slave Counterpoint,* 40.

83. Jacob Read to Seaborn Jones, 14 December 1790, Jacob Read Papers, 30 July 1776–1 August 1812 folder, SCL, USC.

84. Cf. P. Morgan, *Slave Counterpoint,* 40.

85. Hendrich? Hayler? to John Ewing Colhoun, 13 August 1794, John Ewing Colhoun Papers, SCL, USC.

86. George Keckley to John Ewing Colhoun, 7 September 1796, John Ewing Colhoun Papers, SCL, USC.

87. Cf. Giddens, *Constitution of Society;* and Giddens, *Central Problems in Social Theory,* especially 69–73.

88. Scott, *Weapons of the Weak;* and Scott, *Domination and the Arts of Resistance.* Although rightly understanding such actions as forms of dissent, Eugene D. Genovese misinterpreted them as "prepolitical," or "apolitical," a result of "accommodation" to the hegemony of the paternalistic ethos. Genovese, *Roll, Jordan, Roll,* 598 and 659. Scott's thesis correctly relocates these actions in the realm of the political, by emphasizing the constancy of subaltern resistance to oppressive rule.

89. Baird, "Between Slavery and Independence," 110.

90. Washington cited in Scarborough, *Overseer,* 73.

91. Carter cited in P. Morgan, *Slave Counterpoint,* 192.

92. Hendrich? Hayler? to John Ewing Colhoun, 13 August 1794, John Ewing Colhoun Papers, SCL, USC.

93. John Channing to William Gibbons, 4 June 1770, William Gibbons Jr. Papers, 1769–71 file, 1728–71 box, Duke.

94. P. Morgan, *Slave Counterpoint,* 192.

95. Solomon Nash cited in ibid., 320.

96. Baird, "Between Slavery and Dependence," 202.

97. Michael Boinneau to John Ewing Colhoun, 11 June 1798, John Ewing Colhoun Papers, SCL, USC.

98. John C. Grinninger to John Ewing Colhoun, 22 August 1795, John Ewing Colhoun Papers, SCL, USC.

99. John Ewing Colhoun to Mr. Bard?/Mr. Bon?, 20 June 1797, John Ewing Colhoun Papers, SCL, USC. See B. Wood, *Women's Work, Men's Work.*

100. This commercial value became especially important to Virginian planters from the middle of the eighteenth century, when slaves came to be defined legally as real estate rather than personal property. Hening, *Statutes at Large,* 3:333–5; 4:223; 6:432. Cf. Parent, *Foul Means,* 221. For South Carolina see Littlefield, *Rice and Slaves,* 2. Events such as the Revolutionary War caused slave values to increase even more. See for example William Ancrum to Marlow Pryor, 23 December 1776, William Ancrum Account Book and Letterbook, SCL, USC.

101. Cited in P. Wood, *Black Majority,* 331.

102. Bartram, *Travels through North and South Carolina, Georgia, East and West Florida,* 309.

103. Robert Bristow to Thomas Booth, 5 September 1711, Robert Bristow Copybook, L. of Va., 496.

104. 10 November 1787, Robert Carter of Nomini Hall Letterbook, Chauvenet Collection, 6:39. Cf. Robert Carter of Nomini Hall Letterbook, Chauvenet Collection, CWF, 6:165.

105. Joseph Ball to Joseph Chinn, 14 February 1743/4 (o.s./n.s.), Joseph Ball Letterbook, CWF.

106. Agreement between Daniel Parke Custis and Joseph Valentine, 14 November 1755, Custis Family Papers, 1683–1858, VHS.

107. William Ancrum to Marlow Pryor, 30 October 1776, William Ancrum Account Book and Letterbook, SCL, USC.

108. Joseph Ball to Joseph Chinn, 11 April 1748, Joseph Ball Letterbook, CWF.

109. Henry Fitzhugh to Captain Nicholas Battaile [*sic*], n.d., Henry Fitzhugh letterbook, 1746–74, Henry Fitzhugh Papers, Duke.

110. Cf. J. Morgan, *Laboring Women,* 164–65.

111. Henry Laurens to James Lawrence, 1 January 1763, in Laurens, *HL Papers,* ed. Hamer, 3:203.

112. William Lee to Mr. Ellis, 24 June 1778, William Lee's letterbook, 1769–93, Lee Family Papers, 1638–1867, section 115, VHS, 265.

113. 10 November 1787, Robert Carter of Nomini Hall Letterbook, Chauvenet Collection, 6:39. Cf. Robert Carter of Nomini Hall Letterbook, Chauvenet Collection, CWF, 6:165.

114. Cf. P. Morgan, *Slave Counterpoint,* 262.

115. Pennant, "Thomas Pennant's Notebook about America," Warwickshire County Record Office, Warwickshire, U.K., 23–24.

116. Cf. Lockley, *Lines in the Sand,* 34.

117. Baird, "Between Slavery and Independence," 109.

118. P. Morgan, *Slave Counterpoint,* 332.

119. Carter cited in ibid., 327.

120. Ibid., 194.

121. Sandy, "Homemakers, Supervisors and Peach Stealing Bitches," 478.

122. Cf. Mullin, *Flight and Rebellion;* cf. Scarborough, *Overseer,* 80.

123. Simon Sallard to Richard Chapman, 25 January 1737, Simon Sallard Papers, 1732–37 folder, U. of Va.

124. John Blair to Charles Dabney, 1 April 1769, Charles William Dabney Papers, UNC.

125. See Isaac, *Transformation of Virginia,* 342–43; Olwell, *Masters, Slaves and Subjects,* 213.

126. P. Morgan, *Slave Counterpoint,* 326.

127. N. Jones, *Born a Child of Freedom, Yet a Slave,* 205.

128. See, for example, Genovese, *Roll, Jordan, Roll,* 1–148.

129. Baird, "Between Slavery and Independence," 157.

130. John Houstoun to William Steven, 7 April 1781, folder 5A/4, box 2, Houstoun Collection, GHS.

131. Edward Harleston to ?, 30 October 1801, William Moultrie Papers, folder 24, box 2, SCL, USC.

132. Cf. Genovese, "Rebelliousness and Docility in the Negro Slave."

133. Chaplin, *Anxious Pursuit,* 268.

134. Rutman and Rutman, *Place in Time,* 162.

135. Camp, *Closer to Freedom,* 33–34; 62.

136. John Lloyd to E. H. Champion, 14 June 1796, John Lloyd Papers, folder 1, SCL, USC.

137. *South Carolina and American General Gazette* (Charleston), 20 January 1781, cited in P. Morgan, *Slave Counterpoint,* 185n62.

138. The ownership of property by chattels long represented a quandary to jurists in slave societies. But it was a customary right for most African American slaves to cultivate their own food and provisions, usually in their leisure time. They traded these goods at markets that were common in many settlements across the South. The practice also made economic sense to planters, since the crops supplemented the food that slaveholders were bound to provide. See B. Wood, *Women's Work, Men's Work.*

139. Sidbury, *Ploughshares into Swords,* 25.

140. John Houstoun to ?, 17 March 1792, Houstoun Collection folder 5A/5, box 2, GHS.

141. Edward Ambler to Charles Dabney, 14 July 1767, Charles William Dabney Papers, 1715–1845, folder 9, box 1, subseries 1.1: 1716–75, UNC.

142. Charles Dabney to ?, 1770, Charles William Dabney Papers, 1715–45, UNC.

143. B. Wood, *Slavery in Colonial Georgia,* 114.

144. Cf. Scarborough, *Overseer,* 70.

145. B. Wood, *Slavery in Colonial Georgia,* 114.

146. Henry Laurens to Frederick Wiggins, 20 March 1766, in Laurens, *HL Papers,* ed. Chesnutt and Rogers, 5:92.

147. Barclay, *Voyages and Travels of James Barclay,* 27.

148. John C. Grinninger to John Ewing Colhoun, 22 August 1795, John Ewing Colhoun Papers, SCL, USC.

149. See for example Hening, *Statutes at Large,* 1:440; 3:103; 270; 298; 4:132–33; 327; 405; 5:548–49; 6:357–58; B. Wood, *Slavery in Colonial Georgia,* 113.

150. Barclay, *Voyages and Travels of James Barclay,* 25–26.

151. Ibid., 27.

152. *VG* (Rind), 10 August 1769.

153. Wicek, "Statutory Law of Slavery and Race in the Thirteen Mainland Colonies of British America," 274.

154. Olwell, "'Domestick Enemies,'" 23.

155. B. Wood, "Some Aspects of Female Resistance to Chattel Slavery in Low Country Georgia," 613.

156. Laurens cited in P. Morgan, *Slave Counterpoint,* 331n23. Cf. *VG* (Rind), 7 March 1751, 3.

157. Young, *Domesticating Slavery,* 47.

158. P. Morgan, *Slave Counterpoint,* 279.

159. Sandy, "Homemakers, Supervisors and Peach Stealing Bitches," 481.

160. Gronau cited in B. Wood, *Slavery in Colonial Georgia,* 141.

161. Cf. Isaac, *Landon Carter's Uneasy Kingdom,* 211.

162. Hewatt cited in B. Wood, *Slavery in Colonial Georgia,* 141.

163. Fithian cited in R. Brown and B. Brown, *Virginia 1705–1786,* 50; cf. P. Morgan, *Slave Counterpoint,* 282–83.

164. Wicek, "Statutory Law of Slavery and Race in the Thirteen Mainland Colonies of British America," 266–67.

165. P. Morgan, *Slave Counterpoint,* 315.

166. *GG,* 20 August 1766, 3.

167. Lockley, *Lines in the Sand,* 33.

168. P. Morgan, *Slave Counterpoint,* 293.

169. Joseph Ball to Joseph Chinn, 18 February 1744, Joseph Ball Letterbook, CWF.

170. Entry for 18 July 1773, Cabell Commonplace Book, Cabell Commonplace Books, 1769–95, VHS, vol. 4.

171. Entry for 21 August 1773, ibid., vol. 4.

172. Henry Laurens to John Smith, 30 May 1765, in Laurens, *HL Papers,* ed. Hamer, 4:632.

173. Lockley, *Lines in the Sand,* 33.

174. Laurens cited in Dornan, "Women Slaveholders in the Georgia and South Carolina Low Country," 197.

175. P. Morgan, *Slave Counterpoint,* 316.

176. Byrd cited in Lockridge, *Diary, and Life, of William Byrd II of Virginia, 1674–1744,* 114.

177. William Byrd to Mr. Beckford, 6 December 1735, Byrd Family Papers, 1684–1842, bound volume: copy made by Elizabeth Byrd Nicholas in 1876, VHS, 97.

178. Byrd cited in Lockridge, *Diary, and Life, of William Byrd II of Virginia, 1674–1744,* 69.

179. Joseph Ball to Joseph Chinn, 31 August 1754, Joseph Ball Letterbook, CWF.

180. See, for example, entries for 8 February 1709; 17 June 1710; 30 April 1711, in Byrd, *Secret Diary of William Byrd of Westover, 1709–1712.*

Chapter 6: "Insurgents . . . disappointed in their villainous Stratagems"

1. Harman Utterback deposition, 22 September 1782, Ball Family Papers, L. of Va.

2. M. Jones, *Limits of Liberty,* 49; 53. General Clinton's southern campaign did not get underway until late 1778. Ibid., 55.

3. Laurens, *Letter from Henry Laurens to His Son John Laurens August 14, 1776,* 20. Comprehensive surveys of the Revolution in the states under examination here include, for South Carolina, Gordon, *South Carolina and the American Revolution,* and Nadelhaft, *Disorders of War;* for Georgia, Hall, *Land and Allegiance in Revolutionary Georgia;* and for Virginia, Selby, *Revolution in Virginia, 1775–1783;* Tillson, *Gentry and Common Folk.* Holton's *Forced Founders* is an analysis of the war throughout the colonies.

4. M. Jones, *Limits of Liberty,* 46.

5. Cf. Sandy, "Divided Loyalties in a 'Predatory War,'" 383–84.

6. The discussion below takes 1782 as the end date of the Revolutionary War since it was in this year that hostilities ceased in the United States (British forces evacuated Wilmington, North Carolina; Savannah; and Charleston). The Treaty of Paris, formally ending the war, was signed in September 1783.

7. Peter Kolchin cited in Sandy, "Divided Loyalties in a 'Predatory War,'" 359.

8. Camp, *Closer to Freedom,* 9.

9. John Lyon receipt, 21 February 1776, John Gibbons Papers, 1775–79 file, Duke.

10. Mullin, *Flight and Rebellion,* 52.

11. William Ancrum to Marlow Pryor, 7 December 1779, William Ancrum Account Book and Letterbook, SCL, USC. Cf. McDonnell and Hilton, "Patriot vs. Patriot," 241–44.

12. William Ancrum to Marlow Pryor, 27 May 1777; William Ancrum to Marlow Pryor, 23 March 1776, William Ancrum Account Book and Letterbook, SCL, USC.

13. William Ancrum to Marlow Pryor, 7 February 1780, William Ancrum Account Book and Letterbook, SCL, USC.

14. Peter Papot account, 26 March 1779, William Gibbons Jr. Papers, 1774–84 file, 1728–71 box, Duke.

15. For the wartime experience of Charleston, see McCowen, *British Occupation of Charleston, 1780–82,* and Borick, *Gallant Defense.*

16. Hayne, "Records Kept by Colonel Isaac Hayne," 21–23; cf. Isaac Hayne Ledger, SCL, USC.

17. John Lewis Gervais to Henry Laurens, 27 September 1782, John Lewis Gervais Papers, folder 1, SCL, USC.

18. George Washington to Lund Washington, 26 November 1775, in Washington, *Writings of Washington from the Original Manuscript Sources,* http://memory.loc.gov/cgi-bin/query/r?ammem/mgw:@field(DOCID+@lit(gw040113)) (accessed 2 May 2015).

19. John Lewis Gervais to Henry Laurens, 27 September 1782, John Lewis Gervais Papers, folder 1, SCL, USC.

20. Laurens, *Letter from Henry Laurens to His Son John Laurens,* 24.

21. George Washington to Bartholomew Dandridge, 5 June 1782, in Washington, *Writings of Washington from the Original Manuscript Sources,* Series 3H (Letterbooks Varick Transcripts), Letterbook 2 (2 January, 1780–28 December 1782), 319.

22. Margaret Colleton to Robert Raper and Francis Kinloch, 13 July 1778, Margaret Colleton Papers, folder 4, viewed in typescript at SCL, USC.

23. Cf. Isaac, *Transformation of Virginia,* 11–138; Baird, "Between Slavery and Independence," 21.

24. Alexander Gray to Governor Patrick Tonyn, 20 February 1778, Henry Strachey Papers, Clements Library, University of Michigan, Ann Arbor, cited in Young, *Domesticating Slavery,* 68. At the start of the war Patrick Tonyn wrote an illuminating letter outlining Loyalist support in the Carolinas and Georgia. See Coleman, "Letter from Governor Patrick Tonyn of East Florida to George Germain, Secretary of State for the Colonies, 1776," 289–92.

25. Dunmore had "declared all indented Servants, Negroes, or others . . . free that are willing to bear arms, they joining His MAJESTY's Troops as soon as may be," Proclamation of Earl Dunmore, Africans in America, http://www.pbs.org/wgbh/aia/part2/2h42t.html (accessed 16 March 2015). For a thorough account of Dunmore's actions, see Holton, *Forced Founders,* 133–63.

26. Washington cited in Grizzard, *George Washington,* 90.

27. Memorandum book 13, 1773–76, Robert Carter of Nomini Hall Letterbook, Chauvenet Collection, CWF, 175–80.

28. Kulikoff, *Tobacco and Slaves,* 308. See also Kaplan, "'Domestic Insurrections' of the Declaration of Independence"; Robert Carter to Thomas and Rowland Hunt, 18 April 1777, Robert Carter of Nomini Hall Letterbook, Chauvenet Collection, CWF, 3:122.

29. Schama, *Rough Crossings,* 77; 81.

30. Proclamation of Lord Dunmore.

31. And, often, it was a value judgment. Some slaveholders mistook voluntary enslaved flight for British theft, much as they confused the "loyalty" of their bondpeople with a pragmatic desire for the comparative security of the plantation. Yet it is evident that black men and women actively welcomed the war with Britain, convinced that the Dunmore Proclamation presaged general emancipation. Henry Melchior Muhlenburg, a Pennsylvanian Lutheran pastor, wrote that enslaved people everywhere "secretly wished the British army might win for then all Negro slaves will gain their freedom." Muhlenberg, *Journal of Henry Melchior Muhlenberg,* 3:106.

32. Note 20, George Washington to Lund Washington, 30 April 1781, in Washington, *Writings of Washington from the Original Manuscript Sources,* http://memory.loc.gov/cgi-bin/ampage?collId=mgw4&fileName=gwpage077.db&recNum=228&tempFile=./temp/~ammem_gQpl&filecode=mgw&next_filecode=mgw&prev_filecode=mgw&itemnum=2&ndocs=100 (accessed 30 April 2015); cf. Washington, *Diaries of George Washington,* 5:3; 144; 6:549. Frederick's value almost certainly derived from his expertise in plantation management.

33. George Washington to Joseph Reed, 15 December 1775, in Washington, *Writings of George Washington,* vol. 3.

34. And, as a large slaveholder, Dunmore employed overseers. See Edward Snickers Account, 10 January 1774–20 June 1776; 9 April 1785, to Earl of Dunmore, Swem. Sylvia Frey argued that Dunmore made his proclamation for reasons that were "practical rather than moral" and "rooted in military expediency rather than humanitarian zeal." Frey, *Water from the Rock,* 63. See also Blumrosen and Blumrosen, *Slave Nation.*

35. Cf. Schama, *Rough Crossings,* 65–70; 74. Olwell, "'Domestick Enemies'" is a comprehensive account of Loyalist attempts to foment enslaved rebellion in South Carolina at the beginning of the conflict.

36. Laurens, *Letter from Henry Laurens to His Son John Laurens,* 23–4.

37. Ibid., 20; P. Morgan, *Slave Counterpoint,* 283.

38. John Lewis Gervais to Henry Laurens, 27 September 1782, John Lewis Gervais Papers, folder 1, SCL, USC. For the Revolutionary experiences of Henry Laurens's son James, who served as aide-de-camp to George Washington, see Massey, *John Laurens and the American Revolution.* Though his father was a slaveholder, James was an abolitionist.

39. Proclamation, 30 June 1779, British headquarters (Sir Guy Carleton papers), Howard-Tilton Library, Tulane University, New Orleans, cited in Frey, *Water from the Rock,* 113–14.

40. William Ancrum to James Edward Colleton, 14 July 1780, Margaret Colleton Papers, folder 1, SCL, USC. Cf. Frey, *Water from the Rock,* 76; 113–14.

41. Aaron Loocock to Dr. A. Swainston, 12 July 1786, Margaret Colleton Papers, folder 3, SCL, USC.

42. Frey, *Water from the Rock,* 211. For a downward revision of Frey's figures, see Pybus, "Jefferson's Faulty Math."

43. Entry for 27 January 1786, Samuel Stiles' Account Book 1783–1803, Colonial Dames Collection, GHS, 1.

44. B. Wood, "Some Aspects of Female Resistance to Chattel Slavery in Low Country Georgia," 604.

45. John Lloyd to Abraham Lloyd-Stoke, 29 January 1798, folder 1, John Lloyd Papers, SCL, USC.

46. Cf. Schama, *Rough Crossings,* 73; Laurens, *Letter from Henry Laurens to His Son John Laurens,* 11–12.

47. Adams cited in Kaplan and Kaplan, *Black Presence in the Era of the American Revolution,* 25.

48. Schama, *Rough Crossings,* 74.

49. British promises of manumission, coupled with the glaring contradiction between Patriot slaveholders' libertarian ambitions and their suppression of black people, persuaded many bondpeople—including one of George Washington's slaves—to imbibe British libertarian rhetoric ahead of that voiced by the Americans. See Pybus, *Epic Journeys of Freedom.*

50. John Lewis Gervais to Henry Laurens, 14 August 1784, John Lewis Gervais Papers, folder 1, SCL, USC. Cf. P. Morgan, *Slave Counterpoint,* 225.

51. Washington, *Papers of George Washington,* 1:64 and 66.

52. Kulikoff, *Tobacco and Slaves,* 311; McDonnell, *Politics of War,* 227.

53. Cf. Kulikoff, *Tobacco and Slaves,* 310.

54. Accounts Audited of Claims Growing Out of the Revolution in South Carolina, 1775–1856, reel 40, file no. 2172; cf. reel 131, file no. 6814, viewed on microfilm at SCDAH.

55. Memorandum book 13, 1773–76, Robert Carter of Nomini Hall Letterbook, Chauvenet Collection, CWF, 175–80.

56. 6 December 1779, William Gibbons Jr. Papers, 1774–84 file, box 2, Duke.

57. The names of forty-eight Georgian and South Carolinian overseers and stewards from *HL Papers, Butler Plantation Papers—the Papers of Pierce Butler (1744–1822),* the John Ewing Colhoun Papers, the Margaret Colleton Papers, and the John Lewis Gervais Papers were checked against indexes of Revolutionary war pensioners at SCDAH and GDAH. Involvement in the Revolutionary militia did not necessarily imply patriotism. In the South Carolina backcountry, where Scottish highlander immigrants staged a Loyalist uprising, many men tried to avoid taking an oath of fealty to the Revolutionary regime and were enlisted only under compulsion. See Laurens, *Letter from Henry Laurens to His Son John Laurens,* 13.

58. John Lewis Gervais to Henry Laurens, 27 September 1782, John Lewis Gervais Papers, folder 1, SCL, USC.

59. Sandy, "Divided Loyalties in a 'Predatory War,'" 381.

60. Chaplin, "Tidal Rice Cultivation and the Problem of Slavery in South Carolina, 1760–1815," 38; Sandy, "Divided Loyalties in a 'Predatory War,'" 379.

61. Kulikoff, *Tobacco and Slaves,* 311.

62. Francis Lightfoot Lee to Landon Carter, 9 November 1776, in P. Smith, *Letters of Delegates to Congress, 1774–1789,* 5:462.

63. Entry for 8 January 1777, Margaret Colleton account, 25 September 1776 to 28 August 1780, Margaret Colleton Papers, folder 5, SCL, USC; Chaplin, "Tidal Rice Cultivation and the Problem of Slavery in South Carolina, 1760–1815," 38.

64. Sandy, "Divided Loyalties in a 'Predatory War,'" 382

65. Accounts Audited of Claims Growing Out of the Revolution in South Carolina, 1775–1856, reel 101, file no. 5104, SCDAH. John Couturier, whom Colhoun would also later employ, served as a captain in the South Carolina militia during the war. McCrady, *History of South Carolina in the Revolution, 1775–1780,* 3:144.

66. Accounts Audited of Claims Growing Out of the Revolution in South Carolina, 1775–1856, reel 163, file no. 8835, SCDAH.

67. Miscellaneous expense journal, 1771–80, William Gibbons Jr. Papers, Duke.

68. "Petition of Inhabitants of Lunenburg County," 23 May 1776, cited in McDonnell, "Popular Mobilization and Political Culture in Revolutionary Virginia," 967.

69. McDonnell, *Politics of War,* 227.

70. McDonnell, "Popular Mobilization and Political Culture in Revolutionary Virginia," 967. Robert Carter to John A. Washington, 23 November 1775, Robert Carter Letterbooks, vol. 3, Robert Carter Papers, CWF.

71. Kulikoff, *Tobacco and Slaves,* 311; McDonnell, *Politics of War,* 228.

72. Hadden, *Slave Patrols,* 155.

73. See Baird, "Between Slavery and Independence," 223–46.

74. Schama, *Rough Crossings,* 66.

75. See Frey, *Water from the Rock,* 77, and Foner, *Blacks in the American Revolution,* 41, for black involvement in the Patriot cause.

76. William Ancrum to Marlow Pryor, 1 March 1776, William Ancrum Account Book and Letterbook, SCL, USC. Early in the war slave patrols were denuded of military-age men, with the result that overseers and others who were excused from the militia set up ersatz patrol units. See Hadden, *Slave Patrols,* 155.

77. William Ancrum to Parker Quince, 5 September 1778, William Ancrum Account Book and Letterbook, SCL, USC.

78. Stephanie Camp brackets together "runaway," "truant," and "absentee," distinguishing them from the more permanent status of "fugitive." Camp, *Closer to Freedom,* 36.

79. William Ancrum to Parker Quince, 5 September 1778, William Ancrum Account Book and Letterbook, SCL, USC. John Lewis Gervais to Henry Laurens, 27 September 1782, John Lewis Gervais Papers, folder 1.

80. Camp, *Closer to Freedom,* 116.

81. Entry for 30 October 1781, daybook, 1:137, Robert Carter Papers, 1772–94, Duke.

82. See Frey, *Water from the Rock;* Quarles, *Negro in the American Revolution.* For the developing historiographical notion that the Loyalist cause promised the fulfillment of enslaved people's revolutionary ambitions, see Pybus, *Epic Journeys of Freedom,* and Schama, *Rough Crossings.* See also Pulis, *Moving On;* Gibson, *Loyal Blacks;* Foner, *Blacks in the American Revolution.*

83. Hadden, *Slave Patrols*, 156–57. Cf. McIlwaine, *Executive Journals of the Council of Colonial Virginia*, 6:582; Greene, "Colonial South Carolina and the Caribbean Connection," 85.

84. Madison, *Papers of James Madison*, 1:153. George Washington made a very similar pronouncement in December 1775. Schama, *Rough Crossings*, 75.

85. Scott, *Domination and the Arts of Resistance*, 202–3; 223.

86. William Ancrum to Marlow Pryor, 9 November 1779, William Ancrum Account Book and Letterbook, SCL, USC. Henry Laurens used similar martial language to describe rebellious bondpeople. In 1775 he related to his son the "trials of Several Negroes Suspected of plotting an Insurrection." Laurens cited in Olwell, "'Domestick Enemies,'" 33. At the same time, a court in St. Bartholomew's Parish in Charleston ordered the execution of George, an enslaved preacher who had been convicted of "exciting & endeavouring to bring ab[ou]t a General Insurrection." Ibid., 34.

87. Norrece T. Jones has proposed a martial analogy for the struggle between master and slave, invoking John Locke's maxim that "the perfect condition of slavery . . . is nothing else but the state of war continued between lawful conqueror and captive." As Jones argued, "such an analogy not only allows one to perceive lucidly the depth and complexity of the hostilities it stirred, but helps to avoid any puerile interpretations of slave words and actions." N. Jones, *Born a Child of Freedom, Yet a Slave*, 10–11. Walter Johnson arrives at a similar conclusion in "Nettlesome Classic Turns Twenty-Five," rejecting Eugene D. Genovese's hegemonic reading of slaveholder paternalism and replacing it with "something that sometimes looked a lot more like a war." This analogy serves eighteenth-century enslaved resistance well, though naturally it holds most salience for oppositional activity in the Revolutionary War. Hence William Ancrum's fearful estimation that restive slaves were enemy combatants, or "insurgents" in possession of "stratagems."

88. Camp, *Closer to Freedom*, 10; 119; Scott, *Domination and the Arts of Resistance*, 202–3; 223.

89. Cf. Schama, *Rough Crossings*, 77–78.

90. This argument builds on Stephanie Camp's work on a similar phenomenon from the Civil War. See Camp, *Closer to Freedom*, 117–38.

91. John Lewis Gervais to Henry Laurens, 27 September 1782, John Lewis Gervais Papers, folder 1, SCL, USC.

92. See Sidbury, *Ploughshares into Swords*, 25.

93. *South Carolina and American General Gazette* (Charleston), 20 January 1781, cited in P. Morgan, *Slave Counterpoint*, 185n62.

94. *South Carolina and American General Gazette* (Charleston), 20 January 1781, cited in ibid., 185n62.

95. "The Examination of Sundry Negroes Belonging to Sir James Wright Respecting the Murder of Joseph Weatherly," in Hawes, "Minute Book, Savannah Board of Police."

96. "Rival geography" is taken from Camp, *Closer to Freedom*, 6–7. It featured "spaces that gave [bondpeople] room and time for their families, for rest from work, and for amusement." This geography might include the "quarters [and] outbuildings" of their owners' plantations, but it just as likely featured "woods, swamps and neighboring farms as chance granted them." Cf. Egerton, *Death or Liberty*.

97. For Michel Foucault power is a "multiplicity of force relations immanent in the sphere in which they operate"; resistance therefore "depends upon a multiplicity of points of resistance." Foucault, *History of Sexuality*, 95–96. Bondpeople tested the boundaries of this power structure because "any structure of ideas is vulnerable at its margins." Mary Douglas cited in Camp, *Closer to Freedom*, 6.

98. "Examination of Sundry Negroes Belonging to Sir James Wright Respecting the Murder of Joseph Weatherly," 245–57.

99. This is not to deny that the years 1775–82 witnessed large-scale revolutionary movements initiated by the enslaved. Walter Johnson remarks that the American Revolution was "profoundly (and at various turns decisively) shaped by the self-willed actions, both military and otherwise, of

black slaves fighting for freedom, or slave rebels." See Johnson, "Nettlesome Classic Turns Twenty-Five." But the outcome of wartime enslaved resistance was not the complete societal upheaval of which whites were so timorous, and which would later occur (though as a result of dissimilar circumstances) on Saint-Domingue. See Stubbs, "Haitian Revolution"; Jacob Read to General Jackson, 26 February 1796, Jacob Read Papers, folder 3, SCL, USC.

100. George Washington, General Orders, 25 October 1781, in Washington, *Writings of Washington from the Original Manuscript Sources,* http://memory.loc.gov/cgi-bin/query/r?ammem/mgw:@field(DOCID+@lit(gw230293)) (accessed 30 April 2015).

101. Pinckney cited in Sandy, "Divided Loyalties in a 'Predatory War,'" 385.

102. This paragraph draws heavily on social theorist Anthony Giddens's concept of structuration and is influenced by an application of the same theory to power relations in classical slavery. Endeavoring to draw a consensus between traditional structuralist and functionalist models of power, Giddens determined that social actors "are not simply the passive victims of external pressures, but themselves repeatedly reinterpret" social structure, "and so by their actions reproduce the social order." Hopkins, "Novel Evidence for Roman Slavery," 26. See Giddens, *Constitution of Society,* and his collection of essays *Central Problems in Social Theory,* especially 69–73.

103. William Ancrum to James Edward Colleton, July 14 1780, Margaret Colleton Papers, folder 1, SCL, USC; cf. Chaplin, *Anxious Pursuit,* 217.

104. John Lewis Gervais to Henry Laurens, 27 September 1782, John Lewis Gervais Papers, folder 1, SCL, USC.

105. See also Sandy, "Divided Loyalties in a 'Predatory War,'" 388.

106. See, for example, Charles Johnston to Major General William Phillips, 28 July 1779, Bland Family Papers, 1713–1825, section 13, VHS.

Epilogue

1. Douglass, *My Bondage and My Freedom,* 44; 71.
2. Ibid., 71.
3. Ibid., 64.
4. Bigelow, *Curse Entailed,* 136.
5. Hildreth, *White Slave,* 174.
6. Stowe, *Uncle Tom's Cabin; or, Negro Life in the Slave States of America,* 210; 327.
7. Scarborough, *Overseer,* 8; Brinton, *Man Is Love,* 113.
8. Anonymous, "Slave's Story," 615–16.
9. Burke, *Rules for the Government and Management of the Slaves, to Be Observed by the Overseer.*
10. Excerpt from the *Southern Agriculturist,* cited in Olmsted, *Cotton Kingdom,* 440 (italics in the original).
11. Haley, *Roots,* 234.
12. Morrison, *Beloved.*
13. Laurens, *Letter from Henry Laurens to His Son John Laurens August 14, 1776,* 9.
14. Ibid., 20.
15. Genovese, *Roll, Jordan, Roll.*
16. For Sarah Knott "sensibility" celebrated the human capacity for sympathy; "sensibility" was, in turn, central to the mental architecture in which the American Revolution took place. Knott, *Sensibility and the American Revolution,* 79.
17. P. Morgan, *Slave Counterpoint,* 284.
18. And indeed Sarah Knott suggested that sentimentalism also affected much of the rest of society, transcending lines of class and gender. See Knott, *Sensibility and the American Revolution.*
19. Joseph Ball to Joseph Chinn, 30 August 1746, Joseph Ball Letterbook, CWF.
20. Entry for 2 March 1762, Francis Jerdone Memorandum Book, Swem.

21. 22 November 1746, Joseph Ball Letterbook, CWF.

22. Parent, *Foul Means,* 232.

23. Byrd cited in ibid., 232.

24. For examples of Carter's growing moral puritanism, see Robert Carter to Robert B. Carter, 21 November 1778, Robert Carter of Nomini Hall Letterbook, Chauvenet Collection, 3:75; Robert Carter to Francis Christian, 23 June 1779, Robert Carter of Nomini Hall Letterbook, Chauvenet Collection, 3:122; 1791, Robert Carter of Nomini Hall Manuscript Ledger, 9 vols., Chauvenet Collection, CWF, 9:1–2.

25. Robert Carter III to Messrs Jackson and Rutherford, 26 March 1767, Letterbook of Robert Carter III of Nominy Hall, 1760–64, CWF; entry for 30 October 1781, daybook, 4:147, Robert Carter Papers, 1772–94, Duke; Robert Carter to Charles Haynie, 21 April 1784, daybook, 5:248, Robert Carter Papers, 1772–94.

26. Robert Carter III to ?, n.d., Letterbook of Robert Carter III of Nominy Hall, 1769, CWF.

27. David Ramsay cited in P. Morgan, *Slave Counterpoint,* 296; Charles Ball cited in ibid., 298.

28. Petition of Georgetown residents, 4 April 1787, Thomas Pinckney Papers, Library of Congress, cited in ibid., 286.

29. Laurens, *Letter from Henry Laurens to His Son John Laurens,* 21; 9.

30. Levi Shefhall to Seaborn Jones, 15 November 1790, Seaborn Jones Sr. Papers, 1761–1847, folder 1, 1761–93, Duke.

31. Thomas Boone to Margaret Colleton, 29 September 1773, Margaret Colleton Papers, folder 1, SCL, USC.

32. P. Morgan, *Slave Counterpoint,* 285.

33. Joseph Ball to Joseph Chinn, 5 February 1754, Joseph Ball Letterbook, CWF; Joseph Ball to Joseph Chinn, 19 February 1754, Joseph Ball Letterbook, CWF.

34. John Lloyd to E. H. Champion, 14 June 1796, John Lloyd Papers, folder 1, SCL, USC. Lloyd's analysis was that "the excess of labour, the low wages (in comparison to the high prices of provisions, the distress in sickness and the frequent want of articles of the first necessity) make the situation of the common people in England not even a very eligible one."

35. Sarah Pearsall makes a similar point in *Atlantic Families,* 86–87. Being a man or woman of feeling "served as a fantasy for these men and women, in the face of an Atlantic economy, and a political world, in which indifference and even cruelty could be paramount." Likewise Nicole Eustace has argued that emotions "mask[ed] continuing inequalities of power even as they maintained them." Eustace, *Passion Is the Gale,* 69.

36. Robert Carter Nicholas advertisement in *Virginia Gazette* (Purdie and Dixon), 14 January 1767, cited in P. Morgan, *Slave Counterpoint,* 290.

37. *VG* (Purdie), 21 August 1778, 4.

38. John Lloyd to Richard Champion, 16 November 1796, John Lloyd Papers, folder 1, SCL, USC.

39. Robert Carter to Jacob Bruce, 27 July 1772, Robert Carter of Nomini Hall Letterbook, Chauvenet Collection, CWF, 1.

40. Littleberry Apperson to Robert Carter, correspondence of Robert Carter III, Carter Family Papers, 1651–1861, folder 1, VHS.

41. Charles Dabney to ?, 1770, Charles William Dabney Papers, 1715–45, UNC.

42. Laurens cited in Sandy, "Divided Loyalties in a 'Predatory War,'" 368.

43. John Steele to Mary (Polly) Steele, 6 October 1796, John Steele Papers, folder 3, SCL, USC, 2.

44. John Steele to Polly Steele, 1 March 1792, John Steele Papers, folder 2, SCL, USC.

45. Thornton cited in K. Wood, "Broken Reeds and Competent Farmers," 46.

46. K. Wood, "Broken Reeds and Competent Farmers," 46.

47. K. Wood, *Masterful Women,* 52.

48. *VG* (Purdie and Dixon), 3 December 1772.

49. *VG* (Purdie and Dixon), 6 August 1772.

50. See, especially, Wiencek, *Imperfect God.*

51. Ibid., 2; Washington, *Diaries of George Washington,* 6:42. Similar motivation perhaps lay behind the many runaway adverts that demanded the return of the bondperson to the overseer rather than the planter. Thus James Fraser, Pierce Butler's overseer, reported the flight in 1773 of the bondman Johnny and promised that "Any Person that will deliver him . . . to the . . . Overseer . . . shall receive TWO DOLLARS reward." Supplement to *SCG,* 24 March 1773, 4.

52. See, especially, Camp, *Closer to Freedom;* B. Wood, *Slavery in Colonial Georgia;* Dusinberre, *Them Dark Days;* Parent, *Foul Means.*

53. B. Wood, *Slavery in Colonial Georgia,* 155.

54. B. Wood, "Some Aspects of Female Resistance to Chattel Slavery in Low Country Georgia," 608.

55. Baird, "Paternalism and Profits," 151.

56. Camp, *Closer to Freedom,* 3; 144.

57. John Ewing Colhoun to Mr. Bard?/Mr. Bon?, 20 June 1797, John Ewing Colhoun Papers; report of trial at John Ewing Colhoun's plantation at 12 Mile River, 29 August 1798, John Ewing Colhoun Papers, SCL, USC.

58. Affidavit of J. Greene, 29 August 1798, John Ewing Colhoun Papers, SCL, USC.

59. John C. Grinninger to John Ewing Colhoun, 22 August 1795, John Ewing Colhoun Papers, SCL, USC.

60. P. Morgan, *Slave Counterpoint,* 287.

61. Robert Carter to Newyear Branson, 3 February 1790, Robert Carter Letterbook, 9:93, Duke, cited in Mullin, *Flight and Rebellion,* 71.

62. Robert Carter Nicholas to Charles Dabney, 4 September 1773, Charles William Dabney Papers, 1715–45, folder 13, box 1, subseries 1.1: 1716–75, UNC.

63. De Crèvecoeur cited in P. Morgan, *Slave Counterpoint,* 272.

64. The pages that follow discuss accusations of overseer inhumanity as part of the rhetorical assault that slaveholders inflicted on their managers. However, bondpeople played a crucial role in extracting this admission from their owners. Cf. the definition of enslaved resistance provided by Philip Morgan: "wherever and whenever masters, whether implicitly or explicitly, recognized the independent will or volition of their slaves, they acknowledged the humanity of their bondpeople. Extracting this admission was, in fact, a form of slave resistance, because slaves thereby opposed the dehumanization inherent in their status." P. Morgan, *Slave Counterpoint,* xxii.

65. Davis, *Problem of Slavery in the Age of Revolution, 1770–1823,* 23.

66. Laurens, *Letter from Henry Laurens to His Son John Laurens,* 9.

67. Thomas Wadsworth Will, 14 September 1799, SCL, USC.

68. John Channing to [Edward Telfair], 10 August 1786, folder 3, box 3, Edward Telfair Papers, 1761–1847, Duke.

69. See P. Morgan, *Slave Counterpoint,* 271, for the use of bestial language to describe other outsiders, including Irish immigrants.

70. Washington cited in Baird, "Between Slavery and Independence," 112.

71. William Lee to Mr. Ellis, 24 June 1778, William Lee's letterbook, 1769–93, Lee Family Papers, 1638–1867, section 115, VHS, 265.

72. Washington cited in Scarborough, *Overseer,* 94–95.

73. Washington cited in Baird, "Between Slavery and Independence," 168.

74. Cf. Eustace, *Passion Is the Gale,* 175.

75. Joseph Ball to Joseph Chinn, 27 June 1749, Joseph Ball Letterbook, CWF.

76. Entry for 1 November 1777, daybook, XIC, 124, Robert Carter Papers, 1772–94, Duke.

77. Sandy, "Homemakers, Supervisors and Peach Stealing Bitches," 479.

78. Tucker cited in P. Morgan, *Slave Counterpoint,* 329.

79. B. Wood, *Masterful Women,* 53.

80. Hewatt cited in Young, *Domesticating Slavery,* 75

81. Henry Laurens to Abraham Schad, 23 August 1765, in Laurens, *HL Papers,* ed. Hamer, 4:665.

82. Laurens cited in Chaplin, *Anxious Pursuit,* 124. For the effect of humanitarianism on white people's treatment of the enslaved (including the amelioration of the Virginia slave code), see P. Morgan, *Slave Counterpoint,* 228–29; Chaplin, *Anxious Pursuit,* 124; Chaplin, "Slavery and the Principle of Humanity."

83. Chaplin, "Slavery and the Principle of Humanity," 305. Partly slaveholders were influenced by a new philosophical emphasis on empathy. See Hume, *Essays Moral and Political;* Haakonssen, *Adam Smith: Theory of Moral Sentiments.*

84. George Washington to Alexander Spotswood, 23 November 1794, in Washington, *Writings of Washington from the Original Manuscript Sources,* http://memory.loc.gov/cgi-bin/query/r?ammem/mgw:@field(DOCID+@lit(gw340030)) (accessed 2 May 2015).

85. Chaplin, "Slavery and the Principle of Humanity," 301.

86. Newton, *Journal of a Slave Trader 1750–1754,* 111.

87. Ibid., 111–12.

88. Edgeworth, *Popular Tales,* 3:171.

89. Clarkson, *History of the Abolition of the African Slave-Trade,* vol. 2, chapter 9.

90. Robert Carter to Thomas Olive, 8 May 1781, Robert Carter of Nomini Hall Letterbook, Chauvenet Collection, CWF, 8:75.

91. Cf. Isaac, *Transformation of Virginia,* 342–43; Olwell, *Masters, Slaves and Subjects,* 213; P. Morgan, *Slave Counterpoint,* 284.

92. Rutledge cited in Schwartz, *History of the Supreme Court,* 5; 22 April 1776, Robert Carter of Nomini Hall Letterbook, Chauvenet Collection, CWF, 3:18.

93. Josiah Smith to George Austin, 30 January 1770, Josiah Smith Jr. Lettercopy Book, 1771–84, UNC, 157.

94. Josiah Smith to George Austin, Josiah Smith Jr. Lettercopy Book, 1771–84, UNC, 228.

95. Copy of Letter from Young Men of Augusta, Georgia, to President Adams, 2 July 1798, Colonial Dames Collection, folder 94, box 10, GHS.

96. Scott, *Domination and the Arts of Resistance,* 105.

97. Thomas Jefferson to William Wirt, 5 August 1815, in Jefferson, *Works of Thomas Jefferson in Twelve Volumes,* vol. 11, http://hdl.loc.gov/loc.mss/mtj.mtjbib022119 (accessed 30 April 2015).

98. Jefferson, *Notes on the State of Virginia,* 165.

99. Laurens cited in Sandy, "Divided Loyalties in a 'Predatory War,'" 365.

100. Solomon Betton to John Mercer, 6 September 1791, letters from Solomon Betton, Mercer Papers, VHS.

101. Solomon Betton to John Mercer, 6 September 1791, letters from Solomon Betton, Mercer Papers, VHS.

102. Solomon Betton to John Mercer, 19 September 1791, letters from Solomon Betton, Mercer Papers, VHS.

103. Entry for 9 September 1784, daybook, 6:31, Robert Carter Papers, 1772–94, Duke.

104. Robert Carter to Newyear Branson, 16 April 1785, daybook, 6:138; entry for 22 April 1785, daybook, 6:194, Robert Carter Papers, 1772–94, Duke; P. Morgan, *Slave Counterpoint,* 327.

105. Robert Carter to Samuel Straughan, 6 July 177, daybook, 7:307, Robert Carter Papers, 1772–94, Duke.

106. Jefferson, *Notes on the State of Virginia,* 162.

107. Ragsdale, *Planters' Republic,* 126.

108. Isaac, *Transformation of Virginia,* 247.

109. "Wednesday August 22. In Convention," "Debates in the Federal Convention of 1787 as Reported by James Madison," Tansill, *Documents Illustrative of the Formation of the American States,* 590–91.

110. Ragsdale, *Planter's Republic,* 122.

111. Jonathon Boucher to George Washington, 21 May 1770, in Washington, *Writings of Washington from the Original Manuscript Sources,* http://memory.loc.gov/cgi-bin/query/r?ammem/mgw:@field(DOCID+@lit(lw040016)) (accessed 2 May 2015).

112. Jefferson, *Notes on the State of Virginia,* 162; Jefferson cited in Talpalar, *Sociology of Colonial Virginia,* 395; cf. Anburey, *Travels through the Interior Parts of North America,* 371–76.

113. Baird, "Between Slavery and Independence," 75.

114. Breen, *Tobacco Culture,* 86.

115. Jefferson, *Notes on the State of Virginia,* 244. See also Kennedy, *Mr. Jefferson's Lost Cause.*

116. Thomas Jefferson to William Wirt, 5 August 1815, in Jefferson, *Works of Thomas Jefferson,* vol. 11, http://hdl.loc.gov/loc.mss/mtj.mtjbib022119 (accessed 30 April 2015).

117. Robert Carter to Hill Carter, Thomas Nelson Carter, Anne Butler (Carter) Wickham, and Lucy (Carter) Wickham, 12–14 October 1803, viewed in typescript at VHS.

118. Foner, *Story of American Freedom,* 20.

119. "Friday August 10. In Convention," "Debates in the Federal Convention of 1787 as Reported by James Madison," Tansill, *Documents Illustrative of the Formation of the American States,* 511.

120. See for example George Keckley to John Ewing Colhoun, 17 June 1797, John Ewing Colhoun Papers, SCL, USC.

121. William Cantey Will, Colonial Records, Miscellaneous Bonds, Book YI, GDAH.

122. Washington, *Diaries of George Washington,* 6:373.

123. Will of Richard Scammell, Surry County, Virginia Will Book 1, 1792–1804, viewed on microfilm at CWF, 300.

124. Names of men working as overseers from 1750 onward were checked against tax and census indexes for 1782 and 1790; any names that were repeated were discarded.

125. Baird, "Between Slavery and Independence," 115.

126. Ibid., 98.

127. Names of men working as overseers from 1750 onward were checked against the Kentucky census indexes for 1790 and 1800; any names that were repeated were discarded.

128. Names of men working as overseers in South Carolina and Georgia from 1750 onward were checked against the South Carolina census indexes for 1790, and the 1820 census index for Georgia; any names that were repeated were discarded.

129. Chaplin, "Tidal Rice Cultivation and the Problem of Slavery in South Carolina, 1760–1815," 47.

130. Betton cited in Baird, "Between Slavery and Independence," 113.

131. Ibid., 115.

132. John Irby to Henry Banks, 7 November 1797, Banks Papers, 1781–1817, section 1, "John Irby" folder, VHS.

133. Betton cited in Baird, "Between Slavery and Independence," 112, 244.

134. Ramsay cited in Foner, *Story of American Freedom,* 31.

135. Jefferson, *Notes on the State of Virginia,* 163.

136. Genovese cited in N. Jones, *Born a Child of Freedom, Yet a Slave,* 28–29.

137. Cf. Isaac, *Transformation of Virginia,* 211; Foucault, *Discipline and Punish,* 3–31. See Olwell, "'Domestick Enemies,'" 24, for details of exemplary executions of bondpeople who had killed planters and overseers.

138. Gordon S. Wood has shown how even in highly stratified South Carolina, there was strong support among lowlier inhabitants for a more egalitarian order. How differences in approaches to politics within as well as between states influenced assessments of overseers represents another

fruitful area of research. G. Wood, *Radicalism of the American Revolution,* 120. Cf. Baird, "Between Slavery and Independence," 249–53. See, especially, 253 for the effect of evangelical Protestantism on contemporary understandings of freedom and dependence. Further research might also shed light on how these distinctions changed over time. For example Max Edelson has proposed that "the agricultural innovations [colonists] introduced in rice production . . . undermined the effectiveness of the task labor system, long seen by historians as a crucial point of leverage used by the enslaved to limit planters' demands for work." Edelson, *Plantation Enterprise in Colonial South Carolina,* 11.

139. Cf. Stubbs, "Violence, Dependence and Liberty"; Greenberg, *Masters and Statesmen.*

140. See, for example, Kolchin, *American Slavery 1619–1877,* 173.

141. The classic text on scapegoating in philosophical anthropology is Girard, *Scapegoat.* Girard argued that religions keep violence outside societies by deflecting it onto scapegoats whose sacrifices restore social order. Cf. Baird, "Between Slavery and Independence," 29.

142. See for example Chaplin, *Anxious Pursuit*; O'Brien, *Conjectures of Order*; Follett, *Sugar Masters.*

143. Tadman, *Speculators and Slaves,* 183; Gudmestad, *Troublesome Commerce,* 190. Cf. Deyle, *Carry Me Back.*

144. Tadman, *Speculators and Slaves,* 183.

145. Elizabeth Fox-Genovese and Eugene D. Genovese have argued that the slave system of the antebellum South should be delineated a "hybrid system," both "based on slave relations of production and yet deeply embedded in the world market"; we see the stirrings of this tension in the eighteenth century. Cited in Kolchin, *American Slavery 1619–1877,* 173. Max Edelson suggested that "in their entrepreneurial sensibilities, as well as their devotion to production for the market, planters were early modern capitalists. Their plantation businesses were a form of free enterprise, although they centered on slavery rather than free labor, and in the long term, industrial manufacturing proved to be more influential in shaping the evolution of the modern, global economy." Edelson, *Plantation Enterprise in Colonial South Carolina,* 4. See also Breen, *Marketplace of Revolution;* Oakes, *Slavery and Freedom,* 40–79; Young, *Domesticating Slavery.* A recent treatment of the idea of slavery as capitalism is Baptist, *Half Has Never Been Told.*

146. Jones cited in Camp, *Closer to Freedom,* 67.

147. Henson's autobiography cited in Fisher, "Unique Montgomery Property for Sale."

Bibliography

Primary Sources

Archival

Birmingham Central Library Archives, Birmingham, England
Zachary Lloyd Collection
University Library, University of Cambridge, Cambridge, England
Butler Plantation Papers—the Papers of Pierce Butler (1744–1822) and Successors from the Historical Society of Pennsylvania: A Listing and Guide to the Microfilm Collection. Marlborough, U.K.: Adam Matthew Publications, 1996 (microfilm).
Duke University Perkins Special Collections Library, Durham, North Carolina
William B. Berkeley Papers, 1771–1878
Robert Carter Papers, 1772–94 (typescript)
Henry Fitzhugh Ledger
Henry Fitzhugh Papers, 1746–69
John Gibbons Papers, 1758–89
William Gibbons Jr. Papers
William Henry Hall Papers, 1736–82
Seaborn Jones Sr. Papers, 1761–1847
Josiah Tatnall Sr. Papers
Edward Telfair Papers, 1762–1831
Wingfield Papers
Ralph Wormeley Account Book, 1773–84
Georgia Department of Archives and History, Atlanta, Georgia
William Cantey Will, Colonial Records, Miscellaneous Bonds, Book YI
Miscellaneous Bonds, Book O
Georgia Historical Society, Savannah, Georgia
Colonial Dames Collection
Copy of Letter from Young Men of Augusta, Georgia, to President Adams, 2 July 1798
Houstoun Collection
Samuel Stiles' Account Book, 1783–1803
Hargrett Rare Book and Manuscript Library, University of Georgia, Athens, Georgia
Gideon Denison Family Papers
Library of Virginia, Richmond, Virginia
Ball Family Papers, 1680–1785
Robert Bristow Copybook
Francis Jerdone Memorandum Book
Jerdone Family Papers
Martha Washington to Mrs. Powell, 1 May 1797
Aylette Waller Contract
Maryland Historical Society, Baltimore
"An Overseer Doing His Duty, Sketched from Life near Fredericksburg [Virginia]," 13 March 1792, Benjamin Henry Latrobe, Sketchbook, 3:33

John D. Rockefeller Library, Colonial Williamsburg Foundation, Williamsburg, Virginia
Joseph Ball Letterbook (microfilm)
Joseph Ball Letterbook, Library of Congress (typescript)
Robert Bristow Letterbook (typescript)
Letterbook of Robert Carter III of Nominy Hall, 1760–64 (typescript)
Letterbook of Robert Carter III of Nominy Hall, 1769 (typescript)
Chauvenet Collection
Robert Carter of Nomini Hall Letterbook (typescript), 9 vols.
Robert Carter of Nomini Hall Manuscript Ledger, 9 vols.
King George County Inventories 1721–44 (microfilm)
Sol Feinstone Collection (microfilm)
John Spotswood to Alexander Spotswood, 29 November 1722, Alexander Spotswood Papers, Colonial Williamsburg Digital Library, http://research.history.org/DigitalLibrary/View/index.cfm?doc=Manuscripts%5CM4802101.xml (accessed 14 November 2014)
Inventory of the Estate of Charles Stagg, York County, 17 May 1736 (microfilm)
Surry County, Virginia Will Book I, 1792–1804 (microfilm)
York County Wills and Inventories, 1771–83 (microfilm)
South Carolina Department of Archives and History, Columbia, South Carolina
Accounts Audited of Claims Growing out of the Revolution in South Carolina, 1775–1856 (microfilm)
Letters of Administration 1775–78
South Carolina Historical Society, Charleston, South Carolina
Isaac Hayne Ledger, 1765–81 (microform)
Plantation Belonging to the Estate of John Singleton, St. Bartholomew's Parish, South Carolina, May 1795, Theodore Gourdin Collection
South Caroliniana Library, University of South Carolina, Columbia, South Carolina
William Ancrum Account Book and Letterbook
Othniel Beale Papers
Margaret Colleton Papers
John Ewing Colhoun papers
James Glen Papers
Richard Hampton Papers
John Harleston Papers, ca. 1759–74
Louis Kelly Crowder Genealogical Collection
John Lewis Gervais Papers
John Lloyd Papers
William Moultrie Papers
Jacob Read Papers
John Steele Paper
Thomas Wadsworth Will
Manuscripts Department, Southern Historical Collection, University of North Carolina, Chapel Hill, North Carolina
Josiah Smith Jr. Lettercopy Book, 1771–84
Charles William Dabney Papers, 1715–1845
Manuscripts Department, Earl Gregg Swem Library, College of William and Mary, Williamsburg, Virginia
Francis Jerdone Memorandum Book
Fontaine-Maury Papers
James Mercer Slave Pass, 29–30 October 1771 (transcript)
Jerdone Family Papers

Nourse and Morris Family Papers
John Page Diary
Edward Snickers Account, 10 January 1774–20 June 1776; 9 April 1785, to Earl of Dunmore
Alderman Library, Special Collections, University of Virginia, Charlottesville, Virginia
Simon Sallard Papers
Sabine Hall Papers, 1650–1779
Virginia Historical Society, Richmond, Virginia
Banks Papers, 1781–1817
Bland Family Papers, 1713–1825
Byrd Family Papers, 1684–1842 (bound volume: copy made by Elizabeth Byrd Nicholas in 1876)
Lucy Battaille Thornton Papers, 1798–1862 (typescript)
Cabell Commonplace Books, 1769–95
Carter Family Papers, 1651–1861
Robert Carter Papers, 1760–1815
Robert Carter to Hill Carter, Thomas Nelson Carter, Anne Butler (Carter) Wickham, and Lucy (Carter) Wickham, 12–14 October 1803 (typescript)
Custis Family Papers, 1683–1858
John Lee to George Lewis, 29 May 1797
Lee Family Papers, 1638–1867
Mercer Papers
Washington, George, "A View of the Work at the Several Plantations in the Year 1789 and General Directions for the Execution of It"
Warwickshire County Record Office, Warwickshire, U.K.
Thomas Pennant's Notebook about America

Books, Articles, and Internet Sources

"Abstracts from Records of Richmond County, Virginia." *William and Mary College Quarterly Historical Magazine* 17, no. 2 (1908): 73–85.

American Council of Learned Societies. *Surnames in the United States Census of 1790*. Baltimore: Clearfield, 1990.

Anburey, Thomas. *Travels through the Interior Parts of North America*. 2 vols. London: W. Lane, 1789.

Anonymous. "A Slave's Story." *Putnam's Monthly Magazine* 9 (June 1857): 614–20.

Aristotle. *The Politics*. London: Penguin Classics, 1962.

Barclay, James. *The Voyages and Travels of James Barclay, Containing Many Surprising Adventures, and Interesting Narratives*. London: Printed for the author, 1777.

Bartram, William. *Travels through North and South Carolina, Georgia, East and West Florida*. Savannah, Ga.: Beehive, 1973.

Berkeley, Edmund, Jr. "Notes on Often-Cited Persons, Places and Things in Robert Carter's Diary and Letters." In Robert Carter, *The Diary, Correspondence, and Papers of Robert "King" Carter of Virginia, 1701–1732*, ed. Edmund Berkeley Jr., http://carter.lib.virginia.edu/public/Cbiodir.html (accessed 6 May 2015).

Beverley, Robert. *The History and Present State of Virginia*, ed. Louis B. Wright. Chapel Hill: University of North Carolina Press, 1947.

Bigelow, Harriet Hameline. *The Curse Entailed*. Cleveland, Ohio: Isaac I. Bigelow, 1857, http://webapp1.dlib.indiana.edu/TEIgeneral/view?docId=wright/VAC5819&brand=wright (accessed 25 January 2015).

Brinton, Bulah. *Man Is Love*. Philadelphia: J. B. Lippincott, 1873, http://webapp1.dlib.indiana.edu/TEIgeneral/view?docId=wright/VAC5892.xml&brand=wright&field1=text&freeformQuery=bulah&startDoc=1 (accessed 25 January 2015).

Burke, A. J. *Rules for the Government and Management of the Slaves, to Be Observed by the Overseer.* Charleston, S.C., n.d.

Byrd, William. *Another Secret Diary of William Byrd of Westover, 1739–1741,* ed. Maude H. Woodfin. Richmond, Va.: Dietz, 1942.

——. *The Secret Diary of William Byrd of Westover, 1709–1712,* ed. Louis B. Wright and Marion Tinling. Richmond, Va.: Dietz, 1941.

——. William Byrd II to Charles, Earl of Orrery, 5 July 1726. "Virginia Council Journals, 1726–1753." *Virginia Magazine of History and Biography* 22 (1924): 27.

Carter, Landon. "Diary of Col. Landon Carter." *William and Mary College Quarterly Historical Magazine* 14, no. 1 (1905): 38–44.

——. *The Diary of Colonel Landon Carter of Sabine Hall, 1752–1778,* ed. Jack P. Greene. 2 vols. Charlottesville: University Press of Virginia, 1965.

——. "Landon Carter's Crop Book." *William and Mary College Quarterly Historical Magazine* 22, no. 4 (1912): 280–85.

——. "Will of Landon Carter (1770/1779) of Sabine Hall, Richmond County, Virginia," http://files.usgwarchives.net/va/richmond/wills/c6360001.txt (accessed 8 May 2015).

Carter, Robert. *The Diary, Correspondence, and Papers of Robert "King" Carter of Virginia, 1701–1732,* ed. Edmund Berkeley Jr., http://carter.lib.virginia.edu/public/ (accessed 6 May 2015).

Clark, Murtie June. *Colonial Soldiers of the South, 1732–1774.* Baltimore: Genealogical Publishing, 1986.

Clarkson, Thomas. *The History of the Abolition of the African Slave-Trade.* London: L. Taylor, 1808.

Clayton, John. "A Letter from Mr. John Clayton: Giving an Account of Several Observables in Virginia," http://www.virtualjamestown.org/exist/cocoon/jamestown/fha/J1074 (accessed 6 May 2015).

Coleman, Edward M. "Letter from Governor Patrick Tonyn of East Florida to George Germain, Secretary of State for the Colonies, 1776." *Mississippi Valley Historical Review* 33, no. 2 (1946): 289–92.

Cooper, Thomas, and David McCord, eds. *Statutes at Large of South Carolina.* 10 vols. Columbia, S.C.: A. S. Johnson, 1836–41.

DeBrahm, William. *A Map of South Carolina and a Part of Georgia . . . Composed from Surveys Taken by . . . William Bull . . . Captain Gascoign, Hugh Bryan . . . and the Author Wiliam De Brahm. . . .* London: Thomas Jeffreys, 1757. Copy in U. of Va.

de Crèvecoeur, J. Hector St. John. *Letters from an American Farmer* 4, http://avalon.law.yale.edu/18th_century/letter_09.asp (accessed 9 January 2015).

Donnan, Elisabeth, ed. *Documents Illustrative of the History of the Slave Trade to America.* 4 vols. Washington, D.C., 1932.

Douglass, Frederick. *My Bondage and My Freedom.* New York: Miller, Orton, and Mulligan, 1855, http://docsouth.unc.edu/neh/douglass55/douglass55.html (accessed 28 January 2015).

du Monceau, M. Duhamel. *A Practical Treatise on Husbandry.* London: C. Hitch and L. Hawes, 1762.

Edgeworth, Maria. *Popular Tales.* London: Printed for J. Johnson, 1811.

Encyclopaedia Britannica. 3 vols. Edinburgh: For A. Bell and C. Macfarquhar, 1771.

"For the Colony in Virginea Britannia: Lawes Divine, Morall and *Martiall &c.,*" 27, http://www.virtualjamestown.org/exist/cocoon/jamestown/laws/J1056 (accessed 6 May 2015).

Grizzard, Frank E. *George Washington: A Biographical Companion.* Santa Barbara, Calif.: ABC-Clio, 2002.

Haley, Alex. *Roots.* London: Vintage: 1991.

Hamilton, Stanislaus Murray, ed. *Letters to Washington and Accompanying Papers: Published by the Society of the Colonial Dames of America,* http://memory.loc.gov/ammem/gwhtml/ (accessed 13 November 2014).

Harrower, John. "Diary of John Harrower, 1773–1776." *American Historical Review* 6, no. 1 (1900): 65–107.

——. *The Journal of John Harrower: An Indentured Servant in the Colony of Virginia, 1773–1776,* ed. Edward Miles Riley. New York: Holt, Rinehart, and Winston, 1963.

Hawes, Lilla M., ed. "Minute Book, Savannah Board of Police." *Georgia Historical Quarterly* 45 (1961): 245–57.

Hayne, Isaac. "Records Kept by Colonel Isaac Hayne." *South Carolina Historical and Genealogical Magazine* 12, no. 1 (1911): 19–23.

Hening, William Waller, ed. *The Statutes at Large, Being a Collection of All the Laws of Virginia, from the First Session of the Legislature, in the Year 1619.* 18 vols. New York: R. and W. and G. Bartow, 1823.

Hewatt, Alexander. *An Historical Account of the Rise and Progress of the Colonies of South Carolina and Georgia.* London: A. Donaldson, 1779.

Hildreth, Richard. *The White Slave; or, Memoirs of a Fugitive.* Milwaukie [*sic*], Wisc.: Rood and Whttemoore [*sic*], 1852, http://purl.dlib.indiana.edu/iudl/wright/VAC6730 (accessed 25 January 2015).

Holcomb, Brent H., ed. *South Carolina Marriages 1688–1799.* Baltimore: Genealogical Publishing, 1980.

——, ed. *Supplement to South Carolina Marriages 1688–1820.* Baltimore: Genealogical Publishing, 1984.

Hume, David. *Essays Moral and Political.* London: Printed for A. Millar and A. Kincaid, 1748.

"Interest (n.)." In *Oxford English Dictionary.* 2nd ed. Oxford: Oxford University Press, 1989, http://www.oed.com/view/Entry/97735 (accessed 13 February 2014), 3.

Jefferson, Thomas. *Notes on the State of Virginia,* ed. William Peden. New York: Norton, 1972.

——. *The Works of Thomas Jefferson in Twelve Volumes,* ed. Paul Leicester Ford. 12 vols. New York: Knickerbocker, 1904, http://memory.loc.gov/ammem/mtjhtml/mtjhome.html (accessed 30 April 2015).

Jones, Hugh, *The Present State of Virginia.* London, 1724.

Laurens, Henry. *A Letter from Henry Laurens to His Son John Laurens August 14, 1776.* New York: Columbia University Libraries, 1964.

——. *Papers of Henry Laurens,* ed. P. M. Hamer. 4 vols. Columbia: University of South Carolina Press, 1970–74.

——. *Papers of Henry Laurens,* ed. D. R Chesnutt and G. L Rogers V. Columbia: University of South Carolina Press, 1976.

Lawrence, John W., ed. "The Descendants of Daniel Couturier in South Carolina." Unpublished report viewed at SCL, USC, 1990.

Madison, James. *Papers of James Madison,* ed. William Hutchinson et al. 12 vols. Chicago: University of Chicago Press; Charlottesville: University Press of Virginia, 1962–91.

Mandeville, Bernard. *The Fable of the Bees and Other Writings,* ed. E. J. Hundert. Indiana: Hackett, 1997.

McIlwaine, H. R., ed. *Executive Journals of the Council of Colonial Virginia.* 6 vols. Richmond: Virginia State Library, 1925–66.

Morrison, Toni. *Beloved.* London: Vintage, 1997.

Muhlenberg, Henry Melchior. *The Journal of Henry Melchior Muhlenberg,* trans. Theodore G. Tappert and John W. Doberstein. 3 vols. Philadelphia: Muhlenberg, 1942–58.

Newton, John. *The Journal of a Slave Trader 1750–1754: With Newton's Thoughts upon the African Slave Trade,* ed. Bernard Martin and Mark Spurrell. London: Epworth, [1788] 1962.

Olmsted, Frederick Law. *The Cotton Kingdom: A Traveller's Observation on Cotton and Slavery in the American Slave States, 1853–1861,* ed. Arthur M. Schlesinger. New York: Da Capo, 1996.

Pinckney, Eliza Lucas. *The Letterbook of Eliza Lucas Pinckney, 1739–1762,* ed. Elise Pinckney. Columbia: University of South Carolina Press, 1997.

Pringle, Robert, *The Letterbook of Robert Pringle,* ed. Walter B. Edgar. 2 vols. Columbia: University of South Carolina Press, 1972.

Proclamation of Earl Dunmore. Africans in America, http://www.pbs.org/wgbh/aia/part2/2h42t.html (accessed 16 March 2015).

Ryland, Elizabeth Hawes. "Names from a Ledger of a Merchant at Aylett, Virginia, 1781, 1782." *William and Mary College Quarterly Historical Magazine,* 2nd ser., 17, no. 1 (1937): 49–52.

Smith, Adam. *The Theory of Moral Sentiments,* ed. Knud Haakonssen. Cambridge: Cambridge University Press, 2002.

Smith, Paul H., ed. *Letters of Delegates to Congress, 1774–1789.* 26 vols. Washington, D.C.: Library of Congress, 1976–2000, 5:462, http://rs6.loc.gov/ammem/amlaw/lwdg.html (accessed 2 November 2014).

Stowe, Harriet Beecher. *Uncle Tom's Cabin; or, Negro Life in the Slave States of America.* Ware, Hertfordshire, U.K.: Wordsworth Classics, 1995.

Tansill, Charles C., ed. *Documents Illustrative of the Formation of the American States.* Washington, D.C.: Government Printing Office, 1927.

Tinling, Marion. "Cawsons, Virginia, in 1795–1796." *William and Mary Quarterly,* 3rd ser., 3, no. 2 (1946): 281–91.

Washington, George. *The Diaries of George Washington,* ed. Donald Jackson and Dorothy Twohig. 6 vols. Charlottesville: University Press of Virginia, 1976–79, http://memory.loc.gov/ammem/gwhtml/gwhome.html (accessed 30 April 2015).

——. *George Washington's Accounts of Expenses while Commander-in-Chief of the Continental Army, 1775–1783.* New York: Houghton Mifflin, 1917, http://memory.loc.gov/ammem/gwhtml/gwhome.html (accessed 29 December 2014).

——. *The George Washington Papers at the Library of Congress, 1741–99: Series 2 Letterbooks,* http://memory.loc.gov/ammem/gwhtml/gwhome.html (accessed 6 February 2015).

——. *The Papers of George Washington,* ed. W. W. Abbot and Dorothy Twohig. 12 vols. Charlottesville: University Press of Virginia, 1983.

——. *The Writings of George Washington,* ed. Worthington Chauncey Ford. 14 vols. New York: G. P. Putnam's Sons, 1889–93, http://oll.libertyfund.org/titles/washington-the-writings-of-george-washington-14-vols (accessed 30 April 2015).

——. *The Writings of Washington from the Original Manuscript Sources, 1745–1799,* ed. John C. Fitzpatrick. 36 vols. New York: Greenwood, 1970, http://memory.loc.gov/ammem/gwhtml/gwhome.html (accessed 2 May 2015).

Williams, John Rogers. "Journal of Philip Fithian, Kept at Nomini Hall, Virginia, 1773–1774." *American Historical Review* 5, no. 2 (1899): 290–319.

Wroth, Lawrence C. "Report of Executors of Estate of William Parks, the First Printer in Virginia." *William and Mary College Quarterly Historical Magazine,* 2nd ser., 2, no. 3 (1922): 202–9.

Contemporary Periodicals (and Related Works)

Boston Chronicle I, XLII, 26 September to 3 October 1768, in South Carolina Regulators: 2 MPs, SCL, USC, 26 September to 3 October and 3 October to 10 October 1768 file.

Georgia Gazette (microfilm), University of Cambridge Library.

New York Journal; or, General Advertiser.

South Carolina Gazette (microfilm), University of Cambridge Library.

South Carolina Gazette and Country Journal (microfilm), University of Cambridge Library.

Virginia Gazette: Parks (1736–40); Hunter (1751–61); Royle (1761–65); Purdie and Co. (1765–66); Purdie and Dixon (1766–65); Rind (1766–74); Pinkney (1774–76); Purdie (1775–79); Dixon and Nicolson (1779–80); Clarkson and Davis (1779–80).

Osborne, J. A. *Williamsburg in Colonial Times: Incidents in the Lives of the English Colonists in Virginia, during the 17th and 18th Centuries as Revealed in Old Documents and Files of the Virginia Gazette.* 2nd ed. Washington, D.C.: Kennikat, 1972.

Secondary Sources

Anzilotti, Cara. *The Affairs of the World: Women, Patriarchy and Power in Colonial South Carolina.* Westport, Conn.: Greenwood, 2002.

Arendt, Hannah. *The Human Condition.* Chicago: University of Chicago Press, 1998.

Baird, James. "Between Slavery and Independence: Power Relations between Dependent White Men and Their Superiors in Late Colonial and Early National Virginia with Particular Reference to the Overseer-Employer Relationship." Ph.D. diss., Johns Hopkins University, 1999.

——. "Paternalism and Profits: Planters and Overseers in Piedmont Virginia, 1750–1825." In Robert Olwell and Alan Tully, eds., *Cultures and Identities in Colonial British America.* Baltimore: Johns Hopkins University Press, 2006, 147–68.

Baptist, Edward E., ed. *The Encyclopedia of Slavery in the Americas.* New York: Facts on File, forthcoming.

——. *The Half Has Never Been Told: Slavery and the Making of American Capitalism.* New York: Basic Books, 2014.

Bassett, John Spencer. *The Southern Plantation Overseer as Revealed in His Letters.* 1925. New York: Negro Universities Press, 1968.

Beeman, Richard R. *The Evolution of the Southern Backcountry: A Case Study of Lunenburg County, Virginia 1746–1832.* Philadelphia: University of Pennsylvania Press, 1984.

——. *The Varieties of Political Experience in Eighteenth-Century America.* Philadelphia: University of Pennsylvania Press, 2004.

Berkin, Carol. "Clio's Daughters: Southern Colonial Women and Their Historians." In Catherine Clinton and Michele Gillespie, eds., *The Devil's Lane—Sex and Race in the Early South.* New York: Oxford University Press, 1997, 15–23.

Berlin, Ira. *Many Thousands Gone: The First Two Centuries of Slavery in North America.* Cambridge, Mass.: Harvard University Press, 1998.

——."Time, Space and the Evolution of Afro-American Society on British Mainland North America." *American Historical Review* 85, no. 1 (1980): 44–78.

Blumrosen, Alfred, and Ruth Blumrosen. *Slave Nation: How Slavery United the Colonies and Sparked the American Revolution.* Naperville, Ill.: Sourcebooks, 2005

Borick, Carl P. *A Gallant Defense: The Siege of Charleston, 1780.* Columbia: University of South Carolina Press, 2003.

Bradburn Douglas M., and John C Coombs. "Smoke and Mirrors: Reinterpreting the Society and Economy of the Seventeenth-Century Chesapeake." *Atlantic Studies* 3, no. 2 (2006): 131–57.

Breen, Timothy H. *The Marketplace of Revolution: How Consumer Politics Shaped American Independence.* New York: Oxford University Press, 2004.

——. *Tobacco Culture: The Mentality of the Great Tidewater Planters on the Eve of Revolution.* Princeton, N.J.: Princeton University Press, 1985.

Brewer, Holly. "Entailing Aristocracy in Colonial Virginia: 'Ancient Feudal Restraints' and Revolutionary Reform." *William and Mary Quarterly,* 3rd ser., 54, no. 2 (1997): 307–46.

Brown Katharine L., and Nancy T. Sorrells. *People in Profile: Christ Church Parish 1720–1750.* Irvington, Va.: Lot's Wife Publishing, 2002.

Brown, Kathleen M. *Good Wives, Nasty Wenches, and Anxious Patriarchs: Gender, Race, and Power in Colonial Virginia.* Chapel Hill: University of North Carolina Press, 1996.

Brown, Robert E., and B. Katherine Brown. *Virginia 1705–1786: Democracy or Aristocracy?* East Lansing: Michigan State University Press, 1964.

Browne, C. A. Virginia. "Reverend Dr. John Clayton and His Early Map of Jamestown." *William and Mary College Quarterly Historical Magazine,* 2nd ser., 19, no. 1 (1939): 1–7.

Burnard, Trevor. *Mastery, Tyranny and Desire: Thomas Thistlewood and His Slaves in the Anglo Jamaican World.* Chapel Hill: University of North Carolina Press, 2004.

———. "The Sexual Life of an Eighteenth-Century Jamaican Slave Overseer." In Merril D. Smith, ed., *Sex and Sexuality in Early America.* New York: New York University Press, 1998, 93–114.

Camp, Stephanie H. *Closer to Freedom: Enslaved Women and Everyday Resistance in the Plantation South.* Chapel Hill: University of North Carolina Press, 2004.

Chaplin, Joyce E. *An Anxious Pursuit: Agricultural Innovation and Modernity in the Lower South, 1730–1815.* Chapel Hill: University of North Carolina Press, 1996.

———. "Slavery and the Principle of Humanity: A Modern Idea in the Early Lower South." *Journal of Social History* 24, no. 2 (1990): 299–315.

———. "Tidal Rice Cultivation and the Problem of Slavery in South Carolina, 1760–1815." *William and Mary Quarterly,* 3rd ser., 49, no. 1 (1992): 29–61.

Clinton, Catherine. *"The Plantation Mistress": Woman's World in the Old South.* New York: Pantheon Books, 1982.

Clinton, Catherine, and Michele Gillespie, eds. *The Devil's Lane—Sex and Race in the Early South.* New York: Oxford University Press, 1997.

Clukey, Amy, and Jeremy Wells, eds. *Plantation Modernity.* Athens: University of Georgia Press, forthcoming.

Connell, R. W. *Masculinities.* Oxford: Polity, 1995.

Cotterill, R. S. *The Old South.* Glendale, Calif.: Arthur R. Cook, 1939.

Davis, David Brion. "Looking at Slavery from Broader Perspectives." *American Historical Review* 105, no. 2 (2000): 452–66.

———. *The Problem of Slavery in the Age of Revolution, 1770–1823.* 2nd ed. New York: Oxford University Press, 1999.

d'Entrèves, M. P. *The Political Philosophy of Hannah Arendt.* London: Routledge, 1994.

Deyle, Steven. *Carry Me Back: The Domestic Slave Trade in American Life.* New York: Oxford University Press, 2005.

Dornan, Ingeborg. "Women Slaveholders in the Georgia and South Carolina Low Country, 1750–1775." Ph.D. diss., University of Cambridge, 2001.

Dusinberre, William. *Them Dark Days: Slavery in the American Rice Swamps.* New York: Oxford University Press, 1996

Edelson, S. Max. *Plantation Enterprise in Colonial South Carolina.* Cambridge, Mass.: Harvard University Press, 2006.

Egerton, Douglas. *Death or Liberty: African Americans and Revolutionary America.* Oxford: Oxford University Press, 2009.

Ekirch, Roger. *Bound for America: The Transportation of British Convicts to the Colonies, 1718–1775.* Oxford: Oxford University Press, 1987.

Eustace, Nicole. *Passion Is the Gale: Emotion, Power and the Coming of the American Revolution.* Chapel Hill: University of North Carolina Press, 2008.

Falola, Toyin, and Amanda Warnock, eds. *The Encyclopedia of the Middle Passage.* Westport, Conn.: Greenwood, 2007.

Fink, Gary M., and Merl E. Reed, eds. *Race, Class and Community in Southern Labor History.* Tuscaloosa: University of Alabama Press, 1994.

Fisher, Marc. "Unique Montgomery Property for Sale: Uncle Tom's Cabin." *Washington Post,* 13 December 2005, B01.

Fludernik, Monika, and Miriam Nandi, eds. *Idleness, Indolence and Leisure in English Literature.* Basingstoke, U.K.: Palgrave, 2014.

Fogelman, Aaron S. "From Slaves, Convicts and Servants to Free Passengers: The Transformation of Immigration in the Era of the American Revolution." *Journal of American History* 75, no. 1 (1998): 43–76.

Follett, Richard J. *The Sugar Masters: Planters and Slaves in Louisiana's Cane World, 1820–1860.* Baton Rouge: Louisiana State University Press, 2005.

Foner, Eric. *Blacks in the American Revolution.* Westport, Conn.: Greenwood, 1976.
———. *The Story of American Freedom.* New York: W. W. Norton, 1998.
———. *Tom Paine and Revolutionary America.* 2nd ed. Oxford: Oxford University Press, 2005.
Foucault, Michel. *Discipline and Punish: The Rise of the Prison.* New York: Vintage Books, 1979.
———. *The History of Sexuality,* trans. Robert Hurley. 3 vols. New York: Pantheon Books, 1978.
Frey, Sylvia R. *Water from the Rock: Black Resistance in a Revolutionary Age.* Princeton, N.J.: Princeton University Press, 1991.
Genovese, Eugene D. "Rebelliousness and Docility in the Negro Slave: A Critique of the Elkins Thesis." *Civil War History* 13 (1967): 293–314.
———. *Roll, Jordan, Roll: The World the Slaves Made.* New York: Vintage Books, 1976.
Gibson, Ellen. *The Loyal Blacks.* New York: Capricorn Books, 1976.
Giddens, Anthony. *Central Problems in Social Theory: Action, Structure and Contradiction in Social Analysis.* Berkeley: University of California Press, 1979.
———. *The Constitution of Society: Outline of the Theory of Structuration.* Cambridge: Polity, 1984.
———. *Sociology.* 2nd ed. Cambridge: Polity, 1993.
Gordon, John W. *South Carolina and the American Revolution: A Battlefield History.* Columbia: University of South Carolina Press, 2003.
Greenberg, Kenneth S. *Masters and Statesmen: The Political Culture of American Slavery.* Baltimore: Johns Hopkins University Press, 1988.
Greenblatt, Stephen. *Renaissance Self-Fashioning: From More to Shakespeare.* Chicago: University of Chicago Press, 1980.
Greene, Jack P. *Imperatives, Behaviors and Identities: Essays in Early American Cultural History.* Charlottesville: University Press of Virginia, 1992.
Gudmestad, Robert H. *A Troublesome Commerce: The Transformation of the Interstate Slave Trade.* Baton Rouge: Louisiana State University Press, 2004.
Gutman, Herbert. "The World Two Cliometricians Made: A Review Essay of F+E=T/C Positive Labour Incentives and Slave Work Habits." Review of *Time on the Cross: The Economics of American Negro Slavery,* by Robert William Fogel and Stanley L. Engerman. *Journal of Negro History* 60, no. 1 (1975): 117–18.
Hadden, Sally. *Slave Patrols: Law and Violence in Virginia and the Carolinas.* Cambridge, Mass.: Harvard University Press, 2001.
Hall, Leslie. *Land and Allegiance in Revolutionary Georgia.* Athens: University of Georgia Press, 2001.
Hast, Adele. "The Legal Status of the Negro in Virginia 1705–1765." *Journal of Negro History,* 54, no. 3 (1969): 217–39.
Hirschman, Albert O. *The Passions and the Interests: Political Arguments for Capitalism before Its Triumph.* Princeton, N.J.: Princeton University Press, 1977.
Hoffer, Peter Charles. *Cry Liberty: The Great Stono River Slave Rebellion of 1739.* Oxford: Oxford University Press, 2010.
Holton, Woody. *Forced Founders: Indians, Debtors, Slaves, and the Making of the American Revolution.* Chapel Hill: University of North Carolina Press, 1999.
Hopkins, Keith. "Novel Evidence for Roman Slavery." *Past and Present,* 138 (1993): 3–27.
Isaac, Rhys. *Landon Carter's Uneasy Kingdom: Revolution and Rebellion on a Virginia Plantation.* Oxford: Oxford University Press, 2004.
———. *The Transformation of Virginia 1740–1790.* Chapel Hill: University of North Carolina Press, 1982.
Johnson, Walter. "A Nettlesome Classic Turns Twenty-Five." *Common-Place* 9, no. 4 (2001), http://www.common-place.org/vol-01/no-04/reviews/johnson.shtml (accessed 7 June 2015).
Jones, E. L. *Agriculture and the Industrial Revolution.* Oxford: Oxford University Press, 1974.
Jones, Maldwyn A. *The Limits of Liberty: American History 1607–1992.* 2nd ed. Oxford: Oxford University Press, 1995.
Jones, Norrece T., Jr. *Born a Child of Freedom, Yet a Slave: Mechanisms of Control and Strategies of Resistance in Antebellum South Carolina.* Hanover, N.H.: University Press of New England, 1990.

Jordan, Winthrop. *White over Black: American Attitudes toward the Negro, 1550–1812.* Chapel Hill: University of North Carolina Press, 1968.

Joyce, Patrick, ed. *The Social in Question: New Bearings in History and the Social Sciences.* London: Routledge, 2002.

Kaplan, Sidney. "The 'Domestic Insurrections' of the Declaration of Independence." *Journal of Negro History* 61, no. 3 (1976): 243–55.

Kaplan, Sidney, and Emma Nogrady Kaplan. *The Black Presence in the Era of the American Revolution.* Amherst: University of Massachusetts Press, 1989.

Kennedy, Roger G. *Mr. Jefferson's Lost Cause: Land, Farmers, Slavery and the Louisiana Purchase.* Oxford: Oxford University Press, 2003.

Klingsberg, Frank J. *An Appraisal of the Negro in Colonial South Carolina.* Washington: Associated Publishers, 1941.

Knott, Sarah. *Sensibility and the American Revolution.* Chapel Hill: University of North Carolina Press, 2009.

Kolchin, Peter. *American Slavery 1619–1877.* New York: Hill and Wang, 1993.

———. *Unfree Labor: American Slavery and Russian Serfdom.* Cambridge, Mass.: Harvard University Press, 1987.

Kulikoff, Allan. *Tobacco and Slaves: The Development of Southern Cultures in the Chesapeake, 1680–1800.* Chapel Hill: University of North Carolina Press, 1986.

Littlefield, Daniel C. *Rice and Slaves: Ethnicity and the Slave Trade in Colonial South Carolina.* Urbana: University of Illinois Press, 1991.

Lockley, Timothy J. "Crossing the Race Divide: Interracial Sex in Antebellum Savannah." *Slavery and Abolition: A Journal of Slave and Post-slave Studies* 18, no. 3: 159–73.

———. *Lines in the Sand: Race and Class in Lowcountry Georgia, 1750–1860.* Athens: University of Georgia Press, 2001.

Lockridge, Kenneth A. *The Diary, and Life, of William Byrd II of Virginia, 1674–1744.* Chapel Hill: University of North Carolina Press, 1987.

Mancall, Peter C., Joshua L. Rosenbloom, and Thomas Weiss. "Slave Prices and the South Carolina Economy, 1722–1809." *Journal of Economic History* 61, no. 3 (2001): 616–39.

McCowen, George Smith, Jr. *The British Occupation of Charleston, 1780–82.* Columbia: University of South Carolina Press, 1972.

McCrady, Edward. *The History of South Carolina in the Revolution, 1775–1780.* 8 vols. New York: Russell and Russell, 1969.

McCurdy, John Gilbert. *Citizen Bachelors: Manhood and the Creation of the United States.* Ithaca, N.Y.: Cornell University Press, 2009.

McCusker, John J. *Money and Exchange in Europe and America, 1600–1775: A Handbook.* Chapel Hill: University of North Carolina Press, 1992.

McDonnell, Michael A. *The Politics of War: Race, Class and Conflict in Revolutionary Virginia.* Chapel Hill: University of North Carolina Press, 2007.

———. "Popular Mobilization and Political Culture in Revolutionary Virginia: The Failure of the Minutemen and the Revolution from Below." *Journal of American History* 85, no. 3 (1998): 946–81.

McDonnell, Michael A., and Woody Hilton. "Patriot vs. Patriot: Social Conflict in Virginia and the Origins of the American Revolution." *Journal of American Studies* 34, no. 2 (2000): 231–56.

Massey, Gregory D. *John Laurens and the American Revolution.* Columbia: University of South Carolina Press, 2000.

Morgan, Edmund S. *American Slavery, American Freedom: The Ordeal of Colonial Virginia.* New York: W. W. Norton, 1975.

Morgan, Jennifer L., *Laboring Women: Reproduction and Gender in New World Slavery.* Philadelphia: University of Pennsylvania Press, 2004.

Morgan, Philip D. *Slave Counterpoint: Black Culture in the Eighteenth-Century Chesapeake and Low Country.* Chapel Hill: University of North Carolina Press, 1998.

Morgan, Philip D., and Michael L. Nicholls. "Slaves in Piedmont Virginia, 1720–1790." *William and Mary Quarterly,* 3rd ser., 46, no. 2 (1989): 211–51.

Morton, Louis. "Robert Wormeley Carter of Sabine Hall: Notes on the Life of a Virginia Planter." *Journal of Southern History* 12, no. 3 (1946): 345–65.

Mullin, Gerald W. *Flight and Rebellion: Slave Resistance in Eighteenth-Century Virginia.* New York: Oxford University Press, 1972.

Nadelhaft, Jerome J. *The Disorders of War: The Revolution in South Carolina.* Orono: University of Maine at Orono Press, 1981.

Nash, R. C. "South Carolina and the Atlantic Economy in the Late Seventeenth and Eighteenth Centuries." *Economic History Review* 45, no. 4 (1992): 677–702.

——. "South Carolina Indigo, European Textiles, and the British Atlantic Economy in the Eighteenth Century." *Economic History Review* 63, no. 2 (2010): 363–92.

Oakes, James. *Slavery and Freedom: An Interpretation of the Old South.* New York: Alfred A. Knopf, 1990.

Oakeshott, Michael. *Lectures in the History of Political Thought.* Exeter, U.K.: Imprint Academic, 2006.

O'Brien, Michael. *Conjectures of Order: Intellectual Life in the American South, 1810–60.* Chapel Hill: University of North Carolina Press, 2004.

Olwell, Robert A. "'Domestick Enemies': Slavery and Political Independence in South Carolina, May 1775–March 1776." *Journal of Southern History* 55, no. 1 (1989): 21–48.

——. *Masters, Slaves and Subjects: The Culture of Power in the South Carolina Low Country, 1740–1790.* Ithaca, N.Y.: Cornell University Press, 1998.

Olwell, Robert, and Alan Tully, eds. *Cultures and Identities in Colonial British America.* Baltimore: Johns Hopkins University Press, 2006.

Parent, Anthony. *Foul Means: The Formation of a Slave Society in Virginia, 1660–1740.* Chapel Hill: University of North Carolina Press, 2003.

Pearsall, Sarah. *Atlantic Families: Lives and Letters in the Later Eighteenth Century.* Oxford: Oxford University Press, 2008.

Phillips, Ulrich B. *The Slave Economy of the Old South,* ed. Eugene D. Genovese. Baton Rouge: Louisiana State University Press, 1968.

Pocock, J. G. A. *The Machiavellian Moment: Florentine Political Thought and the Atlantic Republican Tradition.* Princeton, N.J.: Princeton University Press, 1975.

Poovey, Mary. "The Liberal Civil Subject and the Social in Eighteenth-Century British Moral Philosophy." In Patrick Joyce, ed., *The Social in Question: New Bearings in History and the Social Sciences.* London: Routledge, 2002.

Prude, Jonathan. "To Look upon the 'Lower Sort': Runaway Ads and the Appearance of Unfree Laborers in America, 1750–1800." *Journal of American History* 78, no. 1 (1991): 124–59.

Puglisi, Michael J., ed. *Diversity and Accommodation: Essays on the Cultural Composition of the Virginia Frontier.* Knoxville: University of Tennessee Press, 1997.

Pulis, John W., ed. *Moving On: Black Loyalists in the Afro-Atlantic World.* New York: Garland, 1999.

Pybus, Cassandra. *Epic Journeys of Freedom: Runaway Slaves of the American Revolution and Their Global Quest for Liberty.* Boston: Beacon Books, 2006.

——. "Jefferson's Faulty Math: The Question of Slave Defections in the American Revolution." *William and Mary Quarterly,* 3rd ser., 62 (2005): 243–64.

Quarles, Benjamin. *The Negro in the American Revolution.* Chapel Hill: University of North Carolina Press, 1961.

Ragsdale, Bruce A. *A Planters' Republic: The Search for Economic Independence in Revolutionary Virginia.* Madison, Wisc.: Madison House, 1996.

Rutman, Darrett B., and Anita H. Rutman. *A Place in Time: Middlesex County, Virginia, 1650–1750.* New York: W. W. Norton, 1984.

Sadlek, Gregory M. "Otium, Negotium and the Fear of Acedia." In Monika Fludernik and Miriam Nandi, eds., *Idleness, Indolence and Leisure in English Literature.* Basingstoke, U. K.: Palgrave, 2014, 17–39.

Salmon, Emily Jones. "Convict Labor during the Colonial Period," http://www.encyclopediavirginia.org/Convict_Labor_During_the_Colonial_Period (accessed 17 January 2015).

Sandy, Laura. "Divided Loyalties in a 'Predatory War': Plantation Overseers and Slavery during the American Revolution." *Journal of American Studies* 48, no. 2 (May 2014): 357–92.

——. "Homemakers, Supervisors and Peach Stealing Bitches: The Role of Overseers' Wives on Slave Plantations in Eighteenth-Century Virginia and South Carolina." *Women's History Review* 21, no. 3: 473–94.

——. "Mary-Anne Schad and Mrs. Brown: Overseers' Wives in Colonial South Carolina." In Marjorie Julian Spruill, Valinda W. Littlefield, Joan Marie Johnson, eds., *South Carolina Women: Their Lives and Times.* 3 vols. Athens: University of Georgia Press, 2009, 1:60–78.

——. "The Role of Overseers in the Management of Slave Plantations in Virginia and South Carolina, 1740–1800." Ph.D. diss., University of Manchester, 2006.

Sarson, Steven. *British America 1500–1800: Creating Colonies, Imagining an Empire.* London: Hodder Arnold, 2005.

Scarborough, William K. *The Overseer: Plantation Management in the Old South.* Baton Rouge: Louisiana State University Press, 1966.

Schama, Simon. *Rough Crossings: Britain, the Slaves and the American Revolution.* London: BBC Books, 2005.

Schmidt, James D. "Overseers and the Nature of Southern Labor Contracts." In Gary M. Fink and Merl E. Reed, eds., *Race, Class and Community in Southern Labor History.* Tuscaloosa: University of Alabama Press, 1994, 87–96.

Schwartz, Bernard. *A History of the Supreme Court.* Oxford: Oxford University Press, 1995.

Scott, James C. *Domination and the Arts of Resistance: Hidden Transcripts.* New Haven, Conn.: Yale University Press, 1990.

——. *Weapons of the Weak: Everyday Forms of Peasant Resistance.* New Haven, Conn.: Yale University Press, 1985.

Selby, John E. *The Revolution in Virginia, 1775–1783.* Williamsburg, Va.: Colonial Williamsburg Foundation, 1988.

Shalev, Eran. *Rome Reborn on Western Shores: Historical Imagination and the Creation of the American Republic.* Charlottesville: University of Virginia Press, 2009.

Shuler, Jack. *Calling Out Liberty: The Stono Rebellion and the Universal Struggle for Human Rights.* Jackson: University Press of Mississippi, 2009.

Sidbury, James. *Ploughshares into Swords: Race, Rebellion and Identity in Gabriel's Virginia, 1730–1810.* Cambridge: Cambridge University Press, 1997.

Simpson, J. A. and Weiner, E. S. C., eds. *The Oxford English Dictionary.* 2nd ed. 20 vols. Oxford: Oxford University Press, 1989.

Skinner, Quentin. "The Place of History in Public Life." *History and Policy* 35 (2005), http://www.historyandpolicy.org/papers/policy-paper-35.html (accessed 17 January 2015).

Smith, Adam. *The Wealth of Nations, Books 1–3.* 3 vols. London: Penguin Classics, 1999.

Smith, Mark M. *Mastered by the Clock: Time, Slavery, and Freedom in the American South.* Chapel Hill: University of North Carolina Press, 1997.

——. "Old South Time in Comparative Perspective." *American Historical Review* 101, no. 5 (1996): 1432–96.

Smith, Merril D., ed. *Sex and Sexuality in Early America.* New York: New York University Press, 1998.

Sobel, Mechal. *The World They Made Together: Black and White Values in Eighteenth-Century Virginia.* Princeton, N.J.: Princeton University Press, 1987.

"Society in East Virginia." *William and Mary College Quarterly Historical Magazine* 22, no. 4 (1914): 221–28.

Somerville, Diane Miller. "Rape, Race, and Castration in Slave Law in the Colonial and Early South." In Catherine Clinton and Michele Gillespie, eds., *The Devil's Lane—Sex and Race in the Early South.* New York: Oxford University Press, 1997.

Stampp, Kenneth M. *The Peculiar Institution: Slavery in the Ante-bellum South.* New York: Alfred A. Knopf, 1956.

Starr, Rebecca. *A School for Politics: Commercial Lobbying and Political Culture in Early South Carolina.* Baltimore: Johns Hopkins University Press, 1998.

Stubbs, Tristan. "The Haitian Revolution." In Toyin Falola and Amanda Warnock, eds., *The Encyclopedia of the Middle Passage.* Westport, Conn.: Greenwood, 2007, 206–8.

——. "Indigo." In Edward E. Baptist, ed., *The Encyclopedia of Slavery in the Americas.* New York: Facts on File, forthcoming.

——. "Rice." In Edward E. Baptist, ed., *The Encyclopedia of Slavery in the Americas.* New York: Facts on File, forthcoming.

——. "Space, Time and Female Resistance to Slavery on Antebellum Plantations," https://www.h-net.org/reviews/showrev.php?id=12259 (accessed 3 November 2014).

——. "Violence, Dependence and Liberty: Representations of the Plantation Overseer in Eighteenth-Century Virginia, South Carolina and Georgia." In Amy Clukey and Jeremy Wells, eds., *Plantation Modernity.* Athens: University of Georgia Press, forthcoming.

Tadman, Michael. *Speculators and Slaves: Masters, Traders and Slaves in the Old South.* Madison: University of Wisconsin Press, 1989.

Talpalar, Morris. *The Sociology of Colonial Virginia.* New York: Philosophical Library, 1968.

Tang, Joyce. "Enslaved African Rebellions in Virginia." *Journal of Black Studies* 27, no. 5 (1997): 598–614.

Tillson, Albert H., Jr. *Gentry and Common Folk: Political Culture on a Virginia Frontier, 1740–1789.* Lexington: University Press of Kentucky, 1991.

Trinkley, Michael, et al. *Investigation of an Eighteenth Century Overseer Site (38CH1278), Christ Church Parish, Charleston County, South Carolina.* Chicora Foundation Research Series 64. Columbia, S.C.: Chicora Foundation, 2005.

——. *Liberty Hall: A Small Eighteenth Century Rice Plantation in Goose Creek, Berkeley County, South Carolina.* Chicora Foundation Research Series 62. Columbia, S.C.: Chicora Foundation, 2003.

Vlach, Michael. *Back of the Big House: The Architecture of Plantation Slavery.* Chapel Hill: University of North Carolina Press, 1993.

Walsh, Lorena S. *From Calabar to Carter's Grove: The History of a Virginia Slave Community.* Charlottesville: University Press of Virginia, 1997.

——. "Plantation Management in the Chesapeake, 1620–1820." *Journal of Economic History* 49, no. 2 (1989): 393–406.

Weir, Robert M. *"The Last of American Freemen": Studies in the Political Culture of the Colonial Revolutionary South.* Macon, Ga.: Mercer University Press, 1986.

Wicek, William M. "The Statutory Law of Slavery and Race in the Thirteen Mainland Colonies of British America." *William and Mary Quarterly,* 3rd ser., 24, no. 1 (1977): 258–80.

Wiencek, Henry. *Imperfect God: George Washington, His Slaves, and the Creation of America.* New York: Farrar, Straus, and Giroux, 2003.

Wiethoff, William E. *Crafting the Overseer's Image.* Columbia: University of South Carolina Press, 2006.

——. "Enslaved Africans' Rivalry with White Overseers in Plantation Culture: An Unconventional Interpretation." *Journal of Black Studies* 36, no. 2 (2006): 429–55.

Wolf, M. Montgomery. "Elite Male Self-Fashioning in Colonial Virginia: The Diaries of William Byrd of Westover, Landon Carter, and Philip Vickers Fithian." Ph.D. diss., Georgia State University, 1999.

Wood, Betty. *Slavery in Colonial Georgia, 1730–1775*. Athens: University of Georgia Press, 1984.

——. "Some Aspects of Female Resistance to Chattel Slavery in Low Country Georgia." *Historical Journal* 30 (1987): 603–22.

——. *Women's Work, Men's Work: The Informal Slave Economies of Low Country Georgia*. Athens: University of Georgia Press, 1995.

Wood, Gordon S. *The Radicalism of the American Revolution*. New York: Alfred A. Knopf, 1993.

Wood, Kirsten E. "Broken Reeds and Competent Farmers: Slaveholding Widows in the Southeastern United States, 1793–1861." *Journal of Women's History* 13, no. 2 (2001): 35–57.

——. *Masterful Women: Slaveholding Widows from the American Revolution through the Civil War*. Chapel Hill: University of North Carolina Press, 2004.

Wood, Peter H., *Black Majority: Negroes in Colonial South Carolina from 1670 through the Stono Rebellion*. New York: Alfred A. Knopf, 1974.

Young, Jeffrey Robert. *Domesticating Slavery: The Master Class in Georgia and South Carolina, 1670–1837*. Chapel Hill: University of South Carolina Press, 1999.

Index